The Terrorist Identity

ALTERNATIVE CRIMINOLOGY SERIES
General Editor: Jeff Ferrell

*Pissing on Demand: Workplace Drug Testing and the
Rise of the Detox Industry*
Ken Tunnell

*Empire of Scrounge: Inside the Urban Underground of
Dumpster Diving, Trash Picking, and Street Scavenging*
Jeff Ferrell

Prison, Inc.: A Convict Exposes Life inside a Private Prison
by K.C. Carceral, edited by Thomas J. Bernard

The Terrorist Identity: Explaining the Terrorist Threat
Michael P. Arena and Bruce A. Arrigo

The
Terrorist
Identity

Explaining the Terrorist Threat

Michael P. Arena and Bruce A. Arrigo

NEW YORK UNIVERSITY PRESS
New York and London

NEW YORK UNIVERSITY PRESS
New York and London
www.nyupress.org

Library of Congress Cataloging-in-Publication Data
Arena, Michael P.
The terrorist identity : explaining the terrorist threat / Michael P.
Arena and Bruce A. Arrigo.
p. cm.
Includes bibliographical references and index.
ISBN-13: 978-0-8147-0715-9 (cloth : alk. paper)
ISBN-10: 0-8147-0715-7 (cloth : alk. paper)
ISBN-13: 978-0-8147-0716-6 (pbk. : alk. paper)
ISBN-10: 0-8147-0716-5 (pbk. : alk. paper)
1. Terrorism. 2. Terrorists—Psychology. 3. Group identity
I. Arrigo, Bruce A. II. Title.
HV6431.A755 2006   363.325—dc22
2006010033

New York University Press books are printed on acid-free paper,
and their binding materials are chosen for strength and durability.

Manufactured in the United States of America
c 10 9 8 7 6 5 4 3 2 1
p 10 9 8 7 6 5 4 3 2 1

For my wife and family, who have provided their unwavering support. —MPA

For my children, Rebecca and Anthony, again and always. —BAA

Contents

Acknowledgments

The authors wish to express a debt of gratitude to several individuals who helped this book come to fruition. We thank our editor at NYU Press, Ilene Kalish, for agreeing to take on this project and seeing it through to final print, and our reviewers for their insightful commentary and suggestions.

Part I

1

Introduction

The tragic events of September 11, 2001, once again thrust terrorism into the international spotlight. Moreover, subsequent attacks in Indonesia, Spain, and England have led to renewed discussions about the nature of violence and the spread of militant extremism around the world. Fundamentally, political and policy pundits, social and behavioral scientists, and security researchers and analysts question what motivates a person or group to commit such heinous acts. Admittedly, over the past several decades, numerous attempts have been undertaken to explain terrorism from a variety of perspectives. Regrettably, however, many of these efforts have been of marginal utility, especially for a profoundly frightened and deeply perplexed public. Thus, we are led to ponder the limits of the existing accounts regarding the phenomenon of terrorism.

While political, sociological, and criminological accounts exist, the majority of the extant literature examines the causes of terrorism from within a psychological framework.[1] Many of these studies regard extremist militant conduct as a function of the individual's psyche and attempt to identify specific personality traits that would compel a person to act so violently. In addition, in his extensive review of the *search for the terrorist personality,* Horgan noted that, statistically, psychodynamic theory has been the most popular of psychologically animated approaches accounting for terrorism.[2] Based chiefly on Freud's psychoanalytic theory, this perspective focuses on various unconscious forces and their deterministic influence on human behavior and social interaction. For example, utilizing such concepts as "repressed desire" and "unresolved childhood conflicts," psychodynamic theorists explain extremist militant conduct as an internal struggle waged within an individual's psyche on the basis of unsettled and traumatic life events. Interestingly, despite this discipline's waning influence on modern psychology, the process of identification is one psychodynamic construct that has received considerable attention throughout contemporary explanations of terrorism.[3]

One theme that appears constant in this research,[4] and subsequent investigations along these lines,[5] is that the identity construct is routinely mentioned as a contributing factor in the emergence and maintenance of extremist militant conduct. For example, in a chapter addressing how individuals join and then sustain their involvement in a terrorist collective, Taylor and Quayle explained how identity was a theme that reoccurred throughout their discussion with an Irish terrorist about his troubled life experiences.[6] This is consistent with the insights of M. Taylor, who observed that there is a particular process of identification that materializes when one assesses terrorism and the terrorist self-concept.[7] As he noted, this identity process functions as an intense motivating factor in the manifestation of extreme militant behavior.

Given these observations, it would seem that the link between identity and terrorism has already been well established in the relevant literature. However, as Horgan notes,[8] the initial research[9] upon which these observations were based are seriously flawed for at least two reasons. First, psychological researchers have been guilty of committing the fundamental attribution error.[10] In short, they overestimate the internal causes for terrorist behavior. Indeed, research supporting the notion that those who commit such acts are intrapsychically flawed, abnormal, and/or psychopathic is rare and typically of poor quality.[11] Second, research based on the psychoanalytic paradigm often suffers from methodological deficiencies.[12] Consequently, while previous research has distinguished identity as an integral factor in explaining terrorist behavior, relying purely upon psychological explanations appears wholly inadequate.[13] Indeed, given much of this research to date, the identity construct remains a fundamental, but elusive, feature of society's efforts to successfully understand this deeply disturbing phenomenon.

The Purpose and Design of the Present Study

The overall goal of this volume is to demonstrate how existing knowledge pertaining to identity and terrorism is limited and, in response, to develop an alternative and, perhaps, corresponding social psychological framework[14] grounded in selected insights derived from structural Symbolic Interactionism.[15] To facilitate this project, the five organizing concepts derived from structural symbolic interactionism (i.e., symbols, definition of the situation, roles, socialization and role-taking, and the emergence of the self) are systematically examined, especially as they are understood by Identity Theory.[16] Moreover, as a way of contextualizing this conceptual undertaking, we evaluate five militant extremist organizations that engage (or have engaged) in terrorism. These extremist collectives include the Provisional Irish Republican Army, the Islamic Resistance Movement (Hamas), the Shining Path, the Liberation Tigers of Tamil Eelam, and racist Skinheads.

The theoretical work undertaken in this volume endeavors to deepen and extend society's understanding of the way terrorist identities are created, embraced, and maintained, as well as the way they influence the behavior of members in a militant extremist subculture. This is accomplished by exploring the delicate relationship that exists among culture, self, and society in the formation and preservation of the terrorist self-concept. Ultimately, this undertaking will contribute to a growing body of research known as the "sociology of terrorism" by building upon the initial work proposed within this area.[17] For example, Alexander[18] utilizes the dramaturgical framework developed by Goffman[19] to describe how acts of terrorism are social dramas performed in a manner similar to a major theatrical production. Within this context, terrorists, like actors in a performance, are expected to fulfill certain role expectations according to a script. Moreover, Kappeler and Kappeler examine how terrorism is constructed as a social threat by exploring terrorist groups' use of techniques such as identifying villains and heroes.[20]

Additional illustrations within this emerging field known as the sociology of terrorism are discernible in the literature. For example, relying upon socialization theory, Oberschall points out how Islamist terrorists are bred through preexisting groups and subcultures maintained in schools and mosques that are viewed as legitimate rather than deviant.[21] By employing the methodology of tethered or positivist constructivism, Silverman provides a detailed examination of the similarity between the Western concepts of "just war" and the Islamic concepts of *jihad*.[22] In doing so, he recognizes the important role identity plays in the motivation of terrorism as individuals learn the social expectations of their behavior and the justifications for their violent actions within a group context. These are identities that come with a set of grievances that serve to fuel terrorist behavior. Appropriating a postcolonial perspective, Brents and Mshigeni explore the construction of racial, religious, and political identity in Zanzibar and the way three distinct self-concepts (i.e., being "Shirazi,"[23] Arab, and African) have been framed and reformulated in the context of conflict.[24] Finally, Akers and Silverman view the motivation of terrorism through the prism of social learning theory and determine that the identity and ideology adopted by terrorists include attitudes, beliefs, and values that justify violent acts in pursuit of a noble end.[25] While social learning theory is grounded in psychology, this cross-disciplinary approach utilizes sociological-type concepts—such as the definition of the situation—to explain how individuals, through identity, come to justify their violent actions. Taken together, these works provide a foundation for the sociology of terrorism. This is an important foundation out of which our own explanatory model of identity emerges.

To be clear, however, we must explain that the suggested framework is not meant to be a comprehensive explanation for militant extremist conduct. No single discipline or theory can accomplish this; no single solution or model can eliminate the commission of violence. Instead, the proposed interpretive framework so central to this book's thesis explores one facet of the complex phenomenon known as terrorism. Moreover, this project endeavors to go beyond the demonization and vilification to which terrorist individuals and collectives have been subjected, given their calculated and vile acts. To this end, the ensuing study does not represent an apology for such nefarious conduct; rather, it signifies a novel contextual basis from within which to understand individual and group participation in such extremist behavior.

The specific terrorist organizations under investigation were selected for two reasons. First, the five groups are quite distinct and heterogeneous. Indeed, they represent diverse regions of the globe and include Europe, the Middle East, South America, Asia, and North America. In addition, they reflect four types of terrorism and consist of nationalist/ separatist, religious, revolutionary, and racial/ethnic militant extremism. Presumably, this miscellany helps advance the explanatory and predictive properties of the overall model while heuristically contributing to the generalizability and credibility of the interpretive framework.

Second, each of the terrorist organizations under consideration has received a substantial amount of attention in both the academic and popular literature. This attention includes the release of various types of primary source documents and correspondences that detail the affairs of the respective militant collectives under review. These data form the basis for the ensuing interpretive analysis of identity and terrorism.

Preliminarily we note that other investigators have endeavored to explain the formation of self-concept in relation to extremist militant violence from within an interactionist framework. For example, although not specified as an interactionist analysis, Aho's examination of Idaho Christian Patriotism identified several interactionist-based themes.[26] One of these is socialization. Aho described it as central to one's involvement in the White supremacist movement.[27] Indeed, as he observed, "right-wing radicals are 'socialized' to this orientation by the words and examples of those with whom they are most deeply bonded: parents, teachers, friends, coworkers, or pastors."[28] In his commentary along these lines, Aho specified a concept integral to the symbolic interactionist's understanding of the socialization process, namely, the *significant other*.[29] Significant others convey the various meanings that attach to symbols. This process contributes to the development of one's sense of self and identity. In addition, Aho discussed the importance of social networks and social structure for purposes of membership recruitment, maintenance, and the adoption of extremist attitudes. As we previously explained, social networks and social structure are important concepts within the interactionist framework.

Although more journalistic in scope and orientation, the influence of interactionist theory resonates in Dillon's examination of the role that religion plays in the Northern Irish conflict.[30] This is especially noticeable in Dillon's comments regarding the experiences of those involved in religious life and terrorism. For example, in a series of interviews with Kenny McClinton, an infamous former loyalist paramilitary leader, Dillon indicated that

> McClinton spoke of the traditional symbols that divided the two communities, the wall painting of King William of Orange on the white charger, and slogans such as "Kick the Pope," which seemed "a part of life, just like breathing." Only retrospectively was he able to detect a philosophy underpinning the sectarianism but in his youth he accepted that the slogans defined him and the rest of the Shankill community.[31]

Not only were these symbols described as having meaning in the lives of the Protestant community; they were depicted as informing McClinton's sense of self and identity during his youth. Elsewhere, Dillon described this former loyalist paramilitary leader as having engaged in anti-Catholic violence as an unconscious desire to further his own status within the working-class community of Shankill. Interactionists, especially those who subscribe to structural Symbolic Interactionism, would see the symbolic nature of social structure, stratification, and the enhancement of one's status as profound influences on the emergence of one's sense of self and, hence, one's (group) identity.[32]

In his exploration of religiously motivated terror, Juergensmeyer argued that terrorism or extreme militant acts emerge from cultures of violence. To those within the collective who share similar perceptions of the world, bloodshed, harm, and destruction signify valid and justifiable means by which to instigate change.[33] Although Juergensmeyer grounded his cultural analysis of terrorism in the work of Michel Foucault, Pierre Bourdieu, and Clifford Geertz, he made frequent reference to the impact of symbols and meanings on acts of political violence. For example, he described "symbolic empowerment" as the process through which individuals gain a sense of control over their lives. This empowerment or enfranchisement unfolds through a four-stage process: (1) a world gone awry; (2) foreclosure of ordinary options; (3) satanization and cosmic war; and (4) symbolic acts of power. According to Juergensmeyer, the final stage represents "the performance of acts that display symbolically the depth of the struggle and the power that those in cultures of violence feel they possess."[34] An instance of this is the taking of one's own life and those of others in an effort to secure martyrdom. One of Juergensmeyer's most compelling arguments relative to this study is that terrorism is as much a product of culture as it is the result of individuals.

Fully embracing an interactionist framework, Berbrier conducted a case study of the right-wing publication entitled *Instauration* and its editor.[35] Berbrier argued that White supremacists utilize the technique of impression management[36] to counteract the negative stereotypes that affix themselves to individuals when assigned the stigmatizing identity of racist.[37] By engaging in such normalizing techniques as intellectualizing, transforming, massaging, and manipulating, White supremacists attempt to redefine the meaning for their involvement in this movement.

In a similar fashion, Arena and Arrigo constructed a social psychological model—based on Mead's intrapsychic, interpersonal, and situational frames of reference—in order to understand membership in and the deviant behavior of White supremacist collectives.[38] On the basis of these three prisms, four thematic categories were systematically investigated: power, identity, sexuality, and the definition of the situation. These categories were considered integral to a systematic assessment of White supremacists and their ongoing social interaction.

Blee's treatment of women involved in racist and anti-Semitic groups (e.g., skinheads, neo-Nazis, Christian Identity, Ku Klux Klan), draws attention to the construction of feminine identities within hate movements.[39] On the basis of in-depth interviews with thirty-four women, Blee demonstrates how one's personal and collective feminine identity emerges through racist knowledge and activism channeled within one's mainstream family and home life. Whether pursuing careers in health care, education, or engineering, these mostly middle-class women experience intense racial hatred because they participate for social rather than political reasons in racist groups. This is a process of identity formation in which such things as advertisements for Aryan cookbooks in white power newsletters instruct women on "proper" domesticity, transforming everyday racism into extraordinary racism.

Collectively, the studies cited above lay the essential groundwork for a more detailed and systematic exploration of the identity construct, especially as manifested, nurtured, and sustained in extremist militant groups. The next logical step is to develop an integrated and seamless model that accounts for the formation and maintenance of one's sense of (social) self within the terrorist collective. From our perspective, the structural Symbolic Interactionist framework, built around the insights of Identity Theory, which understands identity to be those aspects "of the self composed of the meanings that persons attach to the multiple roles they typically [assume] in highly differentiated contemporary societies,"[40] is the most serviceable for this particular endeavor. However, before we move on to a more comprehensive review of the conceptual approach undertaken in this book (see chapter 3), some summary observations on alternative interpretive models by which to explain terrorism are warranted.

Alternative Interpretive Approaches: A Brief Review

There are several approaches within the interactionist paradigm wherein the connection between identity and extremist militant behavior could be investigated.[41] These include social constructionism, phenomenological sociology, ethnomethodology, and labeling theory. Each of these orientations is succinctly described below.

The constructionist framework is based on the premise that people's perception of reality is socially conceived.[42] This organization of reality takes place through the interpretations for, perceptions of, interactions with, and ascribed meanings regarding the symbols in one's environment.[43] In this context, identities are formed through one's personal experience, history, and stock of knowledge, as well as the views that others have about one's self-concept as delineated over time. Of particular relevance here is the study of the way societies or cultures construct social problems (e.g., homelessness, flag burning, AIDS, pedophile priests), including the impact such typifications have on those individuals or groups affected.[44]

Phenomenological sociology is based on the conviction that reality is socially constructed. It is informed by the work of existential phenomenologist Alfred Schutz, among other notable theorists. Schutz[45] maintained that by exploring the everyday, routine dimensions of an individual's social life and the person's conscious experiences of it, researchers can expand and deepen their understanding of the way people construct their reality and assign meaning to it.[46] In this regard, then, phenomenological sociology is "the study of consciousness and social life, [exploring that space] between the shape of social life on the one hand and how people perceive, think, and talk about it on the other."[47] Thus, as an investigatory and interpretive model, phenomenological sociology requires that the researcher provide deliberately detailed descriptions of the individual's cognitive and affective experiences as a way of accessing the contours of the subject's consciousness.[48]

Ethnomethodology is another investigatory model based, in part, on the work of Alfred Schutz.[49] However, as conceived of by Harold Garfinkel, "ethnomethodology (meaning 'people's methods') is the study of how [individuals] actually use social INTERACTION to maintain an ongoing sense of reality in a situation."[50] Garfinkel described the ethnomethodological approach as "the investigation of the rational properties of indexical expressions and other practical actions as contingent ongoing accomplishments of organized artful practices of everyday life."[51] Indexical expressions refer to the interpretation of language, behavior, motives, objects, and events in a given environment, all of which have a multitude of meanings. Therefore, only by submerging himself or herself into a particular environment can the researcher understand these expressions from the actor's unique vantage point. Descriptive in nature, the ethnomethodological model relies on knowledge obtained through experience that is local and situated, including conversational analysis. This approach, then, focuses on the taken-for-granted, routine activities of social interaction and, in an effort to understand the human experience, emphasizes the natural encounters that take place during everyday life.[52]

As an interpretive prism for understanding the complexities of human behavior, labeling theory has specifically been applied to studies on deviance.[53] Also known as the "societal reaction approach," labeling theory is based on the premise that people come to perceive themselves and the meaning of their actions from the responses others have to them. Labeling theorists argue that individuals engage in deviance because various systems of social control (i.e., police, court, juvenile, and correctional agencies) define or stigmatize them as such. At the individual level, these definitions can become a part of a person's self-image and personify one's identity. The more an individual comes to internalize the assigned stigma, the more committed the person will become to a deviant career. In addition, at the societal level, the more socially recognized these deviant labels are, the more likely it is that people will come to expect from others behavior that is defined as deviant.

Although all four of these interpretive approaches offer something unique to the study of self-concept and crime, each of them principally emerged from Symbolic Interactionism and the insights generated from within this intellectual tradition. Consequently, it is this explanatory framework that represents a useful and, perhaps, pivotal foundation from which to engage in subsequent interpretive studies on identity and terrorism. Moreover, each of the aforementioned alternative approaches lacks sufficient theoretical and organizational grounding such that any one of them could provide a testable framework for subsequent empirical investigations relevant to our stated thesis. In other words, accessing the identity construct as a basis to explain one's membership in and allegiance to an extremist militant collective necessitates an appeal to social-psychological constructs integral to an understanding of this phenomenon. Social constructionism, phenomenological sociology, ethnomethodology, and labeling theory either do not consist of such well developed concepts or have only tangentially examined them to date. Accordingly, turning to Symbolic Interactionism—an interpretive field of inquiry devoted expressly to examining the meaning-making process through such concepts as roles, symbols, socialization, the definition of situations, and self-concept—seems as logical as it does prudent.

Certainly there are additional alternative approaches outside the realm of the interactionist paradigm that could be of help in understanding the connection between identity and terrorism. For example, postcolonialism critically examines the aftermath of colonial rule.[54] Common topics of study include the subjugation of indigenous peoples, the means through which such communities are oppressed, and the way in which national, ethnic, and/or cultural identities are constructed, understood, and reclaimed in postcolonial climates by both the colonizers and the colonized. Another alternative strategy is postmodernism. As a broad conceptual approach to the knowledge process, postmodernism scrutinizes the role that language plays in shaping reality. In the context of terrorism, postmodernist inquiry would focus on examining the narratives of race, class, power, ethnicity, identity, culture, and gender.[55] The aim of such an inquiry would be to assess how the prevailing "texts" regarding these narratives foster or impede a more complete regard for social justice,[56] especially in relation to the individual's or collective's involvement in militant behavior. Additionally, feminist inquiry is worth noting. This critical approach to understanding social relationships, harm, and identity focuses on the construction of gender as constitutive of the social person and of social life.[57]

While each of these alternative approaches would be useful in its own right for exploring the dynamics of militant extremism and identity construction, these orientations are decidedly beyond the scope of what this book intends. Our approach uniquely addresses the social psychology[58] of terrorism and the manifestation and maintenance of the social person as militantly violent, within the confines of structural Symbolic Interactionism and Identity Theory. Accordingly, incorporating alternative perspectives within the selected framework does not advance the project's overall and targeted thesis. Having said this, we add that future scholars exploring the sociology of terrorism would do well to more systematically assess the relevance of colonialism, postmodernism, and feminist theory, especially in relation to the interpretive model developed in this book. This task is especially noteworthy given that the intended goal of any genuine attempt to advance the study of terrorism would entail a more complete regard for the way territorial imperialism, language construction and meaning making, and gender and sexuality all figure prominently into the analysis of culture, self, and society.

Organization of the Book

This volume is divided into three substantive sections. Consisting of chapters 2, 3, and 4, part 1 emphasizes theoretical developments and sets the stage for the interpretative analysis contained in subsequent chapters of the book. Specifically, this section examines the conceptual dimensions of identity relevant to the model in question and provides a brief overview of the five terrorist organizations under consideration. Part 2 is composed of chapters 5, 6, 7, 8, and 9 and applies the insights of structural Symbolic Interactionism to the five militant extremist collectives. The five chapters contained in this section demonstrate the explanatory and predictive properties of the interpretive framework as developed in the previous portion of this volume. Chapter 10 represents the third part of the book and addresses the implications of the overall conceptual model. The material canvassed here reviews the general utility of the interpretive framework, highlighting future theory construction, research, policy, and programming.

2

The Psychology of Terrorism

The word "identity" is as much a cultural cliché as it is a technical term common to a host of social scientific disciplines.[1] Simply perusing the extant literature on terrorism reveals that identity is frequently mentioned but often taken for granted and treated as though the mere mention of the concept conveys its powerful influence on one's behavior and on who one is. Indeed, as Jenkins observed, "there is something active about the word [identity] which cannot be ignored. Identity is not 'just there,' it must always be established."[2]

In this chapter, we return to the theoretical roots of identity as developed principally in psychology.[3] Our aim is to reestablish the concept's value in relation to understanding militant extremist conduct. To that end, this chapter focuses on providing a more systematic overview of the way the identity concept was developed and, subsequently, has been used to explain terrorism.

Accordingly, this chapter is driven by four substantive objectives. First, a summary of Erik Erikson's identity concept, its use in his eight-stage developmental model, and the concept's reliance on a *needs fulfillment* perspective are described. This more inclusive commentary is essential to our overall undertaking. In short, as was provisionally explained in the introductory chapter, the majority of the extant research attempts to explain terrorist behavior through the identity construct by utilizing the Eriksonian-grounded psychological/psychodynamic framework.

Second, the existing terrorism research that employs the identity concept in an explanatory capacity is reviewed. Although some of this literature is antiquated, its influence on current studies and interpretations remains evident. This analysis demonstrates the degree to which the psychodynamic perspective has informed contemporary investigations of the way one's self-concept is fashioned, nurtured, and sustained through membership in militant extremist collectives. Some brief observations on the limits of this purely psychological approach are also delineated.

Third, the social psychological explanations of terrorism, originating from Social Identity Theory (SIT), are examined. This examination includes an analysis of related fields of inquiry on the subject emanating from political science and international relations. Collectively, this material indicates what investigators purport to know about the identity construct, especially in relation to militant extremist behavior.

Fourth, the limitations of the extant literature on identity and terrorism are summarily delineated. Although brief, this commentary is essential as it sets the stage for the material that follows it in chapter 3. At issue here is whether and to what extent an alternative interpretive model, informed by the insights of structural Symbolic Interactionism, can deepen and expand the social scientific understanding of terrorism such that it benefits society and those impacted by aggression, violence, and bloodshed.

Origins of the Identity Construct

The theoretical study of identity dates back to the early works of Erik Erikson.[4] Erikson began formulating his ideas on what he called "the ego identity" in the early 1940s, basing the concept on the insights of pragmatist William James and the father of psychoanalysis, Sigmund Freud. Erikson's reliance on the work of James is most evident in his treatise *Identity: Youth and Crisis*.[5] In this volume, Erikson cites a letter James had written to his wife. In the letter James states that

> a man's character is discernible in the mental or moral attitude in which, when it came upon him, he felt himself most deeply and intensely active and alive. At such moments there is a voice inside which speaks and says: "This is the real me!"[6]

Although James used the term "character" in his letter, Erikson envisioned that what he was describing was one's sense of identity that overcomes an individual, providing the person with a sense of self-recognition and self-definition.

In the same text, Erikson[7] also refers to Freud's conceptualization of identity. He cites Freud's 1926 address to the Society of B'nai B'rith. In this address, Freud indicates that

> what bound me to Jewry was (I am ashamed to admit) neither faith nor national pride, for I have always been an unbeliever and was brought up without any religion though not without respect for what are called the "ethical" standards of human civilization. Whenever I felt an inclination to national enthusiasm I strove to suppress it as being harmful and wrong, alarmed by the warning examples of the peoples among whom we Jews live. But plenty of other things remained over to make the attraction of Jewry and Jews irresistible—many obscure emotional forces, which were the more powerful the less they could be expressed in words, as well as a clear consciousness of inner identity, the safe privacy of a common mental construction. And beyond this there was a perception that it was to my Jewish nature alone that I owed two characteristics that had become indispensable to me in the difficult course of my life. Because I was a Jew I found myself free from many prejudices which restricted others in the use of their intellect; and as a Jew I was prepared to join the opposition, and to do [so] without agreement [from] the "compact majority."[8]

After reading this passage, Erikson explained that he understood Freud's "consciousness of inner identity" to be a bitter pride in a people's strength cultivated through centuries of persecution.[9] Moreover, given Freud's observations, Erikson conceptualized his own ideas of positive and negative identities in the following way:

> Freud contrasts the *positive identity* of a fearless freedom of thinking with a *negative* trait in "the people among whom we Jews live," namely, "prejudices which restrict others in the use of their intellect." It dawns on us, then, that one person's or group's identity may be relative to another's, and that the pride of gaining a strong identity may signify an inner emancipation from a more dominant group identity, such as that of the "compact majority."[10]

The comments articulated by James and Freud postulate that one's identity emerges from an internal/external dialectic.[11] In other words, both the internal forces of human nature (James's description of one's internal character) and the external forces of the social environment

(Freud's emphasis on collectivity, ethnicity, nationality, and familial and social relationships) assume an integral role in the creation of one's self-concept. Unique to this more psychoanalytic orientation is the ability to integrate both dimensions of existence. On the basis of these insights, Erikson came to define what he termed the "ego identity."[12] The ego identity refers to "the awareness of the fact that there is a self-sameness and continuity to the ego's synthesizing methods and that these methods are effective in safeguarding the sameness and continuity of one's meaning for others."[13] Consequently for Erikson, identity was the answer to the age-old question, "Who am I?"

Within the field of psychology, Erikson is best known for his contributions to personality theory and life span development.[14] Although trained in psychodynamic thought, Erikson believed that Freud's approach to personality growth focused too much on sexuality as the basis for human behavior. Erikson maintained that in order to mature into a healthy, well-adjusted adult with a fully integrated personality and positive identity, a child had to successfully master a particular "crisis" that presented itself in each of eight stages of psychosocial development.[15] These eight stages of development include (1) trust versus mistrust, (2) autonomy versus shame and doubt, (3) initiative versus guilt, (4) industry versus inferiority, (5) identity versus role confusion, (6) intimacy versus isolation, (7) generativity versus stagnation, and (8) integrity versus despair.

Within each stage, the individual confronts two possible outcomes. The failure to successfully complete or adequately negotiate the crisis fosters developmental delays, personality dysfunction, and the acquisition of a negative identity. Erikson defined a negative identity as one that was "perversely based on all those identifications and roles which, at critical stages of development, had been presented to [the person] as [the] most undesirable or dangerous and yet also as [the] most real."[16] In contrast to Freud's focus on sexual gratification, the overarching theme of Erikson's model cultivated a positive identity. Erikson believed that the establishment of this more prosocial self would help yield a healthy personality and would contribute to the manifestation of a well-adjusted individual.

Erikson argued that the pursuit of identity was especially important during early-to-late adolescence. During this period, individuals are in the fifth stage of psychosocial development and are between twelve and nineteen years of age. This is a phase during which young people are expected to master the crisis of identity versus role confusion. In this phase, adolescents develop a strong sense of self or become bewildered about who they are and the roles they are to assume in life. Appropriately completing this stage means that one possesses a strong sense of direction and a solid set of core values, leading to a healthy, productive life. However, failing to successfully master the psychosocial dilemma of this period produces personality impairments and leaves the individual in a perpetual "identity crisis" for the remainder of his or her life. Erikson theorized that young people with little or no sense of self and belonging were especially susceptible to adopting a negative identity such that they were inclined to engage in behavior deemed inappropriate by society. The assumption here was that these youth sought out social disapproval that confirmed their negative identity and, correspondingly, their own limiting self-expectations.

While Erikson's developmental theory is sensitive to the influence of the family, socialization, and other social forces, it relies heavily on the belief that individuals have a strong internal desire to satiate certain needs (e.g., love, belongingness, attachment, and esteem) in order to develop a healthy personality and live a well-adjusted life. This *needs fulfillment* perspective is perhaps best illustrated in Abraham Maslow's hierarchy of needs theory.[17] Maslow arranged human desires or wants into five categories: (1) physiological, (2) safety, (3) love and belongingness, (4) esteem, and (5) self-actualization. Physiological needs are essential to human life and include such things as food and water. Safety needs consist of stability and the protection from harm. Love and belongingness comprise feelings of affection and affiliation. Esteem needs encompass such things as recognition, approval, status, and success. Self-actualization represents the most advanced level in Maslow's hierarchy. Only those who completely fulfill their potential reach this stage.

Maslow's hierarchical model is sequential. In other words, one must satisfy first-level needs in order to advance to second-level needs and so on. This needs fulfillment perspective is important to an understanding of self-concept. In short, Erikson (and those who based their work on his conceptualizations) viewed positive identity as a psychological need that had to be satiated. Unless the individual successfully fulfills this need, personality deficiencies materialize. Indeed, as the next section illustrates, Erikson's psychosocial theory and the needs fulfillment perspective have received considerable attention in what Crenshaw called "the psychology of terrorism."[18]

The Identity Concept in Terrorism Research

Recognizing identity as an organizing concept, Crenshaw summarized two attempts to explain terrorist behavior through the use of Erikson's psychosocial theory.[19] The first was presented by Böllinger.[20] Specifically, Böllinger found Erikson's ideas quite applicable in his psychoanalytic study of West German terrorists. This particular research endeavor was initiated by the West German Ministry of Defense and utilized the case studies of 250 West German terrorists, including 227 left-wing (i.e., Red Army Faction and the 2 June Movement) and 23 right-wing participants.[21]

As Crenshaw explained, Böllinger believed that the subjects in his study failed to successfully incorporate trust, autonomy, and initiative into their personalities.[22] The inability to trust led to excessive aggression and failed social relationships. The lack of autonomy spawned destructive tendencies, insecurity, and a fear of personality disintegration. The absence of initiative engendered feelings of inadequacy, inferiority, and uselessness.

Böllinger speculated that these outcomes were the product of over-controlling and unaffectionate parental figures who engaged in frequent power struggles with their children, resulting in repeated clashes with society's authority figures. In families like these, the children experienced life through the prism of conflict. These were situations in which constant tension emerged between those perceived to oppress and the recipients of such subjugation. Turning to a life of underground resistance was one way in which the children could regain a sense of strength and power over their own deteriorating lives. As Crenshaw described it,

> According to Erikson, the rage that an individual feels at being helpless is projected onto the controlling figures; it may also engender guilt feelings, which lead to self-punitive actions. Thus, Erikson's theory can help explain the theme of self-sacrifice in terrorist behavior. Similarly, some individuals fail to surmount the crisis of initiative, so that on top of feelings of suspiciousness, self-doubt, powerlessness, and shame come inferiority and incompetence, feelings often resulting from social deficiencies and obstacles beyond the individual's control (such as weak educational background). Thus, for the individuals Böllinger studied, layer on layer of development and experience did not smooth over scars but reopened old wounds. Such individuals reached puberty and

the crisis of identity formation already seriously impaired. They found themselves in social and political circumstances that for different reasons were not favorable to the acquisition of a positive identity.[23]

Thus, as Böllinger surmised, the subjects of his study decided to join terrorist organizations in an attempt to create positive identities for themselves. By submerging themselves into the collective identity, they found meaning in their lives, a sense of coherent structure, and a stable social role to occupy. Indeed, the group provided "the structure and integration lacked by the isolated individual."[24]

Another application of Erikson's theory regarding identification and described by Crenshaw is found in Knutson's work.[25] She examined the adoption of the negative identity among incarcerated terrorists by focusing primarily on Zvonko Busic, a Croatian fanatic.[26] Through a series of interviews with him, Knutson determined that an individual comes to adopt the socially (or, more specifically, the governmentally) defined negative identity when the person perceives him- or herself as having no other alternatives or options. Citing Erikson's developmental observations on the matter,[27] Knutson argued that "a young person who, for reasons of personal or social marginality, is close to choosing a negative identity, that young person may well put his [or her] energy into becoming exactly what the careless and fearful community expects him [or her] to be—and make a total job of it."[28] Thus, as Knutson asserted, Busic was a man who felt socially isolated; he experienced the disenfranchisement associated with belonging to a marginalized ethnic group. Feeling as though he had exhausted all possible avenues for a successful life, Busic adopted a negative identity—one that was socially vilified but gave him meaning, structure, and purpose. Busic's decision to highjack a TWA airliner and plant an explosive device in Grand Central Station was undertaken in an effort to confirm and validate his negative identity and, hence, his commitment to the Croatian cause.

Knutson also noted that there are three equally important factors in the formation of a terrorist identity.[29] First, there is one's socialization toward a basic set of beliefs, attitudes, sociocultural/political values, and favored perspectives in which to see the world. To illustrate, Knutson used Ulrike Meinhof, one of the leaders of the Baader-Meinhof group, who was raised in a home with frequent exposure to radical views. Second, identification is influenced by the *psychological needs intensively pressing [on the individual] for actualization through behav-*

ior and commitment."[30] In this instance, a person "may achieve a feeling of wholeness and of success, and an end to frustration and continual defeat in the unsuccessful pursuit of other identities [not] traditionally and personally defined."[31] This includes the terrorist personality. Third, some catalytic event must transpire. This can include a severe life disappointment (or series of disappointments) that trigger within the individual a realization that access to positive alternative identities is nonexistent.

Additionally, Knutson indicated that explaining the underlying causes for the creation of a terrorist self-concept is complicated by the fact that a "negative identity" is not necessarily or always undesirable.[32] Interestingly, this position is inconsistent with Erikson's thesis that the negative identity encompasses disagreeable or adverse characteristics.[33] However, to substantiate her argument, Knutson reported that Busic was a man who strongly identified with the plight of the marginalized Croatian minority. He embodied strong feelings of ethnic pride and nationalism. From a cultural perspective, this type of pride in one's heritage and identification with the Croatian cause would probably be considered admirable, despite the absence (or presence) of society's approval for the violence that ensued.

Psychodynamically conceived investigations such as those cited above led Crenshaw to hypothesize that Erikson's observations regarding totalitarianism and authoritarian movements provided a significant degree of insight into extremist behavior, including terrorism.[34] Indeed, as Erikson explained, "when the human being, because of accidental or developmental shifts, loses an essential wholeness, he [or she] restructures himself [or herself] and the world by taking recourse [in] what we may call *totalism.*"[35] Applying these comments to the phenomenon of terrorism, Crenshaw provocatively argued the following:

At the stage of identity formation, individuals seek both meaning and a sense of wholeness or completeness as well as what Erikson . . . terms "fidelity," a need to have faith in something or someone outside oneself as well as to be trustworthy in its service. Ideologies, then, are guardians of identity. Erikson further suggests that political undergrounds utilize youth's need for fidelity as well as the "store of wrath" held by those deprived of something in which to have faith. A crisis of identity (when the individual who finds self-definition difficult is suffering from ambiguity, fragmentation, and contradiction) makes some adolescents susceptible to "totalism" or to totalistic collective identities that promise certainty. In such collectivities the troubled young find not only an identity but an explanation for their difficulties and a promise for the future.[36]

Crenshaw posited that people who become involved with militant extremism lack a strong sense of identity and find comfort in an organization's totalitarian dogma. This dogma provides the individual with the opportunity to find his or her own sense of identity within the group. In this way, "the collective identity becomes the individual's identity."[37] Moreover, the group offers the member an explanation for the person's feelings of hardship and a vision for a better, brighter future absent the source for his or her suffering.

Perhaps the most lucid application of psychodynamic theory (and by some logical extension, Erikson's psychosocial model) to the phenomenon of terrorist violence is found in the work of Post.[38] Post furthered Böllinger's observations on the importance of identification when accounting for militant extremism. In particular, Post appropriated the psychodynamic concept of "splitting," arguing that it had a profound influence in fanatical aggression. As he explained it,

> The need to belong—the need to have a stable identity, to *resolve a split and be at one with oneself and with society*—I believe that this is an important bridging concept which helps to explain the similarity in behavior of terrorists in groups of widely different espoused motivations and composition. In the case of the individual who takes up the cause of the politicized ethnic or national minority . . . the *split* derives from the *split within society and is a split in the sense of political identity.*[39]

Elsewhere, Post connects the idea of splitting with the related psychodynamic constructs of "projection" and an "externalized locus of control." As he described it,

> There is the me and the not me, the good and the bad, and if things are not going well, it is not me, it is their fault. And, having projectively identified society as the source of problems, it follows that the way to cure the problems is to destroy their source, is to destroy society. Alone, alienated, on the margins of society, seeking to belong, to find acceptance, to find others who feel the same way, that it's society's fault, that

it's not me, it's them—for such individuals, what a wonderful feeling it is to find that one is not alone, to find other like-minded individuals, to have one's inner doubts quelled and shored up with an ideology, to be accepted at last.[40]

Post argued that those troubled individuals who are isolated and alone find belonging, meaning, self-esteem, and an enhanced self-concept in their group membership; this is a collective identity that they will adamantly defend and, if need be, fight to preserve.[41]

In sum, Post furthered the argument that political violence is driven by internal forces in combination with organizational and group dynamics.[42] In addition, by utilizing a psychodynamic approach and by incorporating social psychological concepts such as group behavior and conformity, Post maintained that militant extremism is the result of "the terrorist's search for identity, and that, as he [or she] strikes out against the establishment, [the person] is attempting to destroy the enemy within."[43] Indeed, as he concluded, "the act of joining the terrorist group represents an attempt to consolidate a fragmented psychological identity, to resolve a split and be at one with oneself and with society, and, most important, to belong."[44]

Relying on Post's contention that individuals join terrorist organizations because they have a need to belong (symptomatic of an incomplete or fractured psychosocial identity),[45] Shaw developed what he termed the "Personal Pathway Model."[46] He argued that an individual's decision to join a militant extremist group is inculcated through socialization, narcissistic injuries, and important life setbacks or failures that serve to divert the individual from traditional social roles. These may include escalatory or catalytic events such as a horrific confrontation with police or personal connections with those involved in violent groups. Shaw summarily described such identification as follows:

Apparently, membership in a terrorist group often provides a solution to the pressing personal needs of which the inability to achieve a desired niche in traditional society is the *coup de grace*. The terrorist identity offers the individual a role in society, albeit a negative one, which is commensurate with his or her prior expectations and sufficient to compensate for past losses. Group membership provides a sense of potency, an intense and close interpersonal environment, social status, potential access to wealth and a share in what may be a grandiose but noble social design. The powerful psychological forces of conversion in the group are sufficient to offset traditional social sanctions against violence. . . . To the terrorists, their acts may have the moral status of religious warfare or political liberation.[47]

Clearly, the underlying premise of Böllinger's,[48] Knutson's,[49] Post's,[50] and Shaw's[51] work is that, fundamentally, the individual who becomes involved in a terrorist organization is in some way divided or wanting. More specifically, the person suffers from low self-esteem, engenders a fragmented identity, is searching for a stable self-concept, is unable to cope with the significant frustrations of life, emerges from an at-risk group, or harbors an intense desire to belong because the individual is a social misfit or communal outcast. In short, the subject is pathological and dysfunctional, experiencing profound personality deficiencies traceable to unresolved psychosocial trauma. Accordingly, it is the terrorist organization that fills a deep intrapsychic void in the life of the individual that cannot be sated otherwise.[52]

A Critical Review of the Purely Psychological Approach to Identity and Terrorism

A cursory review of the more contemporary research on militant extremism indicates that "identity" is a term mentioned routinely as a contributing factor that helps explain the emergence of terrorist behavior. Arguably, this is a result of the identity construct (i.e., Erikson's process of identification) as applied to earlier investigations of terrorism.[53] However, one of the primary criticisms of the purely psychological account is that researchers have principally relied on a positivist[54] perspective to understand the motivation of militant extremism and, as a result, have committed the fundamental attribution error.[55] The premise of this concept is that investigators tend to overestimate dispositional or internal causes for behavior and neglect the situational or external influences.[56] Presumably, this bias contributes to the portrayal of individuals who engage in terrorism as demonic, subhuman, or otherwise dysfunctional.

The above observations are consistent with the work of Silke.[57] Silke noted that, for several years, psychological research had depicted militant extremists as inherently flawed, abnormal, or psychopathic. Not surprisingly, then, the most positive diagnoses affixed to terrorists have been that they suffer from antisocial, narcissistic, or paranoid personality disorders. However, the research supporting these conclusions is sparse and of poor quality. As Horgan asserted, there is simply no systematic evidence indicating that terrorists are psychologically different from their nonterrorist counterparts. Instead, there is a growing body of literature supporting the conviction that militant extremists essentially embody ordinary personality features.[58] Indeed, as Silke observed, "most serious researchers in the field at least nominally agree with the position that terrorists are essentially normal individuals."[59]

Given the above observations, Shaw argued that "the risk of primary attribution errors is even more pronounced in the presence of limited or biased data, as is generally available in the terrorism context."[60] Upon closer examination of the existing psychodynamic research that represents the psychology of terrorism (including the use of the identity construct), Horgan concluded that the application of this perspective is un-convincing and is open to considerable speculation.[61] Moreover, he noted that theories built on psychosocial and psychodynamic premises have been stretched beyond their explanatory and predictive power. For example, commenting on Böllinger's conclusions regarding West German terrorists, Horgan[62] offered the following observations:

> Unfortunately, methodological issues reduce the strength of the assertions from the original research. Not only were terrorists unwilling to meet the researchers (owing to the circumstances in which the interviews were taking place), but researchers also reported a lack of cooperation from local officials. . . . As if not problematic enough, Crenshaw reminds us that the researchers were of course interviewing *suspected* terrorists—apprehended but not yet convicted of offenses: "Since interviews with social science researchers did not have the status of privileged communications, the researchers could have been subpoenaed to give evidence in the cases."[63] The implications of such problems should be borne in mind when examining subsequent discussions[64] that develop the conclusions based on this earlier research.[65]

In addition to the fundamental attribution error and the assorted concerns linked to it, the validity of psychodynamic explanations concerning identity and terrorism can be significantly questioned. This is especially the case when one considers "the unfalsifiability and circular logic of [these] theories, their claim to 'special' knowledge, and [their] characteristic reluctance to share in the rigorous scientific demands of contemporary psychology as far as theoretical development and hypothesis testing is concerned."[66] Issues such as those just enumerated led Horgan to conclude that the research on identity and terrorism, informed by the psychodynamic orientation, is woefully inadequate.[67] Indeed, as he summarized,

> the process of identification (in its present incarnations) will remain a very limited tool [in understanding terrorist motivations] for several reasons, not least due to accounts of terrorists' involvement that easily contradict suggestions about generalising from such an approach. A more sophisticated model of identity, one aware of the need to integrate levels of analysis, might prove beneficial particularly in understanding how a terrorist's own sense of identity forms and develops in response not only to his or her "own" world but to external change.[68]

Throughout all of these early psychosocial and, more specifically, psychodynamic theories that account for identity in relation to militant extremism, internal processes or inadequately resolved intrapsychic crises impede prospects leading to the formation of a healthy, well-adjusted personality. As a result, terrorists are defined by their deficiencies and rendered abnormal, psychopathic, and dysfunctional. As we have described, there are serious limitations to this orientation and, as a consequence, a different direction in the literature seems warranted. One suggestion along these lines comes from Brannan, Esler, and Strindberg.[69] As they argued, terrorism research needs "a more constructive [model] that adequately accounts for the dynamics of the group identity and belonging within a framework of profound cultural difference."[70] From their perspective, the application of Social Identity Theory (SIT) represents one possible solution. This is a perspective that "emphasizes the significance of the subject's social situation, the group member's internally constructed social identity, and the context in which a cohesive group consciousness is installed in the minds and hearts of the members."[71] These researchers conclude that SIT adequately fills the explanatory void because it "offers a means of integrating insights from a variety of analytical models within an intercultural framework."[72] With these thoughts in mind, we now turn to the social psychological and related literatures (including political science and international relations) that have appropriated the insights of Social Identity Theory as the preferred basis by which to account for militant extremist behavior.

The Application of Social Identity Theory in Terrorism Research

Social Identity Theory, or SIT, was formalized in the 1970s and 1980s in the work of Henri Tajfel and his colleagues[73] at the University of Bristol in England.[74] In contrast to its American counterpart, it was developed within European social psychology and took a nonreductionistic approach to understanding human behavior.[75] Instead of focusing on intra- and interpersonal behavior, the European perspective focused on intergroup conduct. Moreover, SIT was formed against the backdrop of the turbulent 1960s, and European social psychologists embraced a view of "humankind [that was not] cohesive, peaceful, or rational; [it was one that] could not be adequately explained by the model of humankind offered by major North American social psychological theories."[76] As a theory of intergroup relations between large-scale social categories (e.g., race, ethnicity, socioeconomic status) and group processes, SIT has become a popular approach to understanding prejudice, discrimination, and intergroup violence.[77] As a result, it has seen significant application to the fields of political science and international relations.

An important aspect of SIT is the distinction among three forms of identity: personal, social, and group/collective. Tajfel described personal identity as corresponding to interpersonal behavior in that all individuals see a differentiation between themselves and others.[78] He defined social identity as "that part of the individual's self-concept which derives from [one's] knowledge of his [or her] membership in a social group (or groups) together with the value and emotional significance attached to that membership."[79] Deschamps and Devos argued that one's personal and social identity represent two ends of a continuum.[80] Personal identity is the feeling of difference from others and social identity is the feeling of similarity to others. Pelham and Hetts summarized this by stating that the social self consists of both personal (i.e., private, individual) and social (i.e., shared, collective) identities.[81] The group/collective identity can be defined as a shared sense of characteristics, values, purposes, statuses, histories, and futures. Within Social Identity Theory, all three dimensions play a significant role in shaping one's self-concept, self-worth, self-esteem, and self-definition.

In line with these definitions, Tajfel and Turner described the three general assumptions underlying SIT.[82] They summarized them as follows:

1. Individuals strive to maintain or enhance their self-esteem: they strive for a positive self-concept.
2. Social groups or categories and the membership of them are associated with positive or negative value connotations. Hence, social identity may be positive or negative according to the evaluations (which tend to be socially consensual, either within or across groups) that contribute to an individual's social identity.
3. The evaluation of one's own group is determined with reference to specific other groups through social comparisons in terms of value-laden attributes and characteristics. Positively discrepant comparisons between in-group and out-group produce high prestige; negatively discrepant comparisons between in-group and out-group result in low prestige.[83]

Clearly, these general assumptions are reminiscent of Erikson's conceptualization of the processes of identification, especially those that relate to enhancing self-esteem and striving for a positive self-concept. On the basis of these underlying presuppositions, Tajfel and Turner articulated three theoretical principles of SIT:

1. Individuals strive to achieve or to maintain positive social identity.
2. Positive social identity is based to a large extent on favorable comparisons that can be made between the in-group and some relevant out-groups: the in-group must be perceived as positively differentiated or distinct from the relevant out-groups.
3. When social identity is unsatisfactory, individuals will strive either to leave their existing group and join some more positively distinct group and/or to make their existing group more positively distinct.[84]

Through group identifications, individuals secure for themselves a positive self-concept and self-definition, as well as enhance their self-esteem. The theory indicates that these needs are satisfied through a process of social comparison and by the devaluing of those who do not belong or are members of the out-group.

Hogg described SIT as having two underlying processes: categorization and self-enhancement.[85] Through categorization, one clarifies his or her intergroup boundaries. These are borders or margins that, in effect, produce group stereotypes, normative perceptions, and interpersonal actions. Self-enhancement guides social categorization so that people gain a sense of esteem and positive self-concept by attaching favorable qualities to their own in-group and less favorable qualities to out-groups. There also is a subjective dimension to SIT; that is, people perceive and experience reality from their own unique perspectives.

In addition, Worchel, Morales, Páez, and Deschamps indicated that SIT has two components: cognition and motivation.[86] For example, from the cognition base, individuals overestimate intergroup differences and underestimate intragroup differences. From the motivational base, individuals may develop prejudice in an effort to enhance their own self-esteem. Pelham and Hetts framed this motivational aspect in terms of the need for positive regard or social approval and the need for coherence or cognitive consistency.[87]

For Tajfel and Turner, the basic hypothesis of SIT was that the pressure to see oneself and one's group in a positive light led to social comparison and, subsequently, an attempt to differentiate between in-groups and out-groups.[88] In order for this process to take place, three variables must be present. The first variable is that an individual must have internalized his or her group membership as a part of the person's self-concept. Simply being identified by others as a member of the group is inadequate. The person must feel as though he or she is truly a member of that group. The second variable is that the social situation must be conducive to intergroup comparisons; for example, there must be some identifiable differences in order for individuals to differentiate. The third variable is that group members will not cognitively compare themselves to every collective; however, they will compare themselves to those groups they perceive as relevant to them. Similarity, proximity, and situational salience all play an integral role in determining which groups are comparable and which groups are not.

Tajfel and Turner argued that the competitive dynamic created through this process of intergroup comparison and derogation gave rise to prejudice, discrimination, and ethnic conflict.[89] As a result, those groups with a negative social identity use various strategies to reduce the psychological discomfort produced by this process. Some strategic examples include assimilation, strengthening the group identity, direct challenge, and violence.

While the application of SIT to terrorism has been relatively limited, it has been used to understand intergroup relations between social groups who frequently employ the technique of terrorism. To illustrate, Cairns[90] used Tajfel's approach to intergroup relations[91] as a framework for conducting a social analysis of the conflict between Catholics and Protestants in Northern Ireland. He explored social identity, social competition, and an individual's need for psychological distinctiveness as factors that contribute to this conflict. By identifying social categorization as a pivotal step in his SIT analysis, Cairns discussed the social construction of ethnic divisions between Catholics and Protestants in the region.[92]

Moreover, by assessing the rift in Northern Ireland through SIT, Cairns suggested that the Catholic community possessed, at one time, the negative identity.[93] Indeed, on the basis of the work of previous researchers who explored the situation in Ireland,[94] Cairns noted that the primary method by which the Catholic faithful shed the negative identity and attained a positive one materialized when they created "a new ideology which involved positively valued distinctiveness from the superior group."[95] In particular, this took place during the second half of the nineteenth century in the form of a Gaelic Irish-Catholic pride movement. The aim of the movement was to recognize and reinvigorate involvement in Irish culture, especially in the form of sport.

Another, more subtle means by which to shed the negative identity undertaken by Irish Catholics was through social comparison, specifically in relation to education. Cairns cited the work of Darby to develop this point.[96] Darby found that in an effort to eliminate the stereotype that Catholic schools were academically inferior to their Protestant school counterparts, Catholic teachers employed in Protestant schools frequently described their educational work environment as cold, rigid, and unfriendly.[97] Conversely, they described the atmosphere in Catholic educational settings as friendly, open, and inviting.

Through the use of Irish pride and social comparison, the minority Catholic community in Northern Ireland came to desire the status of the majority Protestant community. Cairns indicated that during the 1920s and 1970s this was captured in the civil rights movement.[98] However, Tajfel suggested that this status-seeking activity was a consequence of social competition: although Catholics in Northern Ireland wanted to maintain their identity, they also had a psychological need to become more like the Protestant majority.[99] Underpinning this desire for standing was the perception among the middle-class Catholic communities that their social mobility was blocked by Protestant segments, resulting in a more radical response from them and, consequently, intergroup conflict.[100]

Cairns also reported that there was little doubt that the Protestant community had enjoyed the positive identity in Northern Ireland for some time.[101] As he explained it, "this positive social identity seems to be based upon folk memories from the past, particularly related to what is seen as their triumphs in a struggle for freedom and conscience at 'Derry, Aughrim and Boyne,' battles linked with the name of William III, Prince of Orange."[102] Indeed, Protestants' annual celebration of these victories was evidence of their insecurity and their desire to maintain the positive social identity through continual social comparison and competition with Catholics in the region. These and other symbolic representations, such as flying the Union Jack and singing the "Queen," were all meant to ensure psychological distinctiveness and maintain the positive social identity as the exclusive domain of Protestants.

Interestingly, Cairns suggested that the formation of Loyalist paramilitary groups among Protestants might have represented reactions to the perceived threat of losing the positive social identity.[103] Examples of these collectives include the Ulster Defense Association and the Ulster Volunteer Force. In conclusion, though, Cairns reiterated the fact that social categorization and the desire to attain (or maintain) the positive social identity through social competition, social comparison, and psychological distinctiveness all played a major role in the Irish conflict.

In a related study, Cairns and Mercer explored the importance of religious, ethnic, and political social identities in Northern Ireland.[104] In their survey, 991 young people (60 percent Protestant, 40 percent Catholic; 57 percent female, 43 percent male; and an average age of 16.6 years) completed a questionnaire. The questionnaire consisted of eighteen dichotomous adjectives, nine of which described personality traits (e.g., anxious vs. calm, happy vs. unhappy), and nine of which described social identities (e.g., Protestant vs. Catholic, Celtic vs. Anglo-Saxon, Republican vs. Loyalist). The participants were asked to choose the term that best characterized them and then to rank order each of the chosen words. Statistical analyses revealed that the Protestant-Catholic identifier was the most popular among the ethno-political categories. Indeed, this group classification seemed to be the most significant indicator of social identities among the youth of Northern Ireland. However, in their concluding remarks, Cairns and Mercer commented that

> social identity is envisaged as a dynamic entity which may vary both from time to time and from situation to situation. . . . It is unlikely that the situation in which the present data were gathered (an open day at a university) was one in which any of the ethno-political social identities was particularly salient and, therefore, the present results may in fact have underrepresented the importance of these social identities in other situations.[105]

What this suggests is that the authors may have underestimated the impact of the specific situation in which the actual data collection process unfolded for their study. However, the fact remained that their results did provide a firmer understanding of religious, ethnic, and political divisions in the region.

Similarly, Seul used SIT to explain the conflict that arises between religious groups.[106] Relying on the assumption that individual and group identities are by-products of a person's efforts to satisfy basic human needs, Seul maintained that religion's primary function was to provide people with a stable and constant sense of shared meaning. As he explained it, "no other repositories of cultural meaning have historically offered so much in response to the human need to develop a secure identity."[107] Transmitted through rites, collective rituals, song, and prayer, religion serves this purpose by providing people with a shared sense of "locatedness" or a place in the world, as well as history, values, and traditions. For many people, involvement in a religious group satiates their need for stability, safety, affection, belonging, and self-esteem. Indeed, as Little[108] observed, religion contributes to the construction of individual and group identity by transmitting "myths of common origin, doctrines of chosenness and holy struggle, claims of primacy with respect to values that arise from a particular tradition's worldview, actors who sanction individual and group behavior with a sacred authority, and memorials and rituals that commemorate the sacrifices of group members."[109] Accordingly, intergroup comparison and competition based on religious differences become even more pertinent when scarce resources and territorial boundaries come into dispute.

Consistent with Seul's thesis, Worchel claimed that ethnicity, rather than religion, citizenship, race, and socioeconomic status, was of paramount importance when establishing an individual's sense of meaning and purpose.[110] For Worchel, ethnicity is the well-spring of human identity. Using Maslow's needs hierarchy,[111] Worchel asserted that human beings seek self-actualization through three goals in life. These goals consist of finding importance, meaning, and order. A pivotal step in attaining these goals is to form a self-identity. Worchel listed three fundamental processes in acquiring a self-identity. These included Cooley's idea of the *looking-glass self*,[112] Festinger's theory of social comparison,[113] and Tajfel and Turner's Social Identity Theory.[114]

Utilizing SIT, Worchel argued that people enhance their own self-image and self-esteem through affiliation with persons of similar ethnic backgrounds (the in-group).[115] This positive identity is attained at the expense of other ethnic groups (the out-groups). More generally, Worchel observed that the group itself is a willing partner. The collective plays an active role in shaping and molding the group members' behaviors. However, as Worchel noted, membership in that particular assemblage may be a significant dimension to the formation of identity for some individuals but not for others. Explaining the identity-through-ethnicity perspective, especially in relation to terrorism, Worchel observed the following:

> Sean O'Grady was a young lion in the Irish Republican Army (IRA). He had a reputation as being one of its most daring and violent members, directly responsible for the death of three Protestants in Northern Ireland. A colleague of mine interviewed O'Grady and reported a rather surprising statement: O'Grady observed that he did not grow up hating Protestants but had adopted the hatreds of his chosen group. He said: "They [Protestants] are the enemy of my people. The IRA targeted these people, and I was their instrument of death. I carry the hatred of my own group."[116]

Although clearly anecdotal, statements such as this suggest how intergroup relations influence militant extremist conduct. In summarizing these three processes, Worchel linked them all to social interaction and intra/intergroup relations.

While the situational component was not the direct focus of Worchel's analysis, he did recognize its importance in developing and maintaining one's self-identity.[117] For example, he incorporated Taylor and Fiske's idea that being a member of a novel or unique group in a particular type of situation gave that aspect of one's identity more prominence.[118] If the situation endangered that facet of one's identity, then it became more important.[119] Worchel[120] intimated that this notion is one of the major tenets underlying terror management theory.[121] The idea behind terror management theory is that individuals will rush to and defend that aspect of their identity under siege in an impending crisis. A second situational component briefly mentioned by Worchel is the physical environment.[122] As he described it, groups use symbols (e.g., flags, costumes, songs, medallions, personal characteristics) to constantly remind people about the collective to which they belong.

In his chapter exploring the causes of ethnic bloodshed, Worchel listed seven situational catalysts for ethnic group formation and intergroup conflict.[123] These factors include proximity, the impact of ethnic group distribution on nationalism, similarity, ethnic hatred between minority groups, ambivalence, salience, and strangeness of the situation. From a cognitive standpoint, Worchel explained that individuals live in a world of information. When information is collected in close proximity to other data or inputs, it is bundled together and forms schemas. A schema can be defined as "an organized body of knowledge about past experiences that is used to interpret present experiences."[124] People are then placed in categories on the basis of similar physical characteristics, places of residence, and common backgrounds. An illustration of the logic of schemas and categorization is the physical proximity of ethnic communities. The closer they are to one another and the less space is available to them, the more friction created by the proximity.

The impact of ethnic group distribution on nationalism was identified as the second catalyst to conflict and group formation. Nationalism was defined as the desire to promote one nation's superiority over others.[125] Worchel explained that one ethnic group's dominion of a nation could lead to disagreement, tension, and military struggle among subordinate ethnic collectives within the country and, moreover, with other groups outside the region.[126]

Similarity was the third factor identified by Worchel.[127] This construct describes the human tendency to affiliate with those who have similar physical characteristics, values, and attitudes. When threatened, individuals find comfort in the presence of those who are like them.

Worchel also listed ethnic hatred between minority groups as a catalyst for self-identity and (armed) aggression.[128] He noted how ironic (and unfortunate) it was that groups that experience prejudice and discrimination tend to direct similar behavior toward other minorities as a response to their own felt or perceived sense of mistreatment. Thus, not only do minority groups experience disdain by the ruling majority; they also encounter it among other ethnic minorities.

The next catalyst listed as contributing to group formation and conflict was ambivalence. Ambivalence draws attention to the uncertainty of one's identity and group affiliation, which can result in violence. As Worchel explained it,

> The point is that ambivalence about ourselves or the identity of our group may impel us to attack another group. By destroying or damaging the other group, we create a more certain or more positive image of our own group. . . . [C]onditions of ambivalence, threat, or uncertainty can consequently light the fires of hatred toward out-groups. We might post a sign over everyone's bed that reads, "The Most Dangerous Ethnic Group Is One Whose Identity Is Confused or Threatened."[129]

Salience was the sixth catalyst identified by Worchel.[130] Examples of ethnic group differences signifying salience in the environment include such things as culture, language, and physical characteristics. These differences serve as cues and are constant reminders of one's differentiation and variation from others.

The final situational factor giving rise to ethnic group formation and, subsequently, intergroup conflict was strangeness, or fear of the unknown. One's lack of exposure to and contact with others in an out-group creates fear and suspicion of these collectives. Although he does not explicitly state as much, Worchel's observations concerning those situational catalysts contributing to group formation and conflict lead one to conclude that such environmental components are as important to the fulfillment of psychological needs in intergroup ethnic conflict as is anything else.[131]

In an effort to demonstrate globalization's causal link to terrorism, Stevens utilized Social Identity Theory to explain the rise of the militia movement in the United States during the 1990s.[132] He identified the passage of the North American Free Trade Agreement (NAFTA) as a watershed event accounting for such armed mobilization on U.S. shores. NAFTA succeeded in formalizing a more open market for the exchange of goods and services; however, it inadvertently widened the income gap in the United States by increasing immigration. Increases in foreign nationals lowered wages, forced a shift in manufacturing from high- to low-wage countries (e.g., businesses moving from the United States to Mexico), and facilitated the development of technological advancements in production (e.g., robots that replaced human workers).

As a result of these changes, a downwardly mobile in-group was created consisting of lower- to middle-class Americans. These Americans had identified themselves as belonging to an internationally competitive labor group wherein their self-worth was informed by the collective's prestige. Unlike those competitive labor groups that thrived in the robust 1990s economy, this assemblage of disenfranchised Americans came to espouse a decidedly inferior group evaluation—one that contributed to the adoption of a negative identity, as well as sentiments of frustration and dissatisfaction. Regrettably, the in-group members came to believe that shedding their negative group status and identity was highly unlikely. Indeed, the implementation of NAFTA was perceived to be part of a larger, international conspiracy "to establish a new world order whose aims [included] the elimination of sovereign nation-states, the dilution of traditional Western values, and the mongrelization of the races."[133] For these Americans, paramilitary resistance represented the only logical response.

Indeed, for some whose allegiances were tied to this in-group, the militia movement may well have become a means by which to restore their sense of self-worth. The militia's staunch commitment to antiglobalization, anti–gun control, malevolent government, and White supremacy fueled the in-group members' resolve. These principals gave participants "new opportunities to meet their blocked needs for meaning, purposive action, and self-worth."[134]

In an effort to shed their inferior in-group identity that stemmed from the unjust implementation of NAFTA, the downwardly mobile individuals who joined such extremist groups began to favorably compare themselves to selected out-groups (e.g., Hispanics, Jews). In particular, militia movement faithful believed that these out-groups, whether through affirmative action or clandestine control of the world's financial system, were responsible for their felt sense of disenfranchisement and disempowerment. Moreover, these militant extremist collectives enabled their membership to invent new ways of evaluating their in-group status. For example, participants found strength in their perception of themselves as defenders of American values and American sovereignty: they were loyal soldiers fighting against a global plot to create a new world order that promoted unfettered immigration and unrestricted gun control. In this way, the militias' attraction to violence emerged from the shared sense of victimization engendered by its adherents. This victimization was thought to be shared by a host of less vocal, but similarly disheartened, Christian Americans. Not surprisingly, then, a desire to protect other like-minded individuals from the onslaught of globalization and tyrannical government became a beacon of the movement's collective identity.

Taylor and Louis utilized aspects of SIT and a vision of the self that emphasizes collective identity to explore the conditions giving rise to the recruitment of terrorists.[135] They focused on the self-concept, defining it as "a pivotal cognitive process that organizes experience, guides behavior, and provides the individual with meaning."[136] Located within the self-concept are identity and esteem: the former concept answers the question, "Who am I?"; the latter concept represents the evaluation of oneself. In addition, the authors made a second distinction that delineated the difference between the personal and collective self. The personal self refers to those characteristics that individuals believe are unique to them; the collective self refers to those attributes that an individual shares with other members of a category. This leads to the identification of four distinct components of the self-concept: personal identity, personal (self-) esteem, collective identity, and collective esteem. For Taylor and Louis, each of these constructs plays a pivotal role in the development of a healthy sense of self.[137]

Admittedly diverting from traditional theory on the self, Taylor and Louis suggested that a hierarchical arrangement to these four components exists.[138] More specifically, collective identity took psychological precedence over the other three components and personal identity assumed priority over personal (self-) esteem. Taylor and Louis justified their position on these matters by indicating that

> collective identity is a description of the group to which individuals belong, which serves as the normative backdrop against which they can articulate their unique attributes. In summary, without a clearly defined collective identity, an individual cannot engage in the normal comparative processes that would allow for the development of a personal identity. In this sense collective identity is primary.[139]

Moreover, an individual could not develop personal (self-) esteem without a clearly defined personal identity. This is the case because an individual who does not have a firm grasp on his or her unique attributes cannot evaluate him- or herself. Hence, given the authors' argument, it is impossible for one to have a personal identity without a collective identity that serves as a referential basis.

Reminiscent of James's contention that individuals have as many social selves as do the people who know them, Taylor and Louis asserted that everyone "has as many collective identities as the number of groups to which we belong and with which we share characteristics."[140] In addition, consistent with Seul's thesis,[141] cultural religious identities have special status because they are collective identities that purport to cover every aspect of a person's life. Indeed, these collective identities

> provide . . . members with a shared history and a set of broadly based and valued goals, along with detailed informal normative information about how to pursue the valued goals defined by the collective identity. Thus, cultural-religious collective identity is socially defined and represents the individual's most pervasive and all-inclusive collective identity.[142]

In sum, those who have a clearly defined cultural collective identity (which may or may not include a religious component) are able to develop a healthy, functioning self. Furthermore, a clearly defined collective identity is necessary for "engaging in the process of defining a personal identity and, by extension, personal (self-) esteem."[143]

Taylor and Louis applied their conceptual insights to terrorism.[144] They focused on those long-standing collective identities that had been disrupted—that is, collective identities that provided "individual group members with a sense of the structure of society, its rationale, how to navigate life successfully, and what to value and strive for."[145] As the authors noted, young people who are future focused are especially vulnerable to a confused collective identity because there is no mechanism or structure to define them, to promote a positive identity, or to achieve their goals. Consequently, if they face a time in their lives such that they are goal directed and desire to engage in meaningful behavior that will be satisfying, these youth will be prime candidates for committing terrorist acts.

To illustrate, Taylor and Louis described young men and women who languish away in refugee camps.[146] They have no legal status and little opportunity for education, work, sanitation, and social services. Despite the transmission of their cultural and ethnic heritage from their elders, this younger cohort lacks a clearly defined collective identity. Those who cannot generate a collective identity of their own may be attracted to the well-defined collective identity offered by other groups (including a terrorist organization), which provides a basis for explaining their marginalized status. Moreover, the collective identity of a militant extremist group "is not only clear but simplistically clear, it is espoused without even minor variation by every member of the organization, and it is forward-looking with the promise of better conditions for the group and the individual."[147]

The terrorist collective identity provides a framework for individual behavior through a plainly and unmistakably defined set of group norms. Indeed, the group self-concept is clearly demarcated as affiliates are typically a minority in their own society. This standing forces them to develop highly salient, simplistic, and deeply ingrained collective identity norms for participants to follow. "Such clarity satisfies an important psychological need for individual members of terrorist groups and offers insights into why a terrorist organization may be so attractive for certain members of disadvantaged groups."[148] Given their theory of identity, the authors concluded that those who lack a clearly defined cultural or religious collective self-concept are psychologically desperate and that the terrorist organization can fill this void. Terrorist organizations are attractive because they offer a simplistic worldview, an unambiguously defined enemy, and a clearly delineated set of norms of behavior through which the individual and the group can dramatically improve their debilitating conditions.

By harvesting concepts from Social Identity Theory, Moghaddam offered what is perhaps the closest vision of an intercultural framework for understanding militant extremism.[149] He described eleven cultural preconditions, and their corresponding perceptions, that lead to acts of terrorist violence. Commenting on these insights, Moghaddam explained that "it is essential to understand [them] as arising out of a larger culture and being imbedded in narratives adopted by a wider population, rather than being unique to small isolated groups of potential terrorists."[150] Using suicide bombers as an example, Moghaddam indicated that embracing these cultural preconditions allows one to have a better understanding of why individuals choose to engage in such violent conduct.

To conceptually ground his prerequisites, Moghaddam outlined four propositions. First, utilizing a cultural and collective approach to studying terrorism is more effective than dispositional and individualistic analyses. Second, a cultural examination fosters the development of a cultural profile regarding the conditions in which militant extremists are most likely to emerge. Third, the most salient and central feature of this cultural profile is a certain style of perceiving societal change and stability. Fourth, terrorist groups arise out of discrete cultural conditions, such as beliefs, values, and collective systems of meaning; therefore, these prerequisites are universal and will hold true regardless of the type of violent group.

The first cultural precondition that Moghaddam identified as spawning militant extremist collectives is the clandestine nature and subsequent isolation of terrorist organizations.[151] Secrecy and segregation serve to both maintain and strengthen ethnocentrism. This, in turn, supports a "we are right, they are wrong" attitude among affiliates, facilitates group conformity and cohesion, and solidifies the influence of its leadership.

The second cultural prerequisite is a dichotomous categorization of the world epitomized by good vs. evil and us vs. them sensibilities. The combinatory effect of categorization and isolation encourages intergroup bias. This leads to the development of stereotypes regarding the in-group and out-group, within-group minimization (a perception that the collective is more homogeneous than it really is), and between-group exaggeration (a perception that the differences between the groups are greater than they are).

A third cultural precondition is the existence of a belief system that portrays society as illegitimate and unjust. Accompanying this belief system may be a perception that a transgression of a "higher order" (e.g., as related to religion) has been committed. It might also entail a conviction that the government in power does not engender the correct values.

The fourth prerequisite is the discernment that since the present society is illegitimate and unjust, a need for radical change is warranted. This can include the belief that replacing the entire political and economic system is necessary. Indeed, as Moghaddam observed, dissatisfaction with the present social system and awareness of cognitive alternatives are given central prominence in Social Identity Theory.[152]

While group isolation and secrecy act as structural catalysts for the dichotomous categorization of one's reality, this precondition is a psychological medium for the fifth precondition. This prerequisite entails the recognition that an absence of legal means exists by which to change society into its ideal form. Whether real or imagined, this insight leads to mobilization and collective action.

Closely linked to this conviction is the sixth precondition. Because society is believed to be illegitimate and unjust, and because all normative paths to achieving an ideal society are blocked, alternative remedies are sought, including the use of nonnormative means (i.e., murder, criminal activity, suicide). Nonnormative interventions or solutions are deemed necessary and justified in the interests of the jeopardized cultural group.

The seventh prerequisite contributing to the formation of militant extremist organizations is a belief that acts of terror will destabilize society. Specifically, acts of terrorist violence inform the general public about the profoundly illegitimate nature of the existing order. Moreover, they demonstrate the inherent weaknesses of the ruling system.

The eighth precondition is the perception that the terrorist group can bring about societal change. This qualification addresses the vital role militant extremists see themselves as fulfilling in the realization of the new order. These roles are crystallized in the narrative of their past, present, and future. In the isolated context of the terrorist collective, these roles or statuses are deeply ingrained in the members.

The ninth prerequisite is the conviction that societal change realized through terrorism will improve the group's situation. This makes extreme acts, such as a willingness to sacrifice one's life for the good of the collective's agenda, seem logical. This is especially the case given the group's firmly held belief that such behaviors will ultimately benefit family members, friends, and the community as a whole.

The tenth precondition is a protected, unstable, and inflated view of the self. Recognizing that low self-esteem is frequently cited as a root cause for an array of disturbing behaviors—despite research suggesting otherwise—Moghaddam claimed that the problem with the self as it relates to terrorist acts is that participants have an overblown and unrealistic view of themselves (e.g., as revolutionaries, supported by the people, engaged in a sacred cause, leading others toward a better life).[153] This self-image, externalized among members, is protected within the isolated confines of the group.

The eleventh and final prerequisite is the perception that disengaging from the terrorist organization is difficult, if not impossible. Typically, these collectives demand complete and total loyalty, which prohibits any possibility of exit. Interestingly, Moghaddam observed that society's refusal to allow individuals to shed the terrorist label and stigma is ever present, especially as personified in the establishment of tribunals such as military courts.[154] Group members interpret panels such as these to indicate that they will never benefit from a fair trial.

Building upon this work, Moghaddam[155] framed aspects of the cultural preconditions into a metaphor he called the "staircase to the terrorist act." At the ground floor were perceptions of fairness and just treatment as they may pertain to independence or one's sense of personal or collective identity. Those who feel deprived of such liberties or that their identities have been threatened may move to the first floor, where one explores his or her options to fight unfair treatment. Continued perceived deprivation leads the individual to the second floor, where social institutions like the educational system may encourage the displacement of aggression upon an out-group. Moving to the third floor, recruits are persuaded to commit themselves to the terrorist group's morality, where the in-group/terrorist collective is seen as morally just and the out-group/enemy as morally disengaged. Moving to the fourth floor, the recruit becomes immersed in the social relationships and activities of the group, causing a change in perceptions focused on the legitimacy of "the terrorist organization and its goals, a belief that the ends justify the means, and a strengthening of a categorical us-versus-them view of the world."[156] It is at the fifth floor that the recruit side-steps inhibitory mechanisms and acts upon the exaggerated differences between the in-group and out-group. It is through the process of social categorization that civilians are determined to be the legitimate targets of violence in pursuit of the greater good.

The Limitations of Social Identity Theory: The Theory's Application to Terrorist Identities

While Social Identity Theory has made and will continue to make a significant contribution to the study of identity as it relates to militant extremism, it is limited in its ability to provide a complete portrait of the self. As Stets and Burke pointed out, SIT proposes that a person develops a social identity on the basis of the knowledge that he or she belongs to a social category or group.[157] SIT treats groups and categories as being synonymous. As demonstrated in the research just reviewed, category or group members may share a common feature or trait, such as being of the same race, ethnicity, or religion. Within this category or group is a uniformity of perceptions that can be revealed in cognitive (e.g., social stereotyping), attitudinal (e.g., a positive evaluation of the in-group and negative evaluation of the out-group), and behavioral (e.g., participating in a group's culture) contexts. However, following SIT, interaction between group members is not necessary in understanding behavior because mutual perceptions will be reinforced as most of the actors in a category hold the same perceptions, resulting in group formation. Invariably, this will give rise to collectives acting in unison, especially since they all have the same perceptions.

While emphasizing the similarities of actors in a group, SIT neglects the individuality and unique interconnectedness one has to those within the group or interaction context. Indeed, as Stryker asserted, people live in groups, not categories.[158] Citing Deaux,[159] Stryker explained that identities based on group relationships are more central and desirable than are those not based on group relationships. In the group-based identities proposed by SIT, only the actor's perceptions and actions are directly involved; one need not interact with group members.[160] Therefore, Social Identity Theory does not address the way individuals within the group who occupy counter-roles or statuses directly involved in the role performance interact with one another. However, as we contend, this deficiency can be remedied through an appeal to a sociologically animated social psychology—one grounded in the tenets of structural Symbolic Interactionism and Identity Theory.

3

The Sociology of Identity

Although Erik Erikson's use of the ego identity construct[1] proved to be a popular innovation in social scientific inquiry, psychology did not (and does not) own exclusive rights to its study nor to its development. In fact, Erikson was not the only social theorist to be influenced by the work of pragmatist and psychologist William James. Indeed, as Weigert et al. observed,

> A small group of sociologists working within a version of American pragmatism were trying to develop a more adequate sociological psychology for understanding human action as essentially social; they knew of Erikson's work and quickly adopted his term, but shortened it to "identity."[2]

The use of the term "identity" proved to be an attractive addition to an already developing discipline that had explored the self's development through the complex interaction between the individual and the symbols and meanings emanating from his or her social environment. This orientation, which would eventually become known as Symbolic Interactionism, adopted the term "identity" but left behind the intensive focus on the needs-driven, unconscious internal forces of the ego identity. Instead, it favored a view of identity whose formation was the result of an interaction between the self and society.

The purpose of this chapter is threefold. First, a brief, though foundational, overview of Symbolic Interactionism is provided. This overview includes a description of the development of the theory from the Scottish Enlightenment period through American pragmatism to contemporary inquiries on the subject. Second, the development of two approaches within Symbolic Interactionism (i.e., situational and structural) are recounted. Given the nature of our own study on terrorism, however, the structural perspective, its five organizing themes, and its conceptualization of the identity concept are more systematically enumerated. This enumeration includes the application of the interpretive framework in relation to five pivotal structural symbolic interactionist concepts. Third, an in-depth exploration of Identity Theory and the two strands of thought that originated from the structural perspective on Identity Theory (IT) are reviewed, and an explanation as to why a sociologically grounded model of identity is warranted. Collectively, the themes and concepts entertained in this chapter provide the necessary theoretical backdrop from within which to explore the link between identity and militant extremism as embodied in the five terrorist organizations examined in this book.

The Foundations of Symbolic Interactionism: A Brief Review

The phrase "Symbolic Interactionism" is a relatively recent one, especially among North American academics;[3] however, its origins can be traced to philosophers of the Scottish Enlightenment period.[4] Indeed, as Stryker indicated, these social theorists provided the rationale for establishing an empirical basis for studying human beings, their behavior, and the society they inhabited.[5] Intellectual luminaries such as David Hume, Frances Hutcheson, Adam Smith, and Adam Ferguson supported this notion by focusing their attention on the concepts of communication, sympathy, imitation, habit, and custom.[6] The Scottish moral philosophers understood society as being a network of interpersonal communications and the source of the self. Furthermore, their approach emphasized the study of human beings and their behavior from the standpoint of society rather than biology.

The link between the Scottish Enlightenment and Symbolic Interactionism is found in the work of American pragmatists such as William James, John Dewey, Charles Horton Cooley, William Isaac Thomas, and George Herbert Mead.[7] Indeed, as Stryker described it, pragmatism basically echoed the themes of the Scottish philosophers:[8] the mind was an instrument for adaptation, mental activities were natural objects subject to scientific investigation, the mind had an organized and internally dynamic character, and society was connected to the emergence of the individual.

William James developed the premise that people form attitudes and feelings about themselves and, in this way, their selves become symbolically denoted much like the objects in their environments.[9] James envisioned four distinct types of self: the material, spiritual, and social self, as well as pure ego. His conception of the social self proved to be particularly influential in the development of Symbolic Interactionism, especially in Mead's vision of the self as consisting of the *I* and the *me*.[10] James believed that an individual had as many social selves as there were people who recognized that person. He saw the self as a product of social relationships and paved the way for a view of the self as having a multifaceted character.

Expanding on the work of James (and others), Dewey stressed that human beings were unique: they possessed the capacity to adjust to their environmental conditions. Thinking entailed defining objects in their setting, rehearsing possible modes of behavior, imagining consequences of various actions, and eliminating and selecting forms of conduct that would or would not lead to desired outcomes.[11] For Dewey, thinking was both rooted and maintained in the capacity of humans to adapt.

Up until this period, the work informing the development of Symbolic Interactionism had been undertaken by philosophers and psychologists. However, these ideas entered the realm of sociology through the insights of Charles Horton Cooley.[12] Cooley saw the individual and society as representing two sides of the same phenomenon.[13] Neither one existed without the other; their relationship was inextricably interdependent. His contention was that individuals use *sympathetic introspection,* a process through which people use sympathy to cognitively imagine things (i.e., situations) as others would. These ideas were emphasized in what Cooley termed "the looking-glass self." He maintained that one comes to learn who one is through social interaction. Cooley theorized that one's self-idea (a more contemporary translation of this is the self-identity) is developed through three principal elements: "the imagination of our appearance to the other person; the imagination of the other person's judgment of [our] appearance; and some sort of self-feeling, such as pride or mortification."[14] Elsewhere, symbolic interactionists have referred to this self-idea phenomenon as "the mirror theory of identity" in that "we are what others' reflections make us [out to be]."[15]

Additionally, Cooley emphasized what he called "primary groups."[16] These consist of a small number of people with whom an individual has frequent face-to-face interactions. He argued that these individuals have a significant influence on the development of one's self, including the learning of behavioral expectations through the process of reflected appraisals.

Another sociologist to influence the early development of Symbolic Interactionism was W. I. Thomas.[17] As Stryker noted,[18] Cooley focused on delineating the emergence of the self in childhood;[19] however, Thomas was concerned with the process through which people came to redefine and socially construct the adult self. Thomas believed that an adequate account of human behavior included both the subjective and objective aspects of the human social experience. As he explained,

> Preliminary to any self-determined act of behavior there is always a stage of examination and deliberation which we may call the definition of the situation. And actually not only concrete acts are dependent on the definition of the situation, but gradually a whole life-policy and the personality of the individual him(her)self follow from a series of such definitions.[20]

Thomas argued that by way of evolution, human beings acquired an ability to define and construct situations through the symbols of their environment.[21] This was a powerful adaptation because to define the situation is to represent the environment symbolically to the self so that a response can be formulated.[22] This ability was pertinent to human survival. For example, if a cave man or woman saw footprints of a dangerous animal near a burrow, they would have to gear their response accordingly (i.e., leave the area). Therefore, human behavior is based on and is a function of the way in which situations are defined.[23]

By far, the most well recognized influence on the development of Symbolic Interactionism and, hence, sociological social psychology is found in the work of George Herbert Mead.[24] Although Mead was a philosopher and a psychologist, his impact has been most widely hailed within the symbolic interactionist tradition. In part, this is because he offered what no one had done before him: systematic treatment of Symbolic Interactionism's key concepts, analytical depth, and scientific precision.[25] Drawing on the lessons of pragmatism, Darwinism, and behaviorism, Mead developed a social psychology that started with ongoing social processes, and, through these social processes, mind, self, and society emerged. For Mead, humans did not simply respond to stimuli. The self developed through a complex interaction with several key

factors. These factors or processes can be understood through five pivotal concepts: objects, acts and social acts, meanings, role-taking, and
the emergence of the self.[26] Each of these elements is briefly described
below.

According to Weigert et al., an object is "any reality toward which
humans symbolically organize their responses and thus give it meaning."[27] Objects can be conceptualized in one of two ways. First, they
can be conceptualized as concrete objects consisting of physical matter that can be referred to, designated, or acted toward. Objects may
be something tangible in the environment (e.g., berries, wild game).
Through the context of an act, such as searching for food, these objects
come to be meaningful symbols—that is, objects that, in the preceding
example, symbolize the possible satiation of hunger. Through action
and meaning, then, objects become symbols. In an example more relevant to terrorism, a concrete symbol may be a target such as a bank, an
embassy, or a plane belonging to a national airline carrier. These symbols may come to epitomize capitalism or Western influence.[28]

Second, a symbol can also be interpreted more abstractly as a social
object. In this instance, symbolization takes place through communication. Communication is the exchange of meaningful gestures, or what
Mead referred to as the *conversation of gestures*. A stranger yelling an
obscenity in one's direction is a gesture. In this case, it is a socially constructed stimulus or a social object that symbolizes a range of possible
sentiments toward another (e.g., anger, violence, hatred). As Mead observed, "the relationship of this symbol, this vocal gesture, to such a set
of responses in the individual himself [or herself] as well as in the other
that makes of that vocal gesture [is] what I call a significant symbol."[29]
More clearly, when gestures come to mean the same thing to various
others and evoke similar responses in them, the gestures are said to have
common or shared meaning. Through this process, the gestures become
significant symbols. Those symbols that do not have shared meanings
are signs. According to Hewitt, then, "social objects are created as people engage in social acts. . . . Social acts depend upon social interaction
and interpretation. That is, in order for individuals to cooperate with
one another in the creation of social objects, they must orient their conduct to one another."[30]

However, in itself, the act is not a simple process. Mead conceptualized the act as having four components: impulse, perception, manipulation, and consummation.[31] In order to understand the act, one must

assess the interrelationships (rather than the distinctions) among all of these factors.[32] The following illustration helps explain the sequence of experiences, underscoring the social act.

If while walking toward her car in a deserted shopping center parking lot, a woman suddenly sees a man moving on foot in her direction, the woman's initial impulse may be to act (e.g., to search quickly for her keys). However, the woman's conduct depends on her perception of the man's action. For instance, she may perceive the man as simply rushing to his own car, which happens to be situated near hers. Indeed, as Hewitt noted, "the perception and designation of objects and stimuli are strongly influenced by the condition of the organism, so that the actions it undertakes stem as much from its own internal states as from the presence of external events or stimuli."[33] Thus, if the woman had experienced an assault in the past, she might be more vigilant in her perception of the man's behavior. The third component in the sequence is manipulation. In an effort to control the situation or gain a clearer idea of the man's intent, the woman might call out, "What do you want?" According to Hewitt, "This is the overt portion of the act—it is the external manifestation of a process that, until now, has gone on internally."[34] The fourth and final component of the act is consummation. It depends on the social response to an act (in this case, the question voiced by the woman). If the man responds that he just wanted to return the woman's credit card, an item she inadvertently forgot at the store register, and if the woman accepts the card graciously, then the sequence is complete and she might return to her day's activities. The significance of the interaction results in a social object: confidence in the store's personnel.

The third important concept within Mead's social psychology is meaning, and, not surprisingly, it is closely related to symbols.[35] Every social act and object in an individual's environment has significance. Individuals are constantly interpreting the meaning of these symbols, and they respond accordingly. As Mead intimated, "meaning is anchored in behavior. The meaning of an act is neither fixed nor unchanging, but is determined in conduct as individuals act toward objects."[36] Engaging in the interpretation of symbols is essential in the process of assigning significance to both social acts and objects. Typically, the interpretation is focused on the intent of a symbol or object. In the example used above, the woman interprets the man's intent throughout her interaction with him.

This process of interacting with symbols, acts, and meanings also involves taking the role of the other. Mead maintained that human beings were able to anticipate the responses of others by perceiving their own behavior from the other's standpoint.[37] This activity is known as "role-taking." Mead claimed that role-taking was a central mechanism in the development of the self.[38] Moreover, he believed it was the essence of thought and, hence, intelligence. As Jenkins observed, "Mead . . . insisted that self-consciousness, indeed cognition itself, c[ould] only be achieved by taking on or assuming the position of the other, in his terms a social 'generalized other.' "[39] A "basic" definition of role-taking is "the process whereby an individual imaginatively constructs the attitudes of the other and is consequently enabled to anticipate the role [and behavior] of the other."[40]

This definition is congruent with Hewitt's statement that "role-taking is a process in which one person 'gets inside' the perspective of another in a particular situation and 'observes' his [or her] own conduct from the other's point of view."[41] Only when people take on the role of another can they begin to see themselves and their behavior as objects in their own social environment. A process that can be both conscious and unconscious, role-taking provides individuals with the ability to see the various possibilities for their own actions. Moreover, Mead argued that thought and intelligence stemmed from the process of interpreting symbols, ascribing meanings, engaging in ongoing action, and role-taking. As he explained it, "in order that thought . . . exist there must be symbols, vocal gestures generally, which arouse in the individual . . . the response which he [or she] is calling out in the other, and such that from the point of view of that response [the person] is able to direct his [or her] later conduct."[42]

Included within Mead's role-taking concept is the idea of *reference others*.[43] These include both *significant* and *generalized others*. Reference others are the groups of people a person accounts for when he or she engages in behavior. More specifically, the individual cognitively constructs the thoughts and attitudes of these others as a way of guiding his or her own conduct. Generalized others are the collective embodiment of society's attitudes, viewpoints, and expectations.[44] Significant others are those who have a more intimate influence on the development of one's self. Examples include family members, school teachers, friends, and primary caregivers.

The fifth component of Mead's social psychology is the emergence of the self.[45] The self manifests itself during the process of social interaction, especially as the actor begins to experience and negotiate his or her own behaviors in relation to others. This process develops a self that is reflexive—that is, a self that is both the object and subject of social interaction. Mead illustrated the two-dimensional quality of the self in his use of the *I* and the *me* social psychological constructs. Stryker succinctly delineated the meaning of these concepts as follows:

> Anticipated responses with respect to oneself become the part of the self Mead calls the "me." This part of the self is the equivalent of social roles which are the organized attitudes or expectations of others incorporated into the self . . . the "I" represents the responses of the person to the organized attitudes of others.[46]

The interrelated nature of Mead's five social psychological concepts was summarily captured in Hewitt's remarks regarding the formation of the self. Indeed, as he explained it,

> The self can be described as a process of conduct formation that more or less constantly moves between two phases. One phase, which Mead called the "*I*," is impulsive. . . . When an individual's adjustment to a situation is disturbed, there is at first an impulse to act in some way. But as this impulse occurs, the second phase of the self, the "*Me*," comes into play: the individual checks or inhibits his [or her] act, considering how it will be received by others (specific or generalized) and choosing the plan of action he [or she] thinks best. The "*Me*" thus represents the specific or generalized other to whom the individual orients his [or her] act.[47]

Accordingly, the formation and maintenance of the self represents a complex interaction of symbols, meanings, acts, and roles. Mead put these key factors together in a three-stage model in which the self emerges through social processes and becomes an object toward which action can be directed.[48]

Stage 1 is the preparatory phase. During this period, the child simply imitates the actions of those in his or her environment. Throughout this stage, the child learns the meanings of symbols and begins to use them in communication.

Stage 2 is the play phase. During this period, the child learns to pretend to be other people and, in a sense, takes on the roles of others. To illustrate, when the child plays at being a mother, teacher, or police officer, he or she internalizes the stimuli that call out a particular response or set of responses to the role performance. These stimuli are eventually used to build the child's self-concept. The child's ability to play a role presupposes his or her capacity to role-take. This is due to the fact that the child has imaginatively constructed another person's attitudes, allowing him or her to anticipate and imitate appropriate behavior.[49]

A child's ability to play a role is not to be confused with role playing. Role playing is a development of playing at the role. As Lauer and Boardman noted,

> Role-playing refers to the fulfillment of a behavioral pattern associated with a social position. It results from reflective-appropriative role-taking, through which the individual develops a self-concept . . . and appropriates certain attitudes consistent with this self-concept. After the child has played at a particular role (mother, teacher, aggressive or non-aggressive person), he [or she] either rejects or appropriates various attitudes associated with this role. Those he [or she] appropriates become the basis for role-playing.[50]

Stage 3 is the game phase. During this period, the child begins to consider his or her own social position in relation to those around the child and assesses the responsibilities each position entails. In addition, the child responds to the members of his or her social environment on the basis of the roles they occupy. One's ability to role-take is created during this developmental process. This activity is essential to understanding how the self-conscious individual comes to establish identity. More specifically, as Mead intimated, such role-taking is pivotal to comprehending how humans come to assume

> the organized social attitudes of the given social group or community (or of some one section thereof) to which he [or she] belongs, toward the social problems of various kinds which confront that group or community at any given time, and which arise in connection with the correspondingly different social projects or organized co-operative enterprises in which that group or community as such is engaged; and, as an individual participant in these social projects or co-operative enterprises, [the person] governs his [or her] own conduct accordingly.[51]

The social attitudes of the organized community or social group represent the generalized other and, in essence, provide unity to the individual's self. Mead emphasized the importance of this phase, claiming that "the game represents the passage in the life of the child from taking the role of others in play to the organized part that is essential to self-consciousness in the full sense of the term."[52]

Clearly, at the heart of Mead's social psychology was a basic premise: society and the self are reflexive. Indeed, society influences the creation and maintenance of the self, and the self influences the creation and maintenance of society. This fundamental precept was the foundation from which other theoretical developments within the tradition of Symbolic Interactionism evolved. Accordingly, in order to understand how self and society influence identity and behavior, these additional developments require some general elucidation.

The Development of Two Approaches in Symbolic Interactionism

Two approaches to interactionist thought have emerged within contemporary Symbolic Interactionism. These include the situational (i.e., processual) or Chicago School and the structural or Iowa School. These traditions originated as a function of the differing research philosophies of Herbert Blumer and Manfred Kuhn.[53] Blumer believed that in order to create a science of social action, researchers needed to rely on the observance of social processes. Moreover, he claimed that in order to understand these processes, investigators had to enter the world of those who were the subject of inquiry. Thus, Blumer offered a more situated or process-oriented description of Symbolic Interactionism that served as a counterpoint to the macrolevel framework common within the discipline of sociology.

Working at the University of Chicago, Blumer and his colleagues emphasized the processes through which people constructed meaning for the situations they encountered and, hence, the behavior they undertook. The approach focused on the emergence of the self in the face-to-face interactions of everyday life as the self unfolded in its naturally occurring environment. This is an approach in which "behavior is viewed as indeterminate, unpredictable, impulsive, and spontaneous. Scholars focus on how individuals define situations and thereby construct the realities [that] they live."[54] This situational, or Chicago School, approach is consistent with what many investigators today would consider to be the traditional symbolic interactionist perspective.

In addition to the process-animated model of Blumer is the structural approach. Commenting on the latter, Kuhn insisted that "if social scientists were to build a body of knowledge of social life of some relevance and utility they [would have to] to develop procedures that: (1) systematically accumulated bodies of data, and (2) subject[ed] these bodies of data to sustained research."[55] Developed at the University of Iowa, the structural approach took as its focus the organization of the self as a basis for examination as opposed to the self's underlying social processes.

Kuhn's self-theory was symbiotic: he saw the organization and structure of the self as reflecting society and the organization and structure of society as personifying the self. Unlike the situational approach, the structural theory of Kuhn and the Iowa School viewed behavior as both emergent *and* deterministic. Kuhn believed that the self and one's behavior were strongly influenced by antecedent variables, including historical, developmental, and social conditions. In a manner reminiscent of James, Kuhn argued that the self was organized structurally. To substantiate this claim, Kuhn and his associates developed an empirical test called the "Who Am I?" or the "Twenty Statements Test" (TST). Kuhn's structural model had a significant influence on what some considered a third school relative to the development of symbolic interactionist theory. In particular, the Indiana School added a social structural component to the structural aspects of the self.[56] In sum, however, structural Symbolic Interactionism sees structure on two fronts: the self is organized structurally, and the self is influenced by social structure. Moreover, the structural approach, which is grounded in theory, takes a quantitative and positivistic approach to exploring the core issues of Mead's[57] social psychology.[58]

Commenting on the underlying assumptions of structural Symbolic Interactionism, Stryker characterized them on the basis of the following eight synoptic statements:

1. Behavior depends on a named or classified world. The names or class terms attached to aspects of the environment, both physical and

social, carry meaning in the form of shared behavioral expectations that grow out of social interaction. From interaction with others, one learns how to classify objects one comes into contact with and in that process also learns how one is expected to behave with reference to those objects.

2. Among the class terms learned in interaction are the symbols that are used to designate "positions," the relatively stable, morphological components of social structure. It is these positions which carry the shared behavioral expectations that are conventionally labeled "roles."

3. Persons who act in the context of organized patterns of behavior, i.e., in the context of social structure, name one another in the sense of recognizing one another as occupants of positions. When they name one another they invoke expectations with regard to each other's behavior.

4. Persons acting in the context of organized behavior apply names to themselves as well. These reflexively applied positional designations, which become part of the "self," create in persons expectations with respect to their own behavior.

5. When entering interactive situations, persons define the situation by applying names to it, to other participants in the interaction, to themselves, and to particular features of the situation, and use the resulting definitions to organize their own behavior in the situation.

6. Social behavior is not, however, given by these definitions, though early definitions may constrain the possibilities for alternative definitions to emerge from interaction. Behavior is the product of a role-making process, initiated by expectations invoked in the process of defining situations but developing through a tentative, sometimes extremely subtle, probing interchange among actors that can reshape the form and content of the interaction.

7. The degree to which roles are "made," rather than simply "played," as well as the constituent elements entering the construction of roles, will depend on the larger social structures in which interactive situations are embedded. Some structures are "open," others relatively "closed" with respect to novelty in roles and in role enactments or performances. All structures impose some limits on the kinds of definitions which may be called into play and thus the possibilities for interaction.

8. To the degree that roles are made rather than only played as given, changes can occur in the character of definitions, in the names and the class terms utilized in those definitions, and in the possibilities for interaction. Such changes can in turn lead to changes in the larger social strictures within which interactions take place.[59]

Clearly, several identifiable concepts can be isolated from Stryker's description of the basic assumptions underlying the operation of structural Symbolic Interactionism. However, Stryker drew special attention to the following as the five major components constituting the social person: (a) symbols, (b) the definition of the situation, (c) roles, (d) socialization and role-taking, and (e) the self.[60] Although not explicitly described as such, these five elements were also located in the work of McCall and Simmons.[61] Specifically, these five concepts were used as the tools of analysis[62] in creating a framework for understanding how structural Symbolic Interactionism underscores Identity Theory and, subsequently, explains the influence of identity on terrorist behavior. In the subsections that follow, each of these five components is summarily described. At issue here are the powerful, organizing effects both the structure of the self and social structure have on the construction of identity.

Symbols

Structural symbolic interactionists focus on symbols in relation to their power to categorize and classify the social world. This focus is based on Mead's conceptualization of objects becoming symbols through the act (e.g., impulse, perception, manipulation, and consummation), as well as the development of shared meaning and significant symbols.[63] Accordingly, language and symbolic systems are seen in terms of the way in which they represent meanings for human action. Furthermore, shared meanings are passed on through history, culture, socialization, and social structure. Indeed, as Stryker noted,

Symbols focus attention upon salient elements in an interactive situation, and permit preliminary organizations of behavior appropriate to it. Culture may be thought of, from this perspective, as a specification of what is important for interaction by being relevant to goal-oriented activity, a specification representing the cumulative experience of a social unit. As this observation implies, there are frequently ready-made definitions available as quickly as appropriate cues are perceived.[64]

These symbols help to interpret and situate the individual in the interactive environment. In addition, they play an active part in defining and constructing the situation in which one finds oneself.

Definition of the Situation

The symbolic transformation of the social environment is closely related to the development of a second major component of structural Symbolic Interactionism, namely, the definition of the situation. Proposed by W. I. Thomas in the 1920s, the concept is epitomized in his now classic statement, "If men and women define situations as real, then they are real in their consequences."[65] In essence, individuals do not necessarily respond to the objective environment but, rather, to the symbolic transformation of that environment. As Lauer and Handel explained,

> To understand how people define situations, then, is to understand the meaning that the situation has for them and thereby to understand why they behave as they do in the situation. Much behavior that is otherwise perplexing can be understood when we know the definition of the situation that the actor holds. Furthermore, to know how people define situations is to understand why they behave differently in the same situation.[66]

The phrase "definition of the situation" can be seen as describing a process through which people ascribe to and exchange meanings for the symbols in their environment. These meanings are the phenomena to which they respond. However, individuals do not passively accept the definitions people create for them; instead, there is a certain degree of self-activity in which they either accept or reject these expressions.[67] In addition, the definition of the situation can be used "to denote the actual concrete situation as it has been defined, or to denote certain psychic products of group life which are left as residua from the definition of many situations."[68]

Eventually, the individual's entire life encounters and personality are based on the amalgamation of a series of these definitions. As Stryker pointed out, reference groups in their many forms have a significant degree of influence on the way in which situations are defined.[69] Reference groups provide the basic prism through which individuals view a particular situation. Part of the reason people define similar situations differently and, hence, behave differently in them is that they have different reference groups. According to Waller's observations on the definition of the situation,[70] there are certain psychic products of group life that constitute the residua of many situations. Thus, the phrase in question represents a collection of many definitions consolidated into one that is comprehensive. In another words, the definition of the situation is consistent with a worldview.

Roles

A third major component of structural Symbolic Interactionism is the way in which roles, as a part of social structure, influence individual behavior.[71] Our assessment of social roles comes primarily from role theory, as developed by Parsons,[72] Merton,[73] and Gross, Mason, and McEachern.[74] Although we recognize that role theory occupies an important place in understanding roles, structural symbolic interactionists have refined the concept in some meaningful ways.[75]

Role theory contends that "the role is a basic building block of social systems . . . to a considerable degree a social system can be thought of as a network of statuses and their associated roles."[76] Thus, roles constitute the means by which people are connected to social systems. Social roles can be understood as a set of societal expectations associated with the occupation of a particular social status or position in relationship to another status or position. With the adoption of roles comes an adherence to specific beliefs, values, norms, attitudes, codes of conduct, and obligations. Typically, these notions are based on the interpretations that one attaches to particular symbols in use and specific definitions of the situation. Role performance occurs when one conforms to behavioral expectations with the goal of acquiring positive and avoiding negative sanctions.[77] Thus, roles are the site where behaviors and expectations converge.[78]

In addition, social roles avail to society a certain degree of stability and predictability, especially since people who occupy specialized roles are expected to perform them in a particular manner. Occupying a role also yields certain role relationships. These relationships are manifested in kinships, social networks, and role sets. Finally, roles exist prior to the individual. Roles are historically, socially, and culturally rooted. Therefore, roles provide an initial framework out of which interaction can occur. Indeed, without these shared meanings as situated within this framework, society would be chaotic and precarious.[79]

Symbolic interactionists use the positional aspect of social roles in more general terms, especially since they are interpreted as socially recognized categories of actors.[80] Moreover, these positions serve to cue conduct, functioning as behavior predictors for those placed in certain categories. In this sense, social roles, much like behavior, are symbols of social structure. Additionally, the use of roles in language implies the reference to a counter-role. As Lauer and Handel noted, this is the concept of *role sets*.[81] For example, there are no professors without students and no store clerks without customers.

Another refinement to the idea of social roles was developed by R. Turner,[82] through the introduction of role-taking. From the perspective of role-taking, roles are not static; instead, they are constantly being formed, modified, and reconfigured. Following structural Symbolic Interactionism, then, roles are, in a sense, improvisational. Thus, positional or cultural role expectations serve merely as guidelines or points of origin for behavior; however, people rarely *stick to the script*.[83] Instead, role performances are filtered through one's personality and self-conception. The link between behavior and role performance is integral to Identity Theory's conception of the emerging self and is elaborated upon in the next subsections. Finally, through definitions people assign to situations, they come to categorize themselves and others by naming or labeling one another. This process implicates the reflexive nature of the self.[84]

Socialization and Role-Taking

A fourth major component of structural Symbolic Interactionism identified by Stryker is socialization and role-taking.[85] Here the focus is on how individuals come to espouse the appropriate interpretation of symbols, definition of situations, and roles, along with the expectations of others. All of these dynamics influence one's definitions of one's position in society and, correspondingly, the development and organization of one's self. As previously described, socialization is the process through which people adopt roles and learn the expectations for their role behavior. Johnson defined socialization as "the process through which people are prepared to participate in social systems. . . . From the perspective of individuals, socialization is a process through which we create a social SELF and a sense of attachment to social systems through our participation in them and our interaction with others."[86]

Symbolic interactionists view socialization as a life-long process. It involves the acquisition of shared meanings that are manifested through symbolic systems of groups and the attitudes of collective members.[87] Among others, agents of socialization can include family, school, the military, peer/ethnic/cultural groups, the media, the workplace, and the government. Affiliation with some of these socializing agents may consist of an institutionalized period of indoctrination. During this period, individuals are introduced to the basic beliefs, attitudes, or rules of life within that particular group.

A basic function of role-taking is to imaginatively occupy the place of another in an effort to see and experience the world (which includes the behavior of oneself) from the other's standpoint. This is achieved through the use of symbols and the meaning-making process where role-taking subjects anticipate the responses of others in an effort to recognize the various possibilities for their own behavior. Moreover, role-taking is acknowledged as a fundamental aspect of all interaction, whether it is based on cooperation or conflict. As Stryker illustrates, "to effectively engage in war, one must anticipate the responses of the enemy in the same manner as a parent must anticipate the responses of a child when seeking to aid the child through a crisis."[88] In both instances, appropriate action requires that the person adopt the perspective of the other—including the other's reference group (i.e., the community of adversaries; the society of children)—to assess how best to respond to the situation at hand.[89]

The structural approach to Symbolic Interactionism generally adopts the reference group component as an influence on behavior; however, the theory argues that this feature has been mostly overemphasized. This is especially the case with respect to the reference group's capacity to provide a standard for conduct and to shape various frames of reference. In addition, McCall and Simmons noted that theorists have overlooked the most important reference point, namely, the reflective self.[90] This approach to role-taking is more inclusive of the psychological and internal influences of the self on behavior.

Self

A fifth component identified by Stryker as integral to structural Symbolic Interactionism is the self.[91] As previously delineated, the self is a product of society, manifested through social processes that encompass the interaction of symbols, definitions of the situation, roles, and socialization and role-taking. However, the structural approach focuses primarily on the self-defining activities of the person. These activities include the establishment of socially recognized categories, corresponding roles, and the self-meanings that attach to them. Roles, then, are the link between the self and one's relationship to others. Moreover, through the constitution of the self, roles are translated into behavior.

Following James's observation that the self is multifaceted (i.e., people have as many selves as they do those who know them), people also have as many identities[92] or role identities as they do role relationships.[93] Accordingly, identities are "parts of the self composed of meanings that persons attach to the multiple roles they typically play in highly differentiated contemporary society."[94] Recognized as an aspect of social stratification, "identities are 'parts' of the self; [that is,] internalized positional designations."[95] More specifically, they are cognitive self-schemas consisting of the internalized role expectations incorporated into one's sense of self.[96]

Self-schemas can be described as "cognitive generalizations about the self, derived from experience, that organize and guide the processing of self-related information contained in the individual's social experiences."[97] Moreover, as Stryker explained it, identities are "cognitive schema whose meaning lies in expectations for behavior reflecting the role on the basis of which the identity is formed."[98] These identities are numerous but organized within the self. In sum, then, "identities are reflexively applied cognitions in the form of answers to the question 'Who am I?' "[99]

The cursory observations chronicled above on the five components constituting the social person outlined important conceptual features to structural Symbolic Interactionism. With these thoughts in mind, the next section provides a more detailed description of the way society influences the creation, maintenance, and storage of one's identity. In addition, the ensuing commentary explains the way in which the self, through self-processes, influences role performances (i.e., behaviors) and, correspondingly, society. Finally, we note that presenting the five structural symbolic interactionist concepts incrementally served the purpose of simplicity. In other words, all five components work together in the dynamic process of forming the social person. Given these observations, we now direct our attention to Identity Theory and its relationship to structural Symbolic Interactionism.

Identity Theory

The association between social structure and the structural processes of the self that constitute identity is known as Identity Theory. Stryker coined the phrase during a presentation at the annual meeting of the American Sociological Association in 1966.[100] He subsequently published the substance of his presentation under the title "Identity Salience and Role Performance."[101] However, the fundamental tenets of Identity Theory were also espoused in Alexander and Wiley's account of "situated identities"[102] and McCall and Simmons's conception of "role identities."[103] To be clear, the significant degree of similarity among these works can be attributable to the fact that, at the time, these ideas were, quite frankly, in the air.[104]

Initially, Identity Theory was developed in response to the ambiguous nature of Mead's work[105] and the difficulty others had in operationalizing the concepts he delineated. Essentially, Mead provided a framework for the assessment of a basic formula: society shapes the self and the self shapes social behavior. However, he understood this relationship to be reciprocal. In other words, following his framework, the self also shapes social behavior and, in turn, shapes society. In utilizing Mead's framework and formula, Identity Theory endeavors to comprehend society and the self in a manner that lends itself to empirical testing.

Stryker and Burke described the development of Identity Theory, the two distinct (although related) directions the theory has taken, the complementary nature of these two strands of analysis, and the theory's potential for future development.[106] One approach to Identity Theory explains how society shapes the self and, with it, social behavior. Specifically, this orientation "concentrates on examining how social structures affect the structure of self and how structure of the self influences social behavior."[107] A second approach to Identity Theory elaborates on Mead's contention that the self shapes society.[108] Specifically, this perspective "concentrates on the internal dynamics of self-processes as these affect social behavior."[109] Interestingly, while these two approaches examine different aspects of identity, both view it through processes that can be both stable and changeable, given the circumstances.[110]

Delineating the basic premises of these respective orientations to Identity Theory makes it possible to review the fundamental concepts that underscore and inform the theory. Moreover, such delineation enables us to characterize the way these two strands of analysis have been used in conjunction with one another, facilitating our targeted exploration on the construction and maintenance of a terrorist group member's identity. As a general proposition, this sort of integration is necessary as it facilitates a more complete conceptualization of identity and Symbolic Interactionism.

Society Shapes the Self

The basic assumption underlying Stryker's Identity Theory is that social structure constrains, facilitates, and inhibits human behavior, although it does not determine it.[111] The focus of Stryker's approach is on how social structure influences the composition of the self and how this composition impacts social behavior as specified through role-related choices. The theory builds on this assumption, along with additional refinements derived from orthodox Symbolic Interactionism. Stryker noted that traditional interpretative analyses have primarily focused on the varying patterns of everyday interaction and the unstable and continuing flexibility of subjective definitions.[112] However, this line of inquiry tends to overlook the hypothesis that some possibilities are more probable than others. Indeed, one's ability to locate various options is, in part, a function of social structure. Given these insights, Identity Theory represents a more holistic, contemporary sociological view regarding society's influence on the human experience. In this framework, society is understood to be "a mosaic of relatively durable patterned interactions and relationships, differentiated yet organized, embedded in an array of groups, organizations, communities, and institutions, and intersected by crosscutting boundaries of class, ethnicity, age, gender, religion, and other variables."[113]

Another important feature of Stryker's Identity Theory that distinguishes it from traditional Symbolic Interactionism is his contention that people inhabit small and specialized social networks of social relationships.[114] Participation in these networks and relationships is supported by the adoption of roles. These social networks and, hence, the roles are embedded within societal structures. These structures are emblematic of the larger society of which they are a part. Accordingly, society influences the emergence of the self.

Given Stryker's perspective,[115] Identity Theory attempts to address why a person would choose to engage in one form of conduct when others are readily available. More specifically, "given situations in which there exist behavioral options aligned with two (or more) sets of role expectations attached to two (or more) positions in networks of social relationships, why do persons choose one particular course of action?"[116] Thus, Identity Theory endeavors to explain why an individual would select out one set of role expectations and, consequently, particular internalized identities as opposed to any equally worthwhile others.

In response to these sorts of questions, Identity Theory suggests that what is at issue is something deeper (and more profound) than mere volition. Specifically, the theory contends that role choice is a function of identity salience and identity commitment. The central tenet of Identity Theory is that commitment impacts identity salience and salience impacts role performance.[117] An elaboration of this proposition "is that 'large-scale' social structures affect commitment [and this] affects identity salience [which] affects role performance."[118] Thus, underpinning Stryker's Identity Theory is the function of identity salience and commitment in the behavioral choices one makes, the role expectations one adopts, and the internalized identities one embraces.[119]

According to Stryker, identities are organized in a hierarchical fashion.[120] Moreover, the complexity of social relationships (i.e., role relationships) is mirrored in the equally diverse multidimensional aspects of the self. Stryker referred to this conceptualization as identity salience.[121] One dictionary definition of salience is "standing out from the rest; noticeable; conspicuous; prominent."[122] Stryker's theory argued that some identities are more prominently featured than others and, more importantly, that they are arranged in a salience hierarchy.[123] The hierarchy is organized on the basis of the probability of each identity being activated in a given situation.

As Stryker explained, the identity's location on the hierarchy is its salience.[124] A general proposition of the theory is that those identities that are activated more frequently become more conspicuous or assume a higher position on the hierarchy. In addition, when identities are more prominent, they are activated more frequently across situations. The definition of identity salience, then, is "the likelihood an identity will come into play in a variety of situations as a function of its priorities as a cognitive schema."[125] Two factors play a part in whether or not a certain behavior will occur. In brief, these include (1) whether, and to what extent, the salience of the identity will interact with "[the] defining characteristics of situations (such as the degree to which the situation permits alternative identities to be expressed behaviorally), and (2) other self characteristics (such as self-esteem or satisfaction)."[126]

Commenting on his characterization of identities and identity salience, Stryker indicated that four implications can be noted. He summarized them as follows:

[P]ersons "carry" cognitive schemata across situations, predisposing them to perceive and act in situations in line with extant identities; identities (and identity salience) can be self-reinforcing, given the noted process and the reciprocal impact of behavior on self-concepts; identities are motivational, moving people to actions expressing their meaning behaviorally; as a consequence of being transsituational, self-reinforcing, and motivational, identities can influence action independent of relationships supporting the identities—they can be functionally independent of the commitments affecting them.[127]

In essence, then, identities and their salience are not only schematic and trans-situational in nature; they also have a self-reinforcing and motivational component.

This next facet of Stryker's Identity Theory is identity commitment.[128] Commitment can be operationalized as "the degree to which the person's relationships to specified sets of others depends on his or her being a particular kind of person (i.e., occupying a particular position in an organized structure of relationships and playing a particular role)."[129] An individual's commitment to an identity is related to the number of others who recognize the person as playing that role and the importance of those others to the individual.[130] For example, a person will be significantly more committed to his or her identity as a police officer if a considerable number of the person's social relationships and social networks are premised upon the notion that the person in question is, indeed, a police officer. Consistent with this assessment, Serpe described two types of commitment: interactional and affective.[131] The interactional component of commitment focuses on the number and frequency of relationships entered by playing a role. The affective component addresses the individual's depth of emotional attachment to various social networks. Commitment through social relationships and networks, then, provides a realizable example of how society influences social behavior in the form of the self.

The above conceptualization is consistent with McCall and Simmons's contention that role identities are organized into a *hierarchy of prominence*.[132] Aside from some minor differences, these two theories are quite similar. However, McCall and Simmons added some specificity to their model by explaining that the organization of role identities is based on cohesiveness.[133] Cohesiveness refers to the extent to which separate role identities are tightly or loosely interrelated. As the authors indicated,

> In most cases, [role identities] seem to "cluster" in smaller numbers of subpatterns. The basis for this clustering is ordinarily that several role-identities involve similar skills, have the same persons "built into" their contents, or pertain to the same institutional context or period of one's life. These clusters may themselves be linked more or less closely with other clusters or may be quite rigidly "compartmentalized" or dissociated from others.[134]

The role-identity model of McCall and Simmons[135] also differs slightly from Stryker's model[136] in that the prominence or salience of a role identity is based on the degree of self- and social support, the degree of commitment to and investment in a role identity, and the intrinsic and extrinsic gratifications associated with the performance of that role identity. The overall prominence of a role identity, then, will fluctuate with these factors.

Additionally, McCall and Simmons acknowledged that the salience of some identities over others was a crucial aspect in the way role identities translated into behavior; however, their understanding of role-identity salience was contingent upon five factors. These consisted of the following: (a) its prominence, (b) its need for support, (c) its intrinsic gratification, (d) its extrinsic gratification, and (e) its perceived suitability for acquiring gratification in a particular situation.[137] Thus, salience denotes a role identity's order of priority in being called on in a given situation. This characterization is the difference between the *situational self* and the *idealized self*, the former signifying the collective embodiment of the prominence hierarchy.

In assessing the limits of this version of Identity Theory (i.e., society influencing the self), Stryker and Serpe noted that it is selective and narrow in focus.[138] The theory seeks to explain role-related behavior and, even more specifically, role choices. Arguably, social structure allows individuals in certain roles more choices and opportunities than those in certain others. However, this point serves to further the contention that social structure has a powerful influence on the adoption and realization of particular identities.

In an application related to terrorism, Stryker used his version of Identity Theory to explain variations in social movement participation.[139] He divided this application into two portions. First, he assessed the degree to which commitment has an influence on social movement participation variability, independent of identity salience. As previously described, commitment is based upon social networks and relationships. Human lives are made up of numerous social relationships to individuals in various groups. Stryker contended that the commitment concept begged the question, How is social movement participation influenced by both movement and nonmovement social relationships, and to what degree are the views of the two social networks overlapping? In response, Stryker summarized his position in the following passage:

> High commitments to groups outside a movement may reinforce the power of the movement to ask for and get participation from its members if the groups share movement expectations, norms, values, and goals. If, however, outside groups to which persons are highly committed do not share movement expectations, norms, values, and goals, movement recruitment and participation will be dampened.[140]

Returning to his illustration of membership in a militant extremist group, Stryker noted that an individual whose family historically supported Irish Republicanism would be more, rather than less, responsive to the demands of the movement, given these traditional and firmly held commitments.

The second part of Stryker's application dealt with identity salience and its influence on social movement participation variability.[141] This portion of his thesis relied heavily on identities as self-schemas that serve to process self-relevant material. From a more sociologically informed social psychological perspective, Stryker argued that identity schemata are cognitive resources used to construct the definitions of the situations in which people find themselves. The salience of identity schemata is dependent on both internal (i.e., emotional) and external (i.e., situational) cues. The process of identity schemata is also reciprocal in nature in that the higher an identity schema is on the salience hierarchy the more likely it is to be accessed. The more frequently it is activated, the more it will inform the definitions for one's manifold situations.

Stryker also observed that salient identities can be self-reinforcing and self-enhancing.[142] In this context, individuals find more self-esteem from engaging in role performances that reflect their more salient identities. As he explained it,

> Since esteem has motivational force, this argues further that persons will seek opportunities to act out the roles underlying salient identities, that they will define a greater variety of situations, appropriately or not, as opportunities to act these roles out, and when possible they will select situations enabling the enactment of salient identities.[143]

This line of reasoning has been appropriated by other investigators. For example, according to Pinel and Swann, the more salient an identity is the higher the need to confirm it.[144] Moreover, as these researchers argued, people are more likely to become active in social movements whose collective identity is consistent with their more salient identities. Thus, the necessity for social movements is not simply linked to definitions of situations that reflect one's salient identities; rather, they also possess self-affirming value. It is our contention that the interactional processes that account for membership in a social movement as examined through the social psychological insights of Identity Theory resonate quite profoundly with an investigation of terrorism.

Self Shapes Society

The second approach to Identity Theory was developed by Burke and his colleagues.[145] It originated in response to the lack of research addressing the way the self shaped society. As Burke and Reitzes explained, sociological social psychology has done an adequate job of investigating the way society influences the self; however, it has neglected to account for the internal mechanisms of the self that constitute society.[146] Thus, this brand of Identity Theory "concentrates on the internal dynamics of self-processes as these affect social behavior."[147] Moreover, the approach focuses on the active processes of the self, being based on the belief that "individuals capable of reflexive thought and self-initiated action are the agents (sometimes as single individuals and sometimes as members of social movements or institutions) that create, sustain, and change larger social structures."[148] Burke's Identity Theory moves from the internal processes of the self through identities and role performance to the self's subsequent influence on society.

Burke's approach to Identity Theory[149] relied on McCall and Simmons's role-identity model.[150] This model proposes that role identities are a person's idealized visions of his or her self. Using Goffman's dramaturgical language,[151] they explain how a person imagines playing a role or character. Typically, this role identity is idealized, exaggerated, or embellished to a significant degree. For example, a child may imagine standing up to the school bully and, as a consequence, may conjure up feelings of respect and envy from other classmates who similarly had been intimidated by this tormentor. However, role identities are more than just daydreams; they are the source of action plans, dry runs, and vicarious performances for assessing reinforcement from reference groups, including oneself. Indeed, as McCall and Simmons explained, "those actions that are not consonant with one's imaginations of self as a person in a particular social position are regarded as embarrassing, threatening, and disconcerting; if possible, they will be discontinued and superseded by actions more in keeping with one's view of self."[152]

Moreover, in an effort to maintain one's role identities, one constantly seeks to legitimate, verify, or affirm them. This self-validation and self-verification is pursued through the process of role performance and attained with role support. This role support is provided to the actor by his or her audience in the form of reactions (i.e., behavioral responses) that serve to confirm the actor's positional status and imagined conception of his or her role identities. Audiences can include friends, news media, society at large, and, most importantly, one's self. However, role support is not indefinite. Human beings are driven to continuously pursue role support as a way to reassert their role identities. They accomplish this by keeping their role performances in line with their idealized selves. As McCall and Simmons observed, these processes of self-validation and self-verification are crucial to understanding the way role identities translate into ongoing behavior.[153]

On the basis of this model, Burke and Reitzes understand identities to be "a set of meanings applied to the self in a social role or situation, defining what it means to be who one is in that role or situation."[154] This conception of identities entails three characteristics.[155] First, identities are social products formed and maintained through the social processes of naming, which locate the self in socially recognized categories. Indeed, identities consist of interaction with others. This interaction involves the processes of identification and exchange. Moreover, identities necessitate the confirmation and validation of self-concepts by means of self-presentation and *altercasting*. Along these lines, the presentation of the self involves the deployment of tactics used to convey an image of one's self to others.[156] Confirmation is achieved when individuals respond to that image accordingly. However, "not only does our performance [in the form of self-presentation] express an image of who we are, but it also simultaneously expresses an image of whom we take *alter* to be."[157] This secondary expressive process is called "altercasting."

The second characteristic informing Burke's theory is the notion that identities are self meanings formed in particular situations organized hierarchically to produce the self.[158] These meanings are produced in response to the demands of the social situation. Moreover, they are based on the similarities and differences of a role in relation to complementary roles or counter-roles.[159]

The third feature characterizing Burke's Identity Theory is that identities are symbolic and reflexive. "The meanings of the self are learned from responses of others to one's own actions. One's actions develop meaning through the responses of others, and over time, call up in the person the same responses that are called up in others."[160] These actions, words, and appearances come to have shared meaning, making them significant symbols[161] in the social environment.[162] Thus, the link between the self and behavior lies in the shared meanings of identities and roles or, more specifically, the recognition that identities predict behavior when the meaning of an identity corresponds to the meaning of a behavior.[163]

On the basis of a cybernetic framework,[164] Burke and Reitzes developed what they termed the "identity control model."[165] The model demonstrates the way in which self-meanings are related to the meanings of one's behavior. Four central components underscore its operation:

> the identity standard, or the set of (culturally prescribed) meanings held by the individual which define his or her role identity in a situation; the person's perceptions of meanings within the situation, matched to the dimensions of meaning in the identity standard; the comparator or the mechanism that compares the perceived situational meanings with those held in the identity standard; and the individual's behavior or activity, which is a function of the difference between perceptions and standard.[166]

Behavior is pivotal to the model because it is used as a means to align perceived self-relevant meanings with the identity standard of a particular situation. The model frames behavior as being goal directed—that is, motivated by the desire to verify one's identity. In essence, self-verification is the process by which self-relevant meanings are brought into agreement with the identity standard.[167] This agreement is achieved either by altering the current situation or by seeking out or creating situations in which self-relevant meanings correspond with the identity standard.[168] Self-verification is the chief internal mechanism through which the self shapes behavior and, hence, constitutes society.[169]

For Swann,[170] individuals facilitate the self-verification process through a variety of strategies, namely, selective interaction, identity cues, and interpersonal prompts.[171] *Selective interaction* is simply electing to interact with those who confirm one's identities and avoiding those who do not. People use *identity cues* to claim a particular identity. For example, some individuals appropriate a particular clothing style in order to "look the part." *Interpersonal prompts* consist of specific actions or mannerisms that one relies on to elicit a response from others, bringing the self-relevant meanings in line with the identity standard.

Burke and Stets[172] also recognized that alternative strategies could be used to manage the discrepancy between one's self-views and those views of the person harbored by others.[173] One such mechanism is *selective perception*. In this technique, the interactant ignores or overlooks those aspects of the person's behavior that do not match his or her idealized role identities. Another mechanism is *selective interpretation*. In this strategy, individuals interpret audience (or certain audience) responses in ways that are conducive to verifying the person's role identities. What makes this possible is that Symbolic Interactionism acknowledges the highly subjective nature of the interpretive process. The mechanisms of selective perception and selective interpretation represent primary coping strategies or, as McCall and Simmons termed them, "the first line of defense."[174]

When the discrepancy between one's self view and the view of the self entertained by others is too extreme or threatening for the mechanisms of selective perception and interpretation to absorb, five more evasive strategies are utilized. The first is *withdrawal*. Here, the actor removes himself or herself from the interaction entirely because it is simply too difficult to manage. The second strategy is *rationalization*. In this instance, the person alleges that circumstances beyond his or her control were responsible for the discrepant role performance. A third technique is *scapegoating*. In this scenario, the interactant blames another for the individual's poor role performance. More specifically, the actor might claim that someone else failed to properly perform the necessary counter-role, that the other person had an unfair advantage, or that the person did not play by the rules. A fourth mechanism is *disavowal* of the performance altogether. In this situation, the actor asserts that the performance was not to be taken seriously because it occurred out of context or it only represented a joke. The fifth strategy is *rejection,* or the *depreciation* of the audience who refuses to give proper role support for the actors' performance. In this case, actors insist that the audience was just not competent or intellectually sophisticated enough to see the merit of the person's role performance.

McCall and Simmons noted that failure to adequately deal with the discrepancies among role identities, performances, and role support could result in internally driven feelings (e.g., misery, anguish, despair).[175] In the most extreme of instances, these sentiments could manifest themselves in self-destructive behaviors, such as acute risk-taking conduct (i.e., suicide). Thus, McCall and Simmons recognized that emotions were constitutive of the outcomes emanating from the self-affirming process.[176]

The identity control model indicates how emotion is, in part, a consequence of "the relationship between perceived self-meanings in the situation and the self-definitional meanings held in the identity standard."[177] One's failure to verify one's self-meanings (i.e., identities) results in negative emotions. Additionally, the depression and distress that originates from incessant failure in confirming an identity leads to reduced commitment and even abandonment of that identity.[178] Conversely, confirming one's identity through the self-verification process results in feelings of mastery, efficacy, self-competency, and self-affirmation at the individual level, as well as feelings of acceptance and self-esteem at the group level.[179] Moreover, one who continually and consistently confirms his or her identity becomes wedded to that set of self-meanings or identities and most trustful of and committed to those who repeatedly verify it.[180] In sum, the underlying premise of Identity Theory as developed by Burke indicates

> that people seek ways to establish and maintain social situations and relationships in which their identities are verified. These are self-verification contexts that maintain the self. At the same time, the actions (role behaviors) that change the situation and lead to new, identity-confirming perceptions manage the flow of meanings, information, and resources that build and sustain the social structure to which the identity belongs. . . . Self-verification through the manipulation of signs and symbols, thus, has consequences that simultaneously sustain the individual and the social structure in which the individual is embedded.[181]

Up until now, Social Identity Theory (SIT) has been the preferred social psychological prism through which to explore the link between identity and terrorist behavior. One explanation for this is that SIT was designed to explain intergroup conflict[182] and, as a result, this made it an attractive approach for understanding militant extremism whether or not the research was grounded in psychology, political science, or international relations. Interestingly, on the surface, Identity Theory (IT) and SIT may seem quite similar. The reality, however, is that they are not. For example, while both utilize the concept of groups in explaining social behavior, SIT treats groups and categories as synonymous. From this perspective, people are members of groups if they share a common trait, such as race, ethnicity, sexual orientation, or religion. The focus on similarity between these types of characteristics is understandable, especially given that SIT was initiated in an effort to explain racial and ethnic discrimination.

Contrastingly, Identity Theory embraces the distinction between groups and categories. As Stryker observed, people live in groups, not categories.[183] Turning to the insights of Deaux,[184] Stryker explained that identities based on group relationships are more central and desirable than those that are not. Although categories are relevant in that they inform social interaction through social boundaries, it is reasonable to conclude that groups have a more immediate influence on shaping behavior. Identity Theory is rooted in the belief that "membership is a matter of playing a role in a network of reciprocal roles."[185] These roles are tied to group affiliations.

A second important distinction between SIT and Identity Theory is that, at its core, the former is anchored by the desire to satiate certain needs (e.g., self-esteem, belonging). However, IT understands identity to be a natural manifestation of social interactive processes and of social life. Admittedly, Identity Theory does not reject the existence of such primal needs, and, likewise, SIT does not dismiss the impact of social forces in the creation of identities and conflict. However, what distinguishes these two orientations on these matters is the depth of their respective commitments. Stated differently, SIT and IT relegate the other's position on identity construction as ancillary to the project of accounting for human behavior and social interaction.[186]

Part II

4

An Overview of Five
Extremist Organizations

The definition of terrorism has attracted intense debate over the past several years.[1] In an effort to move past this discussion and to resituate the conceptual understanding of identity as it relates to militant extremist behavior in its proper perspective, we embrace the definition adopted by the United Nations Office on Drugs and Crime.[2] This definition was developed by Alex P. Schmid and Albert J. Jongman. As they indicated, terrorism is

an anxiety-inspiring method of repeated violent action, employed by (semi-) clandestine individual, group or state actors, for idiosyncratic, criminal or political reasons, whereby—in contrast to assassination— the direct targets of violence are not the main targets. The immediate human victims of violence are generally chosen randomly (targets of opportunity) or selectively (representative or symbolic targets) from a target population, and serve as message generators. Threat- and violence-based communication processes between terrorist (organization), (imperilled) victims, and main targets are used to manipulate the main target (audiences(s)), turning it into a target of terror, a target of demands, or a target of attention, depending on whether intimidation, coercion, or propaganda is primarily sought.[3]

Embedded within this characterization is the contention that terrorism is a tactic or method of combat. While the Provisional Irish Republican Army (PIRA), Hamas, the Shining Path, and the Liberation Tigers of Tamil Eelam (LTTE) have all been designated by the U.S. Department of State as organizations that employ or have utilized this strategy,[4] racist Skinheads[5] are largely organized and operate as street gangs.[6] However, unlike the more stereotypical utilitarian gang, some Skinhead

groups are ideologically based and attempt to promote a right-wing po-
litical/social agenda (i.e., antigovernment, antimulticulturalism, White
supremacy) through threat, intimidation, and fear.[7] As Quarles argued,
right-wing extremists do constitute a legitimate terrorist menace.[8] Although such extremists are an unsophisticated and loosely affiliated
organization, violent acts (i.e., assault, arson, murder, and vandalism)
committed by racist Skinheads are not simply crimes but politically motivated militant attacks designed to instill trepidation and alarm in the
civilian populations of immigrants, gays and lesbians, Jewish Americans, and people of color.[9]

In this chapter, important background material on the five terrorist
groups under consideration in this volume is provided. In particular, a
serviceable, though limited, description of the group's history, development, organization, leadership, strategies and tactics, and current activities are enumerated. In this context, the cultural realities that inform
and texture the ongoing militant extremism of the five respective organizations are disclosed. Accordingly, these summary observations contribute to furthering our understanding of the subtle relationship that
exists among theory, culture, self, and society in the formation and
maintenance of a terrorist identity.

Provisional Irish Republican Army (PIRA)

The conflict or "troubles" in Ireland can be traced back hundreds of
years to the country's earliest beginnings.[10] Ireland's sectarian division
emerged when the Irish were introduced to Christianity around 500
A.D., after which they became devoted followers of the religion.[11] However, by 1172, the country had been invaded and was under the control
of the Norman king of England. Religious differences and territorial
disputes gave birth to armed conflict. Following the Protestant Refor-
mation of the 1500s, King Henry VIII attempted to implement (and impose) a church similar to the one operating in England. The Catholics
vehemently resisted this forced conversion, and soon the discord was
not just about religion but also about independence.[12] The intense quar-
rel over both nationalism and separatism continues into the twenty-first
century.[13]

By the late 1800s, a group of Irish immigrants calling themselves the Irish Republican Brotherhood (IRB) was formed in New York City in an effort to provide economic relief to their friends and family still living in Ireland.[14] Eventually, the group became a financial supporter for revolution. In the aftermath of the 1916 Easter Rebellion, the IRB leader, Padraig Pearse, drafted a letter outlining his terms of surrender. He signed the letter the "Irish Republican Army" (IRA), thereby officially transforming the IRB into a fighting force.[15] In the years following the surrender in Dublin, the IRA unleashed a violent campaign of terrorism in the region.[16] In 1921, a treaty granted independence to the twenty-six counties of Southern Ireland. In this way, Southern Ireland was partitioned from the six counties of Northern Ireland, which remained loyal to the British Crown.[17] For many years following the implementation of the partition, the Loyalist Protestant majority of Northern Ireland exercised considerable political and economic hegemony over the minority Catholic community, creating a volatile situation in the region.[18]

The ratification of the treaty resulted in the emergence of divergent opinions within the IRA. Although many believed that independence should be extended to all Irish, including the northerners, ideas about how to pursue a unified Ireland differed. Some members argued that with the establishment of a political voice their interests would be better served through peaceful methods and political representation. In addition, while more moderate members wanted to maintain the existence of the IRA as an auxiliary force, others wanted to continue their active role in the armed resistance and splintered from the group. With significantly depleted numbers, the IRA continued its campaign. However, in the mid-1960s, the IRA began to focus on politicizing the movement with Marxist praxis and jettisoned the armed struggle, leaving the group unorganized and mostly unarmed.[19] In August 1969, riots erupted in the Bogside region of Londonderry as a result of the Nationalist Catholic community's longstanding feelings of discrimination and a Loyalist Protestant parade. In anticipation of hostilities, Northern Ireland's security forces, the Royal Ulster Constabulary (RUC), was sent to moderate the crowds; however, sectarian violence soon erupted. Loyalist Protestant mobs, backed by the RUC, invaded the minority Nationalist Catholic community and chased many out of their homes. The violence continued for days until the British government dispatched its soldiers to the island to quell the fighting.

Believing that the IRA had essentially failed to defend the Nationalist Catholic community from Loyalist Protestant aggression, dissident IRA members formed a splinter group known as the Provisional Irish Republican Army (PIRA), or Provos, from the Republican "old guard."[20] Initially, the PIRA endeavored to serve as the defender of the Nationalist Catholic community in Northern Ireland; however, the group's leaders had more ambitious aspirations. As Sean MacStiofain, the PIRA's first chief of staff, explained, "As soon as it became feasible and practical, the [P]IRA . . . move[d] from a purely defensive position into a phase of combined defense and retaliation."[21] PIRA members and their sympathizers argued that, although the British forces were supposed to protect their communities from Loyalist Protestant violence, they were as much the enemy as the Loyalist Protestant aggressors. The PIRA had the opportunity to serve in this capacity on several occasions. "For example, in June 1970 PIRA units were able to repel an invasion of the Catholic enclave of the Short Strand in East Belfast by thousands of loyalists while the army was seemingly nowhere in sight."[22]

As chronicled in its training manual, the *Green Book,* the PIRA came to define its objectives as follows:

1. To guard the honour and uphold the sovereignty and unity of the Republic of Ireland.
2. To support the establishment of an Irish Socialist Republic based on the 1916 Proclamation.
3. To support the establishment of, and uphold, a lawful government in sole and absolute control of the Republic.
4. To secure and defend civil and religious liberties and equal rights and equal opportunities for all citizens.
5. To promote the revival of the Irish language as the everyday language of the people.[23]

Once the PIRA captured the Nationalist Catholic communities' support and gained more support than that of the official IRA, the group launched an intense offensive military campaign lasting from 1970 to 1972.[24] By 1971, the PIRA's strategy of political violence included 1,756 shootings and 1,515 bombings, resulting in 174 deaths. In 1972, these numbers dramatically increased; they were responsible for 10,628 shootings and 1,853 bombings, producing 208 deaths. By the early

1970s, the official IRA had all but withdrawn from the armed struggle to unite Ireland, making the PIRA synonymous with the IRA name.[25] Under the banner of the Republican movement, PIRA and its political arm, Sinn Féin, have worked tirelessly toward eliminating British rule over the north and unifying Ireland.[26]

By the mid-1990s, the PIRA began contemplating support for the Northern Ireland peace process.[27] This caused two factions to emerge: the Continuity IRA, which materialized in 1995, and the Real IRA, which appeared in 1997. Some suggest that despite losing some of its members to these splinter groups and its observance of a 1997 cease-fire, the PIRA maintains several hundred members within its ranks in addition to several thousand sympathizers.[28]

Prior to the cease-fire, Horgan and Taylor described the PIRA as being cellular-based, with a hierarchically organized authoritarian structure.[29] At the top of the organizational pyramid lies the Army Executive. This is a body of twelve experienced veterans elected by the General Army Convention, composed of active volunteers, prison representatives, and members of the command structure. The Army Executive, in turn, elects the Army Council. It consists of the PIRA's leadership and is responsible for strategy and tactics of the group's war efforts. The Army Council is divided into the Northern and Southern command. The Northern command reigns over the six counties of Northern Ireland in addition to its five border counties. This was a key command to the PIRA because the vast majority of its operations were in the vicinity of Northern Ireland. The Southern command refers to a distinct region but also to an operational area. Its territory consists of the twenty-one counties of the Republic of Ireland, where it functions mostly in a logistical support capacity, conducting such activities as supplying and storing weapons, training volunteers, and providing safe houses. Both commands are made up of brigades complete with officers and active service units, typically consisting of four full-time personnel and part-time volunteers who carry out the group's activities. Additionally, the Army Council directs the General Headquarters (GHQ). GHQ was responsible for the overall maintenance and conduct of PIRA activities. Based in Dublin, it managed ten departments: quartermaster (procurement, transportation, and storage of armaments), security, operations, foreign operations, finance, training, engineering (bomb construction, weapons development, etc.), intelligence, education, and publicity.

From 1969 until its acceptance of a cease-fire in 1997, the Provisional Irish Republican Army waged a campaign of urban and rural terrorism.[30] Indeed, as some commentators noted,

> The PIRA's *modus operandi* has incorporated bombings, shooting attacks, beatings, high-profile assassinations and kidnapings. The movement has been extensively involved in extortion and armed robberies, and has a sophisticated financial network not unlike that of any large business. PIRA targets have included members of the security forces in Northern Ireland [i.e., the British Army, the Royal Ulster Constabulary (RUC)—the Ulster police force, the Ulster Defense Regiment (UDR), and the Royal Irish Regiment (RIR)], as well as government and private-sector individuals, including senior British government officials and British military targets in the mainland United Kingdom and in western Europe. PIRA targets have also included innocent civilians in Ireland and abroad, and also members of the security forces in the Republic of Ireland. The organization's militancy has, furthermore, been directed against Northern Irish Protestant paramilitary movements, in the main, groups reactive to the Provisionals' terrorist campaign.[31]

Moreover, although in its earlier years the group's attacks were fairly indiscriminate, the recognition of Sinn Féin as a viable representative of the Republican electorate did cause the collective to become more discerning in its use of violence.[32] While PIRA and Sinn Féin have worked toward the overall goal of ending British rule over the north and the unification of Ireland under the banner of the Republican Movement, it appears that the two have come to recognize that aggression, hostility, and fighting may not be the most effective means of achieving this goal.[33]

Recent progress in the peace process notwithstanding, sectarian violence in Northern Ireland has not subsided entirely. For example, while the PIRA has been relatively dormant in terms of the more large-scale terrorist attacks in recognition of the 1998 Good Friday Peace Accord between Sinn Féin and the government of Northern Ireland, it continues to engage in violence in the form of punishment shootings and beatings. Utilized by both Republican and Loyalist paramilitary groups, these brutal attacks are frequently employed to keep the people of their respective communities from committing antisocial acts, including forms of criminal conduct (e.g., drug dealing, robbery, vandalism, and working as an informant).[34]

While the 1997 cease-fire has provided a fragile peace in Northern Ireland, the Good Friday Agreement offers the best chance for an end to the conflict in the region. Indeed, the agreement has served as the backdrop for the creation of a 108-member Assembly, a fourteen-member executive body consisting of both Catholic and Protestant representatives, a scaling back of the British military presence, and the PIRA's decision to begin decommissioning its weapons. Although the island's divisional quarrels still result in sporadic acts of violence, the governments of the Republic of Ireland, Northern Ireland, and Great Britain, as well as the PIRA, have continued to work toward a peaceful resolution.

Hamas

For centuries, the Middle East has been the backdrop for a violent conflict between Israelis and Palestinians. The roots of this dispute can be traced to the emergence of the Zionist movement in the late 1800s, the dissolution of the Ottoman Empire following World War I, and the subsequent division of the Middle East by the Allied powers.[35] Emerging from Europe, Zionism was the political force behind the reestablishment of a sovereign Jewish state in the biblical land of Israel.[36] While in the midst of war, Great Britain issued the Balfour Declaration in 1917. This document endorsed Zionism and promised to assist in the creation of a Jewish national homeland in Palestine in exchange for Jewish support in the war effort.[37] A similar agreement was made with the Arabs, in which England promised them autonomy in exchange for their rebellion against the Ottoman Empire. However, once the Allied powers won the war, they proceeded to carve up the Middle East into spheres of influence despite the prior commitments they had made.

The League of Nations granted Great Britain the Palestine Mandate in 1922, giving it authority over Palestine and Transjordan (i.e., Israel, Gaza Strip, West Bank, a part of the Golan Heights, and Jordan). With a predominantly Arab population and a growing Jewish minority, the region was divided into administrative units.[38] England transferred its portion of the Golan Heights to France, who held the Syria Mandate. The area east of the Jordan River became the Kingdom of Jordan. The land west of the river (i.e., Palestine) was maintained under a British high commissioner. Despite Great Britain's formal authority over Palestine, the region was plagued by Arab-Jewish violence over the rapid influx of Jewish immigrants, the purchase of land by Jewish settlers, and the overall control of the territory.[39]

In 1936, Palestine erupted in an Arab rebellion. It was inspired by the death of Sheikh Izzidin al-Qassam in 1935, who, along with his band of comrades, led an armed revolt in the north of Palestine against British troops.[40] One organization that was particularly concerned with the plight of Palestinian Arabs was the Muslim Brotherhood. Founded by Hasan al-Banna in Egypt in 1928, the Brotherhood was dedicated to revitalizing the Islamic call (*da'awah*) through education and reform and transforming society into what the Prophet Muhammad had envisioned for it.[41] The Brotherhood mobilized popular support, provided material aid, and secured access to the region through members who joined the Palestinian Arab resistance.[42] The revolt subsided in 1939 when the British implemented a strict quota on Jewish immigration; however, the Brotherhood's presence remained and eventually culminated in the founding of its first official branch in Jerusalem in 1945. This was the foremost religious-political movement of its kind in the region.[43]

The end of World War II brought with it thousands of homeless Jews eager to begin a new life in Palestine; however, restrictions on immigration remained in effect.[44] Skilled in sabotage and small-unit tactics, Jewish militants began attacking British troops in opposition to the immigration policy.[45] Violence in the region soared by 1947, and the British were compelled to commit additional troops and resources in an effort to maintain its loosening grip on Palestine. The United Nations (UN) intervened in April 1947 with a plan to partition Palestine: one portion for Arabs, the other for Jews.[46] The proposal was announced in November 1947 and heavy fighting ensued. On May 15, 1948, one day after a provisional government declared the state of Israel's independence, the armies of Egypt, Iraq, Jordan, Lebanon, and Syria invaded.[47]

United with Arab nationalist forces, despite their ideological differences, the Palestinian branch of the Muslim Brotherhood assumed an active part in the 1948 war.[48] By 1947, the Brotherhood had flourished in Palestine, establishing thirty-eight branches with more than ten thousand registered members.[49] However, in the face of overwhelming odds, the newly formed Israel Defense Forces (IDF) secured a large portion of Palestine and many Palestinian Arabs were obliged to find refuge in surrounding Arab states, the Gaza Strip, and the West Bank.[50] When the UN brokered cease-fires between Israel and its Arab adversaries, 75 percent of Palestine was within the borders of the new Jewish state, the West Bank was under the control of Jordan, and the Gaza Strip was under the dominion of Egypt.[51]

Tension in the region sparked large-scale conflict again in the 1967 Six-Day War. On June 5, Israel launched a preemptive attack on Egypt, believing that its forces, gathered in the Sinai Peninsula, were preparing an invasion.[52] Jordan joined the fight by shelling Israel, while Syria bombed settlements in the north.[53] When the war ended, Israel occupied the Old City of Jerusalem, the West Bank, the Gaza Strip, the Golan Heights, and the Sinai Peninsula. Realizing that a conventional war was futile and feeling abandoned by their Arab neighbors, Palestinian militants found solace in the Palestinian Liberation Organization (PLO), which facilitated guerrilla attacks against Israel.[54] Led by Yasser Arafat, the secular organization became the principal voice behind Palestinian statehood over the next several years. In the meantime, the Muslim Brotherhood laid in wait by avoiding military activities, fortifying its hard-core members in the face of Israeli rule, focusing on institution building, and preparing for *jihad*.[55]

Frustration over the occupation of the Gaza Strip and the West Bank erupted on December 8, 1987, after an Israeli truck collided with an automobile carrying several Palestinian workers. Four persons were killed in the West Bank crash.[56] The accident triggered mass demonstrations and riots that evolved into the uprising known as the *intifada*. On the evening of the following day, the Political Bureau of the Muslim Brotherhood met in Gaza at the home of Ahmad Yassin[57] to discuss how they could utilize the situation to stir up religious and nationalist sentiments.[58] At the meeting, they drafted a communiqué. In their announcement, the Muslim Brotherhood stipulated that "during one week, hundreds of wounded and tens of martyrs offered their lives in the path of God to uphold their nation's glory and honor, to restore our rights in our homeland, and to elevate God's banner in the land."[59] In addition, the document indicated that "the *intifada* of our vigilant people in the Occupied Territories comes as a resounding rejection of the occupation and its pressures, land confiscation and the planning of settlements, and the policy of subjugation by the Zionists."[60] The leaflet was distributed in the Gaza Strip on December 11 and 12 and in the West Bank on the 14 and 15. It was signed "Harakat al-Muqawamah al-Islamiyya" (the Islamic Resistance Movement), along with its acronym HAMAS (Hamas), which means "zeal" or "enthusiasm" in Arabic.

The document's release marked the birth of the Palestinian Covenant of the Islamic Resistance Movement.[61] Through its organized use of street violence, Hamas assumed a central role in the *intifada* and soon gained enough power to play a significant role in Palestinian politics.[62]

As an outgrowth of the Muslim Brotherhood, Hamas has an ideology that represents a combination of religious principles and Palestinian national aspirations.[63] According to the Hamas charter, its ultimate goal is "to raise the banner of God over every inch of Palestine."[64] It stipulates that this can only be accomplished through *jihad,* which is an obligation of all Muslims when an enemy usurps their land. Moreover, the charter contends that "the land of Palestine is . . . Islamic [and] entrusted to the Muslim generations until Judgement Day" and that no Arab state, leader, or organization has the right to relinquish it.[65] In sum, then, the Hamas collective aims to destroy Israel and to establish an Islamic Palestinian state in its place.[66]

Hamas is concentrated in the Gaza Strip and the West Bank. The organization is estimated to have between 750 and 1,200 fighters and tens of thousands of supporters and sympathizers.[67] As an organization, Hamas includes both logistical support and military operations and can be divided into three divisions: public (members are active in institutions and politics), underground network (members are active in organizing demonstrations, transferring funds, and gathering intelligence), and the military wing (members are responsible for initiating attacks on Israeli soldiers and civilians).[68] Hamas's governance is entrusted to a political council whose members live inside and outside the occupied territories.[69] Hamas has developed an extensive social welfare network, including nurseries, kindergartens, schools, mosques, health care clinics, summer camps, and sports clubs.[70] Aside from providing much needed support and human services to the Palestinian people, these efforts are also used to indoctrinate young people, recruit members, raise funds, organize activities, and distribute propaganda. In addition, through its public arm, Hamas endorses individuals who are active in Palestinian-Arab institutions and politics.[71]

Named after the Martyr, Izzidin al-Qassam, the Izz Al-Din Al-Qassam Brigades comprise Hamas's military wing. According to investigators, this wing takes orders from the political council.[72] Over the years, members of the brigades have committed numerous acts of terrorism against Israeli and Palestinian civilians. These acts include assaults, kidnappings, shootings, assassinations, and suicide bombings.[73]

Following the passing of Yasser Arafat, Mahmoud Abbas was elected president of the Palestinian National Authority in January 2005. In the month following, President Abbas, Israeli Prime Minister Ariel Sharon, Egyptian President Hosny Mubarak, and King Abdullah II of Jordan met for a summit in Sharm El Sheikh, Egypt. It was agreed that Israel would release over nine hundred Palestinian prisoners and withdraw from Palestinian cities.[74] In return, the *intifada* was declared to be over. In March 2005, Hamas agreed to a *tahediyeh,* or lull in the fighting, and to participate in the parliamentary elections, which have been postponed until January 25, 2006.[75] Despite scattered violence, the Israeli evacuation of Gaza settlements was completed on August 24, 2005, making way for the establishment of an independent Palestinian state. It remains unclear how Hamas, clearly caught between competing agendas, will deal with its ultimate goal of establishing an Islamic Palestinian state in place of Israel. Indeed, only time will tell how Hamas will elect to resolve the more practical question of creating an independent Palestinian state in the territories occupied by Israel since 1967.[76]

Peruvian Shining Path

Latin America is yet another region of the globe that has faced the horror and devastation of terrorism. Indeed, the area has become infamous for its violent insurgent movements and its equally violent government-sponsored counterinsurgent campaigns. Peru has received a considerable degree of notoriety for playing host to one of the most deadly of these movements, namely, the Shining Path. Rooted in a blend of Maoism and Andean mysticism, the organization has the primary aim of overthrowing the Peruvian government and establishing a communist peasant revolutionary regime.[77]

Its first major action was launched on the night of May 17, 1980. This was the eve of the country's first presidential elections in seventeen years. A group of Shining Path militants stormed the town hall in the small Andean town of Chuschi, stole the voting boxes and lists that were to be used in the following day's elections, and burned them in the town plaza.[78] The press paid little attention to the incident, attributing the attack to local thugs; however, the Shining Path had officially embarked on its "people's war." The terrorist organization's size and proclivity for indiscriminate violence soon grew to mythic proportions.

Eventually, it posed a significant threat to the safety and security of the country's inhabitants. Indeed, it is estimated that the nearly thirty-year campaign has claimed over thirty thousand lives and close to $22 billion in damages to Peru's fragile infrastructure.[79]

The Shining Path was founded in 1970 by Abimael Guzmán Reynoso, a philosophy professor at the National University of San Cristóbal de Huamanga in the Ayacucho region of Peru.[80] Guzmán was born in 1934 to a middle-class family.[81] At nineteen, he became a student at the National University of San Agustín in Arequipa, where he was drawn to Marxist philosophy. Eventually, he earned a Ph.D. in philosophy and another in law. Guzmán's involvement in radical politics is believed to have begun in the late 1950s, when he joined the Peruvian Communist Party. This organization was formed from the Peruvian Socialist Party and was created by one of the country's leading Marxist thinkers of the 1920s, José Carlos Mariátegui.[82]

In 1961, Guzmán took an appointment as an instructor of philosophy at the National University of San Cristóbal de Huamanga in the Ayacucho region.[83] The rugged and remote region is situated high in the Peruvian Andes, some two hundred miles southeast of Lima. The Ayacucho region has a history of being politically, culturally, and economically isolated from the rest of the country and is notorious for being among the most impoverished in Peru.[84] Its population consists primarily of Quechua-speaking Peruvian Indians who live in highland communities. When Guzmán arrived, most of the peasant Indians survived through subsistence farming; others were serfs who belonged to haciendas.[85] The region's debilitating poverty, absence of schools, malnutrition, lack of public services, and utter oppression made many within the peasant community receptive to Guzmán's revolutionary message.[86]

In 1963, Guzmán became disenchanted with the Peruvian Communist Party when the Sino-Soviet split caused the group to pursue the Moscovite path of peaceful revolution from within the state rather than the Maoist line of armed revolution.[87] This fissure prompted Guzmán and other pro-Chinese party members to unite under a Maoist splinter group called the Bandera Roja, or the Red Flag. At its peak, the group claimed to have fifty students, which was about half of the university's enrollment.[88] Meanwhile, Guzmán was appointed the head of planning and personnel at the university. This enabled him to fire rival instructors and hire like-minded supporters. Using his position of power at the school, he arranged for his students to go into the rural countryside under the guise of teaching practice and indoctrinate the university's peasant neighbors.

In 1970, Guzmán and his followers—consisting primarily of university students and junior faculty members—split from the Red Flag and formed the Partido Communista del Perú por el Sendero Luminoso de José Mariátegui, or the Communist Party of Peru by the Shining Path of José Mariátegui.[89] Among its membership, the group would simply be called the Partido Communista del Perú (PCP). To those the group would come to terrorize, it was known as Sendero Luminoso, or the Shining Path.[90] The PCP took its name from the title of a magazine published by Mariátegui that read, "By the shining path of Comrade Jose Carlos Mariátegui."[91] Sometime during 1978, Guzmán and the Shining Path went underground; they were not heard from again until the attack in May 1980.

As the organization developed, it formed a powerful cult around the personality of its charismatic founder. To his followers, Guzmán was considered the fourth sword of communism after Marx, Lenin, and Mao. His ideology was a synthesis of the teaching of Jose Carlos Mariátegui and Maoism.[92] In particular, Guzmán adopted Mariátegui's evaluation of Peru's socioeconomic situation, arguing that prior to the Spanish invasion the country's indigenous population practiced a primitive form of Incan communism. Moreover, the capitalist, semifeudal society established in its place forced the Indian community into a position of servitude. Mariátegui envisioned a rural-based revolution that would mobilize the Peruvian peasantry as an oppressed ethnic minority and class of citizens. To achieve this aim, Guzmán and the Shining Path relied on Mao's theory of guerrilla warfare. This theory calls for the mobilization of the rural population into a "people's army." Operating from a firm rural base, the army would encircle the cities and destroy the bourgeois-led state government.

McCormick explained that after raiding the town hall in Chuschi, the Shining Path launched a series of attacks on the symbols of the fascist state, including police stations, government offices, and various nationally sponsored development projects in the Ayacucho region.[93] By 1981, the group had expanded its targets to include infrastructure sites. These consisted of bridges, rail lines, electric power stations and transmission lines, and telecommunications facilities, as well as various economic objectives. The Shining Path's primary weapon was dynamite procured from the thousands of small mining camps that dotted the Peruvian highlands. They also used Molotov cocktails, pipe bombs, homemade grenades, and weapons stolen from military and police forces.[94]

The Shining Path established zones of liberation in various regions of the Sierra. They gained support by capitalizing on the grievances of the poor indigenous inhabitants of the rural highlands, a rapidly declining economy, and centuries-old government neglect of impoverished peasant areas.[95] Within these zones of liberation, the Shining Path staged "people's trials" to punish landowners, money lenders, rural traders, thieves, cattle rustlers, corrupt officials, village merchants, town leaders, and others who committed crimes against the citizenry.[96] In those villages that resisted, the Shining Path gathered local administrators, community leaders, and traitors and, after a brief trial, executed them for their violations.[97] By 1983, the Shining Path was in full operation and expanded its sphere of influence beyond the Sierra.

At its peak, the Shining Path was a highly sophisticated revolutionary organization that functioned at the national, regional, and local level.[98] Each level had layers of committees, operational cells, and support networks. Nationally, the Shining Path was run by the National Central Committee. This entity consisted of Guzmán and his lieutenants. They made all major decisions regarding the group's ideology, policies, and strategies. Six regional committees were situated under the national committee. These included the Eastern, Southern, Northern, Central, Metropolitan, and Primary areas. Encompassing several departments and unit subdivisions, these regional committees were responsible for the planning, evaluation, and execution of all PCP activities in their respective locales. Under the direction of the regional commanders, the militants[99] initiated attacks; activists developed popular education programming, distributed propaganda, and encouraged civil unrest; and sympathizers provided logistical support and participated in demonstrations.

By mid-decade, nearly every department in Peru was experiencing Shining Path violence.[100] In 1992, it was estimated that the organization had between five thousand to six thousand armed militants and fifty thousand people within its support network.[101] In a desperate move to control the violence that had engulfed the country, former president Alberto Fujimori seized near-dictatorial power in April 1992 by disbanding the Peruvian congress and courts. He claimed they were limiting the country's ability to fight terrorism and, consequently, initiated an aggressive antiterrorism campaign. Although numerous widespread human rights violations were committed, the draconian crackdown severely diminished the Shining Path's operational capacity. Specifically, on September 12, 1992, counterinsurgency forces captured Abimael Guzmán in a middle-class neighborhood in Lima, along with several other high-ranking members of the Central Committee.[102] Charged with high treason by Peru's Supreme Council of Military Justice, Guzmán was sentenced to life in prison at an island navy base.[103] With its leader incarcerated and a subsequent public admission of defeat, the group began to factionalize. Large-scale arrests and desertions significantly diminished its numbers.[104] By the mid-to-late 1990s, the Shining Path's activities had been sharply reduced.

Although the Shining Path no longer poses a serious threat to the national security of Peru, the guerrillas continue to initiate sporadic acts of violence. The group still has roughly four hundred to five hundred armed militants within its ranks, and they have been responsible for numerous acts of terrorism.[105] One of these attacks was the detonation of a car bomb near the U.S. Embassy in Lima that killed ten people. Most recently, the Maoist rebels have conducted several well coordinated operations, including the abduction of seventy-one workers at a gas pipeline in the mountain jungles of southeastern Peru and an ambush on a military patrol.[106] Authorities suspect that the recent escalation in Shining Path violence is related to the increase in coca and poppy cultivation in Peru,[107] from which the group has profited.[108] Moreover, experts speculate that the increased source of revenue is being used to fund operations and recruitment drives. Consequently, the Shining Path's recent resurgence has some fearing that the organization is attempting to revitalize its campaign of terror.

Liberation Tigers of Tamil Eelam (LTTE)

Similar to many continents around the globe, Asia is no stranger to the tragedy of terrorism. One such example is the conflict that erupted over a half-century ago on the 2,500-square-mile island off the southeastern coast of India known as Sri Lanka. Tensions on the island are, to some degree, rooted in sixteenth-, seventeenth-, and eighteenth-century colonialism.[109] In 1595, the Portuguese were the first of the European colonial powers to conquer the island of Ceylon (renamed Sri Lanka in 1972).[110] Upon their arrival, they found three indigenous kingdoms: "a

Tamil Hindu state in the Jaffna peninsula, a Sinhalese kingdom in the central highlands at Kandy, and a second Sinhalese kingdom near the western coast."[111]

The indigenous Sri Lankan Tamils are the descendants of darker-skinned Dravidian migrants from south India. They are predominantly Saivite Hindus; speak the Tamil tongue of the Dravidian family, which is also spoken in the southern Indian state of Tamil Nadu; and live primarily in the northern and eastern provinces of the island. Standing in almost perfect geographic, racial, linguistic, and religious contrast are the Sinhalese. They dwell principally in the southwest area of the island, trace their lineage to the fair-skinned Aryan peoples of Northern India, speak the Sinhala language (an Indo-European tongue), and are chiefly Theravada Buddhists.[112]

The seventeenth century brought Dutch governance over the island, although it was eventually supplanted by British rule in 1802.[113] Prior to the British takeover, the Portuguese and Dutch managed the island as two separate ethnic territories, allowing the Tamils and Sinhalese to live in relative isolation from one another.[114] With British rule came the imposition of a plantation economy and a unified state structure with Colombo as its capital.[115] Communal representation was introduced as a means by which the island's localities could advance, protect, and preserve their interests through the government.[116] In 1931, Ceylon was granted self-rule and universal suffrage. At a time when Great Britain's colonial dominion over India began to dissolve, the island of Ceylon was granted full independence on February 4, 1948.[117]

Constituting more than 70 percent of the island's population, the Sinhalese community won roughly 80 percent of the seats in Parliament.[118] Thereafter, Sinhalese legislators began implementing a series of policies designed to reverse what they perceived to be years of British favoritism for the Tamil minority. One example of this was that, historically, high-caste Jaffna Tamils dominated the government's civil service.

During British rule, foreign missionaries established English schools in the Tamil regions. This created a class of English-speaking Tamil professionals who benefited from preferential treatment, especially for positions as civil servants, lawyers, teachers, and doctors.[119] One of the first measures to be implemented was the Sinhalese-Only Act of 1956. The act proclaimed the Sinhala language to be the island's official vernacular. Founded in 1949, the Tamil Federal Party lobbied tirelessly to eliminate the Sinhalese-Only Act. They feared that if their argot was not recognized as one of the island's official tongues, the Tamil community would not only be forced to abandon its language but also its culture and way of life.[120] The Federal Party responded by staging nonviolent picketing campaigns, or *satyagraha,* in protest of the Sinhalese-Only Act and the subsequent discriminatory policies that followed it. These campaigns led to anti-Tamil riots, state repression, and broken pacts and promises.[121]

Passed in the 1970s, another policy known as "standardization" required Tamil university applicants to have higher entrance scores than their Sinhalese student counterparts. Facing a weak economy, upper-, middle-, and lower-class Tamil men developed a collective sense of hopelessness for their future. By the mid- to late-1970s, the Tamil community began demanding a homeland of their own. Feeling a profound degree of restlessness, frustration, and disenfranchisement, young Tamil men began resorting to violence.[122] These young men, affectionately referred to as the "boys," became the backbone of the Tamil insurgency. In sum, the consequence of the postindependence discriminatory policies of the Sinhalese-dominated government was that "the Sri Lanka Tamil community, once the island's most prosperous, was culturally marginalized and reduced to penury as its per capita income fell below that of the Sinhalese."[123] Given these realities, the Tamils concluded that their very existence and survival was in jeopardy.

Founded in 1972[124] by its leader, Velupillai Prabhakaran, the Liberation Tigers of Tamil Eelam (LTTE) represented one of several militant organizations created in response to the government's discriminatory legislative policies.[125] In their document entitled "A Struggle for Justice," the Liberation Tigers of Tamil Eelam stipulated that the movement

> is committed to the position that the Tamils constitute themselves as a people or a nation and have a homeland, the historically constituted habitation of the Tamils, a well defined contiguous territory embracing the Northern and Eastern Provinces. Since the Tamils have a homeland, a distinct language and culture, a unique economic life and a lengthy history extending to over three thousand years, they possess all the characteristics of a nation or a people. As people they have the inalienable right to self determination.[126]

Finding inspiration and justification in socialist praxis, Dravidian history, and the Indian freedom struggle, the LTTE's armed struggle is aimed at creating a territorially and politically independent state to be called Tamil Eelam for the three million Tamil-speaking people living in Sri Lanka, the elimination of caste ties, and a collective national identity for all Tamils.[127]

After several years of ethnic conflict between Tamil militants and the Sinhalese army, the Indian government intervened by dispatching the Indian Peace-Keeping Force (IPKF) to Sri Lanka between July 1987 and March 1990.[128] Hoping that the detachment would bring an end to the conflict and its militant activists, the 2.5-year campaign left twelve thousand dead and over five thousand wounded.[129] Although the troops did eventually force the Tamil Tigers out of the city of Jaffna, which they had overrun, and into the north-central Sri Lankan jungles, the LTTE solidified themselves as an adaptable, innovative, and viable fighting force.[130]

The LTTE is the dominant force behind the creation of a Tamil homeland.[131] Word of its commitment is legendary, as many Tigers have died by their own hand after ingesting the cyanide capsule they wear around their neck to avoid capture and torture.[132] It is estimated that the organization has eight to ten thousand armed combatants in Sri Lanka, with a core of three to six thousand trained fighters.[133] Its structure includes a military wing complete with a maritime group (known as the Sea Tigers) and an airborne group (known as the Air Tigers), an intelligence wing, a finance wing, a political wing, and a women's wing (known as the Birds of Freedom), as well as the infamous suicide commando wing (known as the Black Tigers).[134] The LTTE has also built a strong financial and material structure within the Tamil community at home and abroad.[135] The organization is rumored to use this international network of contacts to smuggle illegal drugs throughout the world, an allegation the LTTE adamantly denies.[136]

Although the LTTE portrays itself as a guerrilla force that mounts military operations against the Sri Lankan army, it is well known for its use of terrorist tactics. The group has engaged in assassination, sabotage, murder, intimidation, and bombings in an effort to promote its cause and solidify its control over select areas of Sri Lanka. Among its many targets, the group focuses on key government and military personnel, economic strongholds, public infrastructure facilities, and fellow Tamils who do not conform to LTTE rule.[137] The LTTE has also become particularly notorious for its use of the suicide bomber.[138] The Black Tigers are estimated to have carried out a total of 150 to 180 such attacks.[139] Aside from the hundreds of lives they have claimed through strikes on numerous Sri Lankan military facilities and symbols of national infrastructure, their victims have included former Indian prime minister Rajiv Gandhi, Sri Lankan president Ranasinghe Premadasa, and Sri Lankan presidential candidate Gamini Dissanayake.[140]

In total, the fighting between Tamil militants and Sri Lankan and Indian forces is believed to have claimed over sixty-five thousand lives and left thousands more with the psychological scars of living amidst the bloodshed and carnage of a war-torn society.[141] At the time of this writing, the LTTE and the Sri Lankan government have made progress in the peace process through the involvement of a Norwegian delegation who helped broker a cease-fire in December 2001.[142] During the process, the LTTE agreed to consider autonomy in a federal system in an undivided island while the Sri Lankan government contemplated the concession of considerable autonomy to the Tamils. However, the road to peace has not been an easy one. In October 2003, Sri Lankan President Kumaratunga called for the dismissal of the Norwegian general in charge of the peace-monitoring mission, claiming that he was biased toward the rebels. Alleging that then Prime Minister Wickremesinghe had made too many compromises in the peace process, President Kumaratunga suspended parliament and seized control while the Prime Minister was in Washington, D.C., meeting with President Bush to discuss the peace process.[143] In November 2003, the government announced that the peace talks would be halted until the political power struggle was resolved. According to the peace secretariat of the Liberation Tigers of Tamil Eelam, the group remained committed to resuming negotiations once the political crisis was resolved.[144] In December 2004, the island suffered devastating damage as a result of a massive tsunami. In June 2005, the LTTE and Sri Lankan government agreed to share nearly $3 billion in aid among the island's Sinhala, Tamil, and Muslim inhabitants, restoring hope that a peaceful settlement to the conflict could be achieved.[145]

Racist Skinheads

North America is another region of the globe that has experienced the devastation and trauma of terrorism. Racist Skinheads are just one example of right-wing militant extremists who commit acts of violence in an effort to promote their political agenda of White supremacy. The history of racist Skinheads is actually rooted in the rebellious youth subcultures of Great Britain during the late 1950s.[146] As Moore explained, the modern Skinhead scene materialized "in England from a series of almost unrelieved social and political disasters: the Depression of the 1930s; the devastation of World War II; and the continuing condition of deprivation—the endless fall from the old power and glory of the Imperial nation—in which the new welfare state seemed mired."[147] Out of these debilitating circumstances "youth subcultures emerged from a time of want and dissatisfaction" in England.[148]

Born in the working-class streets of South London, the Teddy Boys were the first of England's youth subcultures to be recognized. Dressed in a flamboyant, upper-class Edwardian style and exhibiting a preference for loud rock-n-roll music, the Teddy Boys were soon seen as a threat to society's traditional values.[149] However, the Teddy Boys were eventually replaced by the Modernists, or Mods, who modeled their style of dress after young African Americans and developed a taste for Ska and reggae music, with its distinctive West Indian beat.[150] By the mid-1960s, the Mods divided into two factions: the *smooth* Mods, who hailed from a higher social economic status and maintained a sharper style of dress; and the *hard* Mods, who were unemployed and collected welfare.[151] Confronted with a bleaker outlook on their future, the hard Mods appropriated a tougher exterior, consisting of short, cropped hair, work boots, braces (suspenders), Ben Sherman shirts, and Levis.[152] This early Skinhead look was perceived as embracing a more puritanical and masculine image because it was popular among the British working class.[153] Ironically, this initial Skinhead style was also inspired by Black Jamaican immigrants to England, known as Rude Boys.[154] By the late 1960s, the British Skinheads, with their unique style of dress, distinct musical taste, proclivity for violence, and loathing for the status quo, began to emerge as a separate youth subculture.

Although the original British Skinheads were not overtly racist, they did embody ultraconservative values. In addition, they focused on reclaiming their traditional working-class community from England's new immigrant population and the hedonistic hippies they perceived as a drain on society.[155] Their violent outbursts were frequently directed toward Pakistani immigrants and homosexual enclaves.[156] The Skinheads experienced a momentary decline during the early 1970s as a result of increased police harassment; however, they soon resurfaced with the advent of the punk scene in the mid-to-late 1970s.[157] This time around, the Skinheads took on a distinctly racist attitude by embracing Nazism, and they adopted a new avenue for spreading their hate-filled message, Oi music.[158] Originating from a hybrid of Jamaican-inspired reggae and West Indie Ska, Oi music would eventually become the Skinheads' official means of conveying their anger and rebellion toward the status quo. Their hate-filled message made them a national recruiting target for the adult-based, racist group known as the National Front, who sponsored Skinhead concerts.

The racist Skinhead youth scene eventually appeared in North America in the early 1980s.[159] While some have proposed that it came over as a racist movement,[160] Wood argued that it emerged along with the punk scene but did not become distinctly racist until some time later.[161] Racist Skinheads began recruiting the same type of disenchanted teens from White working-class backgrounds to fill their ranks after adapting to the North American brand of White supremacy. This type of White supremacy was conveyed by right-wing groups like the National Alliance,[162] led by William Pierce, and the White Aryan Resistance, led by Tom Metzger.[163] While there is some variation between the larger White supremacist movement and racist Skinheads, there are three pivotal concepts in the racist right ideology common to both hate groups: White supremacy, radical religion, and anti-Semitism.[164]

Simply stated, White supremacy is the belief that Whites are superior to any other race. The foundation of this conviction stems from racism. The literature on racism has evolved considerably over the last several decades; however, Benedict's comments are as insightful today as they were when first drafted more than sixty years ago. She described the phenomenon as follows:

> Racism is the dogma that one ethnic group is condemned by nature to congenital inferiority and another group is destined to congenital superiority. It is the dogma that the hope of civilization depends upon eliminating some races and keeping others pure. It is the dogma that one race has carried progress with it throughout human history and can alone ensure future progress. . . . Racism is essentially a pretentious way of saying that "I" belong to the Best People. For such a conviction, it is the most gratifying formula that has ever been discovered, for neither

my own unworthiness nor the accusations of others can ever dislodge me from my position. . . . It avoids all embarrassing questions about my conduct of life and nullifies all embarrassing claims by "inferior" groups about their own achievements and ethical standards.[165]

Included within the idea of racism is the belief in White supremacy and White separatism. Members of the movement argue that they should establish a racially sovereign nation governed by Whites and free of Jews and minorities identified as "mud" races.[166] Moreover, within this "nation" members promote the preservation of the White race and exercise self-determination.

The second belief structure is radical religion. Wooden and Blazak identified three forms of radical religion that are particularly popular among racist Skinheads:[167] Christian Identity, Odinism, and the World Church of the Creator (WCOTC).[168] Rooted in British-Israelism, Christian Identity maintains that the ten lost tribes of Israel migrated across the Caucasus Mountains to become the Anglo-Saxon people.[169] The implications of such teachings are that the British are God's true chosen people and that the Jewish people are not. The American brand of British Israelism (i.e., Christian Identity) added the anti-Semitic component to this ideology. They insisted that the Jews are the biological offspring of a sexual union between Satan and Eve, and are attempting to erect a reign of evil over the world; consequently, the world is on the verge of the apocalypse.[170]

A second form of radical religion followed by certain racist Skinhead groups is Odinism.[171] This pre-Christian variant of Scandinavian Norse/ Germanic mythology idolizes Viking deities. Examples include

Odin, the father of the gods who is known for wisdom, ecstasy, and magic; Thor, renowned for his strength and might; Frigga, mother of the gods and also known for her wisdom and concern with family and children; Frey, a god of fertility, love, and joy; and Freya, the goddess of fertility and love who also has a warrior part as well.[172]

In particular, Odin and Thor are frequently portrayed as fierce racial warriors.[173] The relationship between the resurrection of this pre-European, pagan religion within the racist American subculture and the German Nazi leaders' interest in pre-Christian forms of religion is not coincidental.[174] As Kaplan explained,

The Odinist dream is of battle, of Valhalla, and of a world restored to the ancient virtues of folk and of tribe. That this dream is reminiscent of National Socialism is no accident. The borderline separating racialist Odinism and National Socialism is exceedingly thin, and much of the material produced by racialist Odinism contains explicit odes to Hitler and the Third Reich.[175]

The third form of radical religion is the World Church of the Creator (WCOTC). This religion is not rooted in any form of ancient religion; instead, it was founded by Ben Klassen, who was once a member of the John Birch Society, a Florida legislator, and Florida chairman for Governor George Wallace's 1968 presidential campaign. Klassen founded the Church of the Creator in 1973, after publishing the book *Nature's Eternal Religion*.[176] In it, he denounced Christianity, calling for its replacement with Creativity, arguing that race was a religion. Klassen's religion continued to receive considerable attention when he published a second book entitled *The White Man's Bible*.[177] The Anti-Defamation League declared the COTC to be one of the most violent organizations in the radical right during the early 1990s.[178] Klassen committed suicide in 1993; however, in 1995, Matt Hale, leader of the National Socialist White American's Party, changed the name of his organization to "the New COTC" and refocused his efforts from politics to religion. In 1996, he pronounced himself to be the Pontifex Maximus of the World COTC.[179]

The third belief structure embedded within the White supremacist ideology is anti-Semitism. The stereotypical portrayal of the Jewish people is as "cheap, miserly manipulator[s] of money, forever preoccupied with materialism, and consequently possessing virtually unlimited economic power."[180] The strong anti-Semitic theme of the White supremacist movement is identifiable not only in their religious beliefs but also in their political platform. The Zionist Occupational Government (i.e., ZOG) is frequently employed to describe the White supremacist's conspiratorial description of a Jewish-run political structure with the goal of oppressing the White working class for the ZOG's own material gain.[181]

The racist Skinhead scene in North America is not a cohesive group; instead, it is a conglomeration of many small and independent units that operate much like street gangs.[182] In the United States alone, there are thirty-nine active Skinhead chapters, or crews; however, given their migratory nature, this calculation may underestimate their true representation in society.[183] The most violent and best organized racist Skinhead group is the Hammerskin Nation.[184] This particular sect formed in Dallas, Texas, during the late 1980s as the Confederate Hammerskins.[185] The group has since expanded and, in 2000, claimed to have nineteen chapters in the United States and one in Canada. According to one imprisoned Hammerskin, their goal is to achieve international unity among Skinheads.[186]

Building upon the crucial role Oi music played in the development of the early racist Skinhead scene, the Hammerskin Nation affiliates with a number of White power music bands. Believing that music is one of the best ways to reach, inspire, and recruit people, the Hammerskin Nation, along with Panzerfaust Records, regularly sponsors a series of hate rock concerts affectionately called Hammerfests.[187]

Upon their arrival on North American shores in the early 1980s, racist Skinheads have engaged in numerous acts of terrorism. These displays of harm have "catapulted them to perhaps the leading position among hate groups practicing violence in America [today]."[188] They have engaged in vandalism, intimidation, arson, beatings, bombings, and murder directed against minority and Jewish communities. As a result, racist Skinheads quickly became a valuable tool for the organized right-wing movement.[189] While racist Skinheads do not garner the amount of publicity they did during the 1980s and 1990s, they continue to be a violent collective, intent on terrorizing non-Whites, gays and lesbians, those of the Jewish faith, and anyone else who opposes their agenda of White supremacy, racial purity, white separatism, radical religion, and anti-Semitism.

5

The Provisional Irish
Republican Army

     This chapter integrates the conceptual material on structural
Symbolic Interactionism and Identity Theory and applies it to membership in the Provisional Irish Republican Army (PIRA). Of particular
concern is the way identity manifests and sustains itself through the various social psychological dimensions that constitute the social person.
Specifically, these dimensions include symbols, the definition of the situation, roles, socialization and role-taking, and the self. The application
of the interpretative and explanatory framework to the PIRA is significant. In short, it demonstrates how culture, self, and society powerfully,
though subtly, contribute to the emergence and maintenance of identity,
including membership in and allegiance to a militant extremist collective. To be clear, this undertaking does not justify or otherwise condone
the violence, bloodshed, or acts of devastation perpetrated by such individuals; however, it does offer a novel perspective by which to account
for the threat or presence of terrorism.

Symbols

For the Provisional Irish Republican Army (PIRA), there are several
symbols that have influenced its ongoing participation in and continued
commitment to militant violence. One such symbol, identified in the
PIRA's official documents, was the brutal and vicious confrontation that
erupted on August 12, 1969, known as the Battle of Bogside.[1]

    Tensions in Northern Ireland had peaked during the summer of
1969. The Loyalist Protestant marching season was quickly approach-
ing, and the minority Nationalist Catholic community felt its demands
for civil rights were not being acknowledged.[2] One of the biggest Loyal-

ist Protestant marches is the annual Apprentice Boy parade. It takes place every August in Londonderry, Northern Ireland. J. R. White described the history behind the commemoration as follows:

> From 1689 to 1691, James II, the Catholic pretender to the British throne, used Ireland as a base from which to revolt against William of Orange, the English King. In August 1689, Irish Protestant skilled workers, called "Apprentice Boys," were relieved by the English after defending Derry through a long siege by the pretender. The following year William defeated James at the battle of the Boyne River. . . . The Protestants have flaunted these victories in the face of the Catholics since 1690. Each year they gather to militantly celebrate the battle of the Boyne and the Apprentice Boys with parades and demonstrations. It fuels the fire of hatred in Northern Ireland and demonstrates the division between Protestants and Catholics.[3]

Clearly, the annual Apprentice Boy parade and other similar exhibitions have a powerful symbolic meaning for both Nationalist Catholics and Loyalist Protestants. Specifically, for Nationalist Catholics, the event signifies aggression and hostility, as well as an attempt to humiliate them for their defeat in past battles.

As the Loyalist Protestants marched past the perimeter of the Catholic Bogside, sectarian clashes erupted and the community was quickly thrust into an all-out conflict. In a combative effort to quell the violence, the government of Northern Ireland deployed the Royal Ulster Constabulary (RUC), who, with the assistance of a Protestant mob, charged the Nationalist rioters.[4] The security forces were met with stones and petrol bombs while the rioters endured police batons and tear gas. The rioting continued for two days and nights and left thousands (mostly Catholics) homeless.[5] British forces were dispatched on August 14 to help deescalate the situation.[6] Despite their presence, violence against the Catholic community continued: Loyalist Protestant mobs burnt down homes and schools and murdered community members while, in some instances, Northern Irish authorities idly sat by observing the devastation and carnage.[7] According to several sources, the failure of the official IRA to defend the Nationalist Catholic community from Loyalist Protestant mobs following the Battle of Bogside represents the primary catalyst for the creation of the PIRA.[8]

Another symbol identified by the PIRA as pivotal to their involvement in militant extremism was the Bloody Sunday massacre. This event took place in Londonderry, Northern Ireland, on January 30, 1972.[9] As P. Taylor noted, it is important not to view this occurrence in isolation.[10] While Derry[11] remained free, the British army pursued a policy of containment by establishing barricades around Nationalist areas designed to segregate and remove Republican troublemakers.[12] However, despite the government's best efforts, violence persisted. For example, young hooligans made a habit of promoting disorder in the streets. Indeed, as P. Taylor explained,

> For many months, there had been endless rioting in the city. Every day at tea time, there would be a confrontation at the corner of William Street and Rossville Street between soldiers guarding the entrance to the city center and the rioters operating out of "Free Derry." Day after day soldiers would stand there being pelted by rioters and the stone throwers would get in plenty of practice.[13]

In addition to practicing containment, the British army adopted a policy of internment. This policy allowed the security forces to hold suspects without trial. In January 1972, the Northern Ireland Civil Rights Association announced that it would lead an anti-internment march in Derry. Fearing that the march would erupt in violence, the security forces planned to have a strong presence in anticipation of any such hostilities.

The rally was to begin in an area known as the Creggan and end at Free Derry corner, where civil rights campaigners would conclude with a few poignant remarks. The march commenced at 3:30 P.M. At about this time, young ruffians engaged the soldiers by hurling bottles, bricks, and anything else they had at their disposal to throw.[14] Although the exact events that transpired thereafter still remain unclear, investigators believe that the IRA and British paratroopers from the First Battalion, Parachute Regiment exchanged gunfire at around 4:00 P.M.[15] Shortly afterwards, the paratroopers were given the order to respond to the hooligans and proceeded to fire upon the crowd. The shooting took less than thirty minutes. In its wake, the paratroopers shot and killed thirteen parade participants.[16]

Following these events, a full investigation into the shootings was authorized. British paratroopers claimed they had been fired upon first and that they had merely returned the volley, fearing the loss of their own lives. The paratroopers were exonerated of all criminal wrongdoing.[17] The Irish Catholic communities in both the North and the South perceived this outcome to be a grave injustice. In short, "the only explanation that ma[de] sense to them, and there remain[ed] few voices to the contrary, [was] that there were orders from on-high to teach the rebels of 'Free Derry' a lesson they would never forget. This lesson, as the evidence of their eyes told them, was to send a good number of the marchers back home in boxes."[18]

The exoneration of the paratroopers was regarded as yet another symbolic (and literal) instance of injustice and unfairness perpetrated against the Catholic community. Moreover, it helped to crystallize the Irish Republican community's belief that the British forces were present only to protect the Loyalist Protestants and oppress the Catholics; therefore, the British and all those who supported them could not be trusted. Indeed, "they" personified the enemy. In the end, Bloody Sunday served to swell the ranks of the IRA and accelerate the region's cycle of violence between Loyalist and Republican paramilitary groups, leading to security crackdowns by British forces for many years following this tragic event.[19]

A third symbol influencing the formation of identity relative to membership in the PIRA was the Irish hunger strikes of the early 1980s. The importance of this symbol is evidenced in the central role it has assumed within the popular culture of the PIRA and the larger Republican collective. Indeed, it represents the ultimate example of self-sacrifice and martyrdom and is a frequent theme within song,[20] literature, art, and public protest.[21]

In July 1972, the secretary of state for Northern Ireland granted special-category status to all prisoners convicted of terrorist-related crimes.[22] Those who were granted special-category status did not have to wear prison uniforms and were allowed special privileges. In 1975, a government committee recommended revoking this political status, believing that it undermined prison authority. By 1978, special-category status had been phased out. As a result, when the first Republican, Kiernan Nugent, arrived at the Maze prison, he was ordered to wear prison garb.[23] Arguing that he was a political prisoner rather than a criminal, Nugent refused to wear the institution's uniformed clothing. He was subsequently locked in his cell naked for his opposition. Nugent used the blanket from his cot to cover himself. This initiated what would later be known as "the Blanket Protest." By 1978, there were approximately three hundred prisoners involved in this form of resistance.[24]

Failing to secure political status, the Republican prisoners began the "Dirty Protest." This act of protest meant that they refused to bathe, smeared excrement on their cell walls, and poured urine under their doors.[25] In January 1980, the convicts issued their demands: (a) the right not to wear a prison uniform; (b) the right not to do prison work; (c) the right to associate freely with other convicts; (d) the right to a weekly visit, letter, and parcel, and the right to organize educational and recreational pursuits; and (e) full restoration of remission lost through the protest.[26] The remonstrations escalated again when seven prisoners, led by PIRA commander Brenden Hughes, went on a hunger strike.[27] After two months without nourishment and with one striker on the verge of death, Great Britain sent official word that a compromise would be offered. Fearing the impending death of their comrade, the strikers halted the protest after fifty-three days only to find that the government document identified little that would actually change.[28]

Determined to triumph after the first hunger strike fiasco, Bobby Sands, a young PIRA officer in charge at the Maze, began a second hunger strike on March 1, 1981.[29] Sands had grown up in a Protestant region of northern Belfast before his family (along with other Catholics) was forced out by a systematic campaign of Loyalist intimidation. The PIRA propaganda campaign received a colossal boost when, five days after Sands had initiated his hunger strike, a member of Parliament for Northern Ireland suddenly died. Listing his occupation as political prisoner, Sands was nominated and won the seat by a small margin.[30] Sands died on May 5, after sixty-six days without nourishment. In death, he became an icon of martyrdom within Irish Republican history and helped to further the PIRA's cult of self-sacrifice.[31]

The loss of Bobby Sands sparked a tremendous outpouring of anger within the Republican and larger Nationalist communities. One hundred thousand people are believed to have attended his funeral.[32] While Sands was followed into death by ten other prisoners, the strike was eventually halted on October 3, 1981. However, before it ended, the strikers reached the hearts and minds of the Irish Nationalist and Republican faithful. Indeed, within days of the hunger strike moratorium, prison regulations subsided, favoring the demands of those politicos incarcerated.

Definition of the Situation

For the Provisional Irish Republican Army, the problem centers on the marginalization and disenfranchisement of the minority Irish Catholic community in Northern Ireland by an alien, tyrannical government. This subjugation began with the occupation of Ireland by British imperialists, continued with an oppressive Northern Irish regime, and has manifested itself in events like the Battle of Bogside, the Bloody Sunday massacre, and the deaths of beloved comrades in the 1981 hunger strikes. Indeed, the history of Northern Ireland is littered with personal accounts of Protestant mob violence, as well as acts of murder, torture, unlawful imprisonment, and harassment.[33] Frequently, these atrocities are believed to have been perpetrated or facilitated by the British and Northern Irish security forces. While these very entities have been (and are) charged with protecting the Catholic community, they are understood to be impervious to legal prosecution or official rebuke.

In addition to the Loyalist- and British-inflicted atrocities, the Northern Irish community's employment of discrimination was another way to oppress Catholics in the region. These actions further fueled the situation, which Republicans and Irish Catholics in the region define as thoroughly untenable. As the PIRA explained, "discrimination in employment and housing has been used on a large scale by the Unionists against the non-Unionist population. The reason behind this is to ensure that the Nationalist minority never rises above 35% of the population and that where Nationalists are in the majority they are deprived of work and forced to emigrate."[34] Tangible expressions of such favoritism, inequality, and prejudice are found in the territory's economic practices. One Irish Catholic woman residing in Northern Ireland active in the civil rights movement in the late 1960s described the presence of employment inequality in the region. As she observed,

> You had a lot of job discrimination and that sort of thing. You know, you had advertisements in the paper that would have stated "Protestant only need apply." Believe that or not [laughs]. . . . As you got older and started to work you found out in most jobs you had all Protestant supervisors. And that they were put there, they were appointed to that job because they were Protestant. Not that they were any better qualified than a Catholic was, or had any more experience at this job or that job, just because of their religion. And you [Protestants] could never let

a Catholic get the upper hand. You could see that. And all the best-paying jobs went to Protestants. Maybe they were younger than you and you had more experience, but they didn't really give you any reason. Even if you pressed them, "Why did that girl get that job, she's earning four times as much as I am, I'm three years her senior?"[35]

Discrimination practices such as these exist throughout the social and political landscape of Northern Ireland. For example, Cairns and Darby reported that unemployment among Catholics was 18 percent at the time while the rate was 8 percent among Protestants.[36] It was even higher among Catholic men (23 percent) in comparison to Protestant men (9 percent). As a result, Sinn Féin publicly pledged to continue its fight, advocating for social justice in the form of education, security, privacy, social services, affordable and quality housing, the elimination of discrimination in employment, the provision of equal rights, and cultural equality.[37]

Prior to the peace negotiations, the PIRA believed that "only one solution [could] work: full freedom for the people of Ireland to determine their own future, without British interference."[38] For the organization, this entailed the abolition of the two-state partition and the creation of a thirty-two-county sovereign Irish nation. As the group officially indicated,

> Our aims are those of the Republican movement. Briefly, these are to end foreign rule in Ireland, to establish a 32-County Democratic Socialist Republic based on the Proclamation of 1916, to restore the Irish language and culture to a position of strength, and to promote a social order based on justice and Christian principles which will give everyone a just share of the nation's wealth.[39]

The ideals of this "new" Ireland are articulated in the same PIRA document.[40] The document suggests the adoption of a revised constitution that ensures an individual's protection, and a governmental structure that applies this principle by allowing for the maximum distribution of authority. This new constitution would espouse social progress and human justice by encouraging tolerance for others and by promoting the establishment of civil rights. This charter would include the right to citizenship without prejudice on the basis of race, sex, religion, philosophical conviction, language, or political outlook; life, liberty, and security of person; freedom of religion; participation in government; fair and equal access to public services; education, work, and a standard of living worthy of an emancipated citizen (including food, housing, medical care, and security against unemployment, illness, and disability); and equal pay for equal work.

Commenting on these ideals and the formation of a more equitable Irish nation, McLaughlin, a member of Sinn Féin, noted the following:

> What sort of society do republicans want? One where no grouping dominates others by virtue of holding particular religious or cultural affiliations. One where economic opportunities are available, irrespective of creed or political loyalties. The right to live one's life according to one's own particular culture should be guaranteed to all. With rights come responsibilities however, and the freedom to celebrate one's culture should not be abused by intolerance of the rights of others. The institutions' governing society must be open to all, and representative of all. The law must not be used as an instrument to coerce and dominate any section of society, and those charged with upholding and maintaining the law must be drawn from all sections of society. The needs and aspirations of the people of Ireland should be subservient to no other interests.[41]

This characterization draws attention to a redefinition of the situation that Irish Catholics seek. This is one in which the core values of religious and cultural tolerance, equal representation, and justice for all citizens are secured.

In its first few years, the PIRA saw armed struggle as the only practical means by which to resolve the problems of discrimination and oppression that the Irish Catholic community experienced in Northern Ireland. However, as Sinn Féin gained political strength, it adopted the strategy of the "Armalite and the Ballot Box."[42] This strategy supported the armed struggle *and* worked to promote change through the democratic process. Documented in the organization's training manual (i.e., the *Green Book*), a method by which the PIRA and Sinn Féin expected to overcome the problem was clearly articulated. Under the subheading of "Means," the document stipulated what its efforts would include.

1. To organise Oglaigh na hEireann for victory.
2. To build on a spirit of comradeship.

3. To wage revolutionary armed struggle.
4. To encourage popular resistance, political mobilization and political action in support of the objectives.
5. To assist, as directed by the Army Authority, all organizations working for the same objectives.[43]

Clearly, this quotation captures both the militant aspects of the PIRA and its political goal of marshalling the community to effect structural change.

The PIRA's militant efforts were further delineated in its five-fold guerrilla strategy. Summarily, this strategy encompassed the following elements:

1. A war of attrition against enemy personnel which is aimed at causing as many casualties and deaths as possible so as to create a demand from their people at home for their withdrawal.
2. A bombing campaign aimed at making the enemy's financial interest in our country unprofitable while at the same time curbing long-term investment in our country.
3. To make the Six Counties as at present and for the past several years ungovernable except by colonial military rule.
4. To sustain the war and gain support for its ends by National and international propaganda and publicity campaigns.
5. By defending the war of liberation by punishing criminals, collaborators and informers.[44]

This five-fold tactical plan was the framework for implementing the PIRA's war against the governments of Great Britain and Northern Ireland, as well as the realization of its wholesale "Brits out" policy.

Collectively, the PIRA's framing of the problem that Catholics in the region have historically confronted, the means the movement identified by which to address it (i.e., a commitment to shared ideals, a new constitution), and the solutions they proposed to end discriminatory practices (e.g., the use of violence and an appeal to democratic processes) are all quite revealing. In short, they send the message that the established definition of the situation is one in which Catholics exist without self-determination—a state of affairs where they are denied the freedom to govern their own fate. Accordingly, the Irish Nationalist Catholic community will continue to be marginalized, will experience oppression (through armed conflict if necessary), and will be denied the very social justice they seek to obtain for themselves and for all citizens in the region.

Roles

There are several social roles that are pertinent to understanding the identities and role behaviors that members of the PIRA embody. One social role fundamental to comprehending the actions of the PIRA is their status as Catholic. The conflict in Northern Ireland is undoubtedly linked to the fact that religion significantly differentiates, indeed segregates, the society. Both the Protestant and Catholic churches have played a prominent role in maintaining these social boundaries, especially in the form of endogamy and separate educational systems.[45] Historically, the Irish Republican movement has always been tied to Catholicism. After all, Republican paramilitary groups have traditionally drawn their membership almost exclusively from the ranks of the working-class, Irish Catholic communities of Northern Ireland.[46]

However, for Provisional Irish Republicans, the conflict in Ireland no longer is about the fight between the differing religious beliefs of Roman Catholics and Protestants. As Bell explained,

> the British often sell the Troubles as a tribal war between Catholics and Protestants and the Irish Republicans assume that they are engaged in a war of national liberation against an alien presence—and there is ample evidence for those who hold either vision. The Irish Troubles you see is the Irish Troubles you get.[47]

Interestingly, the religious label (i.e., status of Catholic or Protestant) has evolved into more of a social than a theological designation. The marginalized status of being Catholic began with the occupation of Ireland by British imperialists. The oppression and victimization endured by Catholics continued over the years in the form of poor housing conditions, discrimination in employment, denial of equal rights, and targeting for violent attacks. Indeed, in a more generalized context, the history of Northern Ireland is fraught with personal accounts of Loyalist Protestant mob violence directed against Catholic communities. These assaults have resulted in thousands of people seeing their homes destroyed by fire, being subjected to beatings, or succumbing to horrific executions.[48] Consequently, what emerges is a vision of Irish Republicanism and self-identity in which an intense value is placed on the ideal of justice as a response to the inequities Catholic citizens believe they have endured over the years.

Although the PIRA has been adamantly opposed to making the "troubles" in Ireland religiously based, Irish Republicanism is fundamentally laden with Catholic values.[49] Bell identified the importance of the church, service, denial, sacrifice, the nobility of suffering, and the assurances of ultimate triumph as examples of such values.[50] These notions are briefly reviewed.

The PIRA's approach to organizational structure and bestowal of power is similar to that of the Roman Catholic Church. Juergensmyer captured this sentiment as he recounted Tom Hartley's interpretation of Gerry Adams's role as party representative for Sinn Féin. Hartley was also a long-time leader of this political group.

> Catholics like [Adams] were "hierarchical." . . . [I]t was a hallmark of Catholic thinking to assume that all Catholics in a region such as Ireland [we]re part of a unified community, [and that] the leader[ship could] . . . generally count on the loyalty of their people. When Gerry Adams participated in peace negotiations earlier in 1998, he could do so in secret, Hartley said, knowing that his party would stand behind him even if they did not know what the terms of his agreement would be. Adams acted "like an archbishop," Harley acknowledged, and yet his Sinn Féin comrades approved of his position.[51]

The tremendous value attached to the ideals of service, sacrifice, denial, and the nobility of suffering were made abundantly clear during the 1980–1981 hunger strikes. Those PIRA volunteers who forfeited their lives were regarded as heroes and martyrs in support of a worthwhile cause.[52] Underscoring the strikes was the conviction that whoever suffered the most would emerge victorious.[53] Dillon similarly noted this connection when commenting on the conversion of incarcerated Loyalist paramilitary members to the fundamentalist faith versus the entrenched religious proclivities of IRA faithful. As he explained,

> The IRA, with a long history of prison culture, always knew why they were in prison: they perceived themselves as freedom fighters, martyrs

for a cause, and they did not present renewed religious conviction as a testimony to change or as a ploy for early release. Many were indeed pious, and their adoption of the hunger strike strategy, with its overtones of the cult of the martyr, reinforced the connection between faith and violence.[54]

Indeed, as Dillon noted, IRA prisoners did not convert while incarcerated because they already went to penal facilities as devout Catholics.[55] Thus, serving a sentence was just part of their dedication to and sacrifice for a cause they perceived to be noble and just.

Finally, the assurance of ultimate triumph is a pivotal aspect of the Republican movement. It is this notion that gives people a reason for their sacrifice, whether in the form of a prison sentence or the termination of their lives. Provisional Republicans engender the belief that their courageous efforts, suffering, and sacrifice will not be in vain. The ultimate triumph is the creation of a free Irish Republic that encompasses all thirty-two counties on the island. Those who become disillusioned (i.e., through a loss of faith or vision) over the strategy might remove themselves from the Republican fight. However, this is not the case for most. Indeed, in many ways the Catholic role has been made to fit Republican need. It is a role that tolerates, endorses, and even incorporates violence and destruction where necessary.

Another role integral to PIRA membership is being a Republican.[56] Simply stated, Republicans are individuals who favor the establishment of a republic and who espouse the values of a republic. In order to understand the Irish Republican ideal, one must first understand the development of republicanism in European history, traceable to the work of Plato.[57]

The essence of Plato's[58] ideal republic was justice: that "no . . . government provides for its own benefit, but . . . it provides and prescribes what is for the benefit of the subject, seeking the advantage of him [or her] who is weaker, not the advantage of the stronger."[59] Bergerot explained that the ideals of a republic were adopted by Lazare Hoche, a leading general of the French Republic and rival to Bonaparte.[60] Hoche articulated a series of republican maxims. They included the following:

Pity those who do not know how to love the people despite their faults and serve them despite their ingratitude.

Reputations fall, and the people remain standing.

One cannot make the republic loved by devastating property and by carrying sword and flame among the inhabitants.

In the soul of republicans there are sentiments of justice and humanity and the greatest horror for bloodthirsty monsters.

True republicans do not commit crimes.

I have told the Directory twenty times, if it does not allow religious tolerance, it must give up any hope of peace in this country.[61]

The relevance of the above commentary regarding the roots of republicanism in European history should not be dismissed lightly. In short, these observations shed some light on the values and expectations espoused by PIRA faithful within the Republican role. The notion of justice has been a core feature of the Irish Republican movement since its inception. This is the case because those within the movement invariably believe they have not been availed of it. Indeed, many within the Irish Catholic community of Northern Ireland perceive themselves as having been significantly marginalized for centuries. This felt sense of victimization and oppression stems from an alien occupation led by a tyrannical government.[62] Therefore, the Republican role signifies the reclaiming of Irish Catholic identity, pride, and unity quashed at the hands of Protestant militant control. In short, Republicanism is about PIRA members regaining a type of justice that historically has been deferred or denied to Catholic citizens in the region.

The Provisional Irish Republican Army is often referred to as "Oglaigh Na hEireann." This expression means "Irish Volunteers" in Gaelic.[63] There exists within this name a third social role for the PIRA. This is the role of being a volunteer. Comprehending this role is pivotal to understanding how identities influence the behavior of PIRA members.

There are many beliefs that underscore and inform the volunteer role for PIRA faithful. However, perhaps the most enduring conviction is "the unqualified belief that a United Ireland is an intrinsic good, and the demand for Irish national self-determination so pressing, so overwhelming, that this goal must be pursued at all costs but principally and immediately by force of arms."[64] Interestingly, IRA volunteers do not just see themselves as fighting for a united Ireland. They also view themselves as defenders of all those who have been harassed, beaten, and terrorized by the Protestant community, as well as the security forces of Great Britain and Northern Ireland.[65]

The most salient features of this social role are outlined in the PIRA's manual, the *Green Book*.[66] The manual is issued to all new recruits. Volunteers must swear allegiance to the organization and must obey all orders issued by the Army Council. In a general reading of the document, volunteers are informed that they will be expected to show discipline, commitment, morality, and honor. In addition, the Republican volunteers are to demonstrate respect for the public in an effort to earn their support.

The document also provides a code of conduct for its volunteers. Among these rules is the expectation that members will be truthful in their interactions with comrades and honest in all matters relating to the public, especially in terms of their business affairs. Volunteers must commit themselves to equality and promote the elimination of sexism. Those who advance sectarian ideals or display sectarian attitudes are immediately disciplined. Opposed to "racist attitudes . . . typical of an imperialist mentality," PIRA expects volunteers to respect as equals persons representing different nationalities and races, rather than oppress them.[67] Finally, volunteers are to be proud of their Irish culture and must learn the Gaelic language and promote its use. Thus, overall, the social role of being a volunteer encompasses several dimensions. It includes the ideals of republicanism, nationalism, militarism, romanticism, socialism, anti-imperialism, and anticolonialism.[68]

Additional expectations can be gleaned from the IRA's guerrilla handbook.[69] The handbook begins with a brief description of the long tradition guerrilla warfare has had in Ireland, including spotlighting some of its most notorious champions. With this history in mind, the book articulates the beliefs, values, attitudes, and expectations of the loyal IRA volunteer.

> [The individual must] act alone and fight alone with the weapons at his [or her] disposal—and these very often will not be the best. [The volunteer] must find his [or her] own supplies. [The person's] endurance has to be great: and for this [one] needs a fit body and an alert mind. Above all [the individual] must know what he [or she] is fighting for—and why.[70]

In addition to being independent and self-reliant, volunteers must be persistent, bold, and ingenious. Most importantly, "once the fight is joined, it must be carried out relentlessly and to the bitter end. The road may be long, the sacrifice great, but if the guerrilla has this endurance and the will to win, [he or she] cannot be defeated."[71] Volunteers must be inspired by the ideal, fiercely loyal, and disciplined in their fight against the British Crown. Finally, the individual must adhere to "the guerrilla code—desertion, betrayal, breach of confidence in any way— must be severely dealt with on the spot."[72]

Bell elaborated further on the values and beliefs of Republican volunteers in his description of the *provisional prototype,* or *Provo.*[73] The provisional prototype is most often characterized as someone who is an idealist volunteer, festooned with military honors, a skilled professional rebel, fully cognizant of and receptive to his or her Celtic ethnicity, a true survivor, and a force with which to be reckoned. Bell identifies Bobby Sands as the ideal Provo. Sands starved himself to death in a sixty-six-day hunger strike as an IRA prisoner, protesting the British government's criminalization policies. He was active in the movement for only a brief period of time before he got arrested for weapons possession. He was then sent to prison. Consequently, his contribution to the cause was not with a gun but through his self-sacrifice.[74] He continues to be immortalized as the epitome of the Irish rebel, especially through song, poetry, and murals. Many recruits are drawn to this ideal role, believing that living the proscribed status of a PIRA volunteer is as romantic as it is exciting.

Socialization and Role-Taking

The fourth concept influencing the emergence and maintenance of identities for members of the PIRA is socialization and role-taking. Through these two processes individuals come to learn what behavior specific reference groups (i.e., significant and generalized others) expect from them when occupying certain roles. They also acquire knowledge about how to assess their role performances. Socialization is one way in which individuals learn the expectations of the roles they occupy and the roles they perform. White and Fraser noted that members of the Provisional Republican movement are often taught the expectations of being a

Republican by their Republican families.[75] To illustrate, White and Fraser recount the description that one lifelong Republican member provided regarding how his family influenced his internalization of one dimension of the Republican role.

> My mother's mother, was [pause] a great Republican, she was. But prior to—all our lives, and up to the very end, when she died in the early 1960s, she remained true. And her brother died in 1933, who would be a granduncle of mine. I didn't know him now, he died the year I was born, but he was a man—he never accepted any Free State, good, bad, or indifferent. And uh, my grandmother always told me that he would never have changed. There's a funny thing that I, sort of thing there, that I nearly couldn't be anything else only. I was born to that tradition, and that faith.[76]

Moreover, in response to the changing strategies employed by the Republican movement to secure a united Ireland, the respondent likened his allegiance to Republicanism to his Catholic faith commitment. As he explained,

> *Respondent 4*: Nationality and religion and all this sort of—but that was one thing my grandmother always taught was that religion and Republicanism sort of went hand in hand.
>
> *Interviewer*: Oh really?
>
> *Respondent 4*: Well, in the sense that you lived up to certain standards. And Republicanism is something that you have to be very honest—you just can't change for the sake of changing, or you can't change because somebody says to you, "Ahh, we'll go another path." There's a moral thing in it, you know, that kind of thing.[77]

From the above exchange, it is evident that being a "true" Republican meant that the individual was never to accept the Free State established in lieu of a united Ireland. This was so fervently ingrained into the volunteer that he saw this condition as being foundational, intrinsic, and not something to dispense with easily or lightly. The respondent also identified certain similarities between Republicanism and Catholicism. The morality of Republicanism entailed a full commitment, a bond, linked to one's faith, that could not be changed because of convenience.

Interestingly, not all members of the Republican movement learn from their families that militancy is an acceptable means by which to achieve a united Ireland. In fact, the case of Sean, a former member of the PIRA, is a good example of someone whose parents were firmly against such behavior. As Dillon elaborates,

He grew up in West Belfast with parents who were devout Catholic nationalists. In the 1940s one of his maternal uncles was in the IRA but later left the organization and emigrated. Sean's early years were spent in a Catholic ghetto, isolated from the rest of the world and with little awareness of the nature of his society. It was on his grandmother's knee that he learned about Protestants, the hated B Specials and the brave IRA men who had defended Catholic districts in the 1920s. Policemen in his district were nicknamed "the Pigs" and anyone talking to them was regarded with suspicion. At primary school he was in the hands of the Christian Brothers; tough, uncompromising men who used leather straps to enforce discipline. They augmented his small knowledge of history with accounts of British atrocities over hundreds of years, the 1916 Rising, and the execution of its leaders. The Brothers identified Padraig Pearse as the hero of the rising and Sean was taught to recite poems by him. At the age of ten, he could quote relevant passages from Pearse's pronouncements: . . . "The fools, the fools, they have left us our Fenian dead and Ireland unfree shall never be at peace."

It was powerful stuff, and so were the opening lines from the Declaration of the Republic written by Pearse and Connolly and read by Pearse outside the post office in Dublin on that Easter Sunday morning in 1916: "Irishmen and Irishwomen: In the name of God and the dead generations from which she receives her old tradition of nationhood, Ireland, through us, summons her children to her flag and strikes for her freedom." When I learned those lines I identified with them. In a childish kind of way they told me where I came from. It wasn't that I was anti-British or any of that. In fact I was probably more anti the B Specials even though I'd not seen a B Special. Protestants were the Special and the RUC.

One of the memorable events in [Sean's] youth, to which he attributed great significance, was a screening of the film, *Mise Eire*. Through music, commentary and poetry, the film presented the boy for the first time with the story of the 1916 Rising. He was one among thousands of Catholic schoolchildren who had been taken to cinemas throughout

Northern Ireland to see it. Archive footage showed how the British were the oppressors.[78]

Although Sean did not necessarily learn militancy from his family, his grandmother did indoctrinate him with many of the fundamental values and attitudes at the heart of the Republican role. This knowledge was supplemented by additional significant others, including the Christian Brothers. They taught him poems and gave him a history of Ireland that portrayed the Irish Catholic community as innocent victims who were also heroic warriors. Finally, generalized others, in the form of the media, further served to reinforce Sean's internalization of his status and position as a member of the marginalized Irish Catholic community. The powerful influence these socialization agents had on his life is evident as he recounted his initial participation in a Republican event.

> On Easter Sunday 1966 a republican march took place along the Falls Road and, for the first time in more than a decade, ordinary people turned out to watch it, many of whom had no connection with the IRA. Flag bearers wore the IRA's customary dress of black berets, black jackets and black gloves. I walked off the pavement and joined a lot of other young people who swelled the ranks of the marchers. I felt really proud of myself. There was something about it which gave me a thrill. Now I think it was about identifying with my own people. Mind you, I hoped that none of my relatives would spot me and tell my parents. My mother and father would have been angry. They were nationalists and regarded the republicans as a bunch of nutters. My mother knew the history of some of the older IRA men and said they weren't worth a damn.[79]

Sean explained that as an adolescent he was more concerned with girls until he inadvertently became involved in a riot and subsequently got beaten by security forces. Following the government of Northern Ireland's internment campaign, Sean decided to become a full-fledged Provo. Motivated principally by violence, he decided to join the Provisional Republican movement, a decision consistent with R. W. White's observation on the subject.[80] In short, those individuals who became involved in the Republican movement before 1969 did so because of family socialization. However, those persons involved in the movement post-1969 did so because of the culture of violence that pervaded their lives (i.e., as perpetuated by the Protestant community and the governments of Northern Ireland and Great Britain). Commenting on the socialization process in Ireland, Bell argued that "the past is not inherited but shaped for current usage: each generation gets the history not only that it deserves but that it wants and so writes."[81]

Role-taking has been described as taking place when the individual examines his or her imagined projection of self from the standpoint of others.[82] In other words, one imaginatively occupies the position of another, assessing one's behavior from the other's perspective. Children can be observed in role-taking through their engagement with role playing. The same is true of membership in the PIRA. Indeed, as volunteers and their relatives reminisced about what motivated them to participate in the Republican movement, they identified several factors. However, role playing was prominently featured.

> When we were kids we played IRA men and British soldiers. The soldiers had sticks and sometimes they would beat the shit out of you if they organized snatch squads. We were the rioters and usually the IRA won. Everyone wants to be a cowboy. [However,] the game quickly progressed to stone-throwing at passing British Army patrols, and rioting.[83]

This phenomenon of role playing is observable in the childhood experiences of Ernie O'Malley.[84] He joined the original IRA in its early years after having been educated at a Christian Brothers' school and pushed into the direction of Irish Republicanism, following the 1916 Easter Rising.[85] Christian Brothers' schools were run by the Irish Catholic lay teaching order and many taught future revolutionaries the traditional version of Irish history.[86] While incarcerated in a Dublin prison, O'Malley wrote that as a child he hated the British king "and blamed him for everything. [O'Malley] had great daydreams of [him-]self playing the part of a soldier charging at the head of men, and reforming the dream until [he] was satisfied."[87] In this instance, the roles of IRA volunteer and British soldier are learned through daydreaming and childhood games—an unfortunate consequence of growing up in the midst of violence in this troubled region of the globe.

An illustration of role-taking as practiced by PIRA adults is contained in the autobiography of Maria McGuire.[88] McGuire was the former publicity officer for the Provisional Irish Republican Army. The following passage describes the strategy the group used to solicit contributions from Irish Catholics living in the United States.

> Like the Officials, we were quite ready to play for all they were worth the new Republican myths that were being created out of the current campaign. And nowhere was it easier to capitalize on them than in the United States, where whole communities of Irish-Americans were watching the struggle in the Six Counties like spectators at a morality play, with right and wrong, good and evil, delineated in black and white. It was in the United States that our main fund-raising efforts were conducted, and the visiting speakers, who included Ruairí and John Kelly, the Dublin arms-trial man, were carefully briefed as to how the audience should be played. There should be copious references to the martyrs of 1916 and 1920–1922, the period most of the audience would be living in. Anti-British sentiment, recalling Cromwell, the potato famine, and the Black and Tans, could be profitably exploited. By no means should anything be said against the Catholic Church. And all references to socialism should be strictly avoided; tell them by all means that the Ireland we were fighting for would be free and united, but say nothing about just what form the new free and united Ireland would take.[89]

As this excerpt clearly demonstrates, only when PIRA members took on the role of the Irish American people could Republican representatives develop an effective strategy for soliciting and securing contributions. By interpreting their own behavior through the eyes of U.S. citizens and Irish sympathizers, the publicity team identified what to say and what to avoid. In short, they discovered that prosocialist language and anti-Catholic sentiment, especially directed at the Church, would offend potential American donors, reducing their level of financial patronage.

Similarly, the spread of propaganda exemplifies how the role-taking process teaches individuals the expectations of role performance. Propaganda is typically defined as "the spreading of ideas or information to further or damage a cause."[90] Its purpose is to convince, to win over, and to convert individuals to comparable modes of thinking.[91] Propaganda was a tactic frequently employed by the PIRA to gain public support. Wright divided the PIRA's target audience into three categories:

the uncommitted, the sympathetic, and the active.[92] Much as a salesperson markets his or her product to a particular type of customer in order to lure a buyer, each group requires a distinct strategy to establish or secure organizational loyalty. Thus, in order to devise effective propaganda campaigns, PIRA members adopted the perspective of members for each group and disseminated propaganda that encouraged varying degrees of increasing Republican loyalty. In this context, the behavior of PIRA participants served to make uncommitted members committed, unsympathetic citizens sympathetic, inactive members active.[93] This process, then, reaffirms the standpoint that the Republican movement is a favored way of thinking and bolsters the position that participants assume as members of the PIRA.

Self

Society Shapes the Self

According to Identity Theory, society shapes the structure and organization of the self through *commitment*. This concept is based on the degree to which a person is dedicated to playing or occupying a particular role or position as a function of the number of social relationships the individual experiences, contingent on said role or position. White and Fraser explained that because Republicans advocate for revolutionary goals, support political violence, and are in the minority, the governments of Northern Ireland, Great Britain, and the Irish Republic have had a habit of harassing Republican members.[94] They have also kept close tabs on volunteers through surveillance techniques. The authors noted that in the past these efforts created an atmosphere in which Republicans were forced to interact almost exclusively with other Republicans. As one Republican explained in an interview,

> *Interviewer*: Today would most of your friends be Republicans?
> *Respondent 1*: All my friends are Republicans.
> *Interviewer*: Okay. Is that because of the nature of Republicanism?
> *Respondent 1*: No, it's the nature of censorship and black propaganda. . . .
> There's a huge effort to isolate and marginalize and demonize Republicans not just in the political sense but also in the very much social and personal sense as well. . . . [The authorities want] to crush it—us, to isolate you totally. And they did that in the North. They did that by

killing people of course. Ehm, down here they did it by demonizing you. But also by, like, a whole campaign of anybody that had contact with you would get a visit from the [Special] Branch [of the police], or their workplace [would be visited], or if they were young people their parents would be visited and told, you know, who they're associating with. The IRA—that sort of stuff.

Interviewer: So if somebody would move in near you and—

Respondent 1: Oh, like a neighbor or even children that played with your children [would be visited by the Special Branch]. . . . I had that happen to my children, yes. . . .

Interviewer: Does that—does that pressure then make the camaraderie among Republicans greater?

Respondent 1: Well, obviously, yeah.[95]

Clearly, the result of such policies by the security forces of both the North and South has framed the interactions of Republicans. In short, it has forced them to interact almost solely with one another, causing them to become even more committed to their Republican, Catholic, and volunteer identities. These notions cluster together on the salience hierarchy.

The symbols present in one's environment also have a way of activating certain role identities, forcing them to become more prominent on the salience hierarchy. Take, for example, the Battle of Bogside, the Bloody Sunday massacre, and the Irish hunger strikes' effect in terms of support and membership. Indeed, as R. W. White indicated, "the concern or 'rage' experienced by Southern Irish people after events such as [these were] a product of national identity, and identity that emotionally, if not physically, link[ed] Southern Irish people to Northern Irish people."[96] As a result, the intent behind the symbolic events and their contribution to constructing interpretations produced a catalytic effect: they activated individual Irish identities, heightened the sense of similarity between Southern and Northern Irish people and, subsequently, solidified involvement in the armed struggle to aid their oppressed brothers and sisters. As R. W. White explained,

The potential for recruiting Southern Republicans [wa]s at its greatest when the social processes described above—an Irish identity heightened by anti-Irish violence in the North and social connections with Republicans—work[ed] in combination. During the Provisional Irish Republican era, this . . . occurred twice: between August 1969 [Battle of Bog-side] and Bloody Sunday in 1972, and in 1980–1981 [hunger strikes].[97]

Thus, consistent with a symbolic interactionist perspective, people responded to the symbols, their meanings, and to the interpretations of these three representational events and not to the events themselves. Moreover, from a structural perspective, these same symbols and definitions categorized, situated, and reinforced people's positions and statuses within the existing social structure. Again, R. W. White's observations are compelling here.

As their national identity, their sense of Irishness, [wa]s aroused, Southern Irish people examine[d] the existence of Northern Ireland and their own place in the Irish nation. This prompt[ed] involvement in activities like marches and rallies. These [brought] them into contact with active Republicans. Personal connections dr[ew] them into the Republican Movement.[98]

Whether people witnessed these events first-hand or on the news, the events served as cues to remind people of their status and social position within the larger social structure of both Northern Ireland and the Republic. For many, the symbols contributed to their shared sense of injustice and hatred—sentiments that could no longer be ignored. The effect was that many young people sought out opportunities to engage this salient identity by participating in marches, rallies, and protests. Many joined the PIRA, and some became the organization's most notorious leaders.[99]

Self Shapes Society

In this chapter, the Catholic, Republican, and volunteer roles were identified as integral to an understanding of the overall PIRA identity. Indeed, through the process of interpreting symbols, defining the Northern Irish situation, engaging in role-taking and role performance activities, and participating in socialization experiences, the Catholic, Republican, and volunteer statuses became self-meanings embodied within the greater self-schema of PIRA members. In addition, however, the construction of the social person, particularly as a Provo, helped to define the society that Irish citizens inhabited.

One representative illustration that depicts how PIRA self-schemas shaped society is the 1980–1981 Irish hunger strikes undertaken by dedicated members. The symbolic significance of the strike powerfully defined the oppressive situation that Catholics endured under British rule and Protestant control. Socialized by family members and others in the region's historical struggle to eliminate religious persecution, Provo faithful verified through their role-taking performances the relevance and salience of the Catholic identity. Whether they did so consciously or not, the strikers used identity cues to authenticate this self-concept. For example, many of them allowed their hair to grow to shoulder length, and their beards were worn long and unkempt. They abandoned their prison-issue clothing and donned blankets in robelike fashion. The hunger strikers became frail and thin but portrayed themselves as committed young men. Although physically weak and brutalized by a callous, imperialist power, they remained spiritually true to their political and religious beliefs. Images of the hunger strikers, broadcast throughout the world, conveyed a provocative and compelling message: their actions, in the name of freedom and faith, were strikingly akin to those undertaken by Christianity's most celebrated martyr, Jesus Christ. In this respect, then, the self-concept of the Irish hunger strikers informed the constitution of the region and shaped the way Northern (and Southern) Irish people understood PIRA terrorism.

The Catholic identity was also verified through interpersonal prompts. Again, the activities of the hunger strikers were significant here. Through their steadfast participation, they affirmed many of the values held dear to the Catholic religion. As one imprisoned PIRA member observed,

> We were committed to something. Unless someone was coming in and saying "Right, you have your own clothes, you won't do prison work, you have all your demands," short of that we wouldn't have entertained it. It was all or nothing at that stage. The fact that so many people had died made us even more determined.[100]

Embedded within this statement are the Catholic values of self-sacrifice, suffering, and an unwavering commitment to cherished ideals. The media coverage surrounding the hunger strikes not only confirmed the legitimacy of PIRA resistance but also contributed to the region's understanding of Irish Catholic oppression and persecution promulgated by the British government and Protestant Loyalists.

In addition, the Irish Republican role was established and endorsed through the identity verification process. For example, individuals who adopted this role engaged in selective interaction when attending a Republican funeral. Indeed, PIRA memorial services are frequently saturated with Republican imagery. Members dress in their traditional attire.[101] This consists of a black beret, a camouflaged army green uniform, black gloves, and a covered face. Donning this apparel conveys respect and a sense of loss for fallen comrades. It also confirms one's commitment to the efforts of other PIRA members who died so that justice could be secured for the marginalized Irish Catholic community. Clearly, presence at these memorial services verifies the role identities of PIRA members as Republicans through identity cues (i.e., particular style of dress). Moreover, funeral attendance by Provo volunteers confirms the role identity of all those Republicans present, and it demonstrates support for the sacrifices of PIRA members.

While the involvement of PIRA members in the hunger strikes served to verify their Catholic identities, they had a similar effect on their role identities as Republicans. The protest principally centered on the British government's attempt to assign and to affix a criminal status upon the prisoners. PIRA volunteers rejected the label, arguing that they were political prisoners fighting for the entire island's right to self-determination. Thus, the hunger strikes were undertaken in order to verify members' Republican identities and to help ensure the PIRA movement's reputation as a legitimate fighting force in pursuit of social justice. Indeed, members believed that they were engaged in a just war in which the repressive and hegemonic practices of Northern Ireland and Great Britain had to be eliminated.

Finally, the volunteer identity, especially in the context of defending the innocent, was invariably confirmed through interpersonal prompts (i.e., acts of violence perpetrated against the Protestant community and the British establishment). Provos perceived their armed struggle to be righteous because their actions were instigated in self-defense. Self-defense was interpreted as an acceptable and justified response, particularly when a person or community was victimized.[102] Moreover, volunteers rationalized their militant extremism because previous displays of terrorism, enacted by the RUC and the British government, were regarded as unmitigated attempts to oppress Catholic people. Therefore, by defining their violent acts as justified expressions of self-defense, PIRA members verified their identities as volunteers skirmishing for the rights and interests of victims. To date, PIRA faithful have attacked railway stations, local Protestant businesses, and military establishments. In the process, they have confirmed their identities as righteous Irish patriots fighting for the expulsion of British influence and control.

As Irish citizens increasingly embody their Republican, Catholic, and volunteer identities, they become emboldened through them. Indeed, they adopt the PIRA self-schemas assigned to them through their ongoing interaction with society and respond accordingly as political activists, soldiers, and patriots. In the final analysis, though, their self-identifications also contribute to the society that members inhabit, reminding people in the region (Catholic and Protestants alike) that war, conflict, and terrorism are a part of the social landscape given the presence of needless political oppression and religious persecution.

6

The Islamic Resistance
Movement (Hamas)

In this chapter, the insights of structural Symbolic Interactionism and Identity Theory are applied to the formation and maintenance of self-concept, especially as it relates to membership in the militant extremist group known as Islamic Resistance Movement (Hamas). Throughout this commentary, the events surrounding the terrorist attacks on the World Trade Center in 2001 serve as an important, though mostly underexamined, backdrop for comprehending the construction of identity among Islamic fundamentalists that powerfully contributed to these particular expressions of abject violence. What is prominently featured, however, are the religious, cultural, and political differences that inform the Israeli-Palestinian conflict. Reviewing these differences in the ensuing analysis, linked as they are to Islamist groups' typical disdain for Western influences and practices, demonstrates the considerable effect that symbols, the definition of the situation, roles, socialization experiences, and role-taking performances all have on the constitution of the self as a social person. As we argue, these forces explain the construction of identity for Hamas faithful and indicate how terrorism (and its threat) is willingly embraced by its organizational members.

Symbols

Zionism is one of the most powerful symbols to influence Hamas. This is evidenced in Hamas discourse. This discourse stipulates that members wage a "holy war" against a foreign invader that has usurped Palestinian land.[1] Understanding the genesis and evolution of this sentiment is important to comprehending the Israeli-Palestinian conflict and those poignant events during the course of this history that have symbolically informed Hamas identity.

Bickerton and Klausner[2] noted that the first wave of Zionist immigrants began their arrival in Palestine in July 1882 and continued until 1903. European supporters of the Zionist movement portrayed Palestine as empty and sparsely cultivated. A popular Zionist catch phrase aptly conveyed this very point of view. As the phrase described it, Palestine was "a land without a people for a people without a land."[3]

Believing that the purchase of Arab territory was a key to their success, the Zionists created political agencies and allegiances in order to acquire property in the name of the Jewish people.[4] By 1903, the Zionists had purchased about ninety thousand acres of land upon which roughly ten thousand Jews built homes, schools, and farms.[5] As Khalidi[6] explained,

> The process would begin with the purchase of land, generally from an absentee landlord, followed by the imposition of a new order on the existing Arab cultivators—sometimes involving their transformation into tenant-farmers or agricultural laborers, and sometimes their expulsion—and finally the settlement of new Jewish immigrants.

While some Arab farmers were allowed to stay and work their land, a second wave of Russian Jewish immigrants—lasting from 1904 until 1914 and consisting of people content with the socialist ideal of *conquest of labor*—displaced many of the indigenous Arab tenant laborers.[7] This process of territorial acquisition followed by Arab tenant dislocation became a constant source of friction for the region's inhabitants. Moreover, as the arrival of new Jewish immigrants continued into the "Mandate" years, hostilities only intensified. Indeed, symbolically speaking, the activities of Jewish settlers and entrepreneurs were perceived as efforts to wrongfully take and occupy land belonging to Palestinian peoples.[8]

Another pinnacle event in the perceived usurpation of Palestinian territory was the dislocation of roughly 70 percent of the Palestinian Arab population during the 1948 Israeli War of Independence.[9] Experts estimated that between 600,000 and 760,000 Palestinian Arabs left their villages, homes, and farms to find refuge in the West Bank, Gaza Strip, and nearby Arab countries.[10] The official Israeli position was that the

Palestinian Arabs voluntarily abandoned their residences and communities; however, settlers in the region report that they were forcibly removed by the Zionist project. Indeed, they indicate that Jewish foreign occupiers were intent on ridding Palestine of its Arab peoples and/or sympathizers.[11] Commenting on this issue, Morris[12] examined declassified Israeli archival reports. According to his review, the Palestinian mass exodus was facilitated by Jewish military and paramilitary forces that launched a campaign based on threats, instances of intimidation, and acts of terrorism. Their goal was to expel the Palestinian Arabs from the fledgling state of Israel.

In one of the most notorious attacks, Jewish paramilitary forces attacked the village of Deir Yassin on April 9, killing 254 villagers.[13] In published documents, these assaults were described as significantly contributing to the accelerated pace at which Palestinian Arabs fled their villages and communities. Palestinians refer to their 1948 exodus as "*al-Nakba*," or "the catastrophe." This expression captures the helplessness and fear that they felt in the face of the terrorist attacks promulgated by the Jewish forces.[14] Once again, symbolically speaking, Arabs felt as if their property had been unjustly taken from them and that, as Palestinians, they were forced to leave their homes and to forfeit their livelihoods. Accordingly, Palestinians regarded themselves as displaced victims of a grave and vile act of considerable wrongdoing.

Another symbol identified within Hamas discourse and contributing to Palestinian identity is the emergence of the Islamic "awakening."[15] Initially, the Islamist ideology spread to historic Palestine by way of the Egyptian Muslim Brotherhood.[16] In 1954, Egyptian king Abdel Nasir outlawed the organization, fearing it would become an uncontrollable threat to his regime. This proclamation was a devastating blow to both the Egyptian Muslim Brotherhood and the Palestinian branch of the Brotherhood, as many of its leaders and scores of its followers were disbanded, while still other members were forced underground.[17] In July 1957, a member of a secret military cell within the Brotherhood sent a memorandum to the leaders of the group situated in the Gaza Strip. In the communiqué, he recommended that they "establish a special organization alongside their own which [would have] no visible Islamic coloration or agenda but which [would have] the stated goal of liberating Palestine through armed struggle."[18] The suggestion that a national liberation effort be established, absent religious overtones, was dismissed by the Brotherhood's leadership because it would run contrary to traditional Islamist thinking. Nevertheless, a new group calling itself the National Liberation Movement, or Fatah, emerged.

The emergence of the National Liberation Movement put Islamists in a difficult position. As Maqadima[19] explained, the Brotherhood had two alternatives:

> Either to launch guerrilla warfare against Israel, as the PLO had done, using the same individuals who had grown up under regimes and ideologies distant from Islam—so that one is doomed to repeat the errors of the past; or to launch a comprehensive effort at cultural renaissance designed to instill true Islam in the soul of the individual and, following that renaissance, to embark on the path of liberation.[20]

Believing that Palestine could only be freed by "a generation of Muslims committed to their faith and prepared for sacrifice,"[21] the Muslim Brotherhood decided to postpone its involvement in the armed struggle and to embark on a grassroots campaign. This operation was designed to "Islamize" Palestinian society by cultivating a new cohort of citizens in a true Islamic style.[22] Several initiatives were embarked on consistent with this grassroots effort.

From 1967 to 1975, the Palestinian Islamists entered a *mosque-building* phase. This period represented an effort to "mobilize, unite, reorient, and consolidate the faith of a new generation so as to prepare it for the confrontation with Zionism."[23] Between 1967 and 1987, the number of mosques went from 400 to 750.[24]

From 1975 to the late 1980s, the Islamists entered a second phase of *social institution building*. During this period, the Muslim Brotherhood formed and ran Islamic student societies, schools, libraries, sports clubs, and charitable groups.[25] These benevolent organizations provided money to thousands of needy families, made loans to students for their education at Palestinian and Arab universities, and enrolled thousands of children in kindergarten.[26] Through the practices of these diverse societies and organizations, "the Muslim Brotherhood was able to stay in touch with the masses and [was able] to influence them through charitable, social, and religious activities and celebrations."[27]

In 1979, the Muslim Brotherhood witnessed a second group splinter from its ranks calling itself the Palestinian Islamic *jihad* (holy struggle). During the mid-1980s, the splinter group launched a relatively successful terror campaign against Israel. Subsequent to these attacks, members of the Muslim Brotherhood began engaging in cadre formation and mobilization and embraced a more militant stance at rallies and during confrontations with secular-nationalist movements on university campuses.[28] By the late 1980s, a new generation was prepared to accept the burden of *jihad*.[29] As one prominent Jordanian Islamic figure explained, the Brotherhood took "the youth out of their soft childhood to manhood, from nothingness to self realization, from fragmentation and diverse concerns to unity and cohesiveness."[30] Symbolically speaking, then, these concrete efforts designed to promote the Islamic awakening informed Palestinian identity, especially as young male Islamic citizens were indoctrinated into a culture of service and sacrifice on behalf of their people.

A third symbol identified within Hamas discourse was the signing of the Declaration of Principles on Interim Self-Governing Arrangements (DOP) (also called the Oslo Accord). This declaration was endorsed on September 13, 1993, by the Israeli prime minister, Yitzak Rabin, and the PLO chairman, Yasser Arafat.[31] The secret talks that led to this agreement began as an attempt to address economic cooperation but soon broadened to include a possible joint declaration of principles.[32] As a result, the document consisted of two components: mutual recognition for the rights of the Palestinians and the Israelis to exist and the Declaration of Principles. The DOP outlined a set agenda for future negotiations on Palestinian self-government in the occupied territories. Within nine months, the Palestinian people were to elect a council to oversee education and culture, health, social welfare, direct taxation, and tourism. While defense and foreign affairs remained in the hands of the Israelis, the DOP did provide for the establishment of an internal security force called the Palestinian National Authority (PNA). In addition, the DOP endeavored to facilitate economic cooperation in the form of improved labor and trade flows (designed to improve the standard of living for poor Palestinians) and to sustain the peace process.[33] Rabin and Arafat also agreed to revisit their negotiations in a two-year followup. The purpose of this subsequent meeting would be to assess the status of the territories and would result, ideally, in an agreement to convene again after five years to resolve the issue of permanent settlement. The DOP was an interim accord—indeed, a first step toward a peaceful solution.

The DOP was a frequent topic of discourse within Hamas, which was adamantly opposed to the recognition of any settlement with Israel. The principal and most obvious reason for their rejection of the agreement was that it surrendered Palestinian territory believed to be sacred and entrusted to the Arab-Muslim people.[34] In addition, from a more pragmatic perspective, Hamas insisted that the Palestinian economy would suffer if trade with Israel were encouraged.[35] Indeed, as they argued, the Palestinian economy could simply not compete on the open market with an Israeli gross national product ten times its own. In short, such an exchange would only benefit Israel. Reuveny,[36] summarizing the economic concerns voiced by Hamas, indicated that "the process [would] harm Palestinians in that it [would] create economic hardship, intensify Israeli land confiscations, prevent Palestinian control over resources, and increase Palestinian economic dependence on Israel." Contributing to this perspective were high-profile analysts who represented a more mainstream point of view. Unaffiliated with the Hamas collective, they concurred with its assessment, serving only to further validate the group's overall fears and suspicions.[37] This "objective" corroboration cast doubts on Hamas critics who relegated them to the status of merely "backward-minded [Islamists who] propagate[ed] utopian ideas."[38]

The Declaration of Principles was a powerful symbol in the development of the Hamas organization. It served to solidify the group's role as the new champion of the Palestinian resistance, as a guardian of Islam, and as a legitimate voice calling for the establishment of the historic Islamic Palestinian state.[39] While Arafat and the PLO were prepared to sell Palestine out for a concession of territory from Israel, Hamas continued to advocate for *jihad* through the *intifada* and strove for a unified Islamic nation rid of the Zionist presence.[40] Adamantly opposed to the DOP's ratification, Hamas initiated its first suicide bombing in April 1994, killing eight Israeli civilians and wounding thirty-four in an apparent attempt to disrupt negotiations.[41] Over the next several years, the suicide bombing would become Hamas's primary weapon in derailing the peace process and undermining the Palestinian National Authority.

Definition of the Situation

The way in which members of Hamas define the situation they confront can be categorized into three major themes. These include the problem, the goal, and the means by which to obtain the goal or objective.[42] The contribution that each of these elements makes to the way Hamas defines its perceived state of affairs is described below.

For members of Hamas, the problem is simple. In short, it "is the existence of the Jewish state of Israel in the middle of the Arab-Muslim world."[43] Typically, Hamas leadership has argued that the Israeli-Palestinian struggle centers on the forced removal of the Palestinian Arab people from and the occupation of Palestinian land by Zionist[44] invaders rather than any direct or overt hostility toward the Jewish people who subscribe to their religion as devout followers. However, the group's rhetoric is saturated with anti-Semitic themes.[45] Indeed, Hamas has frequently depicted the core problem as religious in nature, setting as rivals Judaism and Islam.

Commenting on this tension, Litvak[46] explained that for Hamas, Zionists who subscribe to the Jewish faith are vilified as the epitome of evil and falsehood; however, Muslims are portrayed as the incarnation of goodness and truth. This perception has been subjected to both Islamic and Western influences. For example, words used by the Palestinian Islamists to describe the Jews, such as the "unbelievers" and "the people upon whom God's anger came," are borrowed from sources such as the Qur'an and the Hadith.[47] This nomenclature is based on Qur'anic teachings that the Jews denounced God's prophets and strayed from the genuine religion passed on to them. Hamas faithful believe that the Jews (and the Zionist entity they created), having evoked God's anger, are intent on destroying human life.

The demonization of the Jews/Zionists by the Hamas organization is also heavily shaped by European Christian anti-Semitism. This prejudice began to infiltrate the Arab world, most notably in the circulation of the 1926 Arabic translation of the *Protocols of the Elders of Zion*.[48] The forged document, which was disseminated throughout Europe in the 1920s and 1930s, was supposedly a report to a secret Jewish committee called the Elders of Zion. It described a worldwide network of covert agencies and surreptitious organizations that controlled political parties, governments, the media, banks, and the economy. Reliance upon this document is evidenced in the group's charter. Indeed, the charter states that the Jews have

> gained control over the world media, . . . financed revolutions . . . in
> pursuit of their objectives[,] . . . established clandestine organizations all

over the world . . . to destroy societies and [to] promote the interests of Zionism[,] . . . [and] controlled imperialist nations and pushed them to occupy many nations to exploit their resources and spread mischief in them.[49]

The *Protocols of the Elders of Zion* also informs Hamas's belief that Israel has hegemonic aspirations that extend beyond Palestinian land. As described in the charter, the counterfeit document identifies the Zionists' wish to expand their reign from the Nile River to the Euphrates. With the help of Western imperialism, perceived to be controlled by or in collusion with the conspiracy, the Zionists aim to destroy the Arab/ Muslim community, *umma,* in an effort to maintain dominion over the resources of the region.[50]

Another component of the problem that defines the situation for Hamas is their regard for the region itself. According to the Islamic faith, the land of Palestine is understood to be holy and bequeathed to all Muslim generations for eternity. After the Muslim armies conquered the territory of Palestine in 638 A.D., the Caliph Umar ibn al-Khatab "decided that the land should remain in the hands of its owners to benefit from it and its wealth; but the control of the land and the land itself ought to be endowed as a *Waqf* [in perpetuity] for all generations of Muslims until the Day of Resurrection."[51] In part, the sanctity of Palestine is based on the belief that the *al-Aqsa* mosque in Jerusalem was the place God selected for the Prophet Muhammad's ascension into heaven and, subsequently, was the first *qibla* (direction of prayer) for Muslims.[52] This profound religious conviction distinguishes the holy land of Palestine from all other Islamic locales. It signifies an eternal connection between the sacred territory and the Prophet Muhammad. This is one of the primary reasons why Hamas has been so adamantly opposed to the Oslo Peace Accords. In short, the agreement concedes holy land to Israel.

Another dimension to the situation that Hamas defines for itself is the objective that the organization seeks. The goal or objective of the Islamic Resistance Movement is "to create conditions conducive to emancipating the Palestinian people, delivering them from tyranny, liberating their land from the occupying usurper, and to stand up to the Zionist scheme which is supported by neo-colonist forces."[53] Once these objectives are achieved, Hamas plans to reestablish an Islamic state in the land of Palestine, extending from the Jordan River to the

Mediterranean Sea. Although their movement calls for the destruction of Israel, Hamas has indicated that members of the Jewish faith will be respected and will be free to live among Muslims under Islamic law in the region. In an interview, Shaykh Ahmad Yasin, cofounder and former spiritual leader of Hamas, articulated this position. As he explained, "We can coexist with the Jews because they are '*ahl dhimma*' [a reference to the free non-Moslem subjects living in Muslim countries who, in return for paying the capital tax, enjoyed protection and safety] and believers in God. We don't aggress the believers. We respect them. Our obligations are mutual."[54] Clearly, what this quotation suggests is that members of other religious faiths will be allowed to live in the Islamic state, provided they accept Muslim rule and pay a special tax.[55]

Despite its lack of support within orthodox Islamic thought, Hamas has also embraced the notion of Palestinian statehood.[56] According to fundamentalist ideology, there is no attachment to a specific territory.[57] Instead, territory is only significant to Islamist thought in the sense of realizing God's sovereignty and rule over the earth. However, the discrepancy between Islamist thought and commitment to Palestinian nationalism merely for the sake of statehood was reconciled as the movement developed a more pragmatic orientation.[58] This strategy was undertaken as a way to attract adherents from the Palestinian community to the cause.[59]

For Hamas, the ultimate solution to the problem of a Jewish state in the Middle East is to raise the banner of Allah over every inch of Palestine from the Jordan River to the Mediterranean Sea. However, the group's struggle is also about validating the righteousness of the Islamic way of life.[60] Commenting on this way of life, Nüsse[61] observed the following:

> The [inability] of the Muslims to prevent the creation of a Jewish state in Palestine and the repeated military defeats against Israel had fundamentally undermined the self-confidence of Muslims and [had] shaken the basis of their beliefs.
>
> . . . Muslims are fighting to reconcile history to Islamic beliefs and convictions. Thus the outcome of the struggle would prove that Muslims are again on the right path and will continue to succeed in the world. This also means that the fight for Palestine can only be won under the banner of Allah—a fact proven largely by the historic examples of Muslim victories over the Christian crusades and the Tartars.

Israel's presence in the Middle East represents a constant reminder that the Islamic *umma* is weak, is in a state of crisis, and is unable to rid itself of this perceived threat. Thus, the struggle for Hamas is not only about the reclaiming of territory or promoting doctrinal superiority; it also entails the group's confirmation that its path is just and virtuous.

Hamas contends that the only way to purge the Zionist presence from Palestinian land is through Islam. In other words, as Hamas faithful define the debilitating and deplorable situation they confront, the method by which to eradicate it is through a steadfast commitment to religion and culture. Moreover, some suggest that previous efforts to improve their situation failed (i.e., 1948 War, Six-Day War, etc.) because Palestinian Arabs acted in the name of statehood without attempting unification in the interest of Islam.[62] Accordingly, the means by which Hamas aims to achieve its goals of (a) an Islamic government in the land of Palestine and (b) the destruction of Israel is through *jihad,* or holy struggle. Similar to many topics found within scripture, *jihad* has shown itself to be the subject of enormous differences in interpretation.

In part, the Islamist interpretation of *jihad* is based on the writings of Sayyid Qutb. Sayyid Qutb was a novelist, poet, educator, journalist, and member of the Egyptian Muslim Brotherhood.[63] For Qutb, *jihad* was an expansionist war to be fought by all Muslims in an attempt to promote Islam so that it ruled over the political systems of the world.[64] The Islamists who constitute Hamas appear to have adopted a somewhat different definition of *jihad.* They perceive it as a defensive struggle against foreign aggressors who invaded Islamic territory. This interpretation is more consistent with and relevant to their immediate situation.[65] Indeed, as Article 15 of the Hamas charter states, "When an enemy usurps a Muslim land, then *jihad* is an individual religious duty on every Muslim."[66]

Facilitating the spread of the uprising throughout the occupied territories, Hamas identified the outbreak of the *intifada* in December of 1987 as the beginning of the *jihad* that would inevitably bring about the defeat of Israel.[67] The group believed that the Islamic nature of the *intifada* was a result of the people's will and, as such, represented the truest form of democracy.[68] Since the rebellion began, Hamas has encouraged people to fight the Israeli occupation on all fronts. This advocacy has included "throwing stones and firebombs, building barriers, burning tires, wielding knives and axes, clashing with the Israeli forces, and attacking collaborators."[69] The organization has also encouraged people to engage in nonviolent forms of resistance. Examples consist of severing economic ties with Israel, not paying taxes and fines, staging commercial strikes, writing slogans on walls, and raising flags, as well as educating new generations about Islamic art, poetry, and writing designed to nourish the souls of those engaged in the struggle.[70]

Hamas contends that the *jihad,* which has taken the form of the *intifada,* is not the final battle in the Palestinian-Israeli conflict; rather, it is only the beginning of a larger Islamic awakening that will unite the Arab states.[71] The *jihad* signifies more than just armed conflict. In brief, it marks the Palestinian people's return to Islam.[72] Members of Hamas believe that sustaining the *jihad* will serve to inspire Arab people as they forego the evils of modern society. For members of the group, modern society is characterized by individualism, egoism, and materialism.[73] Moreover, they hope that by replacing these evils with communal solidarity and civic harmony, they will give Islamic identity a place of prominence within Palestinian consciousness. Indeed, as the collective has described on its website,

> The Hamas movement believes that the conflict with the Zionists in Palestine is a conflict of survival. It is a conflict of civilization and determination that can not be brought to an end unless its cause—the Zionist settlement in Palestine, usurpation of land, and the displacement of its people—is removed.[74]

In short, the Islamic Resistance Movement's definition of the situation is one in which they wage a war over the survival of the Palestinian, Arab, and Islamic people. The consequence of losing this battle is the extinction of their culture, religion, community, and citizens.

Roles

There are several roles that have substantially contributed to the behavior of Hamas members. Three particularly influential roles include being a Palestinian, being an Islamic Fundamentalist or Islamist, and being a *shaheed* (or martyr). Each of these roles, and their corresponding development, is summarily ex-amined below.

Similar to many forms of identity, the nationalist-oriented Palestinian self-concept is one that is firmly rooted in history and has evolved over many centuries. Khalidi[75] categorized the emergence of a uniformed Palestinian identity into three stages. The first phase took place prior to World War I when the Palestinian identity was shared by a relatively restricted circle consisting of the urban, the literate, and the educated. This group, which proliferated in the last decades under Ottoman rule, constituted a new elite class inclusive of middle-class teachers, clerks, government officials, and businessmen. The Palestinian identity entered a second stage during the "Mandate" years when it began to expand beyond the boundaries of social status. The Arabs' losing struggle with Zionism and the British deepened the shared sense of unity and identity within the urban and rural populations. Finally, during the third stage, the events of 1948 (i.e., the war, the declaration of the state of Israel, a massive influx of Jewish immigrants from Europe, and a collection of dispossessed refugees in the West Bank and Gaza Strip) served to erase the class gap between the well-to-do and the poor. In particular, the importance of pre-1948 conflicts was minimized, thereby crystallizing the Palestinian identity. Indeed, as Khalidi[76] noted,

> for in spite of their dispersion and fragmentation among several new successor states and forms of refugee status, what the Palestinians now shared was far greater than what separated them; all had been dispossessed, none were masters of their own fate, all were at the mercy of cold, distant, and hostile new authorities.

With these three stages in mind, specific role sets can be identified that were essential to the development of the Palestinian identity. For example, one counter-role was the Zionists. Although the Palestinian identity did not materialize as a result of Zionism, its refinement was invariably linked to this movement.[77] Indeed, clearly operating within the Zionist role set has been the conspicuous presence of aggressiveness and victimization. Thus, the Palestinian identity has been informed by members' status as victims.[78] One universal expectation stemming from the victim role is self-defense. In part, this interpretation serves to justify Hamas violence among members of the group.

A second role that has contributed to the Palestinian identity among Hamas loyalists is the status of being a hero and a martyr. For example, in 1935, Shiehk 'Izzidin al-Qassam led an armed revolt in the north of Palestine against British troops in the wake of sporadic Islamic violence targeted against Jews who settled in the region between 1920 and 1929.

"The pride that Hamas [took] in the *jihad* of Shiehk 'Izzidin al-Qassam and his followers in particular [was] reflected in the fact that the military arm of Hamas, which was founded in the early 1990s, [was] named the Martyr 'Izzidin al-Qassam Brigades."[79]

A third role woven into the fabric of Palestinian identity, particularly for militant Islamic collectives such as Hamas, is the Muslim status. Indeed, as Khalidi[80] noted, those who constitute these groups "subsume Palestinian nationalism within one or another form of Islamic identity." Hamas has made the Muslim role a reality by characterizing the achievement of Palestinian statehood as a religious obligation.[81]

The behavior of Hamas members and the construction of their collective identity can also be interpreted through the role that Islamic fundamentalism assumes in their lives. Islamic fundamentalism is a descriptive term. It characterizes individuals who seek to establish an Islamic state based on the "fundamentals" of the religion or, more specifically, governed by Islamic *shariah* (holy law).[82]

Taylor and Horgan[83] identified the four fundamentalist positions of Islam. These include its claims to universal validity, its theocratic demands extending to all aspects of life, the sanctification of Islamic law and its teachings, and the general equation of the Palestinian state with the implementation of Islam. These four tenets or positions represent an inexorable bond between religious and political ideology situated within the greater Islamic fundamentalist movement. Often demonized and frequently misunderstood by Western society,[84] Islamic fundamentalist thought was shaped by and cultivated within the movement by the Egyptian Muslim Brotherhood founder, Hasan al-Banna, and past leader, Sayyid Qutb.[85]

Davidson[86] described four basic assumptions of Islamic fundamentalism. The first of these is that the Muslim world is in a state of disorder brought on by political and moral decay. This devastation is the result of those in both the private and the public sector who have failed to live by the dictates of the Islamic religion. The second supposition is that this decay has made it possible for Western colonialism to flourish and to infect the region with its own destructive and hedonistic values. These values include a commitment to secularism, materialism, and nationalism. This Western influence has essentially fractionalized the Islamic *umma,* or community. The third assumption is that the only way to combat this perceived moral and political decay, as well as damaging cultural propaganda, is to "re-Islamize" the Muslim world. This would require the reaffirmation of Islamic law, or *shariah,* and the purging of Western influences. Finally, the fourth presupposition is that

> the only way to re-Islamize society is to re-politicize Islam itself. As fundamentalist reasoning goes, Islam began as a religion that preached the rejection of false gods and corrupt practices. The West and Westernizers now represent precisely these evils. . . . Islam, representative of a total worldview, is the path to justice and socioeconomic equity.[87]

In addition to adopting these four assumptions as a basis for comprehending the Islamic role and its significance for contributing to the construction of Hamas identity is the belief that Muslims must behave in accordance with the accepted code of Islam.[88] This belief comes with a number of role expectations. For example, the five pillars of Islam indicate that all Muslims must (a) testify that there is no God but Allah and that his prophet is Muhammad, (b) offer prayer, (c) pay an obligatory charity, or *zakat,* (d) make a pilgrimage to Mecca, or *hajj,* and (e) fast during the month of Ramadan (*al-Bukhar*). However, there also is a very specific social doctrine to which Islamic fundamentalists must adhere. As a set of norms or rules for Islamic behavior, they are most notably dictated in the word of God (Qur'an) and in the word or example of the prophet Muhammad (*hadith*).[89] These rules constitute Islamic holy law (*shariah*), which, in essence, is a unification of theory and practice. Although there are far too many laws to list, some examples are worth noting. Women are to be subservient to men and must cover themselves, leaving visible only their hands and face. Muslims are to be politically active and strive to create a polity shaped by Islamic law and values. Muslims are to refrain from drinking alcohol and are to defend themselves when confronted with the enemies of Islam.[90]

A third role crucial to understanding the behavior of Hamas members and the construction of their identity is the suicide bomber, or *shaheed,* status. The act of sacrificing oneself in the name of Islam was first documented thirteen centuries ago during the power struggle that followed the death of Muhammad.[91] Hamas does not use the term "suicide bomber"; instead, it employs the expression "*istishhadi.*" Roughly speaking, this translates into "self-chosen martyrdom."[92] As Dr. Abdul Aziz Rantisi, one of the cofounders of Hamas, explained, the term "suicide bomber" implies an impulsive act by a deranged individual. Those who engage in the act of *istishhadi* partake of deliberate, carefully chosen conduct as a function of their religious duty. Indeed, as Kushner[93] described,

> *Karbala* [a historical reference to the act of self-sacrifice] is not an act of suicide; Islam forbids the taking of one's own life. Rather, it symbolizes the supreme willingness to submit to the will of Allah with the understanding that rewards will come after death. Islam emphasizes that life on earth is merely a transition to a better life. A suicide bomber is making a transition that will put him or her alongside the other heroes of Islam and next to Allah.

Thus, when a Hamas loyalist sacrifices his or her life on behalf of the holy struggle, the person is granted lasting symbolic immortality and is elevated to a higher spiritual plane, that of a martyr, sitting with Allah in the kingdom of heaven.

The beliefs surrounding the *shaheed* role are informed by Hamas recruiters and clerics who promise young bombers entry into a paradise. This is a heavenly realm where rivers flow with sweet honey and holy wine, where seventy-two virgin brides exist for their pleasure, where seventy free passes to this paradise are made available to their friends and relatives, where financial stability is ensured for their families, where scholarships are provided for their siblings, and where compensation for the family's resettlement is guaranteed should Israeli retribution claim their homes.[94] Those who volunteer are deeply pious, brave, and willing to embrace death.[95] Moreover, a young *shaheed* recruit knows that his or her sacrifice will be honored after death. The pictures of *shaheeds* are transformed into posters and plastered on buildings, schools, mosques; they are also dispersed in a form similar to baseball cards. All of these activities commemorate their heroism and martyrdom.[96] For Hamas *shaheeds*, self-chosen martyrdom is looked upon as the most honorable of deeds. As Sayed Abu Musamah, editor-in-chief of the Hamas newspaper *Al-watan*, described it, *shaheed* is "the highest form of courage."[97]

Closely linked to the *shaheed* values of self-sacrifice and courage is role-taking action promulgated by others Palestinians. Contenta[98] interviewed the family members and friends of twenty-one Palestinian suicide bombers. He identified the group portrait of these individuals and found that they were weighed down by poverty, embodied deep religious commitments, and had experienced traumatic encounters with

Israel's military occupation of the West Bank and Gaza Strip, either personally or through intimates. Thus, as one father of a suicide bomber explained, "Every Palestinian home, if it doesn't have someone killed, has a relative or a neighbor or a friend killed . . . this pushes the Palestinian people to seek revenge."[99] As such, *shaheed* invites clear expressions of role-taking action among Palestinian people and, especially, among Hamas faithful.

Socialization and Role-Taking

Initiated by the Palestinian branch of the Muslim Brotherhood, the Islamic awakening in the region has been described as a cultural and educational campaign designed to nurture and rear individuals of the new generation in a true Islamic fashion. This indoctrination did not end at the outbreak of the *intifada*. Instead, this cultural and educational immersion experience, built around a militant version of Islam, represents a mainstay of the organization's strategy. As witnessed in the organization's charter under the subheading "Training the Muslim Generation," Article 16, Hamas articulates its determination to continually replenish its resistance efforts with an endless supply of Palestinian Islamic soldiers.

> We must train the Muslim generation in our area, an Islamic training based on performing religious duties, studying God's book very well, and studying Prophetic tradition (*sunnah*), Islamic history and heritage from its authenticated sources with the guidance of experts and scholars, and using a curriculum that will provide the Muslim with the correct world view in ideology and thought.[100]

What this statement exemplifies is that the group's intent is to socialize young people to believe in the "correct" worldview.

Hamas has continued its grassroots approach to Islamizing Palestinian society, or *Islamization from below.*[101] Through its various social institutions such as day-care agencies, religious schools, youth and sports clubs, clinics, nursing homes, and financial programs, Hamas has worked to persuade its patrons, both young and old, to embrace "true Islam."[102] The group has created summer camps where Palestinian boys are taught a martial blend of religion and soldiering skills. As Stack[103] observed, young boys march around the campgrounds in cadence with their drill instructor's orders. Their activities at the camp include reciting religious ballads and viewing a cartoon history of Genghis Khan's raid on Baghdad. Exposure to the latter teaches the recruits about the long-standing struggle between the Muslims and their infidel foes. In an interview, Ismail Abu Shanab, a leader in the movement, explained the significance of this socialization. As he noted, "The Israelis think that we might forget, but we teach this [Islamizing from below and socialization] to our children and our children will teach it to their children."[104] The realization of the Brotherhood's goal, namely, to create a generation of Islamic warriors who will work to secure a Palestinian homeland and sacrifice their lives if necessary, is evidenced by the numerous young people who volunteer to be suicide bombers.

Upon closer examination of the *shaheed* act, we note that there is a significant degree of anticipatory socialization that prepares young Palestinians to fulfill their religious duty on this front. Indeed, as Alexander and Martin[105] explained, Islamic religious leaders from extremist groups like Hamas "promote 'martyrdom' among Palestinians from an early age."[106] To illustrate, Palestinian children living in the Israeli-occupied territories are bombarded with images venerating the sacrifice of martyrs and are fed a steady diet of anti-Semitic messages through the popular media.[107] In addition, Hamas oversees classes that teach children about Israeli's "illegal occupation" of the West Bank and Gaza Strip and its barbaric "treatment" of Palestinians.[108] Interestingly, while the initial focus of the instruction is on politics and religion, it eventually gives way to lectures about martyrdom and self-sacrifice.[109]

Other ritualized patterns are used to legitimize and indoctrinate Hamas members and commit them to fulfilling the expectations of the martyr role. One such ritual is that the young volunteers are brought to the cemetery at night and told by their trainers to lie in empty gravesites hooded with a white shroud.[110] White shrouds are used to cover bodies for burial, and this is done as a way of preparing the individuals for death. Once their day of judgment has arrived, some volunteers prepare themselves mentally for the event that will end their mortal lives and transform them into martyrs. As Kushner[111] noted, they "leave for their missions directly from their mosques, after completing many days of chanting the relevant scriptures aloud with their spiritual handlers. A favorite verse reads: 'Think not of those who are slain in Allah's way as dead. No, they live on and find sustenance in the presence of their

Lord.'" This sentiment sustains volunteers' impulse to complete the expectations of martyrdom, believing that their actions are just, necessary, and holy. Thus, for the Islamic fundamentalist, or Islamist, the act of giving one's life to the cause transcends death.

Palestinian children also learn the expectations of roles through their engagement in role-taking when playing childhood games. This process is evidenced by the various images of Palestinian boys (and girls) dressed in camouflage fatigues, marching in the streets carrying toy machine guns and burning the Israeli flag.[112] As Hendawi[113] explained,

> The violence has also found its way into play time and games mirroring aspects of life in recent months have evolved. One is "Arabs and Jews," which is a local version of Cowboys and Indians. There is also "Checkpoints," a game in which children try to flag down passing cars—as happens to Palestinians crossing checkpoints manned by Israeli troops checking the identity of passengers. There is also *"shaheed,"* a game in which children take turns being carried by friends shouting "with our blood, our souls we sacrifice you"—as in the funeral processions.

Dickey[114] offered similar observations in his descriptions of how young boys in the Israel-occupied territories love playing would-be suicide bomber with pretend, improvised explosive devices made out of cardboard. Moreover, Assadi[115] observed that toy stores in the West Bank city of Jenin were

> packed with plastic arsenals of rifles, miniature tanks, missiles and artillery pieces. Outside, boys with toy guns organize street battles reminiscent of those fought between Palestinian gunmen and Israeli troops. . . . Children, some dressed in military costumes, roam Jenin's alleys— where damage from Israeli raids is plainly visible—with plastic M-16 rifles slung over their shoulders. Others lie on their stomachs and aim guns at playmates, mimicking Israeli troops searching for Palestinian militants.

Through this role-taking process, young Palestinians assume the statuses of Hamas fighters, *shaheeds,* and Israeli troops. In addition, however, they learn the expectations of the respective roles they perform.

The notion of role-taking is also useful in that it sheds some light on how the leaders of Hamas responded to the DOP and how the accord inevitably reshaped the role identities of the group. From the beginning, Hamas emphatically rejected the acceptance of anything less than a historic Palestinian state and openly proclaimed that it would force the participants of the agreement to abort the negotiations, if need be. Indeed, while Arafat was shaking hands with heads of state who never defended the Palestinian cause,[116] his police force was receiving assistance from Western intelligence organizations as it launched a fervent campaign to apprehend militant Islamists for their violent attacks.[117] This notwithstanding, Hamas continued to serve the Palestinian people through its social endeavors and charitable institutions.

Moreover, Nüsse[118] suggested that Hamas intentionally provoked Israel's collective punishment of the Palestinians by waging bombing campaigns against Jewish settlers. The intent here was to make the Palestinian Authority look incompetent and to illustrate the symbiotic relationship between Hamas and the Palestinian community as a way of winning their support to the collective's more militant extremist cause. In this respect, then, "Hamas was playing its role as an opposition force using the armed attacks to highlight and exploit the difficult situation its political enemy Arafat put himself in with the peace-agreements: building a Palestinian sovereignty by serving Israel's interests."[119] Other investigators have commented on this role-taking strategy, noting that, indeed, "even though Hamas advocated armed struggle against Israel, its leaders were forced to anticipate the expected responses of Israel and the PA and, given the wide public support for the peacemaking process, also of the Palestinian population in the West Bank and Gaza Strip."[120] In sum, by taking on the role of the Israeli government and the oppressed Palestinian masses, Hamas was able to modulate its own behavior in an effort to maximally garner public sympathy and political support.

Although the members of Hamas continued to employ violence against Israel, they practiced considerably more restraint when responding to those Palestinians[121] and surrounding Arab nations that supported the peace accords. For example, careful not to antagonize their Arab brethren, "Hamas did not react to the Oslo Agreement by organizing demonstrations, turning its weapons against the PA, or resorting to the assassination of officials."[122] Although they did attack the content of the peace accords, they refrained from waging personal attacks against the participants and its significant number of supporters.[123] Moreover, Hamas loyalists moderated their political discourse because they feared that excessive criticism of the agreement would marginalize them or, worse, would lead to a civil war.[124] Recognizing the potential political fall-out and the negative repercussions that would have befallen the movement had a more strident position concerning the DOP been adopted, Hamas adopted a strategy that illustrates the group's ability to see its own behavior from various points of view.

What the above observations on role-taking indicate is that, consciously or otherwise, Hamas has embraced the role of various reference groups (i.e., Israeli government, Arab neighbors, and fellow Palestinians), has assessed its actions or potential actions from that perspective, and has adjusted its behavior accordingly. Consequently, Hamas has learned about the existing and new expectations of its manifold roles. Moreover, and perhaps most profoundly, members of Hamas have "moved away from dogmatic positions in a quest for innovative and pliable modes of conduct, the opposite of doctrinaire rigidity, ready to respond or adjust to fluid conditions without losing sight of their ultimate objectives."[125]

As a result of adjusting their behavior to comport with the changing political and social climate surrounding the Israeli-Palestinian conflict, members of Hamas have garnered (and maintained) public support, have secured compliance among their rank and file, and function as a key power broker for the Palestinian people. Thus, by taking on the role of the generalized other (in its various Palestinian, Arab, and Israeli forms), Hamas has modified its political strategies, presumably making the group the legitimate voice of the Palestinians and Allah in the region.

Self

Society Shapes the Self

The Palestinian, Islamic fundamentalist, and *shaheed* identities were noted because each is intimately related to the overall identity of membership in or affiliation with Hamas. In this sense, then, the invocation of one of these self-schemas serves to cue or activate the others. According to this version of Identity Theory (i.e., society shapes the self), a person becomes committed to these role identities through his or her interaction in social relationships and social networks. Thus, for example, take the process through which individuals align themselves with the Palestinian self-concept. Many of the social interactions and, hence, role relationships Palestinians have are contingent upon their identification as Palestinians. Indeed, those relationships that unfold and those social networks that exist on a daily basis, whether in the refugee camps where they live or the deteriorating schools where they attend class, serve to commit Palestinians to their identity.[126] The same is true in the case of role relationships with Israelis. As Khalidi[127] observed,

> The quintessential Palestinian experience, which illustrates some of the most basic issues raised by Palestinian identity, takes place at a border, an airport, a checkpoint: in short, at any one of those many modern barriers where identities are checked and verified. What happens to Palestinians at these crossing points brings home to them how much they share in common as a people. For it is at these borders and barriers that the six million Palestinians are singled out for "special treatment," and are forcefully reminded of their identity: of who they are, and of why they are different from others.

In the interactions described above, social relationships are created when an Israeli security agent identifies, interrogates, and searches a Palestinian traveler or when a border guard checks the work permit of a Palestinian who relies upon a job within the Israeli border that serves as his or her livelihood. These social relationships are constant reminders of one's identity as Palestinian. In the illustration above, this identity encompasses a disenfranchised status in the overall social structure and, as a result, must be singled out for "special treatment." However, as relationships increasingly are based on the Palestinian identity, the frequency of one's mobilization along these lines will similarly rise. Correspondingly, as this identification materializes and solidifies itself, the more attached a person will become to the self-schema and the more salient it will be on the person's identity hierarchy.

A similar argument can be made in regard to the influence significant others play in facilitating the adoption of the *shaheed* role-identity. Interestingly, Contenta[128] found that more than half of the twenty-one suicide bombers he examined were close friends. The mother of Ismail al-Masawabi, a twenty-three-year-old Palestinian who blew himself and two Israeli Army sergeants up on June 22, 2001, explained this process of identity in relation to the *shaheed* role. As she noted, "I was happy when I heard. . . . To be a martyr, that's something. Very few people can do it. I prayed to thank God. In the Koran it's said that a martyr does not die. I know my son is close to me. It is our belief."[129] Moreover, in the interview she stated, "I hope my other children do the same."[130]

Maternal support for the *shaheed* role was also evident in the case of Muhammad Farhat, who killed five yeshiva students in the Atzmona settlement in March 2002. In an interview with *Al-Sharq Al-Awsat,* a Saudi-owned Arabic daily published in London, his mother, Umm Nidal, explained how she and others had instilled a love for martyrdom in her son at a very young age.[131] She noted that during the first *intifada* she had hidden 'Imad 'Aql, a commander of Hamas's Izz Al-Din Al-Qassam, in her family's home for fourteen months. As a result, Muhammad Farhat became 'Imad 'Aql's pupil and a member of the brigades at the age of seven. Indeed, Muhammad watched as 'Aql planned operations and coordinated with the other Hamas militants. Commenting on this society-shapes-self identity process, Umm Nidal explained that

> this was the source of Muhammad's love of martyrdom. . . . This is the atmosphere in which the love of martyrdom developed in Muhammad's soul. I, as a mother, naturally encouraged the love of *Jihad* in the soul of Muhammad and in the souls of all my sons, all of whom belong to the Al-Qassam Brigades.[132]

Prior to initiating a suicide attack in the Jewish settlement of Dugit in the Gaza Strip in June 2002, twenty-three-year-old college student and member of Hamas, Mahmoud el-Abed, appeared in a videotaped last testament holding an assault rifle. His rifle-carrying mother, Naima al-Obeid, stood next to him expressing great pride in his plans for martyrdom.[133] In the video, Mahmoud's mother exclaimed, "God willing you will succeed . . . may every bullet hit its target, and God give you martyrdom. This is the best day of my life." Mahmoud retorted, "Thank you for raising me."[134] Naima got her wish when Mahmoud killed, in an ambush, two Israeli soldiers guarding the gate into the settlement; Mahmoud was also killed in the attack. In an interview with Al-Sharq Al-Awsat, Naima explained that for years she had raised her son to commit suicide for the homeland and rejoiced when her teaching succeeded.[135] She went on to say that the morning after Mahmoud set out on his mission, he returned home after having second thoughts. Naima told her son that she was infuriated and Mahmoud promised that he would complete his act of martyrdom the next day.

Perhaps the most poignant illustration of the role that significant others play with respect to instilling the martyr identity within extremist militants is observable in a photo Israeli soldiers found in the family album of a Hamas gunman in Hebron in 2002. The photograph featured the gunman's infant son dressed in military fatigues complete with a suicide bomber's harness.[136] Although not all significant others in a fledgling martyr's life are supportive of such an identity, classmates, teachers, fellow recruits, parents, and family members serve to repeatedly remind some of their *shaheed* path, obligation, and destiny. Indeed, the social relationships and networks based on one's self-schema as a fledgling martyr and the extrinsic gratification one receives from significant others causes one to become more committed to this identity. This heightened and intensified commitment increases the identity's salience and its proclivity to be activated in a variety of situations. While not all significant others in the suicide bombers' environment are supportive of such an act (i.e., *shaheed*), some parents have found it difficult to shield their children from Hamas recruiters.[137]

Self Shapes Society

The verification of an individual's role identities as Islamic fundamentalists can be observed in the form of identity cues and interpersonal prompts. For example, in order to bring a person's self-meanings in line with the identity standard of an Islamic fundamentalist, individuals use dress as an identity cue. As previously described, Hamas operates many forms of social institutions as a way of promoting the religion and group. One such institution is football (i.e., soccer) clubs. One member described how the athletic organization was distinct from other clubs whose primary membership stemmed from secular Palestinian militant groups like Fatah or the Popular Front for the Liberation of Palestine. As the club member explained, "this club is different; it is Islamic; it represents Islamic men. In other clubs, morality is sometimes low; maybe they drink alcohol in other clubs, maybe they don't pray. There is a big difference."[138]

The role expectations of Islamists are that they live in accordance with Islamic law. One such rule is that men and women dress modestly. One member stated that "first and foremost, we wear long slacks when we play. Morals in the club are very high: we are all Muslims."[139] While the players do not wear slacks, they are dressed in long shorts down to their knees under their football shorts. This is their way of living by the norms prescribed in the Qur'an.[140]

Interpersonal prompts are another technique used to verify one's identity as an Islamic fundamentalist. Jensen[141] observed that the men interrupted their training sessions when the *muezzin* was called for prayer. Although their prayer was short (four *rak'as*) because they wanted to return to the game, it did serve to verify their identities and to shape the environment around them.[142] In another instance of interpersonal prompts that served to verify the Islamic fundamentalist identity, Chartrand[143] noted that a group of thirty teenage boys on the streets of Gaza squirted black paint on women who were not properly covered. Their mission was to reprimand and, if necessary, punish girls, young women, mothers, and daughters who chose to appear in public without their veils. One nineteen-year-old boy, who claimed to be acting on orders from the Islamic Resistance Movement, stated that "this will keep our morals and traditions intact. . . . Only through Islam can we defeat Israeli intelligence agents who use loose women to lure Palestinians into spying for them."[144] In this way the Islamist identity was verified through behavior that further shaped and contributed to Islamic culture.

To verify one's identity as a *shaheed,* one must fulfill the most important expectation—sacrificing one's life for the cause. However, for the martyr-in-training, identity verification takes place through techniques like identity cues and interpersonal prompts. As Mishal and Sela[145] noted, "Hamas and the Islamic *Jihad* adopt . . . the same procedure of finding a candidate for a suicide operation, training and preparing him psychologically, writing a farewell letter, and making a videotape before his mission." These videotaped testimonies, circulated within the Palestinian community in Gaza and the West Bank, are both memorials to the young men who gave their lives and recruiting devices to show potential volunteers. After viewing one such video, Juergensmeyer[146] recalled the following:

> In a videotape . . . that portrays funeral ceremonies for these young self-martyrs, a group of young men is seen entering the crowd, masked and carrying rifles. The crowd roars in frenzied approval. These were "living martyrs," those who had already committed themselves to self-martyrdom and were awaiting their call to action.

A common sight at Hamas rallies and funerals, "living martyrs" are those who commit themselves to self-martyrdom (i.e., to be a suicide bomber) and await their call to action.[147]

For selected events, the living martyrs typically dress in white robes. The robes symbolize the death shroud. A white hood conceals their identity, and a green headband is featured displaying white lettering. In translation, it reads, "no God, but God and Mohammed is the Prophet of Allah."[148] By engaging in rituals such as this, young Palestinian men morally bind themselves to the initiation of their own deaths. This public display of commitment, especially in front of their peers, places a tremendous degree of pressure on the *shaheed* recruits to complete their suicide bombings as this act informs and sustains the culture into which they were born.[149]

Moreover, by using identity cues, the living martyrs verify their self-schemas. They don symbolic attire, brandish rifles, and present themselves to the crowd as persons ready for self-sacrifice. In this way, the successful fulfillment of the role identity of past suicide bombers continues to engulf the lives of future *shaheed* in the form of song, video, prayer, posters, and other symbols of self-sacrifice. Thus, for the young *shaheed* recruits, the act of giving one's life to the cause transcends death and shapes the society that they inhabit.

7

The Peruvian Shining Path

Underscoring the interpretive framework central to this book's thesis is the conviction that the explanatory model extends to all regions of the globe and accounts for all forms of terrorism. Thus far, political and religious forms of militant extremism emanating from Ireland and the Middle East have been examined. In this chapter, however, economic (and social) liberation is showcased, especially as it relates to the violent activities of the Latin American terrorist group known as the Shining Path. As this chapter makes clear, symbols and their meanings, the definition of the situation, role performances, and socialization and role-taking experiences all powerfully contribute to the emergence of the self. In the context of one's membership in the Shining Path collective, this includes the manifestation of identity in which violence, destruction, and discord are all prominently featured.

Symbols

In March of 1982, twenty-one months after the initiation of the "people's war," the Communist Party of Peru (aka PCP) distributed an official document entitled *Let Us Develop the Guerrilla War.*[1] It was written by Comrade Gonzalo,[2] and its release marked the first time the organization made its position on the insurrection public.[3]

Within the document, the PCP claimed responsibility for twenty-nine hundred incidents that had weakened and undermined "the social and economic system of the ruling exploiters," shaken "the semi-feudal foundations of the state, unleashing armed vindicating actions against big land owners[,] lords of the new and old type," and "hit directly the interests of Yankee imperialism, the principle imperialist power on our soil." The document also claimed to have struck a blow against "the Chinese embassy, the sinister cave of the revisionist Deng Xiaoping . . .

and vile traitor to the international communist movement" and carried out important actions "against the state . . . [and] its repressive apparatus."[4] In the process of describing these targets, the PCP identified many of the symbols that informed and sustained its violent existence.

One such symbol was "the social and economic system of the ruling exploiters."[5] For the Shining Path, the existence of this symbol dates back to the arrival of the Spanish conquistadores in 1532.[6] Prior to their landing, the Inca Empire relied upon a system of communal property ownership and a tradition of communal labor for sustenance.[7] The farmers were given military and divine protection in exchange for their labor. After their arrival, the Spaniards swiftly destroyed this cooperative agrarian system and, in its place, established a colonial economy based on mining silver and gold for export to Europe.

The conquistadores relied on Indian laborers, who were often uprooted from their settlements by force and abused in the harsh working conditions of the mines.[8] In the Andean highlands of the Sierra, the Spaniards established large haciendas to supply agricultural produce to the mines and coastal towns. The haciendas were organized along feudal lines where Indian peasants (or *campesinos*) received plots of estate land in return for their labor. They were forced to pay tribute to the Spanish Crown and buy imported artifacts at inflated prices. The native population was economically exploited, culturally isolated, and racially despised.[9] Colonial Peru soon became an apartheid society separated along ethnic and class lines. Even after gaining its independence, the nation continued to maintain a highly compartmentalized social structure divided between Whites and Indians, the coastal region and the Sierras, the capitalists/landowners and the urban workers/miners/peasants, and the exploiters and those who were exploited.[10]

According to the Shining Path, the Indian peasantry continues to be oppressed by the semifeudal, neocolonialist hacienda system, which still exists in the Andean countryside of modern-day Peru.[11] This interpretation is largely based on the critique and analysis of Marxist theorist José Carlos Mariátegui, considered to be the father of Peruvian communism.[12] In one of his most prominent works, *Seven Interpretive Essays on Peruvian Reality*,[13] Mariátegui argued that the dilemmas for the Indian were socioeconomic and connected to the use and ownership of the land. As he explained, "The problem of the Indian is rooted in the land tenure system of our economy. Any attempt to solve it with administrative or police measures, through education or by a road building program, is superficial and secondary as long as the feudalism of the *gamonales*[14] continues to exist."[15]

To the Maoist militants, imperialist intervention created a capitalist/ landowning class whose power was (and is), in part, rooted in the "semi-feudal foundations of the state."[16] Western "Yankee" imperialism just happens to be the current incarnation of foreign influence. This influence continues to dominate Peru today.

A second symbol that has contributed significantly to the behavior of Shining Path militants is revisionism. To these Maoist revolutionaries, anyone who strays from the "official" interpretation of Marxism/Lenin-ism/Maoism is considered a revisionist. While the Soviet Union was condemned for its corruption and treasonlike ideology, Guzmán and the group were particularly haunted by the 1978 overthrow of the "Gang of Four"[17] perpetrated by Chinese Communist Party moderates.[18] Their fear stemmed from a concern that a counterrevolution, similar to the one Deng Xiaoping led in China, would take place within the PCP. The PCP came to believe that it was Mao's indulgence of party moderates that piloted the downfall of the Cultural Revolution and toppled the Gang of Four.[19] As a result, the Shining Path was particularly harsh on Deng Xiaoping and the Chinese leadership for its betrayal of Mao Zedong.[20]

In addition to labeling the communist Chinese establishment an enemy within PCP rhetoric, the group directed attacks against it. For example, Shining Path cadres threw dynamite at the embassy of the People's Republic of China in Lima in March 1986. The attack was undertaken out of "revenge for the betrayal of the ideas of Mao."[21] In an effort "to prevent an overthrow from within and preserve its dog-matic view of revolution,"[22] the group was also particularly harsh on those within PCP ranks who espoused revisionist ideals.

Since the fall of the Gang of Four, the Shining Path has considered itself the vanguard of revolutionary orthodoxy and the future of world insurrection.[23] Guzmán's followers even elevated him to the status of Marx, Lenin, and Mao, referring to him as the "fourth sword of Marx-ism." Guzmán explained the symbolic importance of revisionism for the Shining Path's struggle in a July 1988 interview[24] with *El Diario*.[25] *El Diario* is a Lima-based newspaper and was considered to be the party's semi-official mouthpiece.[26] In the interview, Guzmán stated,

> Revisionism strives to falsify and twist scientific socialism in order to
> oppose the class struggle and revolution, peddling parliamentary cre-

tinism and pacifism. All these positions have been expounded by the revisionists, who have aimed for and continue to aim for the restoration of capitalism, the undermining and blocking of the world revolution, and to denigrate the conquering spirit of our class.

The leader went on to explain that revisionism represented an agent of the bourgeoisie in the ranks of the proletariat that provoked splits within the communist parties. He likened revisionism to a cancer that needed to be "ruthlessly eliminated," swept away like a "colossal pile of rubbish."

A third symbol motivating the behavior of the PCP is the counterrevolutionary response of the Peruvian government. The importance of this symbol is also evidenced in *Let Us Develop the Guerrilla War*.[27] This work includes a chapter entitled "Counterrevolutionary Action Fuels Our Struggle." Within the chapter, the PCP accused the "demagogic" government of using its military and police forces to trample upon the most basic, universally recognized rights of the people. Indeed, the PCP alleged that the forces

> brutally [broke] and [stole] from whatever homes they'd wanted; . . . persecuted, arrested, and jailed whomever they want to; . . . burned, robbed, raped, and murdered with impunity[;] . . . gorged their dark, reactionary zeal on savage beatings of the masses[;] . . . generalized the use of torture, trying to crush their will and extract false confessions, despicably and perversely humiliating people so as to bend the revolutionary morale and annihilate the combatants; . . . [and] used rapes as an infamous, vile, and abusive means to force submission and to tarnish the pure, resolute, and firm spirit of the daughters of the people.[28]

In addition, the PCP explained that the Peruvian government's repressive practices and genocidal actions directed toward the peasantry exposed the government as a treacherous farce that espoused a "sinister plan to crush the people through counterrevolutionary violence." However, as the PCP asserted, this brutal victimization only served to focus the group's resolve and strengthen its bond with the masses.

Putting aside the Shining Path's rhetorical observations and its own human rights abuses, there is no doubt that the Peruvian government used an excessive degree of force in its efforts to quell the Shining Path insurrection. For example, not long after the group began its armed resistance, the military declared emergency zones in those departments plagued by the militants. By 1990, over 50 percent of Peru's population lived in these crisis areas.[29] In addition, the constitutional liberties of those residing within the zones were suspended, and the local governmental authorities were brought under the army's control. Moreover, at various points, security forces launched extremely heavy-handed counteroffenses. These military efforts employed brutal methods of repression and clearly featured genocidal leanings.[30] Unable to distinguish between Senderistas (i.e., revolutionary guerrillas who were servants of the people fighting for social justice and a communist utopia) and their victims, the soldiers frequently operated on the premise that entire villages were Shining Path conspirators. One ranking commander was quoted as saying, "In order for the security forces to be successful, they will have to begin to kill Senderistas and non-Senderistas alike. . . . They will kill 60 people and at best three will be Senderistas, but they will say that all 60 were Senderistas."[31]

Definition of the Situation

As the Shining Path saw it, Peru faced a major economic and political crisis. The organization alleged that the masses suffered the most from the uncontrollable growth in inflation; the increasing budget deficit; the rising unemployment rate; decreasing wages; deteriorating working conditions; and the tightening stranglehold of Western capitalism on the country's natural resources, commerce, and finances.[32] Indeed, the PCP vehemently disputed claims that the land problem had been resolved and, instead, insisted that the government tried

> to fool the peasants with the botched "farming and cattle-raising programs" at the same time as they advocate[d for] the development of the "associative property" to cover up the return of the big landowners to promote bureaucratic capitalism in agriculture under the control of the big banks and with the direct participation of Yankee imperialism.[33]

Guzmán believed that Peru had incurred roughly thirty years of economic crises at the hands of the state's fascist government because of its reliance on an outmoded and moribund system, namely, bureaucratic capitalism, derived from semifeudalism and imperialism.[34] He believed

that as long as the incompetent leadership within the Peruvian administration continued to utilize a semifeudal structure that effectively subju-
gated the poor and as long as the government turned to "Yankee" capital as the engine for such economic development, there would never be
an end to the country's depressed economic system in which the masses
were harshly exploited.

At first glance, it might seem somewhat ironic that the Shining Path
collective would launch its "people's war" just when Peru was returning
to democratic rule. However, since its inception, the PCP has viewed
Peru's democratic institutions with contempt.[35] The group clearly expressed this sentiment when arguing that the political system was nothing more than a corrupt falsification of democracy used by the bourgeoisie to promote an unequal distribution of wealth. Indeed, as the
PCP noted, it was a system that hid "behind the mask of democracy
and its phony concern for the masses" only to promote "servile subjugation" of the exploited masses.[36] This felt sense of grievance and injustice was so deeply ingrained that any change in leadership through the
electoral process was greeted with suspicion and dismissed not only as
irrelevant but as "parliamentary cretinism" and "electoral opportun-
ism."[37] As a result, the PCP saw the Peruvian parliamentary system as
illegitimate and beyond reprieve.

According to Guzmán and the Shining Path, the solution to Peru's
problem was communism itself and the establishment of a collectivist
state. This state would be termed the "New Democratic People's Republic."[38] One PCP document defined communism as

> the society of "great harmony," the radical and definitive new society
> toward which 15 billion years of matter in movement—the part of eter-
> nal matter of which we know—is necessarily and irrepressibly heading.
> . . . A single, irreplaceable new society, without exploited or exploiters,
> without oppressed or oppressors, without classes, without state, with-
> out parties, without democracy, without arms, without wars.[39]

This description led members of the Shining Path to believe that their
struggle for social justice was a righteous cause and that their ultimate
goal was more cosmic and transcendent in nature. Only by way of the
utter destruction of the status quo, as well as the elimination of any
resistance, could the movement create a communist utopia.[40]

The PCP's vision of utopia was heavily influenced by Mariátegui's beliefs. He felt that the indigenous population practiced a primitive form of communism and that they were the direct descendants of Peru's socialist tradition.[41] As a result, the blueprint for Andean socialism was situated within the pre-Columbian peasant community.[42] It was also largely guided by Mao's conceptualization of the interim state structure Mariategui called the "New Democracy."[43] As Tarazona-Sevillano[44] explained, Mao realized that moving China's long-standing social, political, and economic order directly into true communism would be difficult. The New Democracy was to be a transitional system until the remnants of colonialism and feudalism were eliminated. Its implementation included replacing Japanese imperialism and ancient warlord feudalism with a joint dictatorship that united all the revolutionary classes. This unification included the proletariat, peasantry, intelligentsia, and petite bourgeoisie. Economic reform consisted of the nationalization of commercial enterprises, such as banks, factories, and industry. These efforts would limit the political influence of private capital.

Large feudal landholdings were expropriated and distributed among the peasantry; however, some private property titles were still permitted. The existing culture, which Mao believed was feudal and imperialistic, was replaced with a strict adherence to Marxist beliefs based on scientific facts. The New Democracy would introduce the people to genuine equality and a clear path by which to achieve the ultimate goal of true communism.

Although highly influenced by Mao's New Democracy, Guzmán's vision of the New Democratic People's Republic was far more radical. This is the case because it was an end in and of itself. There was no transitional period: industry, foreign trade, the use of currency, a national market economy, and a banking system would all be eliminated immediately.[45] In its place, the PCP would implement a communal village-oriented economy based on a system of barter exchange and the nationalization of all means of production.

In keeping with its back-to-the-Incas philosophy, the state would reject modern technology because its devices were regarded as tools of imperialist control. In its place, the state would return to pre-Conquest agricultural techniques.[46] In addition, there would be no private holdings, as Guzmán believed this strategy would eliminate class differences. Any remaining components of social or economic rank would be abrogated through popular education, and those who were unable to adapt to the new system would be summarily executed.[47] Eventually, the scope of the revolution would be expanded to encompass all of the Quechua-speaking peoples of Bolivia, Columbia, Ecuador, Argentina, and Chile. The insurgent movement's ultimate goal, then, was not just to overthrow the government in Lima but to spark a larger Latin American revolution. Ideally, this effort would unite the entire Quechua nation under the banner of a new socialist state.[48]

According to the Shining Path, "armed struggle [was] the only revolutionary road possible."[49] Therefore, the use of force, violence, and terror (or, what has been termed the "popular war") were the only means by which to attain true communism and establish the New Democratic People's Republic. In a modified version of the three-phased theory of protracted war developed by Mao, Guzmán conceived of a five-stage strategy for achieving victory over the Lima government.[50] These stages included (a) agitation and armed propaganda, (b) sabotage and guerrilla action, (c) generalized violence and guerrilla warfare, (d) conquest and expansion of support bases, and (e) all-out civil war to cause the fall of cities and total collapse of the state. These stages are not necessarily mutually exclusive from one another. In fact, each of them functions simultaneously. A brief description of these phases is chronicled below.

The first stage, agitation and propaganda, took place between 1970 and 1980. It was designed to raise the class consciousness of the peasantry by exacerbating existing class conflicts, by drawing attention to instances of economic inequality, and by reminding the poor that the system was corrupt.[51] In addition, the first stage was structured to mobilize a base of support in the countryside, establish a dedicated cadre to serve in the guerrilla army, and lay the groundwork for an expanded armed struggle.[52] During this stage, the group integrated itself into the indigenous villages of the Peruvian region, built a core base of support, initiated its political indoctrination campaign, and established a "shadow government."[53]

On May 17, 1980, the Shining Path embarked on its second stage of revolution, sabotage and guerrilla action, when it inaugurated the use of violence as a political tool.[54] Over the next several years the organization launched a systematic assault on Peru's socioeconomic system by attacking "the symbols of the fascist state."[55] Examples include such things as police stations, government offices, and government-sponsored development projects; and infrastructure targets, such as bridges, rail lines, electric power stations and transmission lines, and telecommunication facilities.[56] The organization also created safe houses and supply networks and established "zones of liberation."[57]

The PCP entered the third stage, generalized violence and guerrilla warfare, in 1982.[58] Its objective was to broaden its control and intensify its attacks against governmental authority. During this stage, it continued to polarize society and initiated attacks in the cities through a network of urban supporters.[59]

The movement's fourth stage, conquests and expansion of support bases, involved the growth of territory for the purpose of establishing additional support bases. These installations would be used to launch hit-and-run operations against the military forces and to strengthen its guerrilla army.[60] Some analysts believed that the group reached this stage in 1988 because it established support bases in fifteen of Peru's twenty-four departments.[61]

The fifth and final stage entails the fall of cities and the total collapse of the state. During this phase, Shining Path militants intended to force the country's municipalities into submission by surrounding them and by choking off their supply routes.[62] During the implementation of this stage in 1992, the organization suffered a debilitating blow when Guzmán was arrested.

Roles

A remnant of the country's colonial legacy, Peruvian society has long been burdened by a pervasive caste structure. This structure has given rise to distinctive role positions and intense class divisions.[63] Traditionally, there have been three major groups in Peruvian society: creole,[64] *mestizo*,[65] and Indian.[66] During colonial times, most creoles viewed the Indians as an inferior race who were lazy, drunken, coca-addicted, pagan worshipers worthy only of exploitation.[67]

The apartheid system the creoles inherited from the Spaniards treated the Indians as chattel: persons who were destined to serve as an expendable labor force in haciendas and mines. The racism espoused within this system frequently afforded social and economic advantages to creoles and some *mestizos* while relegating the Indians to a second-class citizenry status. As is often the case, these distinctions were represented geographically. The creoles "are concentrated in the wealthier parts of

Lima and in some provincial capitals; *mestizos* in lower-class and slum areas; and Indians in the slums and the rural Andes and Amazon."[68] In the rural Andes where the Shining Path began, the *mestizo* elites acted as provincial lords and officials who ruled over the Indian and *mestizo* peasants.[69] These two roles would prove crucial to the formation of the Senderista identity.

While some consider the Shining Path to be a messianic or millenarian movement rooted in the Andean Indian culture, it is as much a *mestizo* movement. In fact, its leadership has always consisted of small-town, *mestizo* intellectuals whose lineage is traceable to the Andean seignorial system.[70] Armed with a vision of Peruvian society informed by socialism and class conflict, these leaders carried on a long tradition of promoting regional emancipation for the indigenous peasant population, while, in the process, challenging the aristocratic power structure of the upper-class creoles who dominated the Lima-based government.[71] These *mestizo* intellectuals have also carried on the tradition of provincial elites. In other words, they have "embraced *indigenismo* (glorification of Indian customs and traditions) as a reaction against the *hispanismo* (glorification of Hispanic customs and traditions) of the Lima upper classes."[72] To be sure, these leaders were dedicated, college-based revolutionaries.[73] They hailed from the University of San Cristóbal de Huamanga, a liberal institution that provided an education oriented toward social change and "notions of social justice, set against the background of severe poverty and inequality in Ayacucho."[74]

Despite their identification with the Indian plight and the self-perception that they were intellectual warriors who served the exploited masses, the *mestizo* leaders espoused the same racist authoritarian attitudes as did the old provincial *mestizo* elites.[75] As Cadena[76] noted, this sense of paternalistic power over the indigenous population has long been an underlying feature of the relationship between intellectual insurgents and Indians. Within the group, "Shining Path's leaders take on the role of the traditional authoritarian teachers who believe they possess the truth and, therefore, ought to have the absolute power over their students."[77]

This very sentiment was conveyed in Guzmán's approach to the revolution. Consider the following pronouncement:

the masses have to be taught through overwhelming acts so that ideas can be pounded into them . . . the masses in the nation need the leadership of a Communist Party; we hope with more revolutionary theory and practice, with more armed actions, with more people's war, with more power, to reach the very heart of the class and the people and really win them over. Why? In order to serve them—that is what we want.[78]

Within this statement is a particular belief about the poor citizenry of the region. Simply stated, in order to "serve" the masses (i.e., Indians) who occupied the counter-role of student within this role set, it was necessary to direct an overwhelming degree of violence against them. The espousal of such an extreme authoritarian attitude toward the indigenous population provides some explanation as to why the majority of the Shining Path's victims were Indians.[79]

Similar to those who made up the organization's leadership, a large percentage of its rank-and-file were *mestizos*, who came from peasant backgrounds. In fact, a "clear majority of the cadres who [were] captured—a statistically relevant sampling—[were] provincial *mestizo* youths, whose families were peasants in the recent past."[80] In addition, as M. Smith[81] observed, the Shining Path attracted a following of de-peasantized youth consisting of "rural youth who [were] no longer satisfied being peasants but [could not] find adequate employment or opportunity in urban Peru." For "those marginalized *mestizos* who remain[ed] unintegrated in the present system[,] Sendero promise[d] to destroy the existing order and replace it with a rural-oriented utopia."[82] Similarly, as del Pino[83] explained, a strong collaborative bond existed between young people (both *mestizo* and Indian) and the Shining Path. This is the case because the movement gave assurances that poverty, inequality, and the exploitation from which they suffered would all end.

While the Shining Path encouraged the abandonment of Indian customs and traditions (i.e., religion, holidays, calendars, etc.), it drew upon a handful of attitudes, expectations, values, and beliefs espoused within the Indian peasant role in an effort to mobilize the indigenous community.[84] For example, the group capitalized on the Indians' traditional resentment for *mestizo* elites, capitalists, and merchants.[85] As Berg[86] pointed out, within Indian culture there is a social expectation of reciprocity. Indian households rely on a system of mutual assistance as a means of economic survival, particularly relative to agricultural production. Thus, as he noted,

The meanings of friendship, kinship and affection are closely related to economic aid; all relations between people are defined and maintained by exchanges of labor and goods. In some ways the society consists of a complex mesh of instrumental friendships.[87]

Those Indian peasants who become entrepreneurs, refuse to speak Quechua, reject the cultural traditions of the community (e.g., the bond of reciprocity), and adopt the culture of the towns are resented for *acting* like *mestizos*. They no longer are viewed as peasants and are considered to have placed themselves outside the community's moral economy. Consequently, when the Maoist rebels entered villages, they would immediately identify these individuals, submit them to a people's trial, and execute them. These actions garnered Indian peasant support[88] and fueled their desire to seek revenge against those "upwardly mobile, well-off peasants who had exploited them in the past."[89]

The Shining Path also proved to be particularly adept in its strategic use of Andean symbolism and mysticism. For example, one traditional Andean belief manipulated by the Shining Path was the legend of Inkari (Inca-Rey, Inca-king).[90] This myth was derived from the sixteenth-century Inca uprising led by Tupac Amaru I. After suppressing the revolt, the Spanish decapitated Tupac Amaru I and placed his head on a pike. His remains were soon buried when it was learned that his followers had been worshiping the relic at night. As the legend goes, the Inca's head is growing a new body underground and will return to restore Peru to its pre-Conquest order.

The Shining Path capitalized on this messianic myth by representing Guzmán as the modern-day incarnation of the Inkari. This is evidenced in the organization's posters in which "Guzmán occupies the center, dressed in a suit, wearing glasses, book in hand, surrounded by masses carrying rifles and flags, with the great red sun setting behind him."[91] To the Shining Path's Indian followers, Guzmán is referred to as *puka-inti* (Quechua for the "Red Sun"). In Andean mythology, the appearance of the red sun signals the return of Inkari.[92] He is attributed mystical powers, revered with God-Sun adoration—much like the pre-Columbian Inca emperors—and seen as the messiah who will deliver his chosen people, the Quechua-speaking "cosmic race," to salvation.[93] While the Shining Path overtly avoided any ethnic distinctions in its rhetoric, its covert manipulation of Indian attitudes, expectations, and beliefs has allowed the organization to incorporate the motivating power of ethnic survival into its recruitment strategies and militant practices.[94]

The third role influencing the behavior of the PCP's membership is that of the Senderista. As Tarazona-Sevillano[95] explained, at the heart of this role is "the belief that one's personal situation offers little or no hope for social or economic mobility." This victimized aspect of the *mestizo* and Indian role is wedded to the party, the guerrilla army, and the new state through the primary functions of the Senderista. These functions consist of being a "true" Communist, a combatant, and an administrator.[96] These role expectations are taught to individuals in schools, through *El Diario,* and through a variety of other indoctrination outlets.[97]

A "true" Communist is fully committed to being a Marxist-Leninist-Maoist. This is someone who vigorously fights against revisionism and embraces the two-line struggle and accepts self-criticism.[98] As a member of the PCP, the Senderista's task is to "raise the banner of [PCP] ideology, defend, and apply it, and to struggle energetically so that it will lead and guide the world revolution."[99] True Communists assume the responsibility of being initiators of the revolution, adhere to Gonzalo's Fourth Sword ideology, recognize the need for urgency in acting against the "sinister system" of the fascist government and its "imperialist masters," and demonstrate absolute loyalty and obedience to the party.[100]

In addition, Senderistas are obligated to free themselves from oppression. They do this by taking up arms and by joining the People's Army.[101] A soldier displays and sustains "great values, like honor, dispassion, virtue, and bravery."[102] Senderistas are to forfeit their lives as an offering to the movement. Guzmán maintained that it was necessary not only to fight for the revolution but also to die for it; this was referred to as "the quota."[103] Thus, sacrificing one's life for the revolution was not only an obligation but was expected. Moreover, Senderistas are encouraged to be optimistic and to espouse the conviction that the armed revolution is infallible and cannot fail. This is the case because it endeavors to apply "the universal truths of Marxism" by a party that is the vanguard of the proletariat.[104]

Senderistas strive toward the establishment of an ordered society within its "zones of liberation." During their Peruvian popularity in the 1980s and 1990s, they worked toward this goal by implementing a puritanical moralization campaign. The campaign outlawed drinking, delinquency, prostitution, adultery, drug abuse, domestic violence, and robbery.[105] Not surprisingly, these moral and legal constraints fostered behavioral expectations. Senderistas were to abide by and enforce a strict code of conduct espoused within the "eight warnings."[106] Included among these warnings were the following: (a) speak courteously, (b) honorably pay for what is bought, (c) return everything borrowed, (d) pay for everything damaged, (e) do not hit or harm the people, (f) do not trample crops, (g) take no liberties with women, and (h) do not mistreat prisoners.[107]

Finally, the Senderista role hosts a series of role sets. For example, within the movement there was a charismatic leader-follower relationship between Guzmán and the rank-and-file members who played the part of his disciples.[108] In addition, the Senderista serve in a patron-client relationship with the peasant coca growers.[109] Moreover, the PCP also has a number of counter-roles. Examples include opportunists, revisionists, sell-outs of the workers, and members of the Tupac Amaru Revolutionary Movement[110] and the Peruvian Civil Guard.[111]

Socialization and Role-Taking

From its inception, socialization has been a crucial aspect of the Peruvian Communist Party movement. Its initial socialization campaign began during Guzmán's tenure at the National University of San Cristóbal de Huamanga. The charismatic young professor attracted a committed group of student followers. They fervently absorbed his brand of communist ideology through his classes, political meetings, seminars, and study groups.[112] He eventually formed and directed the university's School for Practical Studies. Indoctrinated students would then return to their native rural communities[113] and spread Shining Path's revolutionary message to illiterate peasants under the guise of liberating teaching practice.[114] Indeed, many of these student teachers "returned to the countryside to become primary and secondary school instructors for the express purpose of leaving the movement's mark on the upcoming generation."[115] The Shining Path viewed children as more open to the wisdom of Gonzalo's insights because they had little to no political past. Thus, children were encouraged to participate in the popular war and to adopt the ideology of the proletariat.[116] The aim was to ensure that school-age youth took part in the armed struggle and, in turn, planted the seed of revolution in future generations.

By 1978, Guzmán's power over the university began to diminish, and the group went underground by relocating to the relatively inaccessible areas of the Peruvian countryside.[117] Its efforts to instill the values of the movement into poverty-stricken citizens continued throughout the 1980s, essentially in the form of "popular schools." The collective established these schools throughout Ayacucho and in the neighboring communities of Apurimac and Huancavelica.[118] The popular schools served as a forum to increase class consciousness among the peasantry, working class, and students.[119] They disseminated the Shining Path's ideology "by emphasizing the failures and inadequacies of the present state, the unjust and corrupt nature of the existing socioeconomic order, and José Carlos Mariátegui's Marxist interpretation of Peruvian reality."[120] The programs themselves stressed the need for class struggle, the incompetence of parliamentary democracy, the Shining Path's plan for securing the New Democracy, as well as various role expectations such as hostility toward revisionism and sacrificing one's life for the cause.[121]

During this time, the Shining Path was rumored to have established education camps targeted toward children identified as "orphans of the revolution."[122] Secondary school-age students were particularly susceptible to recruitment as the eroding economy left them with dismal educational and employment opportunities and a wealth of pent-up hostility toward the existing social order.[123] According to some police intelligence reports, there were about five hundred "people's schools" operating in Lima at one time.[124]

The socialization process continued even after the Senderistas entered the criminal justice system. For example, in a visit to one of Lima's major prisons, Renique[125] found that one of the institution's four-tiered, eighty-cell pavilions had been transformed into a Senderista-style revolutionary school. In the pavilion's courtyard, a quotation from Mao Zedong had been painted at the top of a ten-meter wall. Provocative in content, the passage read as follows: "The strength of iron militants permits them to conquer the highest altitudes."[126] A series of murals illustrating the phases of the "popular war" were also displayed on the walls. One of the paintings featured a portrait of a paternal and wise Comrade Gonzalo against a backdrop of a rising sun and masses of peasants and workers. Inside the pavilion, almost every wall was covered with quotations by Guzmán. One quotation emphasized the importance of a healthy body, clear and pure ideas, and strong morals, while others praised the "iron militants."

In addition, military training was a part of the daily routine for imprisoned Senderista. Moreover, a small library, complete with the works of Carlos Mariátegui and Mao Zedong, had been established for the intellectual development of those incarcerated. Indeed, as one inmate tour guide explained, "as prisoners we have not lost our position [as] soldiers in the Popular Army. . . . [W]e learn how to discuss, how to explain the party line without making concessions, how to be clear but strong. We practice physical and oral belligerence."[127]

For security purposes, the Peruvian government eventually decided to refurbish the island prison of El Frontón in order to house the Shining Path guerrillas. A full cell block was dedicated to the captured militants. In a visit to the facility, Gorriti[128] observed that the prisoners went about their everyday lives with "obvious military discipline." As he watched inmates waiting in line for lunch, they would shout slogans regarding Marxism-Leninism-Maoism, and the guiding thought of Comrade Gonzalo, "with the precise and sharp emphasis of a disciplined and trained group."[129] Similar to other correctional facilities in Peru, the Maoist rebels had turned the prison into a center for training, internal advancement, planning, and indoctrination. Indeed, as one correctional official explained, prisoners "arrive here without training, and they leave [as] expert[s]."[130]

Perhaps the most poignant example of how role-taking contributed to the acquisition of roles and the formation of self within Sendero Luminoso membership was located within the group's use of critique and self-criticism. The idea behind this post facto method of analysis was that in learning and implementing the communist party line, an individual, along with peers, engaged in mutual censure and self-appraisal. In particular, each person was expected to analyze his or her thoughts and actions by comparing them to the standards set within communist praxis.[131] Persons were to criticize their own shortcomings, accept the disparaging evaluations of others, and identify the failings of comrades. As the Moscow trials of the 1930s and the Chinese Cultural Revolution of the 1960s demonstrated, this political ritual represents an efficient form of intellectual policing used to elicit conformity.[132] Indeed, the intense social pressure associated with censure and self-criticism persuades individuals into changing their beliefs, attitudes, and conduct so that they are consistent with those in authority. As a result, unquestioned obedience is encouraged if not altogether guaranteed.

Similar to the communist movements before it, the Shining Path incorporated reprimand and self-valuation into its teachings. However, as Gorriti[133] observed, its version typically included "the admission of error, describing [one's] mistakes in the harshest of terms, implacably lashing [oneself], thanking others for having [been] attacked, [and] declaring that [one's] subjection to the party, its guiding thought and general line, slogans, plans, and programs, was complete, absolute." Except for Guzmán, every militant had to go through this process of self-degradation and reprimand in order to affirm himself or herself as a true Communist. Presumably, this ritual helps account for why there were few challenges to Guzmán's leadership and why so few individuals defected from the organization.[134] This notwithstanding, in order to complete this immersion process, Shining Path faithful cognitively assumed the role of their reference group and generalized other (in this case the PCP) in order to recognize their errors and to modify their thoughts and behavior so that their performances were consistent with the party's expectations.

Gorriti[135] offered two detailed descriptions of how self-criticism was used by the Shining Path to purge its ranks of moderates and, inevitably, to encourage the acquisition of roles. The first took place at the Central Committee's Second Plenary Session in March 1980. The meetings were intended to discuss and outline the organization's plan for launching the "people's war." As the proceedings commenced, a faction within the committee expressed doubt that the movement was ready for armed struggle, given its membership weaknesses and military inexperience. Guzmán immediately identified these concerns as those of rightist opportunists and argued that the "correct" position (understood to be his) was that the movement was prepared. As he contended, the "two-line struggle" was needed in order to readjust the party's internal mechanisms. After an ensuing debate, during which Guzmán overtly lambasted the dissenters, the opposing committee members were forced to abandon their pessimistic concerns, and the conference concluded with the decision that the armed struggle would be initiated.

A second example of how self-valuation and criticism were employed to cleanse the movement of non–party faithful and dissidents occurred immediately following the Central Committee's Second Plenary Session meetings. The Shining Path began a military school with the expressed purpose of translating the group's rhetoric into reality and providing the organization's leadership with the necessary skills for carrying out the "popular war." During the discussions surrounding the school's establishment, the "rightist opportunists" who previously voiced nonconforming views were compelled to engage in additional sessions of self-criticism. The veteran leaders were made to appear before students and face a barrage of accusations about having suspiciously strayed from communism's true course. With bowed heads, these experienced followers then thanked their young accusers for recognizing and articulating their misguided ways. Day after day the "rightist opportunists" were made to appear before the students, to admit new errors, and to engage in renewed expressions of self-appraisal designed to rectify their ideological shortcomings. Following the figurative beheading of non-repentant followers, students were encouraged to voice their opinions regarding the role of the two-line struggle and to engage in their own self-criticism. These exercises were incorporated into lessons about the importance of battling against the ill-advised Right and about what it meant to be a "true" Communist. As these examples suggest, the techniques of self-criticism and critique have been commonly used to secure conformity among the membership of the Shining Path collective throughout its militant history.

Self

Society Shapes the Self

According to Identity Theory, the level of commitment individuals have to their role identities is related to the number of social relationships they possess that hinge on those status-generating self-concepts. Consistent with the other militant extremist organizations explored in this book, the Communist Party of Peru significantly influenced the social relationships of membership identity, especially given the group's more clandestine cellular structure. While authority on matters related to ideology, policy, and strategy belonged to Guzmán, the organization was highly compartmentalized.[136] For example, on a day-to-day basis, the cells or units were self-sustaining and appeared to execute their tactical agendas autonomously. The guerrillas traveled from village to village in small bands of five to eight cadres, launching attacks and then disappearing into the countryside.[137] Each cell had one leader who linked the group to the next higher level in the chain of command.[138] Moreover, the maintenance of the Shining Path movement was facilitated by a network of safe houses, sleeping spots, and supply sources. Members were observed resting in caves where they received food, shelter, clothing, and other forms of assistance from sympathizers.

The operational details of the Shining Path's cellular structure, as well as its activities, were described by one former cadre affiliate who became involved in the group during his second year of high school.[139] After attending meetings in his community, the young man and his comrades began traveling to various villages, appropriating livestock and grain, as well as conducting operations on behalf of the organization. The size of the group grew quickly, and the cellular unit began holding meetings twice a week in different communities. Clearly, under these circumstances, steadfast involvement in the group limited the number of intimate social relationships a member could experience or enjoy with those from outside the organization. Indeed, Isbell's[140] observation that the Senderistas were known as *puriqkuna* in Ayacuho (a term interpreted to mean "people who walk or travel" but do not belong to one place), supports the nomadic nature of the cells. Consequently, according to Stryker's[141] Identity Theory premise, this tight-knit cellular structure served to activate the Senderista self-concept more frequently, causing individual members to become increasingly committed to that particular role identity.

Another instance that demonstrates how the PCP dominated social relationships is found in its decision to perform marriages between its members. As Strong[142] observed, couples married "in the name of Chairman Gonzalo and the Communist Party of Peru." Moreover, the ceremony was conducted by a party moderator who, at the conclusion of the event, declared the pair "husband and wife, [who, through their union, would] support, help and assist each other and thereby better serve the revolution."[143] The couple also had to take an oath of fidelity to their partner, to the party, and to its leader. The marriage was then sealed with a quotation from Marx. Thus, through the institution of marriage, the ceremony itself bound (and sanctified) the Senderista identity. Joined ideologically through their coupling, the husband and wife pairing promoted, indeed, ensured, group membership and PCP identity formation.

A more extreme example of how the PCP dominated the social relationships of cadres is found in Renique's[144] and Goritti's[145] respective descriptions of their visits to two Peruvian prisons. Similar to the total institution of a military boot camp, the daily routines of convicts were steeped in the Shining Path's iconography (e.g., paintings, murals). This fervent commitment to the movement was also expressed through drills and ceremonies, the chain of command, the institutional rhetoric, and the regular articulation of party-line views that inmates adopted. Indeed, as was previously reported, one cadre commented on life behind Peruvian bars and noted that "as prisoners we have not lost our position [as] soldiers in the Popular Army."[146]

A similar type of pro-PCP environment was created in July 1990 when some three hundred individuals under the direction of the Shining Path invaded a fifteen-hectare parcel of land adjacent to Lima's Central Highway.[147] Given the strategic value of its location, the settlement was enclosed with a twelve-foot-high adobe wall with guard towers that possessed only two entrances. New settlers were absorbed into the encampment, and the population grew to fifteen hundred within a few months. Describing the operation of the enclosed community and the Shining Path's regulation of it, Kent[148] observed the following:

> The Shining Path strictly controlled the social life of the settlement. The entrances were guarded at all times; no strangers were permitted inside; and all visitors were registered and accompanied during their stay. Residents participated in political indoctrination sessions, communal work parties, community garden projects, military exercises, and collective meals.

Moreover, while researching the daily life and social relations of militant cadres and collectives living in three Shining Path bases, del Pino[149] found that affective ties between inhabitants were prohibited. Residents (including children) could not refer to one another by familial role, such as "*papá*" or "*mama*"; instead, they adopted such terms as "*compañero*" or "*camarada*" in their interactions with them. Clearly, these examples of life in prison and on compounds/bases illustrate how the PCP, as an organization and social system, attempted to regulate every facet of a member's interpersonal exchanges. Not surprisingly, then, one's identification with the Shining Path ostensibly dominated all other social relationships. As a result, this role identification process was most salient in the member's identity hierarchy, assuming a commanding presence among all other possibilities.[150]

Self Shapes Society

The members of the PCP employed a number of techniques to verify their identities as Senderistas. One such tactic included interpersonal prompts. As McCormick[151] explained, before a new recruit was adopted into an operational cell, the person first underwent a lengthy vetting process composed of progressively more difficult tasks. These missions had to be carried out under the watchful eyes of other members. The completion of each task proved the recruit's loyalty and commitment to the organization and eventually placed the individual beyond the limits of the law. In the final step of this vetting process, the recruit was sent out to slay a police officer and was required to return with the murdered officer's weapon.[152] In this context, then, "The killing [represented] a self-defining act, severing the new member's ethical tie to society and bonding [the individual] to the organization."[153]

A Senderista's engagement in the act of self-criticism could also be interpreted as a means of verifying his or her identity. As Gorriti[154] explained, "the supposed honesty and objectivity of the exercise was a way not only to recognize one's errors but also to affirm oneself before others as a true Communist." Moreover, as Gorriti[155] and Renique[156] both recounted, cadres continued to verify their identities in prison. Indeed, as one imprisoned member noted, "agitation, production and military action: These are the basic principles for any member of the Popular Army, and we fulfill every one of them."[157]

In cases such as these, individuals purposely engaged in behaviors that elicited reactions from the audience (i.e., the correctional facility inhabitants; the Shining Path faithful). These reactions aligned PCP members' self-relevant meanings to those of the identity standard (i.e., the PCP movement's perspective on being a "true" Communist). Therefore, any activity completed on behalf of the organization, whether it was an assassination, an act of sabotage, or participation in a round of self-criticism, served to confirm among party loyalists that they were fulfilling the Senderista identity standard.

Another technique the PCP used for identity management was selective perception. During the early 1980s, the Peruvian government passed Law Decree Number 46. This antiterrorism legislation significantly enhanced the discretion of authorities and allowed the controlling regime to fight the PCP as militant extremists. In response, the PCP stated that the law was being used to "swing their rotten club on the sons and daughters of the masses, imposing monstrous punishments that even some reactionaries . . . criticized for being vile and counter-productive."[158] Moreover, the PCP argued that

> to label the armed struggle as "terrorism" is nothing but the demagogic and reactionary position of Yankee imperialism, raised up in order to oppose the armed revolution, seeking to cover it in a cloak of slander while they [the Peruvian government] mount the bloodiest repression and genocide.[159]

Commenting on Law Decree Number 46 and what it really signified, Guzmán[160] argued the following:

> This is how they attempt to discredit and isolate us in order to crush us. This is their dream. . . . We always have to remember that, especially in present-day war, it is precisely the reactionaries who use terrorism as one of their means of struggle, and it is, as has been proven repeat-edly, one of the forms used on a daily basis by the armed forces of the Peruvian State. Considering all this, we can conclude that those whose reasoning is colored by desperation because the earth is trembling beneath their feet wish to charge us with terrorism in order to hide the people's war.

The effect of Guzmán's observations, especially in relation to member-ship self-concept and its ability to shape the Shining Path's collective identity, should not be overlooked or dismissed. Indeed, by focusing on the government's repressive tactics and by ignoring its own ruthless and senseless violence perpetrated against innocent noncombatants, PCP faithful aligned their own self-relevant meanings with those of the iden-tity standard.

In addition, during his interview, Guzmán was asked to address charges that the PCP was a demented, messianic, blood-thirsty, Pol Pot-ian, dogmatic, sectarian, narco-terrorist organization that had trapped the peasantry in the midst of "two fires." Guzmán[161] offered the follow-ing response:

> To me they represent lies and the inability to understand [the] people's war, and I understand that the enemies of the revolution will never be able to understand [the] people's war. With respect to the charge that

the peasantry is caught between two fires, this is an elaborate invention because it is precisely the peasantry that makes up the vast majority of the People's Guerrilla Army. What must be understood is that the Peruvian State, with its armed forces and repressive apparatus, wants to drown the revolution in blood. This is our understanding, and we would recommend that these gentlemen study a little about warfare in general, revolutionary war, and mainly about [the] people's war and Maoism. Although I doubt that they would understand it, because to do so requires a certain class stand.

It is worth noting that in this passage Guzmán utilized the technique of rejecting and depreciating the audience's assessment of the PCP's behavior. In particular, he asserted that those who made these charges lacked sufficient sophistication to comprehend the nature and validity of the armed struggle. Moreover, the government's inaccurate conception of the peasantry's situation further detracted from the credibility of their overall assessment.

8

The Liberation Tigers of Tamil Eelam

Asia is yet another region of the globe where the construction of a terrorist identity can be noted. In this chapter, the manifestation and maintenance of militant extremist violence off the southeastern coast of India is featured. In particular, the ongoing hostilities found in Sri Lanka are showcased. At issue here is the destruction and discord surrounding the indigenous Sri Lankan Tamils who principally inhabit the northern and eastern provinces versus the majority Sinhalese who dwell mostly on the southwest portion of the island. As we demonstrate, a number of social psychological forces have sustained the presence of terrorism in the region. Indeed, symbols and their meanings, the definition of the situation, role performances, and socialization and role-taking experiences all have fueled the formation of the social person and his or her membership in the movement known as the Liberation Tigers of Tamil Eelam (LTTE). Similar to the previous application chapters, the analysis that follows systematically indicates where and how culture, self, and society interact to fashion identity, thereby helping to account for both the presence and the threat of terrorism.

Symbols

As evidenced in both primary and secondary source material, several symbols assume an important role in the identities of LTTE militants. One particularly salient example is the discriminatory policies enacted by the Sinhalese-dominated government.[1] Passed in June 1956, the Sinhala-Only Act was the first of many initiatives to have a detrimental impact on the Tamil minority. Specifically, the act provided that Sinhalese would be the island's sole, official language and that it would be used in all governmental proceedings, including civil service, court-room, and tribunal settings, as well as all orders, reports, pleadings, and judgments.[2]

The Sinhala-Only Act was intended to win favor among the upper echelon of the Sinhalese community and the vernacular-educated villagers who exclusively spoke Sinhalese and who had little chance of securing admissions to universities, civil service jobs, or professional positions.[3] As a result, urban middle-class Tamils were particularly impacted by the efforts to redistribute jobs among the Sinhalese majority. For example, Shastri[4] noted that the proportion of Tamils in public service rapidly dropped following the legislation. In addition, those Tamil civil servants who refused to study or do business in Sinhala, despite offers of promotion and incentives, were dismissed from their positions.[5]

The backlash to the Sinhala-Only Act from the Tamil community was strong. To illustrate, Sinhalese Ministry of Transport officials dispatched buses to Tamil-dominated areas that displayed the Sinhala-language *Sri* lettering on their license plates.[6] In response, angry Tamils painted over the lettering on license plates and other public signs. In their place, they wrote the same letter in the Tamil script.[7] The government's pro-Sinhalese actions initiated what came to be known as the anti-*Sri* campaigns. These campaigns sparked numerous instances of civil disobedience that eventually led to violence against Sri Lankan Tamils.

For young Tamils who were especially affected by the state's discriminatory policies, two additional legislative efforts proved to be the catalysts behind a full-fledged Tamil nationalism movement.[8] The first was the passing of the 1972 Constitution, which gave special protection to those of the Buddhist faith. This enactment was a serious blow to the Tamils, given that most Tamils are Hindu.[9] The second legislative initiative was termed "standardization." Essentially amounting to reverse discrimination, the policy implemented a weighted scoring system for university applicants. In effect, "a Tamil medium student had to obtain a higher total [number] of marks than a . . . Sinhala medium [student in order] to enter the university, specially the medical, engineering and science faculties."[10]

The government-sponsored practice of standardization became one of the primary forces that mobilized the Tamil youth community. This is the case because they not only were barred from public service positions but also were denied the opportunity to seek higher education. Thus, these two legislative efforts symbolically instilled within the Tamil minority the importance of Tamil unity—regardless of class or caste distinction—and they sowed the seeds of Tamil separatism.

A second significant symbol included the anti-Tamil rallies and protests. These pogroms took place in 1956, 1958, 1977, 1981, and 1983.[11] Following the initiation of the Sinhala-Only Act, Tamil leaders staged a protest in the open space known as Galle Face Green, close to the Parliament building in Columbo. The protest erupted in anti-Tamil violence led by organized mobs of Sinhalese.[12] The violence quickly spread to other areas of the island, resulting in an estimated 150 deaths, many of which were Tamils.[13] The most infamous of these rallying events was the one that took place in July 1983.

The initial riot was ignited by the massacre of thirteen Sri Lankan Army soldiers who were ambushed by a cadre of LTTE militants in Jaffna on the night of July 23, 1983. In his partisan account of the motivations for the ambush, Piyadasa[14] explained that days earlier the Sri Lankan Army unit had been responsible for the deaths of two LTTE guerrillas and the gang-rape of a Jaffna Tamil girl. Thus, the LTTE ambush was a retaliatory action. The waylay marked the largest number of casualties suffered in one attack by Sri Lankan military or police forces since the beginning of the armed insurgency.[15] The next morning, the Sri Lankan Army responded by rampaging through the ambushed area, indiscriminately killing approximately fifty Tamil civilians.[16] When the bodies of the slain Sinhalese soldiers arrived at the cemetery in Borella, Columbo, they were met by an angry mob of about ten thousand Sinhalese. Rioting ensued within hours, and by July 25 the city's Tamil residents were under attack.

Mobs of Sinhalese rioters were armed with axes, poles, iron rods, clubs, knives, daggers, petrol bombs, and firearms. They beat, murdered, and raped innocent Tamils.[17] Moreover, at Welikade prison, a hostile mob of Sinhalese protesters pushed past guards to murder Tamil militants who were serving time in the facility.[18] Representatives in the Tamil community accused the Sri Lankan government of playing a covert role in the riots. Tamil members believed the administration's complicity was evident in the Sinhalese gang's reliance on official vehicles and electoral lists, which they used to systematically comb the area, resulting in the identification and destruction of many Tamil residences and businesses.[19] Although the exact casualty totals and material losses were impossible to cite—especially since the Sri Lankan government did not hold a public inquiry—it is estimated that the week-long mêlée resulted in the death of over four thousand Tamils, with damage to Tamil homes and establishments exceeding several million rupees.[20] As a consequence, hundreds of Tamils were left homeless and were forced into refugee camps.[21]

Senaratne[22] described the anti-Tamil riots of July 1983 as a watershed event in postcolonial Sri Lankan history. The horrific accounts of victimization spread rapidly throughout the Tamil community. Indeed, stories were recounted of how women had been sexually assaulted in the streets; of how passengers on a minibus had been murdered when trapped inside while it was set ablaze despite their cries for mercy; of how thousands of Tamil dwellings had been ransacked and burned, some while women and children were still inside; and of how hundreds of thousands of Tamils had become refugees. These atrocious events unfolded while several Sri Lankan police and military personnel observed the destruction and mayhem and, in some instances, participated in the massacre.[23] As a result, the Tamil community found a new appreciation for the militants' struggle for nationalism. According to Swamy's[24] estimation, none of the Tamil militant groups had more than fifty active members prior to the event. However, following the rioting and bloodshed,

> hundreds of young Tamils—school and college students—in Sri Lanka's northeast began approaching local militant leaders whom they had shunned until then, clamoring for membership and arms. Many boys ran off from their homes, leaving terse notes that they were going away to fight for Eelam.[25]

Clearly, the symbolic nature of the ensuing violence perpetrated against Tamils was as provocative as it was powerful. In short, it represented yet another impetus for young people to involve themselves in the struggle for Tamil Eelam and its liberation.[26]

A third symbol informing the identity of LTTE dissidents and the violent military extremists in the region are the various broken and thus unmet promises the Sinhalese-dominated government has made to the Tamil minority.[27] The abrogation of agreements or accords is a recurring theme in LTTE literature. As such, it functions as a symbolic underpinning for the Sri Lankan conflict.[28]

One such example is the Bandaranaike-Chelvanayakam Agreement of 1957 (BC Pact). This agreement was signed on July 26, 1957, by Prime Minister Bandaranaike and Federal Party leader S. J. V. Chelvanayakam.[29] As an "interim adjustment" to the Sinhala-Only Act, the agreement was designed to allow the Tamil dialect to be recognized as belonging to that of a national minority and, consequently, to represent a parallel language of administration to Sinhala in the northern and eastern provinces. Moreover, provisions would be made for "reasonable use" of the Tamil vernacular in the seven Sinhalese provinces. Interestingly, Prime Minister Bandaranaike tore up the agreement before it could be implemented. He claimed that the disobedience expressed by the Tamils in the anti-Sri campaigns led him to this decision. However, a more plausible explanation is that the prime minister buckled under pressure from the Buddhist clergy who alleged that the agreement was designed to wrongly appease the Tamils and would only serve to divide the country.[30]

Another act perceived as a shattered promise was the breach of the 1987 Indo–Sri Lanka Peace Accord. In an effort to bring an end to the Tamil conflict, Indian prime minister Rajiv Gandhi[31] and Sri Lankan president Junius Jayewardene signed the agreement on July 29, 1987, in Colombo, Sri Lanka. The accord, which was the basis for the Indian Peace Keeping Force's intervention, included a provision that India would not allow its land to be used as a staging ground for activities that jeopardized the unity, integrity, or security of Sri Lanka.[32] While the LTTE was intentionally excluded from the negotiating table, it did reluctantly agree to the agreement's terms. The catalyst for the island's return to violence was the interception of an LTTE boat off Point Pedro on October 4, 1987.[33] Along with the Indian Navy, the Sri Lankan Navy captured the militants and their cargo of arms while traveling from Tamil Nadu, India, to Point Pedro, Sri Lanka.

The LTTE alleged that the cadres were moving furniture and documents from a former base in Tamil Nadu and that the weapons and ammunition were in their possession for purposes of self-defense.[34] Interpreting the incident as a direct violation of the accord, the Sri Lankan national security minister insisted that the militants be brought to Colombo for interrogation. While in custody, the twelve militants consumed cyanide capsules.[35] In the aftermath of their suicides, violence broke out between the LTTE and the Indian Peace Keeping Force (IPKF). What little harmony the accord provided over the brief three-month period came to an abrupt halt. As the LTTE alleged, Sri Lankan leaders broke their pledge to Tamil leaders and Indians by demanding that the cadres be brought to Colombo for interrogation.

Definition of the Situation

According to members of the Liberation Tigers of Tamil Eelam, the problem they confront is that Tamil citizens are innocent victims of government-sponsored Sinhalese persecution. This is an oppression that emerged when Sinhala national chauvinism identified the Tamil community's dominance over the state apparatus and plantation economy as a threat to the region's development.[36] Through discriminatory legislative action (e.g., the Sinhala-Only Act, the practice of standardization) and the denial of equal human rights, the Sinhala majority has "unleashed a systematic form of oppression that deprive[s] the Tamils of their linguistic, educational and employment rights."[37] In addition, the government's efforts to encourage physical violence against the Tamil community were evident, at least to the LTTE, in the July 1983 anti-Tamil protests. Finally, the Sinhala leadership victimized the Tamil people when it failed to deliver on its pledges to the Tamil citizenry. Indeed, as Thirunavukkarasu[38] observed, "Making promises and then reneging on them—this is one of the techniques of oppression and deceit adopted by the Sinhalese leadership which feels no compunction in breaking its pledges overnight." Thus, as the LTTE has interpreted it, "The objective of the chauvinistic ruling class is nothing other than to inflict maximum injury [on] the Tamils[,] to terrorize, subjugate and destroy the aspirations of our people for political independence."[39]

The LTTE equates the government's oppressive efforts as akin to a racial holocaust.[40] Indeed, as the LTTE has asserted, "The features of Sinhala state oppression clearly indicate a devious plan calculated to destroy the national identity of the Tamil people."[41] The group's sense of desperation is further conveyed in the belief that the oppressive measures have been implemented with "genocidal intent involving a [strategic] plan aiming at the gradual and systematic destruction of the essential foundations of the Tamil national community."[42] For LTTE loyalists, the massive extermination of Tamil life, theft of land, and destruction of their property following the communal massacres are clear indicators that the Sinhalese intend to ensure genocidal outcomes.[43] In a more recent report of oppression, the LTTE claimed that the Sri Lankan government unleashed a full-fledged war to suppress the Tamil struggle for political independence. Specifically, in the Northeast,

> a series of war crimes of grave nature [were] committed against Tamils under the camouflage of offensive military operations. The military occupied areas in the Northeast have turned into massive concentration camps where Tamils [have been] subjected to arbitrary arrests, detention without trial, rape, torture and murder. There is [also] documentary evidence to substantiate over 500 cases of disappearance in Jaffna.[44]

Moreover, in southern Sri Lanka, political opponents are subjected to harassment, intimidation, arrest, detention, and assault at the hands of Sri Lankan armed forces.[45]

The LTTE contends that the Tamils will never peacefully coexist with the Sinhalese in a single state; therefore, the only solution to the Sri Lankan conflict is a homeland in which they have the right to self-determination.[46] Indeed, as Prabhakaran noted in his 1993 Heroes Day speech,[47] "We are firmly convinced that the creation of an independent sovereign state of Tamil Eelam is the only and final solution to the Tamil national question."[48] The LTTE has maintained that its goal of seeking national liberation through armed struggle was not an arbitrary decision. It was based on the articulation of the collective will of the Tamil people as embodied in the mandate for political independence and statehood. This mandate was determined at the 1977 general elections.[49]

Prabhakaran articulated the LTTE's solution when explaining that the Tamil Eelam he envisioned would be an "economically self-sufficient and self-reliant [society. It would be] a democratic system in which the people [would] have the right to rule themselves. And there [would] be economic equality among the working people."[50] He went on to point out that "we [the LTTE organization] want to establish a socialist society. Ours will be a unique socialist model, neither Soviet nor Chinese nor any other."[51] This was to be a pro–women's rights society that encouraged its citizens to practice the religion of their choice.[52] In short, Prabhakaran envisioned the establishment of "an egalitarian society where there [would be] no class contradiction and exploitation of man by man; a free, rational society where human freedom and rights [would be] protected and progress enhanced."[53]

History also plays an important role in the LTTE's response to the Sri Lankan conflict and the meaning or definition that attaches to the situation in which the movement finds itself. The LTTE places considerable emphasis on the ancestral greatness and glory of the Tamil kingdom. The most salient example of this is the group's use of the springing tiger as its emblem. Francis[54] elaborated on the springing tiger's link to Tamil's renowned past:

> The LTTE connects its ideology with a judicious use of symbols rooted in Tamil myth such as the tiger, the symbol of one of the most favourite Tamil gods, Murugan. It was the emblem of the ancient Chola emperors, the concept of *maram* (wrath), the concept of *vira tayar* (brave mother) and the *vira pen* (brave woman) who sacrifice their loved ones for the war. This is a recurring theme in Purananuru poetry of the Sangam period between 500 B.C. and 200 A.D."

Commenting on the symbol of the springing tiger itself, Hellmann-Rajanayagam[55] noted that it signified

> an integral part of the royal emblem of the Chola Kings under whom Tamil language, Hinduism, Tamil culture, and the vast Tamil kingdom flourished. This indicates that the true power base of the LTTE is not Marxist ideology, but the ancient glory of a people and a race.

Relative to their solution (i.e., nationalism), the LTTE's connection to the ancient Tamil kingdom is located in the group's proposed borders for Tamil Eelam.[56] The LTTE insists that the sovereign state should not only encompass the North and East but also western districts as far as Mannar and southern districts as far as Puttalam, Chilaw, and Negombo. The organization stipulates that these regions should be included as a part of the state because the inhabitants share a linguistic heritage with the Tamils.

The LTTE also maintains that armed struggle is the only means by which to achieve self-determination and continued life as a citizenry. Although the group has been open to possible political negotiations with the assistance of international mediation forces, it has remained skeptical about the probable success of such initiatives. This skepticism is traceable to past cease-fire failures and broken promises.[57] Until recently, the Sri Lankan government has been hesitant to engage in such peace discussions, arguing that the Tamil problem is an internal conflict.[58] However, the LTTE claims that the Sri Lankan government's reluctance stems from their refusal to recognize the standing of the LTTE as a major force to be reckoned with in the region. Moreover, observers note that the Sri Lankan administration fears that the Tamil people will find a sympathetic ear in the international community wherein any negotiations would invoke the anger of the Sinhala Buddhists.[59]

The LTTE believes that its armed struggle is justified because it is one of self-defense. As the collective contends,

> the Tamils have resorted to arms to defend themselves and the war being waged by the Liberation Tigers is a defensive war. Unlike the measures adopted by the Sri Lankan government, this struggle is not aimed at domination; instead, it serves to protect the sovereign identity of the Tamil people."[60]

Thus, it is the Sinhalese-dominated Sri Lankan government's oppression that has generated the group's demand for secession.[61] Moreover, the LTTE vigorously alleges that the Sri Lankan administration is responsible for compelling the Tamil people to respond violently. Indeed, as one publication explained,

> The Tamils took up arms when they were presented with no alternative other than to defend themselves against a savage form of genocidal oppression, when peaceful agitations were violently repressed, when constitutional paths and parliamentary doors were effectively closed, when Sinhala ruling elites callously rejected the demands for justice and equality. Therefore, the Tamil armed struggle for political independence and self-government is the historical product of decades of racist oppression and injustice.[62]

Clearly, as this passage indicates, only after being forced to retaliate and defend themselves did the Tamils resort to violence. Moreover, this was an effort to ensure self-protection where aggression was only employed as a last resort.

From the LTTE's perspective, the Sinhalese-dominated Sri Lankan government has concealed its genocidal motives through its solution to the Tamil problem. As a consequence, the existence of the Tamil community (and its people) has been placed in jeopardy. Not surprisingly, then, the LTTE's fight for a homeland is perceived as integral to the citizenry's very survival. This is why compromising on the establishment of a sovereign Tamil state is unacceptable to group members. Indeed, speaking on behalf of the LTTE, Prabhakaran[63] observed that "after facing so many genocidal attacks, the Tamils realise there is no solution other than Eelam for them if they are to live in peace and security." Understanding this orientation to the Tamil problem and conflict illustrates how the LTTE group has come to perceive itself as a collection of freedom fighters engaged in a legitimate struggle for self-determination. In the final analysis, if members fail to accomplish their goal, they believe this will lead to their eventual and complete extinction. This is how members define the situation they confront.

Roles

Several social roles are integral to one's membership in the Liberation Tigers of Tamil Eelam. Specific examples include being a Sri Lankan Tamil,[64] a freedom fighter, and a martyr. Each role comes with its own set of values, beliefs, and expectations that have been revived and re-created through the Tamil struggle.[65] These matters are examined in this section.

Anthropological research suggests that Tamils from the Tamil Nadu region of southern India began settling the northern areas of Sri Lanka as early as the third century B.C., and that from Jaffna they began moving into the eastern provinces.[66] Differing migratory trends caused distinctions to emerge between the Jaffna Tamils (i.e., those from the Jaffna peninsula and the Northern Province) who were dominated by the Vellalar caste and the Batticaloa Tamils (i.e., those from the eastern coastal region) who are dominated by the Mukkuvar caste.[67] One distinction was that the Jaffna Tamils benefited from the English schools set up by the Christian missions in the northern region.[68] This enabled the Jaffna Tamils to find prestigious employment within the colonial infrastructure.[69] Another distinction was that the East had remained relatively shielded from the orthodox religious influences of India, enabling the area to retain the popular forms of Hinduism and cultural folk traditions that are now extinct in the North.[70] These distinctions eventually led to stereotypes.[71] For example, the urbanized Tamils in the North tended to perceive their eastern counterparts as "backwards and uncivilized, while those in the east perceived the northerners' attitude as that of high caste arrogance."[72]

These regional distinctions aside, the Tamils' caste structure further subdivided the community.[73] For example, in Jaffna members of the lowest caste, the "untouchables," were not allowed to buy land, cremate their dead, enter temples, or frequent high-caste homes.[74] When those in the untouchable caste began demanding social rights, the Vellalar caste used violence to suppress their efforts.[75] Moreover, prior to the nineteenth century, identification as a Tamil was synonymous with being a landowning citizen Vellalar.[76] As a result, lower-caste people were simply not considered Tamil. Although the regional and caste distinctions caused divisions within the Sri Lankan Tamil community, it would eventually be united in the face of a common threat.

As a role set, casting the Sinhalese in the adversarial position dates back to ancient Tamil traditions; however, "by the nineteenth century these accounts had passed into legend and the Sinhala enemy had become mythical and abstract."[77] The enemy reemerged when the government began passing legislation that was perceived to be anti-Tamil. This forced the consolidation of a composite Sri Lankan Tamil role.[78] Thus, as Palacinkam[79] observed, "Sinhala chauvinism and its violent manifestations have helped the polarisation of the heterogeneous masses of the oppressed Tamil nation, with different class elements and castes towards a determined revolutionary struggle for political independence." Indeed, as one Jaffna inhabitant explained,

> adversity has been a great leveler of Jaffna's stratified, hierarchical society. Everyone, from the upper-class government servant down to the humblest laborer, stands in the same queue for kerosene and cooking oil. Everyone, from the Government Agent [district administrator] downwards, travels by bicycle.[80]

A second significant social role for members of the LTTE entails being a freedom fighter.[81] For many cadres, Prabhakaran is the embodiment of Eelam and the Tamil people.[82] Indeed, he has achieved demigodlike status among his cadres[83] and is the central figure in the Tamil struggle.[84] As a result, he is the chief iconic spokesperson for this role. Not surprisingly, then, many of the values, beliefs, expectations, and attitudes of the freedom fighter status can be extrapolated from his words and deeds. As the title of the role implies, there is an intense focus on the value of freedom. Indeed, as Prabhakaran commented in his 1992 speech, "Freedom is a noble ideal. It is the highest virtue in human life.

It is the basis for human progress and development. It is freedom that gives meaning and wholeness to life. The yearning for freedom arises as the deepest aspiration of the human spirit."[85]

A belief espoused by freedom fighters is that the Tamil people will continue to fall victim to the ruthless genocidal aims of the Sinhalese government if they are not opposed. This belief can be extrapolated from Prabhakaran's 1992 Great Heroes Day[86] address in which he proclaimed, "Our enemy is heartless and committed to war and violence. . . . We have no alternative other than to continue our struggle."[87] In addition, the Tamil citizenry believe that their actions are justified and righteous. For example, in Prabhakaran's 1993 Great Heroes Day speech he told the people that "we are standing on a strong moral foundation. We are fighting for a just cause. Our political objectives conform with international norms and principles. . . . We must be firm in the cause of our struggle because truth and justice are on our side."[88] Connected to this belief is a sense of retribution and vengeance, given the suffering endured by the Tamil community. As one young man who contemplated joining the ranks of the LTTE intimated, "The harassment that I and my parents have suffered at the hands of the [Sri Lankan] army makes me want to take revenge."[89] For this individual, vengeance was a matter of Tamil pride.

Prabhakaran has also identified certain expectations for his freedom fighters. In taking the oath of allegiance, cadres accept that their primary duty is to further the achievement of a Tamil motherland.[90] Prabhakaran's adoption of the springing tiger as the organization's emblem[91] conveys the message that "the LTTE cadre is expected to conform to the ideals of the past. A failure is not that of an individual, letting down the organization, it is the failure to live up to the ideals of a glorious past."[92]

The expectations of the role are also conveyed in the LTTE's code of conduct. These monastic-like practices include no smoking, drinking, or marriage, as well as chastity and a renunciation of all familial ties.[93] Based on the traditional Tamil and Hindu classics, these norms of conduct encourage cadres to adhere to the traditional hero-ascetic image found in ancient Tamil myths. For pragmatic purposes, Prabhakaran incorporated the code's relational aspects into the LTTE constitution. This is because he believed that any family relations or love affairs would impede one's commitment to the cause.[94] However, the code was eventually altered and cadres were allowed to marry after a certain age and following a certain number of years of service.[95]

The attitude with which freedom fighters are to fulfill their duty is described in Prabhakaran's 1992 Heroes Day speech. Commenting on the resolve of the Tamil loyalists, he noted that "the strength of our struggle arises from the fierce determination of our fighters. Their firm commitment and their courage to act without the fear of death are the force and resource of our struggle."[96] This statement alludes to the expectation that cadres are to espouse absolute devotion, total commitment, and unwavering resistance to compromise.[97] This attitude is exemplified in the wearing of the cyanide vial by organizational members.[98] Indeed, as Roberts[99] explained, "Once the cyanide vial was adopted and put into practice by the early Tiger martyrs in their own world, the pro-Tiger circles, the cyanide capsule around the neck was a testimony of commitment, a symbol of *esprit de corps*." Following the completion of their training, new soldiers are draped with the necklace in the "passing out parade" by the local commando leader.[100] All cadres are expected to wear the necklace and use its contents if the situation necessitates it. This intense focus on self-sacrifice has led to what some have termed a "cult of martyrdom."

A third role pertinent to LTTE membership is that of *mavirar*. The word translates into "great hero," but is frequently used to describe an LTTE martyr. Schalk[101] described this role as follows:

> There are four elements to this hero role that are significant for the LTTE: [1] the projected belonging to a group of *maravar*, i.e. professional fighters; [2] the relentless toiling, the not giving up, or the permanent resistance; [3] the fact that the hero is predestined to do evil in the form of killing, but the element of self-redemption is not made explicit anywhere in any LTTE text, still less the element of self-redemption for the people or for humanity; [and 4] the hero has to die a violent death, for which he gets no compensation in this or the next life. The LTTE hero is a "secular" hero.

This honorable title is bestowed by the LTTE leadership an all cadres who have died in battle or in an attempt to avoid capture.[102] According to the LTTE, in order to become a martyr, "[one] gets killed in the very act of killing that intends to make the holy aim come true."[103] Moreover, the only reward for martyrdom is the satisfaction that the person died destroying the enemy and will experience the promise of honor in death.

Schalk[104] further explained that other Tamil words are employed by the LTTE that frequently translate into "martyr"; however, all of them have parallel meanings. For example, "*tiyaki*" (one who abandons) and "*tiyakam*" (abandonment) are typically converted into "martyr" by LTTE members.[105] "*Tiyaki*" is a variation of the Sanskrit word "*tyagi.*" The term was revived from ancient Indian culture in the people's struggle for independence from British rule. The LTTE has attached a specific meaning to the term. In short, it implies a voluntary abandonment of life in the act of taking another's while trying to reach an end state that has been declared holy. Moreover, *tiyakam* represents a reaction to encountering the death of a comrade. In an act of rage, the *tiyaki* is slain in the process of killing. Similar to "*mavirar,*" the title "*tiyaki*" is reserved only for the veneration of the dead. Thus, there is a distinction between the *tiyaki* and the *tiyaki*-to-be. In life, it is anticipated that the *tiyaki*-to-be will possess extraordinary moral and mental qualities.

LTTE cadres are expected to conform to the ideals of the past, to demonstrate self-restraint by resisting temptations, and to ready themselves to suffer a representational death for the people of Tamil Eelam.[106] Although one does achieve *tiyakam* by ingesting cyanide when facing capture, the ideal act of the *tiyaki* is to purposefully use one's life as a weapon, for example, becoming a suicide bomber.[107]

The LTTE's concept of martyrdom is rooted in the sacrificial themes of ancient Tamil culture and history.[108] For example, themes such as dedication and asceticism have been invigorated from the Tamil *bhakti* religious tradition and help equip the LTTE cadres with a sense that their struggle for independence is more celestial or cosmic in nature.[109] Moreover, Francis[110] explained that the LTTE's cult of martyrdom "has deep roots in Tamil myth and ideology. The Purnananuru, an ancient Tamil epic, makes several references to the practice of ancient Tamil warriors sacrificing themselves for the leader. It was considered the ultimate tribute." Other religious and secular dimensions of Tamil martyrdom are also discernible. Indeed, as Schalk[111] described, there is also a "Christian element expressed in the concept of a *catci,* 'witness,' 'martyr,' " a Subhasism element "expressed in the justification of armed struggle and in the concept of *balidan,* 'gift (of life) as sacrifice,' " a Dravidian nationalist element which provides for the "concept of a linguistic Tamil nation-state," and a martial feminist component. Finally, there is the utilization of sacrificial language as communicated in such terms as "*arppanippu,*" which means "dedication (of man to go)" and "*pali,*" which means "sacrifice."[112]

Socialization and Role-Taking

As illustrated by the life of the LTTE's leader, Velupillai Prabhakaran, the process of learning and adopting the social roles necessary for membership in the LTTE begins at an early age. Prabhakaran was born on November 26, 1954, to parents who were members of the Karaiyar caste and resided outside of Jaffna in a village known for fishing and smuggling.[113] The youngest of four children, Prabhakaran was his father's favorite and was often found by his side.[114] Prabhakaran's father was a popular man who frequently engaged in discussions with friends about the worsening ethnic relations in the country. He lamented over the ill fate of the Tamils. These conversations, to which Prabhakaran would listen attentively, would serve as his initial introduction to the plight and struggle of Tamil citizens.

As Prabhakaran grew older, he attended political meetings where speakers reinforced many of the opinions expressed at home by detailing Sinhalese atrocities and by emphasizing the importance of building Tamil resistance.[115] Prabhakaran recollected how these experiences impacted him. As he explained,

> The shocking events of the 1958 racial riots had a profound impact on me when I was a schoolboy. I heard of horrifying incidents of how our people had been mercilessly and brutally put to death by Sinhala racists. Once I met [a] widowed mother, a friend of my family, who related to me her agonizing personal experience of this racial holocaust. During the riots a Sinhala mob attacked her house in Colombo. The rioters set fire to the house and murdered her husband. She and her children escaped with severe burn injuries. I was deeply shocked when I saw the scars on her body. I also heard stories of how young babies were roasted alive in boiling tar. When I heard such stories of cruelty, I felt a deep sense of sympathy and love for my people. A great passion overwhelmed me to redeem my people from this racist system.[116]

Prabhakaran was exposed to similar values and opinions while he attended school. For example, he recalled that while in the eighth standard, he had a teacher, Mr. Vernugopal, who instilled within his students the belief that the Tamils should take up arms against the Sinhalese.[117] In an interview, Prabhakaran[118] recalled the influence of Vernugopal's lessons:

It [was] he who impressed on me the need for armed struggle and persuaded me to put my trust in it. My village used to face military repression daily. Hence, even as a child I grew to detest the Army. This hatred of military repression, combined with Mr. Vernugopal's persuasive stress on armed struggle and the thirst for liberation, generated an inner dynamism within me and friends of my age flocked behind Mr. Vernugopal.

Clearly, while significant others socialized Prabhakaran into the Tamil-Sinhalese conflict (e.g., his father, his teacher), the great heroes of history taught him the intricacies of being the leader of a struggle for freedom and justice. As a child, Prabhakaran[119] described himself as being a voracious reader. He enjoyed reading biographies that chronicled the exploits of Alexander the Great and Napoleon Bonaparte. He was particularly drawn to the martyrs of the Indian freedom struggle like Subhash Chandra Bose,[120] Bagat Singh, and Balagengadhara Tilak. As he explained it,

Above all [else], Subhash Chandra Bose's life was a beacon to me, lighting up the path I should follow. His disciplined life and his total commitment and dedication to the cause of his country's freedom deeply impressed me and served as my guiding light.[121]

These Indian folk tales instilled in him the desire to fight (and to resist) what he perceived to be foreign oppression. They also taught him about the ideal behaviors one should embody as a revolutionary. As Prabhakaran[122] noted,

The books that I read dealing with national liberation struggles conveyed one clear message to me: "A freedom fighter should be pure, selfless and ready to sacrifice himself for the people." So I would say that the various books I read impelled me to struggle for the freedom of my people.

Another way in which Prabhakaran learned the role of a revolutionary was through role-taking experiences. For example, as a child he recited dialogue from the movie *Veerapandia Kattabomman*.[123] Through the film, he imagined himself to be the legendary warrior who fought against the British invaders.[124] In addition, Prabhakaran practiced martial arts and when his parents noticed their sons' fascination with anything related to combat, they nicknamed him *"veeravan"* or "brave one." Moreover, he and his friends worked at building bombs intended for enemy forces. And, in preparation for his life as a revolutionary, Prabhakaran "would tie himself up, get into a sack and lie under the sun the whole day. . . . He even inserted pins into his nails. At other times, he would catch insects and prick them to death with needles to gain the mental preparation to torture the 'enemy.' "[125]

When Prabhakaran[126] was fourteen years old, his burgeoning thirst for freedom led him and seven other like-minded youngsters from school to form a militant collective. As the leader, Prabhakaran explained that their focus was to buy guns, build bombs, and stage an attack on the Sinhalese Army. However, the group eventually abandoned its plan, given the members' inability to raise enough money to purchase a weapon. At sixteen, Prabhakaran dropped out of school and began mixing with Tamil militant activist gangs.[127] On July 27, 1973, he shot and killed the Tamil mayor of Jaffna because he was a member of the Sri Lanka Freedom Party. The political assassination earned him nationwide notoriety and the prestige of being a wanted man. In sum, as Prabhakaran[128] explained, "This is how I spent my youth, filled with thoughts about struggle, freedom and the urge to do something for our people."

As detailed in Prabhakaran's childhood experiences, he was not the only one influenced by the processes of socialization and role-taking. Indeed, comparable experiences have been documented by other Tamils who joined the LTTE. Commenting on this indoctrination process, one Tamil militant indicated that "we used to hear our elders constantly speak about Sinhalese atrocities. . . . [The description of these horrible acts] influenced us greatly."[129] In addition, the passage of discriminatory legislation reinforced and confirmed group members' views regarding the continued victimization of the Sri Lankan Tamils, whose only available recourse entailed the use of violence.

Presumably, these early childhood experiences informed the LTTE's campaign to groom new cadres. In fact, when asked about his fervent interest in the welfare of small children whose lives have been adversely affected by the ethnic war, Prabhakaran[130] explained,

The future generation is the foundation of the nation we hope to build. Therefore, I consider bringing up the future generation and molding its character and ideals as important as building up the nation. . . . My ambition is to mold a new generation of youth who will be the architects of our country's future. . . . I consider it our paramount duty to educate these children and bring them up on the correct lines as the architects of the future of our nation. That is why I pay very special attention to them.

In line with these beliefs, the LTTE has implemented a multifaceted conditioning program. The program is designed to instill within youth the values, attitudes, and expectations that constitute the Sri Lankan Tamil, the freedom fighter, and the *mavirar/tiyaki* roles.

As described by the University Teachers for Human Rights,[131] the LTTE's indoctrination strategies include both socialization and role-taking techniques. As they observed,

> The methods employed included displaying cutouts and poster pictures of dead cadres all over, patriotic songs, exhibits of representations of Sri Lankan Army atrocities, meetings in schools, LTTE versions of history in school curricula with compulsory tests and a general exhibition of military glamour. Even children's playgrounds and parks were designed with mock weapons to give children a feeling that they were playing in battle grounds. A common picture seen everywhere in Jaffna in 1990 was an LTTE soldier holding children on either side and walking towards a hill top where a gun was planted upside down. This symbolically portrayed the vision of the LTTE.[132]

Moreover, this conditioning process is particularly evident in environments where the LTTE has a captive audience. For example, the LTTE sponsors a number of orphanages in Jaffna, "where children are taught to sing songs with godly veneration for the Leader and his vision."[133] The educational system in northern Sri Lanka is essentially run by the LTTE, providing the group with an opportunity to impose its version of history and its definition of the situation on students.[134]

Members of the LTTE's political wing frequently address school children and target midteens. These youth are subjected to intense propaganda and are encouraged to screen "action" videos. Developed by the LTTE's video unit, the films often entail glorious military battles.[135] In a government-funded school in an LTTE-controlled region of Sri Lanka, C. L. Joshi[136] observed several six- to eight-year-old boys viewing war movies in a classroom. Their teacher noted that the "young students

[were] shown LTTE war movies and [were] given speeches by members of the political wing of the Tigers."[137] The most extreme example of the LTTE's socialization strategy is found at *Punniapoomi* (Sacred Land). This school is located in Oddusuddan, where children are molded into LTTE soldiers.[138] Here, too, socialization and indoctrination techniques are employed to ready Tamil youth to take up the (violent) cause for liberation, self-determination, and nationalism.

Self

Society Shapes the Self

Research on the Liberation Tigers of Tamil Eelam indicates that membership in the collective saturates almost every aspect of a cadre's life. Commenting on this immersion, one Tamil activist explained the pivotal "test" that a recruit must undergo before becoming a full-fledged affiliate. "The most important test is detachment from the family. Cadres no longer belong to their family; the movement becomes the family."[139] Moreover, as the University Teachers for Human Rights[140] found,

> Children who joined [the LTTE] were quickly hidden away and parents were denied contact. The first [person] to express a wish to go home was humiliated and given a sound thrashing in front of his mates, which effectively deterred others from expressing any such wish.

Members are so engulfed in the LTTE identity that they literally live, eat, sleep, fight, and die together.[141] This cultural immersion extends to the battlefield, where every aspect of a cadre's life is spent with the others in the collective.

In addition, for those group members who wish to marry, the Liberation Tigers of Tamil Eelam perform special wedding ceremonies. Adele Balasingham,[142] sociologist and wife of the LTTE's British-educated ideologue, Anton Balasingham, commented on this ritualized practice, during more than twenty years of her husband's involvement with the organization. As she explained, the weddings were arranged by the head of the LTTE's political wing and conducted at a local office. The ceremonies combined the more positive elements of Tamil culture but dismissed the more reactionary features of the movement. As an institution, the ceremony served to join together both the Sri Lankan Tamil and freedom fighter roles. For the bride and groom, the politico-religious service helped to crystallize their commitments to one another, to the movement, and, perhaps most profoundly, to their self-concepts as LTTE followers. Moreover, the LTTE-sponsored event functioned as a social gathering for members, friends, and colleagues whose relationships hinged on their ongoing group affiliation.

Another way in which an individual becomes committed to the LTTE identity is by living a proscribed life. After the interception of the LTTE boat off Point Pedro in October 1987, the IPKF began a military campaign in northeastern Sri Lanka aimed at decommissioning the extremist group's military armaments. During these instances, the IPKF became notoriously adept at large-scale cordon-and-search missions, including systematic patrols that entailed the quarantining of various Tamil village areas where homes and buildings were carefully inspected.[143] Not only did the operations drive many militants underground, but they also allegedly resulted in the victimization of numerous Tamil communities.

Choosing to remain with her husband and to live on the run, Balasingham[144] reduced the couple's belongings to the bare necessities. They distributed their expansive collection of textbooks to local families. She wrapped her family photo album in plastic and buried it in the ground, hoping to retrieve it at a later time. Adele explained that her efforts were similar to those of other LTTE cadres who were forced to leave spouses, children, family, and friends behind. Once Balasingham, her husband, and a group of LTTE faithful fled the country, they felt "united by the common danger [they confronted] and [their] urgency for shelter and safety."[145] According to her recollections, the couple's social relationships were extremely limited. Because the threat of informants was ever present, they were forced to associate almost exclusively with trusted LTTE cadres and sympathizers.

As they moved between safe houses seeking refuge, the renegades were often given a warm welcome by their hospitable supporters. Young children acted as lookouts by reporting the latest troop movements while the village women prepared hot meals and warm beds for the visitors. Balasingham also explained that many of her hosts would share stories of personal hardship inflicted by the government or the victimization suffered at the hands of the Sinhalese and IPKF soldiers.

The life experiences of those would-be suicide bombers who fill the ranks of the Black Tigers are also representative of the societal influence on one's identity commitment. The Black Tiger squads receive specialized training and are frequently made to operate as a self-contained unit.[146] Their isolation from the rest of the LTTE collective during training and operations preparation presumably has made them an extremely tight-knit group.[147] The bond shared among Black Tiger members is vividly captured in the film *tayakkanavu,* or "Dream of the Motherland."[148] The movie was produced by the LTTE's official television station and features a young boy who joins the suicide squad after his friend is killed in a Sri Lankan army bombing raid. The volunteers undergo an arduous training regime and develop a strong sense of fellowship in the process. This is particularly evident between the film's hero and another volunteer. For example, in one scene, the two are observed feeding each other by hand, a sign of their intimacy. Eventually, the film's hero is chosen for a mission that he successfully executes. His comrades are also shown mourning his passing.

Those martyrs-to-be who are selected to conduct "off-the-battlefield" suicide operations deep inside Colombo are sent to live in safe houses where they become members of a cell.[149] Once in enemy territory, the operatives are ordered to collect intelligence information and to rehearse dry runs in order to develop their speed and stealth.[150] After preparations are completed, the Black Tiger executes his or her mission. Sri Lankan sources estimate that in addition to LTTE intelligence operatives who support suicide operations, approximately thirty Black Tiger sleeper units are active in Colombo.[151] Although the exact number of cell members remains a mystery, those assigned to such a unit are expected to ready and support the martyr-to-be in that person's planned attack. While covertly residing among members of their cell, almost all of the bombers' social relationships are based on their identity as would-be martyrs. Indeed, for members of the Black Tiger group, one thing is clear: their commitment to the martyr identity, informed by the thought of their mission, is ever present.[152]

The Self Shapes Society

The processes of selective perception, selective interpretation, and rationalization help explain how members of the LTTE deny their label as ruthless terrorists and verify their identities as freedom fighters. Those involved in the militant Tamil movement first received their proscribed status in 1979, when the Jaywardene government passed the Prevention of Terrorism Act.[153] As Ponnambalam[154] noted, the draconian law provided the Sri Lankan military forces carte blanche in their fight against the Tigers. In response to the act, the LTTE sent an official letter of protest to Sri Lankan prime minister Premadasa arguing that it was the Sri Lankan state police and armed forces that were guilty of terrorism and not the Tamil Tigers.[155] Since then, the LTTE has asserted that the Tamil Tigers' actions represent those of freedom fighters, rather than those of a "band of bloodthirsty terrorists bent on anarchism," as the Sri Lankan government routinely portrays them.[156]

Selective perception is one technique used by the LTTE to manage the discrepancy between the identity standard of being a freedom fighter versus behavior characterized as consistent with that of a terrorist. For example,

> with a few exceptions, the LTTE has claimed responsibility only for the suicide-attack operations it has conducted against military targets in Sri Lanka's northeastern region. The organization refrains from claiming responsibility for operations against VIP targets as [well as] non-military infrastructures.[157]

In short, the LTTE has simply ignored or dismissed its culpability for those actions deemed to be the product of militant extremists because these depictions conflict with their internalized identities of themselves as noble and just freedom fighters.

The process of selective interpretation is evident within LTTE rhetoric. The discourse frequently employed or featured includes opinions of those audience members who verify group participants' identities as freedom fighters. For example, in one such propaganda piece, the LTTE cited the views of Ms. Karen Parker, an attorney specializing in international and human rights law.[158] After an extensive explanation pertaining to her credentials as an authority on the matter, she observed the following:

> I have been asked to set out my views on whether the LIBERATION TIGERS OF TAMIL EELAM (LTTE) is a "terrorist" organization. I state categorically that the LTTE is not a "terrorist" organization, but rather an armed force in a war against the government of Sri Lanka. Charac-

terization of the LTTE as a "terrorist" organization is politically motivated having no basis in law or fact.[159]

Ms. Parker supported her position, drawing upon several points. She indicated that the Sri Lankan conflict represents a civil war between two armies: the Liberation Tigers of Tamil Eelam and the Sri Lankan Armed Forces. She noted that the struggle centers on the national liberation of a people who have chosen to exercise their right to self-determination.[160] Finally, she explained that neither the LTTE nor the Sri Lankan government could be characterized as terrorist organizations because only a few soldiers have violated the rules of armed conflict by attacking noncombatants.

Another instance of selective interpretation comes from the movement's frequent reference to international law, especially those passages or documents that support the LTTE cause.[161] For example, in a paper presented by the International Federation of Tamils (IFT),[162] its authors argued that because the LTTE's armed struggle entails an escape from domination rather than the domination of others, its activities are justified. Identified as a collective under the control of LTTE front organizations,[163] the IFT cited the General Assembly Resolutions on Friendly Relations among States (Resolution 2625) and on Definition of Aggression (Act 7), as well as the 1977 Additional Protocol I to the Geneva Convention of 1949 (Act 1 C4) for "legal" support. These decrees account for (and defend) the use of violence as a last resort when people exercise a right to self-determination. Moreover, proponents of the LTTE movement indicate that by denying the Tamil people their right to self-determination, the Sri Lankan government has clearly and unequivocally violated Articles 1(2), 1(3), 2(4), and 56 of the United Nations Charter.

A more evasive management strategy used by LTTE members wherein the discrepancy between terrorist behavior and the freedom fighter identity standard is negotiated is rationalization. To illustrate, when confronted with photographs that depicted civilians brutally attacked by Tamil militants, Prabhakaran explained that

> they [the Sri Lankan government] have got these Home Guard thugs who are armed and trained by the Armed Forces. They dress like civilians but are almost like death-squads [who] let loose on Tamil civilians

now and again—to loot, burn, destroy. In some cases we have attacked them. They look like civilians. In some areas there are Sinhalese-Tamil civilian conflicts. These conflicts take place when the Sinhalese are brought to the Tamil areas to forcibly occupy the land. Clashes do take place to protect the land.[164]

Prabhakaran went on to intimate that the pictures were used merely as propaganda to spread lies and other falsehoods about the LTTE and its just cause.

In another interview, Prabhakaran was asked if the LTTE had killed innocent civilians during its military offensives. He stated that "the LTTE has never killed any civilians. We condemn such acts of violence. There were occasions when we had to kill home guards. But they are not civilians. They are trained non-combat draftees who carry guns."[165] Once again, within this passage, Prabhakaran stipulated that the LTTE did not target civilians and, although it might appear that they had been injured or killed, the so-called civilians were, in fact, armed Sri Lankan government officials. Whether or not Prabhakaran's understanding of these events was based on reality, he utilized the techniques of rationalization and disavowal to manage the large disconnect between militant extremist behavior and the freedom fighter identity standard.

9

Racist Skinheads

Thus far, our efforts to examine the construction of identity among various militant groups have focused on the international scene. In particular, expressions of terrorism in Northern Ireland, the Middle East, Peru, and Sri Lanka have all been investigated. However, militant extremist organizations also exist within the United States. One such collective is the right-wing political group known as racist Skinheads. The antigovernment, antimulticulturalism, and White supremacy ideology of this organization, and the violence perpetrated in furtherance of the group's cause, is based on intimidation, fear, and hate. Thus, racist Skinheads constitute a legitimate terrorist menace[1] whose collective behavior is the source of considerable speculation.

One facet to understanding this behavior is the emergence and maintenance of membership identity within the organization. Accordingly, this chapter explores those social psychological forces that contribute to establishing the racist Skinhead identity. Along these lines, insights from structural Symbolic Interactionism and Identity Theory are woven together to fashion a portrait of how the social person is constituted and how affiliation in the organization is ensured. Thus, symbols and their meanings, the definition of the situation as interpreted by group members, role performances, and socialization and role-taking experiences are all examined. As the chapter makes evident, the social psychological theory employed helps to illuminate the delicate relationship that exists among culture, self, and society, especially in attempts to account for identity construction, terrorist behavior, and the maintenance of both among members of racist Skinhead collectives.

Symbols

There are many symbols that are pivotal to the construction of identity and the manifestation of violently extreme conduct among racist

Skinheads. One such symbol is the devalued social status of White men. This is particularly poignant for young people involved in the movement. Indeed, their interactions with the symbols of their environment indicate that being a White male is no longer the preferred ascribed status. Instead, it represents a threatened and endangered social standing.

The centrality of White men and their devalued status to the overall White supremacist movement was articulated by Daniels.[2] In particular, she drew attention to an illustration that is regularly published by the White Aryan Resistance movement, a southern California–based organization that has had a powerful influence on the violent activities of racist Skinheads.[3] In the picture's foreground, a White man points to the reader and is dressed in working-class attire that includes a hard hat, a plaid shirt, and a sleeveless insulated jacket. In the picture's background, a bridge, skyscrapers, and an airplane are featured. The caption reads "WHITE MEN *Built* this nation!! WHITE MEN *Are* this nation!!!"[4]

Admittedly, Daniels explained that the image conveys many messages. Among the possible meanings is the link among race, whiteness, and masculinity. In the illustration, White men are depicted as the only visible actors. As such, they are the only individuals identified as having made a "real" contribution to building the strength of, in this case, the United States. Moreover, this contribution entitles White men to a privileged position in the social structure. Another, more abstract message is present in the routine publication of this singular image. In brief, Aryan male power and privilege is in serious jeopardy. Consequently, the regular publication of the illustration signifies a reminder that this deplorable situation must change.

Similar themes concerning social status are found in Blazak's[5] ethnographic work on racist Skinheads. Specifically, Blazak addressed the effects of perceived loss of standing among young White men, as well as the ensuing experience of societal alienation, and the way racist Skinhead groups utilized such felt marginalization to attract, manipulate, and indoctrinate juveniles into a world of terror. Moreover, Blazak proposed that the threat to White male hegemony employed as a basis to recruit young people into Aryan Skinhead collectives was organized into four categories.

The first category entailed a threat to ethnic and racial status. Group members identified this perceived threat by drawing attention to the growth in the minority student population, the increase in minority student organizations or events, shifts in favor of multicultural curricula, and racial conflict in which educational institutions appeared to support minority groups or interests. The second category included a perceived risk to gender status. This threat takes the shape of conflict over female participation in male activities, the emergence of feminist activist groups, and anti–sexual violence programs or initiatives. The third category is the danger posed to the heterosexual status. Group members identify sexual minority organizations, gay pride events, and inclusiveness movements or sponsored dialogue as elements of this threat. The fourth and final category is the challenge to economic status. This risk is manifested in factory layoffs, large employer downsizing efforts, stiff competition for manual labor, and the erosion of service sector jobs.

Blazak[6] argued that individuals internalize these meanings through their interaction with the objects and social objects that symbolize these threats. For instance, a young man's belief that the White middle class is suffering from downward economic mobility is represented and reinforced when a local company is compelled to lay off employees due to outsourcing practices or factory closings. In addition, some people may perceive television shows that depict women as working professionals and gay men in starring sitcom roles as symbolizing the loss of traditional heterosexual male authority and power. Both illustrations indicate how perceived loss of social standing, linked to policies that benefit other non-White male collectives, can be manipulated to advance Aryan political and ideological goals.

Another symbol influencing the identities of racist Skinheads is the Zionist Occupational Government, which is commonly referred to as the ZOG. This acronym is frequently employed by extreme right-wing Aryan activists to describe a conspiratorial entity consisting of Jews identified as having seized power over the government and as intending to eliminate the White race.[7] Following his interactions with racist Skinheads, Christensen[8] defined the individual terms that constitute this expression. These include "Zionist: Someone who will sacrifice any person, anything, or any nation for the greater good of Israel. Occupational: Possession by force, rather than by voluntary agreement. Government: Control of a population."[9]

Based on the teachings of White supremacist groups such as the National Alliance and the White Aryan Resistance, racist Skinheads contend that the ZOG controls every aspect of society, including the banking system, the media, law enforcement, the judicial system, immigration policy, foreign affairs, the U.S. economy, and many more.[10] Presumably, this fictitious entity is an outgrowth of the conspiratorial theory described in the *Protocols of the Elders of Zion*,[11] which was distributed throughout Europe. As previously described (see chapter 4), this forged document was supposedly a report to a secret Jewish committee called the Elders of Zion. The report described a worldwide network of camouflaged agencies and covert organizations that controlled political parties, governments, the media, banks, and the economy.

The ZOG expression appears to have first become known outside the right-wing subculture when the *New York Times* ran a story on December 27, 1984. The article chronicled the operations of the racist terrorist group known as the Order (aka the Silent Brotherhood).[12] Moreover, the article explained that the group raised money to fight a war against the U.S. government, which the militants identified as the ZOG. Robert J. Matthews, leader of the Order, had appropriated the ZOG expression from *The Turner Diaries*.[13] This work inspired him and his comrades to form the Order.[14]

Largely accepted as the racist bible,[15] *The Turner Diaries* describes the exploits of Earl Turner and his band of White guerrillas who fight in a race war against non-Whites and the evil ZOG. Turner is described as an honest, hard-working, mild-mannered family man who is forced to defend his race and White heritage. He does this by attacking government installations and law enforcement officials identified as the ZOG's primary instrument of oppression.[16]

William Pierce, the author of the book (he used the pen name Andrew MacDonald), was also the founder of the neo-Nazi organization known as the National Alliance. The National Alliance has a powerful influence on racist Skinheads, especially through the production of hate rock by its subsidiary, Resistance Records. Both the National Alliance and Resistance Records have had a considerable influence on racist Skinheads. Indeed, when members of this collective speak of overthrowing the "evil empire" through acts of violence, it is the ZOG to whom they refer.

A third symbol crucial to understanding the identities and subsequent militant behaviors of racist Skinheads is their sustained indulgence in hate music. The contemporary version of Nazi Skinheads hate rock first emerged in 1977. This is the period when racist Skinheads began to find direction in the music of Ian Stewart and his band, Skrewdriver.[17] Although the group's early recordings were not decidedly racist, they did speak to the White working-class youths who felt frustrated and alienated by the status quo.

In 1982, the group completed its racist evolution, as evidenced in its recording of "White Power." Skrewdriver inspired a musical genre as it toured Europe and developed an intense cult following. The group recorded additional albums, such as "Hail the New Dawn" in 1984 and "Blood and Honour" in 1985. Both albums were emblematic of unbridled disdain and extreme violence toward non-Whites as well as the establishment. For example, titles such as "White Warrior," "Take the Sword," "Fists of Steel," "Heads Kicked In," "Reich 'n' Roll," and "Blood and Honour" left little to the imagination as to the content of their respective verses. However, the vile and aggressive imagery conveyed through the lyrics of several Skrewdriver hits is worth noting. Consider the following lines from three representative songs:

> Strikeforce, white survival, strikeforce
> Strikeforce kill all rivals
> (from "Strikeforce")

> We will fight against them with a hammer and a gun
> And when our people start to rise, the traitors'
> Time will come.
> (from "Power from Profit")

> We live on the streets now; we fight for our lives,
> We fight for the flag, we are all willing to die.
> (from "Flying Flag")[18]

It is clear from these brief excerpts alone that a message of hate, anger, violence, and White survival are all vividly and provocatively communicated.

Since its inception, Oi music and its progression into hate rock has been a hallmark of the racist Skinhead movement. It also continues to be a symbol of White working-class protest, Aryan survival, and the warrior-hood mentality.[19] In North America alone, there are more than seventy White Power music groups.[20] The leading producer of hate rock, Resistance Records, is believed to gross around $1 million a year in sales.[21] Christensen[22] suggested that White Power music is so popular because it serves to arouse a primitive rage in those who listen to it and reinforces the idea of racial and religious discrimination. In addition, the message embedded within the words themselves tells Skinheads that they are heroic warriors fighting for the survival of the White race. Skinheads are repetitively bombarded with this lyrical theme as Oi music and hate rock are a frequent part of their activities. These activities might include something as simple as congregating in a park or something as staged as attending a White Power concert.

In a survey of thirty-two self-identified racist and nonracist Skinheads, Wooden and Blazak[23] found that the racist teenage cohort agreed with the statement that their music espoused violence. Moreover, the researchers drew attention to a possible connection between violent music preferences and childhood abuse, especially since these same youths reported prior abuse by their parents. Thus, it is reasonable to argue that by implication the music is quite symbolic. In short, it fuels, nurtures, and confirms the importance of militant behavior among listeners, especially given their membership standing in the collective.

Definition of the Situation

For racist Skinheads, the problem is that those of Aryan descent are in danger of losing their "racial purity" and integrity as a result of the rapid influx of non-Whites into the United States, increased acceptance of race mixing, and the waning existence of traditional White male hegemony.[24] Indeed, the battle between good and evil rages on in modern-day society for those group members who subscribe to Christian Identity beliefs. This is particularly salient for participants who allege that the evil ZOG exercises its authority and influence over the government in order to eliminate Christianity and with it the White race, culture, and heritage.[25] Moreover, religion teaches Aryan adherents that the world is on the brink of the apocalypse and as God's chosen people it is they who must triumph over evil (i.e., the Jewish conspiracy). Similarly, Odinists believe that the White race is nearing extinction. Consequently, it is their obligation to preserve and protect it from any non-White person who challenges their preferred way of living or any individual who favors multiculturalism.

Moreover, racist Skinheads are convinced that as an endangered group, Whites are subjected to discrimination, loss of rights, and the inability to express personal and collective pride in their racial heritage. Some Aryan supremacists contend that this has resulted in psychological damage, more specifically, a deflated self-esteem. As Berbrier[26] pointed out, an article in the *NAAWP News*[27] even claimed that the higher suicide rate in White males was the result of their alienation from society.[28]

In its most extreme form, this group's ideology claims that the White man's freedoms are being forcibly removed by the ZOG-dominated government and its functionaries (e.g., legislators, federal/state authorities). For White supremacists like racist Skinheads, clear evidence of this deplorable condition is discernible. For example, the August 1992 stand-off between Randy Weaver and U.S. federal agents at Ruby Ridge and the April 1993 siege on David Koresh and the Branch Davidians in Waco, Texas, are visible indicators of the eroding rights and liberties otherwise enjoyed by Aryan men.[29]

To illustrate further how group members define the situation they experience, consider the following statement made by a nineteen-year-old Atlanta, Georgia, Skinhead named Jack:

> Man, it's obvious that the world is seriously fucked up. My mom and step-dad work their asses off and it just keeps getting worse for them. It really sucks, especially for the working man. Look at all the money the Jews have. For doing what? Some guy busts a gut in a factory all day long then gets laid off so the Jew owner can hire some dumb spic who will work for half the price. People wonder why things are so bad. Because no one can make an honest living, that's why. There's no good job for me, they were all given to losers.[30]

Arguably, Jack's anger was triggered by his interpretation of the symbols in his surroundings. This includes the devalued status for the White working-class population to which his mother and stepfather belong. Jack assigns meaning to the (concrete and abstract) symbols in his environment and this leads him to form a definition of the situation he (and his family) confronts. In short, the "working man" has been victimized and the "world is seriously fucked up."

Many racist Skinheads share the belief that the inevitable race war in America "will [produce] an 'autonomous Aryan homeland in the Northwest' (as the *Volksfront* newsletter describes it), the ultimate goal [being] an America that has been ethnically cleansed of all enemies, including White race traitors."[31] Moreover, commenting on the importance of achieving White separatism, one member of the Confederate Hammer Skinheads, the predecessor to the Hammerskin Nation collective, offered the following explanation:

> To me, the term white separatism is simply a statement of our objectives. Any rational person must accept the fact that other races and cultures are not going to simply disappear, therefore, in order to continue our own cultural and perhaps genetic evolution, separatism represents the best interests of our people.[32]

Explaining this idea at more length, and minimizing the violent aspects of their particular organization, another Hammerskin member described the rationale behind the effort to self-segregate.

> If you listen to the government and the media, we are trying to start a race war. In reality, though, we are just trying to build a healthy environment for our children to grow up in. Meaning a sufficiently independent alternative to the host society. A free haven of thought and action ruled by our own standards. Obviously we can't take over the planet to do this, so as a brotherhood we will segregate ourselves and do things for the benefit of our brothers and our families. We will build a steadfast brotherhood throughout the western world.
>
> We chose as an organisation the road to self-segregation as the most achievable solution to a society we don't like. Attempting to change the world with pointless rhetoric is pure laughable utopia. Society is shaped by economy not by ideals. All the White Pride in the world won't beat the almighty dollar. Self-segregation is the only solution.[33]

Clearly, statements such as those quoted above indicate that the ultimate solution is to create a sovereign community in which the survival of the White race is assured. There is a degree of pragmatism found within these passages. Indeed, realizing that world domination is not feasible, group members are prepared to settle for a region ruled only by Whites. This would be an Aryan territory free of the perceived threats posed by minorities, Jews, and those living alternative lifestyles.

According to Dobratz and Shanks-Meile[34] the idea of self-segregation along racial/territorial lines emerged within the larger White supremacist movement during the early 1980s. In an initiative referred to as the Northwest Imperative, White separatists plan to carve out a homeland in the Pacific Northwest within the borders of Washington, Oregon, Idaho, Montana, and Wyoming. Their goal is to reestablish White Aryan sovereignty in which participants are free to practice self-determination.

The White Aryan Resistance (WAR), which was created by John Metzger in Southern California, notes that White racialists would achieve this goal (i.e., self-determination) by moving to the northwest region, buying land adjacent to other Whites, and procreating on a massive scale.[35] Children would be raised in the long-standing tradition and fighting heritage of the White race. The nation-state would only extend citizenship to Aryans. This would include having voting rights, owning property, serving in the military or law enforcement, and holding a political office. According to WAR, class barriers would be eliminated and leaders would emerge on the basis of "blood and brains."[36] Group members believe that only through this strategy of self-separation and victory in the coming race war will the White race be able to ensure its survival. Conversely, failure would result in the extinction of the White race.

The means by which racist Skinheads seek to solve the problem they identify is by preserving the White race. This sentiment is expressed in the popular phrase "the 14 Words." The expression reads as follows: "We Must Secure the Existence of Our People and a Future for White Children."[37] This saying was popularized by David Lane, who was a member of the Order.[38] Similarly, WAR has issued a proclamation. It espouses a more reactionary stance. For example, as the collective asserts, "The Great White Aryan race must be advanced and protected at all costs and above all other issues."[39] Influenced by organizations like WAR, racist Skinhead groups believe that violence is the only feasible means by which to safeguard the blood line of the White race. Moreover, books like *The Turner Diaries*[40] facilitate racist Skinheads' adoption of the view that evil non-White hordes will eventually emerge, forcing Whites to fight for their lives. Indeed, if Aryans are prepared to stand united, they can defeat their adversaries and create a homeland for themselves.

In support of these convictions, many racist Skinhead groups have adopted the RaHoWa battle cry. "RaHoWa" translates into "Racial Holy War."[41] Commenting on this notion, one WCOTC Skinhead observed that

> since the beginning of time, it's been an ongoing "holy" war waged by
> the Jews against Nature's most magnificent Creature, the Noble White

Race. Therefore, we wish to fight fire with fire, and we make no bones about it. RAHOWA is our battle cry![42]

Clearly, then, racist Skinheads define the situation they confront as one that necessitates violence. This is particularly the case if the White race is to be protected at all and any costs. Accordingly, members function as foot soldiers for the movement. As Christensen[43] explained,

Racist skinheads created a subculture of people whose purpose is to act as soldiers assigned the task of cleaning America of unwanted elements, and they even have the power to decide which elements. They have been taught by the upper-echelon white supremacist organizations that the white culture is on the decline, a result of minorities having large families and whites being manipulated by the Jewish-controlled government to abort their children. They have been brainwashed to believe the white working man is duty-bound to fight to return America to the white men who built it.

Consistent with this sentiment, Robert Miles, a longtime leader of White supremacist groups, noted that Skinheads therefore serve an important role in the movement's efforts to secure their vision of change for group affiliates. Indeed, as he concluded, "If there's a future for the right wing, [skinheads] will be the first racial wave. They're what Nazi stormtroopers were in the early '20s."[44]

Roles

Fundamentally, there are three tangible roles that serve to inform the Skinhead identity. These include being a member of the White working class, being a man, and being a heroic warrior. In general, members of the White supremacist movement, of which racist Skinheads are a part, believe Whites are routinely victimized by society.[45] They claim that policies such as affirmative action have oppressed them by promoting reverse discrimination practices. Members maintain that the discrimination promulgated by such practices has made the White male category the new disadvantaged social position.[46] Moreover, adherents claim that given this double standard, Whites have lost the right to express pride in their culture, heritage, and race. As a result, they are inhibited from making any displays along these lines, succumbing to shame, stigma, and ridicule when public declarations of pride are expressed.

Any attempt to advocate for the elimination of affirmative action or to form White groups is labeled as racist. In essence, Aryan supremacists argue that "Whites are being treated differently from others—told by amorphous and impersonal factors such as 'the system' not to take pride in their 'heritage' but rather to 'hate their own' kind."[47] Consequently, on the basis of this brand of institutionalized discrimination, White supremacists are convinced that the very survival of their race is at stake, that they represent an endangered species, and that their felt victimization is comparable to ethnic cleansing.

A second component of this particular role entails being a member of the working class. Since the beginning of the racist Skinhead movement, members have always been self-conscious of their working-class roots. In many ways, they embrace the Protestant work ethic described by Max Weber.[48] This ethic emphasizes an unwavering commitment to religion and a disciplined regard for the value of labor. Moreover, the role of the honest, hard-working, blue-collar employee concerned with financial sustenance rather than material wealth has always been an important feature of the racist Skinhead mindset.[49] To illustrate, consider the following caption from a pamphlet distributed by the movement. It reads, "SKINHEADS OF AMERICA, like the dynamic skinheads of Europe, are working class Aryan Youth. We oppose the capitalist and the communist scum that are destroying our Aryan race."[50] In addition, in his study of American Skinheads, Hamm[51] found that of the twenty-two terrorist-type Aryans he interviewed, four came from white-collar backgrounds, seventeen from blue-collar backgrounds, and one was unemployed. These data suggest that the racist Skinhead perspective overwhelmingly gravitates toward working-class sensibilities.

Combined with the blue-collar ethic of this role is "White male privilege." Among other things, this authorizes White men to benefit from, at the very least, a middle-class standing, provided they are hard working.[52] This notion of privilege leads to a second crucial role that informs our understanding of the Skinhead identity. In short, this entails being a man. The traditional image of masculinity conveyed and sanctioned by society includes the expectation that one should not engender stereotypic feminine qualities. In other words, the individual should refrain from expressing emotion, openness, or vulnerability, and, at the same time, should demonstrate success in his endeavors, including work and sports; display aggressiveness when dealing with others; initiate and control his (hetero)sexual relationships; and possess traits such as dominance, self-reliance, courageousness, and bravery.[53]

A cursory analysis of racist Skinhead discourse and imagery reveals that members embrace aspects of these conventional "male" roles. For example, hyper-masculine depictions of racist Skinheads often appear in their artwork.[54] Participants are frequently portrayed as shirtless, with their muscles bulging, or wearing a skin-tight shirt that reveals every curve of their chiseled physique.[55] Teeth clenched and eyes opened wide and focused in vigilant anticipation, they may be snapping out a Nazi salute, stomping on an unfortunate minority member with their steel-toed Doc Marten boots, or destroying some form of the Jewish entity.[56]

Another crucial (and related) aspect of masculinity, especially for those within the White supremacist movement, is the use of physical violence. More specifically, if an individual's maleness is challenged or is otherwise threatened, there is only one honorable means by which to reestablish it: the exercise of force.[57] Appropriating violence when one's masculinity has been threatened is especially important for racist Skinheads because victimization is related to violence. Therefore, by internalizing their oppressed status, racist Skinheads are expected to engage in hostility, cruelty, and bloodshed. These acts are then justified through the discourse of self-defense. Commenting on the place of violence and self-defense in the construction of the racist Skinhead identity, Hamm[58] offered the following observations:

> As seen by subcultural members, it [violence] is a necessary means of protecting group values. As such, the role of the deviant peer seems to be an inconsequential factor in the formulation of this norm. In other words, there is nothing sociologically or legally deviant about self-defense. Instead, self-defense is a cherished value of American nationalism.

Moreover, from the perspective of the social psychological framework in question throughout this chapter (and book), not only is self-defense an American value; it is also a male value.

The focus on the male gender role is not intended to insinuate that women do not take up or play an active part in the racist Skinhead subculture. Indeed, as a counter-role, women constitute a role set along with male racist Skinheads. Specifically, within the larger White supremacist movement, women are most often represented as subservient or are otherwise relegated to a secondary position.[59] This view was supported by Hamm,[60] who found that racist Skinheads are predominantly male oriented. In addition, women are viewed by male racist Skinheads as a support structure. As such, they are valued for their domestic capabilities, such as homemaking and child bearing.[61] This status is consistent with their importance to the continuation of the White race—a status that, for some women, has enabled them to hold more meaningful positions within the Aryan movement.[62]

Linked to the gender role of being a man is the ascribed status of defending White women and of safeguarding the Aryan race. Indeed, for White supremacists like Nazi Skinheads, "the highest duty and honor [bestowed upon] a White man, according to white supremacist discourse, is to preserve the white family and with it a hierarchy of race, gender, and sexuality."[63] Thus, in part, the masculine role entails loyalty to one's collective (i.e., racist Skinheads) and responsibility to those females in the group.

The third pivotal role that contributes to the identity of movement affiliates is that of the valiant warrior who fights for the survival of the White race. This is a popular theme within the racist Skinhead organization.[64] To illustrate, consider the following message written in a pamphlet distributed by an Aryan gang:

SKINHEADS worldwide are warriors. We never run away, back down, or sell out. We despise the traitors, the cowards, the apathetic, and the limp wristed queers. We will fight forever to defend our people and our land. Our heads are shaved for battle.[65]

Additionally, Wooden and Blazak[66] noted that Skinheads frequently like to view themselves as heroic saviors of their White brethren, seen as societal outcasts unwittingly fashioned into cultural underdogs. This theme is often depicted in Skinhead art and tattoos in which the Viking warrior rescues his people from "evil Jews and subhuman mongrels."[67] A pamphlet circulated by the White Aryan Resistance movement describes some of the basic expectations of the racist Skinhead warrior role:

> The attitude of a skinhead is generally ready to fight and on guard all the time. Skins do not usually go around and start trouble. Its [*sic*] only when people start to make the jump on skins. When that happens, the skins end up winning! Skinheads are mad and tired of the system screwing them over.
>
> Skinheads are the All-American white youth. They love mom and love their flag. The dress of the skin (is) rough, smart and clean. All in all, the skinhead uniform is working class, ready to fight because our heads are shaved for battle.
>
> Skinheads are against non-white immigration because these people take our jobs and land and give nothing in return. Skinheads are Anti-Semitic, because we know the Jews have extorted us for there [*sic*] personnel [*sic*] means. Skinheads are anti-abortion, we all know that abortion is another form of genocide, the nonwhite races and the jews [*sic*] sit and laugh at our self-annihilation.[68]

In exploring the construction of the warrior Skinhead culture, the work of Etter[69] is particularly useful. His identification of concerns and values for this group was consistent with Miller's[70] examination of youth gangs situated in communities of low socioeconomic status. Thus, according to Etter,[71] the Skinhead warrior role consists of a series of elements or focal concerns.

The first element of the warrior role is *trouble*. This concern is summed up in anxiety over confrontations with real or imagined rival groups. For Skinheads, their enemies include collectives such as law enforcement personnel, non-Whites, and the ZOG. Moreover, these adversaries occupy the counter-role status to the warrior role. The second element is *toughness*. This focal concern encompasses one's sense of physical prowess, fearlessness, courage, and traditional masculinity. The third element is *smartness*. It entails one's verbal agility, quick-wittedness, and the belief that "street smart" skills are superior to formal education. In relation to racist Skinheads, this notion is exemplified among members who assert that they possess the mental acuity to see through the ZOG's elaborate ploys to deceive the White man. For example, while the majority of Whites believe that teaching multiculturalism throughout the primary and secondary educational curriculum encourages tolerance and respect for diversity among today's children, Skinheads recognize that the "real" intent is to eliminate the White race and its culture of pride and power.

The fourth element of the warrior role is *excitement*. Within the Skinhead warrior image there is a thirst for thrills that is often quenched only through combat. The fifth concern is *fate*. Typically, the belief is that as warriors, members are predestined to fight and, if need be, to die. Moreover, the conviction is that their lives are somewhat incidental in comparison to waging the good fight. For instance, consider the eerily predictive lyrics of one of Ian Stewart's last songs before a car accident unexpectedly took his life:

> If suddenly, I am forced to take my leave,
> Will you carry on with the things that we believe?
> One day if suddenly they take my life away,
> Will you be fighting to win a bright, new day?[72]

The last element of the warrior culture is *autonomy*. Racist Skinheads make it clear that they reject the current established authority, believing that it is under the control of ZOG.[73] Members contend that only through bloodshed, frequently depicted as a racial holy war (or RaHoWa), will the movement be able to overthrow the government. Again, the aim is to reestablish a country free of those deemed not to belong or to ensure their own self-segregation.

White supremacists, like racist Skinheads, often combine the warrior image with religious undertones to elevate the role to the level of nobility.[74] This is especially true for those group members who are devout followers of the Christian Identity, Odinism, and/or the World Church of the Creator (WCOTC) sects. These racist Skinheads believe that they have been ordained by their religion to promote the preservation of their race and that undertaking such an endeavor is both honorable and just. Indeed, reminiscent of the fate element found in the warrior culture, giving one's life for the cause is perceived as warranting praise, admiration, and martyrdom. Clearly, then, religion is crucial to understanding this role. This is the case because faith serves as a schema through which opposing groups are vilified to a point that they are not only the enemy of the Aryan group but are an adversary of God.[75] Thus, by demonizing and degrading Jewish people, non-Whites, and homosexuals, young group affiliates conclude that they are advancing humane (and legitimate) interests, facilitating and rationalizing the use of violence in their cultural, ancestral, and heroic struggle.

Socialization and Role-Taking

Racist Skinheads learn the expectations for their behavior and their position within society's social structure through socialization. It would appear that significant others have a powerful socializing effect on the adoption of roles pertinent to being a racist Skinhead. Indeed, a Skinhead's comrades undoubtedly indoctrinate a new recruit with belief systems that espouse hatred for Asians, African Americans, Hispanics, Jews, and homosexuals. As Fangan[76] observed,

> The National Socialist Skinheads maintain that to understand how the conspiracy works one has to read a certain amount of heavy literature. The more of this one reads, the more one is able to see through "the falseness of the system," and one thus becomes skilled in reading between the lines of the news.[77]

For the Hammerskin Nation, this indoctrination is likely to take place during the three-month probationary period in which prospective members are required to put in a certain amount of "face-time."[78] In addition, new recruits learn about the organization's proclivity toward violence during the hostile (though customary) rite-of-passage encounter to which they are subjected. This is the day the initiate is "jumped in" by other members.[79] Finally, a racist Skinhead recruiter may be the first to introduce a fledgling candidate to the conspiratorial concept of the ZOG. Oftentimes, however, such individuals have already been exposed to racist attitudes.

According to Wooden and Blazak,[80] racist Skinheads typically emerge from racist environments. What this suggests is that significant others, such as parents, close family members, and friends, lay the groundwork for young men (and women) to be recruited into the racist youth subculture and to adopt its conspiratorial ideology. Interestingly, however, the academic literature examining whether racist Skinheads come from abusive homes is mixed.[81] This notwithstanding, according to some investigators, racist Skinheads generally do self-identify themselves as having been bullies or troublemakers in grammar school.[82] Arguably, these aggressive adolescents derive satisfaction from harassing other youngsters. Developmentally speaking, hurting one's peers becomes a means by which to gain power. Thus, parental influences, the child's home environment, and an unruly temperament may all play a part in constructing the adolescent bully. In adulthood, the impact of such youthful experiences—stemming from a home life in which racism and anti-Semitism are espoused by significant others—can foster the Skinhead identity.[83]

The impact of generalized others in the formation of the racist Skinhead identity is also worth noting. Indeed, according to Etter,[84] the glamorized warrior image of the 1980s and 1990s widely embraced by the middle and working class had a profound socializing influence on the racist Skinhead subculture. To illustrate, in his work *Warrior Dreams: Paramilitary Culture in Post-Vietnam America*, Gibson[85] traced the development and (re)making of the historical warrior archetype into the contemporary paramilitary fighter between the post-Vietnam era and the end of the twentieth century. Essentially, the Vietnam War represented the first military campaign that the United States had lost. As a result, many American servicemen who fought abroad and many of their homeland supporters began to question the firmly held belief that the men of the United States were the undisputed champions of the battlefield. This led them to reevaluate their masculinity, the righteousness of their country's armed conflicts, and their overall self-image.

This insecurity was heightened by the civil rights and feminist movements of the 1960s and 1970s. These events were perceived as threats to the White male's hegemonic status in society. A massive influx of immigrants, an unfriendly economy for the working class, and increased crime and drug usage added to this turbulence in collective consciousness. Indeed, as Gibson[86] noted,

> Lacking confidence in the government and the economy, troubled by the changing relations between the sexes, uncertain of their identity or their future—[American men] began to dream, to fantasize about the powers and features of another kind of man who could retake and reorder the world. In the New War he fights the battles of Vietnam a thousand times, each time winning decisively. Terrorists and drug dealers are blasted into oblivion. Illegal aliens inside the United States and the

hordes of nonwhites in the Third World are returned by force to their proper place. Women are revealed as dangerous temptresses who have to be mastered, avoided, or terminated.

Given these conditions, the 1980s and 1990s represented a tumultuous period during which men began to construct a new male role, namely, that of the paramilitary warrior.[87]

The paramilitary warrior was epitomized in movies like *Commando*,[88] starring Arnold Schwarzenegger; *Invasion U.S.A.*,[89] starring Chuck Norris; and *Rambo*,[90] starring Sylvester Stallone.[91] The paramilitary warrior is fictionalized as someone who, relying upon his intimate knowledge of military tactics and weapons, rids the country of an invading communist force, contests rogue spies who betray the United States for money, or, metaphorically, refights the Vietnam War and wins. Enemies are destroyed by the dozens with assorted weapons of warfare. These weapons might include small arms, various explosives, or even hand-to-hand fighting techniques when necessary.

Typically, the paramilitary warrior is portrayed as a mild-mannered man, often a family man or someone who is looking to live a peaceful life but finds himself in extraordinary circumstances. It is only when his back is against the wall that he is forced to unleash the cunning killer that lurks within him. A generation of males cognitively played this new role of the paramilitary warrior. Their fascination with this military mindset sparked a lucrative subculture complete with its own trade magazine, *Soldier of Fortune*. These warrior dreams, images, and aspirations were quickly adopted within the American White supremacist movement and, subsequently, they trickled down into a number of racist Skinhead groups.[92]

Research conducted by Burris et al.[93] revealed that White supremacists are particularly adept at using the Internet to establish social networks, to promote their message, and to recruit new members. For example, the White Aryan Resistance and National Alliance collectives have established elaborate websites as a means of reaching out to young people. Most recently, both sites have begun offering downloadable video games in which the player assumes the part of a character with the mission of killing enemies of the White race. Called "advergames," they are designed "to sell young players on careers, ideas, and identities."[94] According to the available research, this medium appears to be one of the best ways of marketing to young men. In particular, 60 percent of boys ages thirteen to seventeen and 72 percent of young men ages eighteen to twenty-four now head to game sites when they go online.[95]

Although not racist Skinhead specific, one such game is "KABOOM! The Suicide Bombing Game." This Flash-based game is housed on WAR's official website, www.resist.com. The player's objective is to play the part of a Palestinian suicide bomber and attempt to detonate the improvised explosive device strapped to his or her body when the highest number of Jewish men, women, and children are in the closest proximity. The player directs the suicide bomber down the city streets of Israel before finding just the right moment. After the explosives are detonated, the blood, heads, and body parts of the suicide attackers' victims are splattered along the pavement, while the body of the suicide bomber simply disappears into oblivion. A score card then appears marking how many men, women, and children were killed in the attack.

The most blatant example of a hate video game that features role playing is "Ethnic Cleansing," produced by Resistance Records. Released in 2002, it is based on popular games such as "Doom" and "Quake" in which a player assumes the role of the character and controls his or her actions. After choosing to be a character, such as a Ku Klux Klan member or a racist Skinhead, the participant is thrust into the midst of a race war taking place in a city that most resembles New York. The character roams the streets and subways killing "predatory subhumans" and their Jewish "masters" in an effort to save the world.[96]

The game's background is loaded with sharp details. Plans for world domination, signs reading "Diversity, It's Good for Jews," and billboards for the National Alliance are seen throughout the city's streets. When the player kills African Americans they make monkey and ape sounds; when the player kills Latinos they say, "I'll just take a siesta now!" and "Ay Carumba!"; and when Jewish characters are killed they say, "Oy vey!" At the final level, the player battles with a rocket launcher yielding Ariel Sharon in his "subterranean lair." He is heard hurling insults such as, "We have destroyed your culture!"; "We silenced Henry Ford!"; and, as he dies, "Filthy White dog, you have destroyed thousands of years of planning." Through these hate video games, young people learn the expectations of social roles by engaging in role playing and, subsequently, role-taking. Currently, no research exists indicating how successful these games are as recruiting tools for racist Skinheads or the larger White supremacist movement. However, the United States Army reports that its version of the role-playing-based game "Operations" has prompted 15 to 30 percent of the roughly thirty-five thousand people a day who access the game's website to then check the Army's recruiting site.[97] On the basis of this finding, one can reasonably speculate that a notable portion of those who play the hate-based video games are subsequently inclined to peruse the websites of White supremacy movements like racist Skinhead organizations.

Self

Society Shapes the Self

According to Identity Theory, the structural and organizational composition of the self is influenced by society. One way in which society shapes the contours and operation of the self is through commitment. This concept is based on the degree to which a person is dedicated to taking up or living out a particular role as a function of the number of social relationships contingent upon the said role or position. At times, an individual's membership in a racist Skinhead collective is relatively easy to discern, given the person's chosen style of dress and overall appearance. Examples of this are delineated below.

The traditional Skinhead look is a shaved head, industrial steel-toed Doc Marten boots, polo or T-shirt, denim jeans rolled to below the knee, braces (suspenders), a military flight jacket adorned with a variety of racist patches, and numerous tattoos.[98] The white laces in Skinheads' boots stand for the purity of the Aryan race and for White pride; red laces symbolize the spilt blood of their enemies.[99] Yellow laces are also worn to communicate hatred for the police or that a participant has killed a law enforcement officer.[100] Braces of varying colors may be used to signify regional affiliations, and if suspenders are down over the shoulders, as opposed to up and over them, it means that the person is looking for a fight.[101]

According to Young and Craig,[102] "the skinhead uniform itself and the symbols and rituals adopted by group members combine to achieve obvious hyper-aggressive and hyper-masculine effects." Moreover, Wooden and Blazak[103] found that racist Skinheads in comparison to nonracist Skinheads were more likely to agree that their peers viewed them as troublemakers; this identification represents just one aspect of the heroic warrior social role confirmed through the observations of others. In addition, making a conscious effort to "look the part," racist Skinheads typically thrive on society's imagined perception of them—a perception based on a reputation of indiscriminate violence toward community members.[104] Their look is designed to intimidate their enemies and evoke fear in others.

Every time a pedestrian or passerby avoids members' stares or declines to respond to their verbal assaults, the behavior not only heightens participants' feelings of power; it also confirms their identities as affiliates of a feared organization. In addition, though, it serves as yet another social relationship built on their role identities as members of a dreaded group. Indeed, individuals become committed to this identity because it invariably is manifested in nearly every social situation to which members are involved, given their distinct style of dress and the semipermanent features (e.g., closely cropped hair, tattoos) participants engender. As a result, their role identities as racist Skinheads become the foundation upon which many of their social relationships are formed, further committing them to this unique social person status. Moreover, with the knowledge that their association in the group is so easily recognizable, arguably racist Skinheads purposefully seek out situations in which their membership identities are activated.

Some additional (though cursory) observations regarding identity commitment are warranted here. These comments further suggest how members' dedication to their social person status is maintained through external (i.e., societal) factors. The organization and operation of racist Skinheads have been described as akin to those of street gangs.[105] In addition, the migratory nature of affiliates supports the hypothesis that a significant portion of their within-group role relationships (i.e., those with their comrades/peers) are based on membership in these respective organizations.[106] Finally, for those who hold steady jobs as laborers, role relationships based on the White worker identity can reinforce the commitment of affiliates to their position within the White working class as well as their role identities as members of a racist Skinhead group.

Self Shapes Society

Through the self-verification process the racist Skinhead aligns his or her self-relevant meanings with those of the identity standard. Consequently, being a member of the White working class is verified through identity cues. For example, the chosen style of dress, the closely cropped hair, the industrial steel-toed Doc Marten work boots, the denim jeans, and the suspenders are worn by members in recognition of their White working-class roots.[107] Moreover, and specifically in relation to the Hammerskins, their patch consists of two crossed hammers. This symbolically indicates that participants embrace their working-class background. Then, too, Skinheads "believe that their shaved heads, flight jackets, and boots show everyone what they believe."[108]

The use of interpersonal prompts is a technique that aligns one's self-meanings for maleness with the identity standard. Located within this identity standard are aspects of power and aggression. Some individuals become involved in the racist Skinhead movement in order to gain a sense of authority and control over their lives. Indeed, as Young and Craig[109] noted, "Many physically unimposing young men are attracted to the subculture because it provides a chance [for them] to feel 'more powerful.'"[110] Moreover, the appearance of members intimidates others and evokes fear in those around them. Along these lines, "the skinhead uniform itself and the symbols and rituals adopted by group members combine to achieve obvious hyper-aggressive and hyper-masculine effects."[111] Additionally, reclaiming aspects of their masculinity is expressed through violence framed within the discourse of victimhood. By internalizing these varied aspects of manhood (i.e., power, aggression, nationalism), racist Skinheads justify their violent behavior behind the guise of self-defense.

The heroic warrior role identity is also confirmed or verified through engagement in hostile confrontations. In these instances, racist Skinheads regard themselves as fighting for the White race against non-Whites, Jews, homosexuals, and all those suspected of being instruments of the evil ZOG. For example, Hamm[112] found that 89 percent of the Skinheads he interviewed ($N = 36$) reported that they joined the group to fight for the survival of their race.

In one particularly chilling incident, Hamm recalled the events surrounding the death of Mulguletta Seraw, an Ethiopian immigrant, at the hands of Kenneth Murray Mieske. Mr. Mieske was a member of the East Side White Pride organization, a Portland Skinhead, and the vocalist for the heavy metal band Machine. Mieske is currently serving a life sentence for the 1988 brutal murder of Mr. Seraw. The circumstances that led up to the slaying are well documented.

At about 1:30 on the morning of November 13, 1988, Kenneth Murray Mieske (a.k.a. Ken Death)—a stocky twenty-three-year-old singer with a heavy-metal band called Machine—drove his car through the rainy streets of Portland, Oregon. At his side were twenty-year-old Steven Strasser and nineteen-year-old Kyle Brewster. Mieske, Strasser, and Brewster were members of a skinhead gang called the East Side White Pride and they were intoxicated on beer. Their hair was cut short and they wore jeans, bomber jackets, and black steel-toed boots.[113]

Meanwhile, Wondwosen Tesfaye, accompanied by his friend Tilahun Antneh, sat double-parked in a car, saying good night to a third friend, Mulguletta Seraw. All three of the men were Ethiopian immigrants. After shouting some orders to move the car, the Skinheads exited their own vehicle.

Just as Seraw backed away, Mieske, Strasser, and Brewster approached Tesfaye's car. Mieske carried a baseball bat. He smashed the front window of the Dodge, spraying Tesfaye and Antneh with shattered glass. Then he turned on Seraw. "No please!" cried Seraw. "Please!" Using all the power of his strong young body, Mieske then beat Seraw in the head with the ball bat as Strasser and Brewster kicked the 100-pound immigrant with their boots. When they were finished, Mieske had fractured Seraw's skull in two places, killing him. Twenty-four hours later, Portland police searched the three-room apartment of Strasser and Brewster. In the first room, they discovered a collection of baseball bats and clubs. In the second, they found racist propaganda published by a Southern California organization known as the White Aryan Resistance (W.A.R.). And in the third room, they found a small library on the rise and fall of Nazi Germany.[114]

In this case, the process at work entailed interpersonal prompts. Mieske had collected racist propaganda published by WAR. This organization frequently depicts racist Skinheads as heroic racial warriors, and he expressed his violent fantasies through his music. On this tragic night, Mieske and his comrades found themselves in a situation that was conducive to the confirmation of the heroic racial warrior role identity. The most obvious and conventional role performance for the heroic warrior is victory against his (or her) foes. In this situation,

Mieske's enemy was a 100-pound Ethiopian immigrant. Clearly, the efforts undertaken by Mr. Mieske and his comrades to confirm their statuses through bloody victory were promising, if not altogether assured.

Interspersed with the heroic warrior role is that of the noble savior, especially for one's White brethren. For example, consider the following incident recounted by a twenty-two-year-old Portland Skinhead.

> There was a fight at [Walker] High School between a Black kid and a White kid and everyone was supporting the Black kid who had been picking on this White forever. Typical bullshit, right? But we knew that there were Whites there who were sick and tired of being called "racists" just for sticking up for themselves. So we went down there one day, right, when school was letting out and beat the shit out of some gangster-looking nigger. The next day everyone at Milwaukee was talking about, "Oh man, did you hear that the skinheads kicked some nigger's ass?[115]

In yet another instance, a twenty-year-old Skinhead from Florida offered these comments:

> It's a fun Saturday night for us. We go down to Visage and drink beer, slam dance and pick up some punk chicks and fight. All it takes is one Spic to start something and we just open a can of whoop ass. It's great for us because we know that half the white kids there are getting harassed by the Hispanics in their school and they are just waiting for someone to stick up for them. I've had these totally straight looking kids come up to me later, maybe a month later, and say, "Hey, that was really cool what you did. I wish you guys would come to my school and kick some ass."[116]

Once again, interpersonal prompts are the primary technique through which the Skinheads align their self-relevant meanings (i.e., warrior identity) with the significance assigned to their behavior (i.e., battle, victory, savior of Whites in need).

Additionally, the technique of selective interpretation can be observed in the previous passages. Specifically, consider the concluding comments offered in both statements but especially in the first one. The Skinhead member exclaims, "The next day everyone at Milwaukee was talking about, 'Oh man, did you hear that the skinheads kicked some nigger's ass?' " Here, the group member uses selective interpretation; he defines the student's remarks as supporting, indeed glorifying, the collective's assault on the African American student. This is substantiated by the student's reported use of a racial slur to describe the victim. In this case, the racist Skinhead employed the technique of selective interpretation to verify the alignment of his role identity as a noble warrior and savior with his ongoing (violent) behavior.

Part III

10

Conclusion

The conceptual and applied work undertaken throughout this book suggests that selected facets of structural Symbolic Interactionism and Identity Theory can be integrated to fashion an interpretive and explanatory model that accounts for the emergence and maintenance of identity among various terrorist organizations. Consistent with this thesis, the first section of the text emphasized theoretical developments and provisional remarks on militant extremism germane to our overall enterprise. The second section stressed the linkage between theory and practice by systematically reviewing five different terrorist movements from around the globe that featured various types of militant and violent behavior (e.g., nationalist, religious, political, racial). Admittedly, the five applications were not exhaustive; however, this was not our intention. Instead, the aim was to assess the relevance of the proposed framework for purposes of meaningful and practical social science inquiry as well as for potential programmatic reform.

On the basis of the foregoing analysis, it appears that accessing and examining the formation of identity is quite revealing, especially in the context of explaining the terrorist threat. This is a significant preliminary finding. Generally speaking, what it implies is that the prevailing research would do well to appropriate a more interpretive lens, built around the insights of social psychology, as investigators endeavor to explain, predict, and prevent future acts of terrorist violence at home or abroad. It is this realization that underscores and informs the sundry issues entertained in this book's final chapter.

In particular, several summary observations are detailed in this concluding chapter. These observations return the reader to the text's original thesis, the various facets of the conceptual framework that governed our more empirical analyses, and the rich data elicited through the respective applications to the distinct terrorist collectives. Accordingly, we globally review Identity Theory and sociological social psychology, remaining mindful of how the suggested template sensibly accounts for deviant or criminal behaviors, including militant extremism. In addition, the five fundamental elements of our explanatory model are represented. Our exploration of these elements in relation to the terrorist organizations under consideration formed the basis for our contention that culture, self, and society profoundly interrelate. Indeed, as a complex network of human social interaction, the maintenance of identity textures the society that terrorist group members inhabit. Moreover, the lifeworlds to which affiliates are exposed and immersed informs their militant self-concepts. Several thematic and synoptic comments along these lines are provided.

This chapter also focuses on implications. Although clearly provisional and certainly speculative, these remarks draw attention to future research, programming, and policy. In particular, the significance of the model for purposes of police administration and management are featured, including recommendations relevant to local and federal law enforcement practices, military preparedness, intelligence-gathering strategies, and counterterrorism interviewing approaches. In addition, attention to law and public policy is highlighted. Among other things, the suggestions here focus on surveillance and civil liberties, peace negotiations and international affairs, and governmental initiatives that employ violence as a response to terrorism. Finally, the conceptual framework's ability to account for other forms of criminal conduct (e.g., gang affiliation) is briefly assessed, and the model's overall contribution to understanding the identity construct is tentatively discussed.

Identity Theory and Sociological Social Psychology

The contention that identity plays a significant role in the commission of terrorism is not necessarily novel. Indeed, an examination of previous research revealed that the application of Erikson's process of identification to terrorist motivations was a popular approach during the late 1970s and early 1980s.[1] In turn, these investigations informed the popular view that militant extremists engender a fragmented or nonexistent identity, compelling them to join organizations whose totalitarian dogma satiates this need to establish a self-concept.[2] However, as Horgan[3] argued, this early research suffered from several significant limitations. Chief among them was that social scientists committed the fundamental attribution error and, as a result, their respective inquiries were methodologically flawed.

In sum, relying on this purely psychological explanation for terrorism (i.e., that individuals behave violently because they are in search of an identity) has inevitably contributed to the false assumption that there is something profoundly unhealthy, dysfunctional, or incomplete about such persons. Accepting the notion that "terrorists are essentially normal individuals,"[4] this book rejected the psychological position largely because it did nothing more than pathologize, vilify, and demonize group members.[5]

In response, we argued that the cognate field of social psychology offers a more accurate and seamless depiction of identity's influence on extremist violence. This is the case because the conceptual framework attempts to understand behavior as an interaction between the internal psychological factors and the external sociological forces of the human experience. Along these lines, several studies were reviewed that suggestively indicated how a psychologically animated social psychology (i.e., Social Identity Theory) could be used to explain terrorism. However, as we stipulated, this perspective fell short of providing a complete picture of the process of identity construction, the emerging self, and, for purposes of this project, their respective influences on militant extremism. In part, this is the case because Social Identity Theory views the creation of the social person as linked to one's belonging to various categories or collectivities in which a uniformity of group perceptions is promulgated. However, this focus on intergroup, as opposed to intragroup, dynamics neglects the unique interconnectedness one has to those within the membership collective or the specified interaction context.[6]

Accordingly, we maintained that Identity Theory, grounded in sociological social psychology and structural Symbolic Interactionism, addressed these shortcomings. Indeed, the proposed interpretative framework offered a vision of identity based on social roles and the exchanges people partook in based on their corresponding role or position relationships. Thus, in effect, this book endeavored to create a rich, conceptual model that both interpreted and explained human social be-havior in various organizational settings or contexts. More specifically, this model was designed to explore the nature of symbols and their meanings, the corresponding definitions of the situation that group members encountered, the roles that affiliates lived out, and the socialization experiences and role-taking performances participants embodied. By accessing and investigating these dimensions of the identity construct, the relationship among self, society, and culture was made manifest, especially in the context of explaining terrorist behavior and/or its likely threat.

Symbols and Their Meanings

Several symbols were identified as having a powerful influence on the actions of those members aligned with the extremist organizations under examination. For the Provisional Irish Republican Army three symbols were prominently featured. These included violent attacks on Nationalist Catholics by Loyalist Protestant mobs during the Battle of Bogside; the shooting deaths of unarmed civil rights protesters in the Bloody Sunday massacre; and the prisoners who sacrificed their lives in the face of a punitive British regime during the Irish hunger strikes. The pertinent symbols for Hamas consisted of Zionism, a religious and economic ideology perceived to have wrongfully led to the usurpation of Muslim territory; the advent of the Islamic awakening, a theological movement that returned the Palestinian people to their religious roots in pursuit of reclaiming their homeland; and the Oslo Accord, a peace agreement that illegitimately forfeited Islamic holy land to Israel. For the Shining Path, notable symbols comprised the social and economic system of the ruling exploiters epitomized in the oppressive, semifeudal, neocolonialist hacienda system located in the Peruvian countryside; revisions to the group's fundamentalist interpretation of Marxism/Leninism/Maoism; and the brutality perpetrated by the Peruvian government's counterrevolutionary forces. The discriminatory policies enacted by the Sinhalese-dominated Sri Lankan government, the anti-Tamil programs, and the broken promises made to the Tamil minority by Sinhalese authorities represented the pertinent symbols for the Liberation Tigers of Tamil Eelam. Finally, for North American racist Skinheads, pivotal symbols included the devalued status of White men in the United States, exemplified by threats to their (privileged) ethnic, racial, gender, heterosexual, and economic standing; their belief in the Zionist Occupational Government (i.e., ZOG), understood to control the government, the media, and the economy; and hate music, recognized as an expression of protest against efforts to marginalize the status quo.

In exploring each of these symbols for the respective organizations, we provided important background information. This information was useful in that it described how the symbols developed shared meanings within individual groups and among their respective memberships through exposure to history, culture, socialization, and social structure. Moreover, it was noted that the symbols led to action for militant affiliates, especially as conveyed through the organization's official discourse or channels of communication.

A cursory review of the various symbols and their corresponding meanings as located across the five different terrorist organizations indicates some thematic points of similarity. Most especially, for each collective an identified concrete or abstract symbol personified the wrong or injustice that had been perpetrated against the militant extremist group. Some additional observations on this matter are warranted.

For the PIRA, the mistreatment and violence perpetrated against the minority Catholic community in Northern Ireland by Protestant Loyalists, British authorities, and other sympathizers conveys this felt sense of harm. For Hamas, the occupation of holy Muslim land that was "stolen" through Zionist colonialism symbolically communicates this notion of wrongdoing. For the Liberation Tigers of Tamil Eelam, their ongoing exposure to discrimination, oppression, and disrespect as a minority citizenry sends to them a profound message of injustice. For the Shining Path, the dictatorial governmental system, the ideological assault on the true path of Marxism/Leninism/Maoism waged by revisionists, and the ruthless acts of the Peruvian counterinsurgency forces against the country's peasant inhabitants personify members' lived sense of unfairness. For racist Skinheads, the loss of the preferred (and privileged) White, male, heterosexual status in American society communicates a deep sense of mistreatment and inequity.

To be clear, these symbols are more than just representations of grievances provided in the rhetorical stylings of an extremist group. Instead, according to the structural Symbolic Interactionist perspective and Identity Theory, all of these symbols have the power to classify the social world. In the case of those terrorist groups examined throughout this book, they served to cast the members of a particular ethnic, racial, religious, or political segment of society into what was perceived as a threatened, though cherished, position or status.

Definition of the Situation

In addition to classifying the social world, these symbols contributed to the construction of each group's definition of the situation. Interpreting the meaning of these symbols and acting as a reference group, these five organizations provided their members with a basic prism through which to view their existences. Along these lines, the text explored the definition of the situation for each movement within the parameters of a problem, a solution, and a strategy for achieving that particular result. This approach was undertaken because, inevitably, social problems are created through a totality of interactions. Reducing the definition of the situation to a few select, though pivotal, concrete situations would have overlooked the true essence by which group members came to perceive their world and the way this perception subsequently influenced their identities and corresponding behaviors. Moreover, failing to include descriptions of the way members of the respective militant organizations envisioned their future and focusing instead on the way affiliates resorted to violence in an effort to affect that forecasted outcome would be similarly limiting.

For the PIRA, the problem centers on the marginalization of the minority Irish Catholic community in Northern Ireland by an alien tyrannical government and an intractable Protestant Loyalist majority. While the PIRA traditionally has viewed armed struggle as the only viable means by which to eliminate its oppression, the movement came to adopt a more moderate platform with the increased influence of its political wing, Sinn Féin. This entity encouraged change through political mobilization and grassroots empowerment. The PIRA's proposed solution to their problem entails the unification of a thirty-two-county sovereign Irish state, devoid of British influence. This sovereign nation-state espouses social justice, civil rights, and religious tolerance. The organization's inability to achieve this solution would result in the continued oppression of the Irish Catholic community.

The membership of Hamas views its principal problem to be the exile of the Palestinian people from their rightful land and the existence of a Jewish state in the middle of the Arab-Muslim world. The organization's goal is to emancipate the Palestinian people from occupation, to liberate and reclaim their holy land, and to topple the Zionist regime that is supported by neocolonialist influences. In its place, Hamas plans to reestablish an Islamic state encompassing all of historic Palestine, from the Jordan River to the Mediterranean Sea. For Hamas faithful, the Palestinian-Israeli conflict is a struggle for survival; failure to successfully achieve their desired goal means that the Palestinian Arab people will, in time, become extinct.

The Shining Path collective regards its primary problem as economic and political. This is a wholesale crisis in which Peru's indigenous masses have suffered at the hands of the fascist government through its reliance on bureaucratic capitalism. The latter was derived from the regime's commitment to semifeudal and imperialistic practices. The identified solution to the militant group's dilemma was to establish and implement a collectivist state based on a fundamentalist interpretation of Marxism/Leninism/Maoism. In order to achieve this goal, the collective argued that it needed to engage in armed struggle. The violence and terrorism that followed was designed to reestablish Andean socialism and to protect true communism from the ideological assaults of revisionists.

The problem identified by the Liberation Tigers of Tamil Eelam is that the Tamil people have been the innocent victims of government-sponsored Sinhalese oppression. Discriminatory policies, anti-Tamil initiatives, and broken promises are just three symbolic representations of this oppression. For the LTTE, the means by which to end this subjugation is to carve out a Tamil state based on egalitarian principles. The only perceived approach by which to achieve self-determination and to ensure a sustainable future is through armed struggle.

For racist Skinheads, the fundamental dilemma is that those of Aryan descent are in danger of losing their "racial purity." This perception is traceable to members' belief that a rapid influx of non-Whites into the United States has occurred, that increased acceptance of racial mixing has taken place, and that the waning existence of traditional White male hegemony continues unabated. For this extremist collective, violence is used to intimidate others and as an expression of power over those deemed to be undesirable. Group members contend that the coming Racial Holy War will lead to large-scale violence between the races. This will result in the Aryan people establishing an independent state in the Pacific Northwest where affiliates can freely advance their quest for racial purity. Participants maintain that failure to achieve this goal will result in the extinction of the White race.

The definition that each militant extremist group attaches to the hostile situation it encounters is quite significant. Indeed, recalling the words of W. I. Thomas, "If men and women define [their] situations as real, then they are real in their consequences."[7] Thus, if new recruits, established affiliates, and/or hard-core members truly embrace the meaning the organization assigns to the cultural/political/religious situation the group itself encounters, then members will interpret their predicament as grave. In short, they will perceive their identities as unjustly placed in disrepute and all those who embody the collective's perspective as wrongfully under siege.

On the basis of a rigid belief system that defines the situation dichotomously, members regard their struggle for movement identity as a fight between good and evil, oppressor and oppressed, aggressor and victim. This steadfast view informs the terrorist organization's contention that it knows what is best for its citizenry, and that achieving the desired outcome (e.g., economic liberation, nationalism, self-determination, racial purity) is worth sacrificing the lives of innocents. This is especially true for movements such as Hamas, the Shining Path, and racist Skinheads. As militant collectives, they tend to be more apocalyptic and are driven to reestablish some aspect of a past social order based on their respective fundamentalist interpretation of religion or ideology. For the members of the five terrorist organizations examined in this book, prospects for continued discrimination and oppression—as well as the likelihood of extinction and genocide—are all considered very real. As a catalytic dimension of the situation the respective groups define and adopt for their membership, affiliates believe that immediate and sustained action is not only warranted but is essential. This belief system includes the use of terrorism and other forms of violence to rectify their felt sense of victimization and impending doom.

Roles

Several themes emerge when we assess the various roles that inform membership in the five militant organizations examined in this book. The two most salient of these are briefly reviewed in this section. These include the victim and martial roles.

Within all of the groups examined, there is the adoption of a common role that is threatened or under assault, contributing to a perceived sense of persecution. This is the victim role. Consistent with role theory, the conventional aspects of such a position include the experience of unequivocal harm and unquestioned blamelessness (i.e., not responsible for the harm that befalls them), such that a sympathetic response to the group's plight is merited.[8]

For the PIRA, this sense of victimization emerges as members occupy the Irish Catholic role. Both inherent in and fundamental to this role is the conviction that the Irish Catholic community historically has been economically and politically marginalized by the British government and by the Protestant community in Northern Ireland. Similarly, the Palestinian role espouses the belief that Palestinian Arabs have been disenfranchised and oppressed by Israel. Moreover, the Islamic fundamentalist status perceives continued exposure to Western influences as eroding the Islamic *umma*. For members of the Shining Path, the *mestizo* role comparably functions, although it includes some variation. Specifically, the *mestizo* intellectuals who composed the Shining Path's leadership identified with the exploited and marginalized standing of the indigenous Peruvian Indians. However, at the same time, they conveyed an intrinsic attitude of superiority to the peasantry—citizens they purportedly assisted. Conversely, within the *mestizo* and Indian peasant roles, resentment for the *mestizo* elites, capitalists, merchants, and the colonial invaders who oppressed them through the Andean semifeudal system informs the group's felt sense of victimization. The Sri Lankan Tamil role is based on the belief that the Tamil population was subjected to persecution by the Sinhalese-controlled government, especially in the form of unjust programs, discriminatory policies, and broken promises. Finally, for racist Skinheads, the experience of victimization is traceable to their membership roles as White, working-class males endeavoring to survive amidst a hostile, pro-minority environment.

The second type of common role that contributes to the formation of the self is the martial role. Drawing upon aspects of the victim-oriented role, the martial status demands some sort of violent response to the experience of subjugation.[9] The response is designed to reclaim what was lost or stolen, or to confront a counter-role that endangers one's very existence or chosen way of life. For the militant extremist collectives investigated throughout this text, these roles are based on mythology and romanticism, rather than historical fact, in which ancient warrior images prevail.

Grounded in conventional practices with corresponding societal expectations, the martial role has been appropriated by the respective terrorist organizations and performed by individual members. Moreover, for each collective, this role does not exist or function in a vacuum; rather, it is significantly connected to other statuses that members faithfully occupy. This point is crucial to understanding how self-meanings (i.e., identities) are generated and how their subsequent inclusion into self-schemas influences the way in which the roles are internalized, organized, and expressed.

To illustrate, a cursory review of the Republican, volunteer, Islamist, Senderista, freedom fighter, male, and racial holy warrior roles reveals some striking commonalities. These are all statuses or positions in which justice, equality, self-determination, freedom, autonomy, and self-sacrifice are valued. Moreover, it is expected that those who assume these roles will be courageous and loyal, disciplined and strong, determined idealists, obedient to the movement's moral and ethical code of conduct, and committed to the ideals of the past. Among the five terrorist organizations examined, the most extreme roles include the Shaheed and the Mavirar/Tiyaki. This is because affiliates are expected to willingly sacrifice themselves as they violently take the lives of their enemies. This particular feature makes the martial role distinct from the Christian or Western conception of a martyr.[10] However, the most important similarity among the martial roles embraced by the different militant collectives is that those who undertake this performance are perceived as heroic protectors of a people, defenders of the group's faith, ethnicity, ideology, or race.

Socialization and Role-Taking

Socialization is a process through which individuals learn and adopt social roles. Moreover, through exposure to socialization, people are prepared to participate in social systems, create social selves, and attach themselves to the systems in which they participate. The application chapters identified a variety of socializing agents that can be categorized into significant and generalized others. Several summary comments that illustrate the activity of socialization are delineated below.

In the case of the PIRA, family members, as significant others, were identified as pivotal to teaching children the values and expectations of being a Republican and, more specifically, living the role of a Catholic. Interestingly, the family does not need to immerse the subject into every aspect of a particular role in order for the person to occupy it. For example, in the case of Prabhakaran's childhood experiences, he explained that relatives exposed him to the plight of the Tamil freedom struggle and to Sinhalese-perpetrated atrocities at a young age. Other Tamil militants articulated similar sentiments. However, within these interactions, no indication that family members advocated for the use of violence was ever made. This fact notwithstanding, exposure to such socialization functioned as a foundation on which the core values, expectations, and attitudes of the victimization role were communicated and upon which the martial role could be built. The same argument applies to the case of racist Skinheads. Their socialization homelife typically consists of racism and bigotry. While family members do not necessarily indoctrinate their offspring to take up the martial facet of the warrior role, the home-based socializing encounters of youth with racism operate as one of its fundamental components.

Specifically within an educational context, former members of the PIRA recalled the Christian Brothers who taught them the lessons of British atrocities, the heroic acts of the 1916 Easter Rising, and Republican poetry in primary school. Additionally, Hamas has established and funds kindergartens—as well as daycare centers and youth and sports clubs—for purposes of training the next Muslim generation. This campaign is particularly noteworthy, especially with respect to Hamas's efforts to attract fledgling Shaheeds and to prepare them for suicide operations. Moreover, Guzmán and the Shining Path conducted socialization campaigns through university "outreach" programs. Here, student-followers went into the local countryside to teach in primary and secondary schools. Finally, Prabhakaran recollected the importance of a particular teacher who introduced him to the necessity of armed struggle as a mechanism to establish Tamil liberation. Collectively, these instances demonstrate the profound importance of socialization (i.e., instructional setting) through significant others (i.e., teachers) in the formation and maintenance of identity.

The educational forum continues to be a staple of the LTTE's multifaceted conditioning program. Indeed, in those school systems under Prabhakaran's control, students are indoctrinated with a decisively pro-LTTE curriculum. In an even more extreme example of socialization, martial roles are taught during an institutionalized period of immersion for young Tamil youth.

Additional efforts at educational socialization can also be noted. To illustrate, Hamas created summer camps for kids, the Shining Path established popular schools in the countryside and in prisons, and the LTTE formed its Punniapoomi (Sacred Land) school. These indoctrination initiatives are all quite revealing. What they suggest is that instructional institutions, and their agents of socialization, serve the interests of the extremist organization by exposing and inculcating recruits to the important aspects of the martial role.

Examples of the way the generalized other socializes individuals into the terrorist collective's social system are apparent in a variety of contexts or outlets. For members of the Provisional Irish Republican Army, the generalized other is expressed through popular, medialike art. These include films, murals, poetry, and song. For the Hamas movement, manifestations of the generalized other take the form of the many posters and playing cards that blanket communities along the West Bank and Gaza Strip. These items are distributed to Palestinian people in order to venerate the self-sacrifice of a Shaheed.

The Shining Path's use of murals and artwork in its makeshift popular prison schools conveyed a similar message. Moreover, Prabhakaran's reliance upon printed materials that chronicled the exploits of heroic Tamil figures throughout history enabled citizens to learn the role components of being a revolutionary. This activity is also a representation of the generalized other. Similar to the Hamas organization, media devices such as posters and pictures that commemorate fallen soldiers, patriotic songs, and action videos are utilized by the LTTE. Finally, for racist Skinheads, the influence of the paramilitary warrior image is significant. As portrayed in popular movies, hate music, and print material, it conveys many of the core features of the racial warrior role. The various print and electronic outlets by which this image is communicated are expressions of the generalized other and its ability to socialize group members.

Related to socialization is role-taking. Role-taking was described as a process through which individuals learn and adopt social roles. By imaginatively taking the place of another, one comes to perceive the possibilities for one's own behavior. Two forms of role-taking were described in this text. The first of these is more rudimentary and is typically observed in childhood game playing. Several examples of such role-taking performances are discernible among the various militant extremist collectives.

To illustrate, members of the PIRA explained how, in their youth, they pretended to be IRA men versus British soldiers. Additionally, a popular childhood game found in the villages of the West Bank and Gaza Strip is "Arabs and Jews." Moreover, the LTTE's creation of playgrounds that feature mock weapons simulating battlefield conditions encourages young people to imitate the martial role. Similarly, for racist Skinheads, the production and viewing of hate video games clearly demonstrates how role-taking activity functions. Participants in these games assume the role of a White supremacist intent on killing those who belong to a minority community.[11]

The second form of role-taking is a more sophisticated variant of the one previously described, requiring a heightened degree of intellectual gymnastics. In brief, members of the respective militant collectives endeavor to interpret the way others might view their activities and attempt to reframe their behaviors (and their rhetoric) in ways that promote sympathy and respect for their causes. Examples of this process are discernible from the activities of the various extremist organizations reviewed in this book.

In their attempts to secure financial support, PIRA members assumed the position (and attitude) of American donors. In doing so, they refrained from mentioning the group's socialist leanings and displayed no hostility toward the Pope. Had PIRA loyalists not adopted this role-taking strategy, their fund-raising efforts would have been seriously jeopardized. PIRA faithful employed a similar strategy in the production and dissemination of propaganda designed to sway members of the Irish Catholic community toward the movement's militant cause. In adopting the perspective of the Israeli government, its Arab neighbors, and fellow Palestinians, the Hamas leadership was able to develop an effective response to the Oslo Accord and other land agreements the group found abhorrent. In this way, Hamas smartly reaffirmed its role as the true guardian of Palestinian interests. Members of the Shining Path who engaged in rounds of criticism and self-appraisal also participated in the role-taking process. Specifically, they predicted potential weaknesses among affiliates and cognitively developed responses that would satisfy inquisitors. This role-taking activity enabled participants to demonstrate that they embraced and espoused the true teachings of Marx/Lenin/Mao.

Self

The fifth structural symbolic interactionist concept that enables one to access identity and to account for the subsequent behavior of extremist group members is the self. Thus far in this portion of the chapter, we summarily reviewed the various symbols that lead the militant collectives to classify the social worlds they respectively inhabit. Through the interpretation of these concrete and abstract symbols, the groups establish a definition for the situation they confront. This definition includes the belief that their ways of life—indeed, their very existences—are in danger of extinction, a reality necessitating immediate and direct action.

The way the victim and martial roles inform and sustain this situated definition for each collective was also delineated. Both of these roles endeavor to address past injustices and to ensure the group's survival. Through socialization experiences and role-taking performances, these roles become internalized self-meanings in the form of role identities. However, the manner in which individuals live them out is a function of society's influence on the self and the impact of the social person on his or her lifeworld. These matters are discussed in the following subsections.

SOCIETY SHAPES THE SELF

This variant of Identity Theory focuses on how social structure affects the composition of the self.[12] Based on the notion that the social person is comprised of several role identities, this line of thinking proposes a salience hierarchy. Moreover, an identity's prominence on this hierarchy is a function of the frequency with which it is activated. Whether or not a specific role identity assumes behavioral form is contingent upon its prominence, its intrinsic and extrinsic gratification, and its suitability for acquiring gratification in a particular situation.[13] A second component to this form of Identity Theory is identity commitment. Identity commitment is based on the number and quality of role relationships one has based on a particular role identity. The more role relationships an individual has that are contingent upon a given identity, the more committed the person will be to that identity. This project argued that different societies function to wed individuals to those role identities that are pertinent to participation in militant groups. Summary examples of this are delineated below.

According to reports from PIRA affiliates, the friends of members are Republicans. In large part, this is the case because the British government isolated the Republican community. Thus, many of the role relationships among PIRA participants hinge on their Republican role identity. Moreover, events such as the Battle of Bogside, the Bloody Sunday massacre, and the Irish Hunger Strikes of the 1980s caused individuals to seek out opportunities to perform their role identities as occupants of a marginalized position. They accomplished this by participating in marches and rallies, and by joining the Provisional Irish Republican Army.

For members of Hamas, Palestinians become committed to this identity through the varied social relationships they establish in the secluded refugee camps and communities of the West Bank and Gaza Strip. This role identity is also enhanced through the "special treatment" affiliates receive from Israeli authorities. Moreover, as we maintained, the salience of being a would-be Shaheed is augmented by significant others (i.e., teachers, principals, and parents). They zealously support young people who express their intentions to fulfill the self-sacrificing martyr role.

The nomadic nature of the Shining Path's operational cells suggests that their role identities were emboldened through the tight-knit social relationships of the group. For example, Sendero's success at regulating virtually every aspect of a member's life, including marriages and the routine activities of those imprisoned or living in compounds, reflects an absence of role identities unrelated to the Senderista status on the identity hierarchy. Similarly, the LTTE collective involved itself in practically every facet of a cadre's life. More specifically, the LTTE made concerted efforts to deny to its members competing role identities. To illustrate, when LTTE affiliates were forced to avoid capture by negotiating their way through an underground network of contacts and safehouses, nearly all of their social relationships were based on their outlawed identity. The racist Skinhead role identity is easily recognizable through members' chosen style of dress and semipermanent features (e.g., tattoos, close-cropped haircuts). As we explained, this role identity forces all of the social relationships of affiliates to be contingent upon it, especially when members are clothed in such attire. Moreover, we indicated that the salience of racist Skinheads' role identity enables them to (re)gain a sense of power and strength through a reputation for bullying and intimidating others.

According to the chapter-by-chapter assessment and the foregoing summary comments delineated above, each of the role identities for the respective groups clusters together on the salience hierarchy to form the martial role identity.[14] Consequently, for each extremist collective, the expression of one role identity is, in a sense, a manifestation of the others. This position implies that while some terrorist operatives may have few role relationships contingent upon their covert identities as members of a militant organization, seeking out opportunities to perform one such role identity would, in a sense, serve to mobilize others. For example, an individual involved in a White supremacist collective might not have many role relationships based on that identity; however, the person's attendance and participation at a Christian Identity church, complete with corresponding friendships and associations, would function to energize the martial role identity. Ultimately, one's efforts to verify the martial role—a status that seeks to secure justice, equality, and self-determination—is the point at which the act of terrorism is committed, embraced, and endorsed.[15]

SELF SHAPES SOCIETY

The other variant of Identity Theory that helps to illuminate the cyclical and symbiotic nature of the society-self relationship is the influence of the social person on his or her lifeworld. In this instance, individuals attempt to align their self-relevant meanings with the identity standard presented by society. Thus, the self shapes society through the self-verification process. This process is facilitated through a number of identity management techniques. These include selective interaction, identity cues, and interpersonal prompts,[16] as well as selective perception, selective interpretation, rationalization, scapegoating, disavowal, and rejection/depreciation.[17] To be clear, society only shapes the self in the sense that it provides culturally prescribed meanings and expectations for the identity standard; it does not cause the social person to act. Inevitably, individuals engage in role-taking performances whereby their personality moderates the way these meanings are internalized and expressed through behavior. This approach to Identity Theory accounts for why some individuals gravitate to militant organizations while others do not. The five application chapters demonstrate how these identity-management techniques are used to verify a group member's role identity. Select examples of this process are delineated below.

A number of identity cues were depicted as verifying the Catholic identity, especially through those hunger strikers who took on a Christ-like appearance. The Islamic fundamentalist identity was confirmed when affiliates wore modest clothing on the football field. The would-be Shaheed[18] identity was verified when participants clothed themselves in the death shroud. The racist Skinhead White worker identity was confirmed when adherents dressed themselves in the attire of the blue-collar laborer.

The identity management technique of interpersonal prompts was described as being useful, especially in verifying several role identities for each of the militant collectives. For the Irish Catholic identity, acts of self-sacrifice and suffering confirmed this status; for the volunteer identity, acts of violence as self-defense verified this status. For the Islamic fundamentalist identity, heeding the call to prayer and engaging in Islamic street justice served as interpersonal prompts verifying this status; for the would-be Shaheed identity, the interpersonal prompts of making videotaped testimonies confirmed this status. For the Senderista identity, fulfilling a lengthy vetting process and affirming one's true commitment to communism through criticism and self-evaluation functioned as interpersonal prompts that verified this identity. For racist Skinheads, the male identity was confirmed through expressions of hyper-masculinity; the heroic warrior identity was verified through acts of violence.

The identity management strategy of selective perception was another technique used among the respective militant collectives investigated in this text to confirm their specified role identities. For example, the Senderista role was verified when affiliates drew attention to the atrocities committed under the auspices of the Peruvian government's counterinsurgency efforts in response to the passing of antiterrorism legislation. The freedom fighter LTTE role identity was similarly confirmed when the group claimed responsibility only for those attacks launched against armed combatants.

The five extremist collectives employed the technique of selective interpretation in a comparable fashion. For example, the LTTE appropriated this strategy when relying on passages from international law documents to support the legitimacy of the group's cause. Moreover, anecdotal comments glorifying assaults committed by racist Skinheads were offered as evidence that Aryans were indeed noble saviors for other, less capable Whites.

The more evasive techniques of rationalization and rejection/disavowal were also employed as management tools to verify group identity. For example, when confronted with the murder of unarmed citizens in a Sri Lankan village, the LTTE's leader asserted that those slain were really Home Guard thugs (i.e., armed soldiers) in disguise. The strategy of rationalization was used because, as the militant leader suggested, honorable warriors do not murder innocent civilians. Additionally, the PIRA incorporated the technique of rationalization to justify its attacks in response to those launched by Northern Irish forces.

Examples of the use of rejection and disavowal to verify specific role identities are also discernible. Two such instances are worth noting. The refusal on the part of PIRA hunger strikers to accept their status as common criminals is one illustration. The contention among Shining Path affiliates that critics of their efforts simply do not understand the significance of the people's war is another.

Implications

In this concluding section, three broad themes are examined. These include a restatement of the book's overall thesis, with due attention to those studies that have offered comparable analyses; an assessment of the text's (and the conceptual framework's) limitations; and a summary review of the study's tentative implications. On this last point, comments related to police administration and management, law and public policy, and the theoretical model's applications to other forms of criminal behavior are all provisionally featured.

Rethinking Our Thesis

As an interpretive and explanatory study, this book endeavored to advance both the field of terrorism research and Identity Theory as understood through key insights derived from structural Symbolic Interactionism. Preliminarily, we note that the field of terrorism research can be positioned within a variety of investigatory levels. For example, Hugh Stephens divided the field into three such domains of analysis.[19] The *Immediate Level* considers practical matters, including operational or tactical issues for law enforcement, intelligence, or military personnel. The *Secondary Level* focuses on strategic analysis, trend identification, and the long-term planning of operations, intelligence gathering, and emergency response intervention. The *Contextual Level* addresses discursive issues, consisting of descriptive and situated accounts of militant extremism from a more general or global perspective. Although law enforcement officials, intelligence analysts, and policy makers may not always see the direct benefits of contextual research, it informs their understanding of terrorist behavior and the taken-for-granted rationale through which these disturbing actions assume lived meaning.

This text endeavored to address the contextual level of analysis. The aim was to provide a more accurate and generalizable framework for comprehending the emergence of identity, especially in the context of explaining the social psychological motivations and forces behind terrorist behavior. To be clear, aspects of the framework are not necessarily novel. For example, several authors have noted the importance of socialization or related topics in regard to the commission of terrorist conduct.[20] Similarly, several investigators have drawn attention to the significance of victimization in propelling extremist violence. Along these lines, Berbrier[21] explored the symbolic construction of persecution in members of the White supremacist movement. Olweean,[22] too, addressed the militant group's victim identity, claiming that the collective carried a "deeply held myth of itself as . . . martyr or even champion of a higher good—sometimes the good of all." Indeed, drawing from aspects of Social Identity Theory, he contended that

> when two groups in conflict each bear a deeply embedded ethos of victim, there is the greatest danger of blind, brutal treatment toward a dehumanized and demonized "other." Absolute wrongness allows for absolute righteousness, and inhumane treatment allows for inhumane treatment in the guise of just retribution toward evildoers.[23]

Rouhana and Bar-Tal[24] explored how both Israelis and Palestinians have relied on history to understand their respective roles as victims of the other's persecution. Moreover, Silke[25] assessed the function of victimization and vengeance in motivating individuals to become involved in terrorist organizations.

Unlike the cited works, this endeavor's chief contribution to the field of terrorism research is that it effectively coalesces many of these themes within a useful organizing framework. At the same time, this project offers several contextual examples of the way identity is established and maintained such that it influences human behavior. Moreover, the conceptual model focuses on the mostly unexamined connections among individuals, groups, society, and culture in relation to militant extremism. Commenting on this type of integration, Crenshaw[26] specifically indicated that this unique feature has remained elusive, especially in the theoretically oriented research on the psychology of terrorism. The same argument applies to the case of sociology, political science, international relations, and other disciplines predisposed to accounting for militant extremism and its global threat. Indeed, as Crenshaw[27] noted,

> We can analyze terrorism at the level of the individual practitioner or the collective actor, the terrorist group. In turn, both actors, individual

and group, must be seen in relation to society as a whole. Similarly, terrorism alters the behavior of individuals, collective actors such as the terrorist organization or the government, and societies.

[However,] the integration of these levels of analysis is a significant problem for research on terrorism.[28]

Thus, by utilizing and integrating key concepts emanating from structural Symbolic Interactionism and Identity Theory, this book accessed the powerful, though subtle, self-and-society relationships that exist in the construction and operation of the terrorist identity.

Limitations

Admittedly, the conceptual and explanatory framework as applied to the five extremist organizations suffers from some methodological limitations. Legitimate criticism could be levied against the model because, in large part, a secondary analysis was undertaken. In other words, the interpretative framework relies on source information not originally collected for purposes of this specific inquiry. Commenting on the shortcomings of such an approach, Champion[29] warned that secondary analysis can be quite problematic. In short, "researchers must often speculate about the meaning of phraseology in various documents, and they lack the opportunity of obtaining further clarification from respondents."[30]

Additionally, the significance of this book's findings are restricted in that various statements, events, and actual language could have unintentionally been taken out of context or otherwise misinterpreted. Thus, material collected and reviewed from previous research studies might be incidentally related to the goals and interests of this project. Indeed, even primary source data from official documents or personal interviews could still be subjected to criticism. This is especially a concern for those source items not originally produced in English. Under these circumstances, the true meaning and essence of language might be lost in translation, which would confound or undermine the arguments presented in this volume. Finally, when one is developing a project built around secondary analysis, published accounts intended for public consumption (e.g., newspaper and magazine coverage, Internet sites) might lack credibility. This is the case because such reporting might not communicate a true and accurate representation of an organization's beliefs, attitudes, or activities. More troublesome, these narrative descriptions might even exacerbate certain aspects of a terrorist event or collective in an effort to persuade a particular audience.

These are all legitimate concerns; however, militant extremist groups are secretive and clandestine in nature. Clearly, then, this very feature makes it especially difficult to access this unique assemblage of violent affiliates or the hostile collectives to which they profess allegiance. As a result, terrorism research demands that investigators take full advantage of the available material, incomplete or suspect though it might be. Typically, these works are authored by investigators representing various academic disciplines. These are social scientists or news journalists who have witnessed militant extremist behavior firsthand or have found a way to penetrate the security and privacy of such closely guarded groups. Consequently, in responding to the criticisms of terrorism research based on secondary source data, Crenshaw[31] offered the following rebuttal:

> Analysis of terrorism must be interdisciplinary, relying on secondary sources from history, political science, and sociology that provide case studies of individual terrorists and terrorist groups. Theoretical insights are often borrowed from other sources . . . and adapted to an interpretation of terrorist activity and its consequences.

Although clearly speculative, this study fully embraced the recommendations of Crenshaw. It represented a preliminary, though sorely needed, interdisciplinary and integrative step toward explaining the terrorist identity and the threat of militant extremism at home and abroad. Thus, to be sure, the work that lies ahead entails a more exhaustive empirical examination of the interpretative model, focusing on its capacity to validly and reliably explain, predict, and prevent domestic and international violence.

Tentative Implications

APPLICATIONS FOR THE LAW ENFORCEMENT, MILITARY, AND INTELLIGENCE COMMUNITIES

Counterterrorism strategies necessitate that those in the law enforcement, military, and intelligence community be equipped with concrete information pertaining to an individual's motivation to join or support a militant extremist collective. This study offered an explanatory and interpretive framework that addresses these very practical concerns. Specifically, the model could enable security personnel charged with profiling, tracking, detecting, and apprehending suspected affiliates to better understand the social psychological, as well as cultural, political, economic, and religious, dynamics that lead to terrorist violence.

As a practical matter, the recommended framework might have considerable utility for the law enforcement, military, and intelligence communities. In particular, the model ostensibly represents a more comprehensive portrait of how the identity construct manifests itself in support of extremist subcultures and in the furtherance of terrorist violence. Indeed, security forces and counterterrorism personnel who track, detect, apprehend, and deter those suspected of perpetrating such acts often rely on outdated and underdeveloped surveillance and profiling approaches, as well as those that are unduly influenced by individual, disciplinary, organizational, or cultural biases.[32]

More specifically, criminal investigators charged with counterterrorism or counterintelligence duties might find the framework helpful in the context of an interview. Here, the explanatory model has potential utility when accounting for why group members embrace particular self-schemas and role sets. To illustrate, in the wake of the 9/11 attacks, U.S. law enforcement officials assigned to counterterrorism initiatives verified and validated aspects of their role identities as entrusted police personnel. In doing so, however, they espoused sentiments of persecution and marginalization, especially in their efforts to uphold justice, defend freedom, and protect Americans from others who threatened or otherwise undermined the country's national security interests or way of life. Similarly, a member or supporter of a militant organization suspected of gathering intelligence, providing logistical support, or coordinating sleeper cells in this country might be working to confirm these same role components that make up that person's identity. Along these lines, knowledge of important symbols and their meanings, familiarity with the way suspects define the victimizing membership situations they confront, awareness of the pertinent roles that influence the behavior of militant participants, and training in the way affiliates both learn and adopt those positions or statuses can all be used to elicit, interpret, and coordinate intelligence information. Consequently, the social psychological model examined in this text offers greater insight surrounding these identifications and activities that could yield better information for those authorities entrusted to protect our communities.

Moreover, the conceptual model could benefit military personnel working to reduce the threat of terrorism to its forces and the civilian populations it protects. Specifically, soldiers who plan, develop, and implement civilian affairs and psychological operations might consider incorporating aspects of the conceptual model into their overall peacekeeping strategies. Designing campaigns intended to reduce support for violent extremists and assisting security forces in their ability to penetrate militant movements are activities that require forethought into the way symbols, roles, and situations take on distinct meanings for a terrorist collective.

Along these lines, one application would entail the facilitation of role conflict between mainstream society and a country's militant extremist group through propaganda campaigns. This could be accomplished by identifying the customary cultural, religious, political, ethnic, etc., statuses (along with their corresponding elements) appropriated by that society and juxtaposing them against those counter-roles embraced by the terrorist collective. The point here would be to exploit the inconsistencies. For example, honor has been specified as a powerful expectation and value within the warrior type role identity, especially among various violently extremist organizations. The production of electronic and print media that documents the lack of honor in murdering noncombatants could help to undermine the support and sustained membership of a terrorist collective.

Another example comes from the activities of the Hamas movement. This collective conceived of and implemented an intensive campaign to socialize young children into the value of self-sacrifice through martyrdom on behalf of the Palestinian cause. However, accessing the role set of motherhood, the counter-role of being a son or daughter, and the societal expectations of family unity among Arab relatives could result in clear and cogent efforts to undermine the value assigned to this indoctrination activity. Moreover, identifying and publicizing role-identity commonalities across tribal, ethnic, or nationalist boundaries could facilitate peace or abate violence. Clearly, these are merely suggestions; however, the framework provides multiple campaign theme possibilities that military personnel could pursue relative to their civil affairs and psychological operations.

Finally, intelligence analysts charged with connecting disparate pieces of information together and with forecasting future behavior might find the framework useful. In short, the model represents a more accurate prism through which to develop collection plans, problem solve, assess threats, challenge existing assumptions, and make informed recommendations. One facet of such intelligence analysis that could be bolstered by the proposed model is "link" or "association" analysis. Based on social network theory, association analysis is a popular means of studying relationships and interactions among individuals, collectives, or entities, especially those involved in the criminal enterprise or a delinquent network.[33]

Ideally, a structural assessment of the role relationships among leaders, lieutenants, foot soldiers, and supporters enables these networks to be disrupted by the identification and targeting of key nodes. A frequently cited illustration of this analytical technique's power is identifying and then removing a key player who is a vital communications link within a terrorist cell, resulting in the erosion and/or disruption of its operational capabilities. In a similar example, it has been argued that those individuals on the fringes of a social network with weaker links, numerically and qualitatively, might be more vulnerable to influence by authorities.[34] Arguably, this is the case because they might be less committed to their role identity as a group member. In an example based on the proposed model, identifying and extricating cell affiliates suspected of facilitating the process of role performance and verification may cause fellow group participants to become more vulnerable as they seek out alternative avenues of self-confirmation.

By strengthening the power of link analysis, intelligence analysts could make a broader variety of recommendations concerning those affiliates that should be targeted for additional surveillance, recruitment as confidential informants, or, if necessary, immediate apprehension. Thus, by utilizing aspects of the interpretive and explanatory framework, analysts would be better equipped to conduct more in-depth examinations of such networks and draw more meaningful conclusions from their often limited sources. In sum, law enforcement, military, and intelligence training emphasizing the symbols, meanings, roles, socialization methods, and self-concepts that underpin identity formation and membership in terrorist groups could go a long way toward predicting and preventing unwanted aggression, social disorganization, and the human misery resulting from such heinous acts.

APPLICATIONS TO LAW AND PUBLIC POLICY

Another area where the preceding analysis finds utility is in the realm of law and public policy. For example, the recent spread of Islamic extremist violence into the Western world has forced many democratic governments to rethink several constitutionally charged issues such as privacy, detention without trial, and the right of assembly. Arguably, a thoughtful and reasoned assessment of the model's capacity to inform and educate might assist legislators and policymakers to develop the most appropriate responses to the threat and presence of terrorism. Clearly, this suggestion resonates deeply, especially given the post-9/11 climate. This assessment argues that terrorism is, in part, a reaction to the perception of marginalization, alienation, victimization, and/or disenfranchisement.

In line with this interpretation, terrorists may continue to emerge as certain groups of people repeatedly interpret the symbols of their oppression as staples of their existence and come to believe that the only possible means of achieving a particular solution is through violence. As a result, government-sponsored actions that rely on tactics such as racial, ethnic, or religious profiling, collective punishment, and large-scale violence to excise belligerent extremists and their loyalists might inevitably (and unwittingly) help to create the symbolic events and interpretations that serve to fuel and sustain martial roles. These are roles that inform the terrorist identity and, subsequently, perpetuate the cycle of violence.[35] Thus, it is imperative that those responsible for making and amending the law have an informed and firm understanding of the motivations behind terrorism (and the groups who initiate such violence) before enacting specific responses to it.

Within the realm of foreign policy, the interpretive framework could also have a significant impact for furthering international affairs. For example, relative to peace negotiations, government officials who utilize aspects of this model could become quite adept at assessing and comprehending the rationale that informs terrorist violence, especially if such personnel effectively adopted the mindset and roles of combatants. One clear application of this strategy exists in the struggle for peace between Israelis and Palestinians. For example, both the Palestinian and Israeli role identities are saturated with themes of victimization, passed on and reaffirmed from one generation to the next. For Palestinians, this persecution dates back to the early 1900s, especially the advent of

Zionism. More recently, it emerges through the occupation of the Gaza Strip and West Bank and the confinement of young men held without trial in administrative detention settings. For Israeli Jews, victimization stems from centuries of persecution, the trauma and inhumanity of the Holocaust, and the unrelenting fear that perhaps one day a suicide bomber will, once again, attack a local grocery store or pummel a favorite discotheque, killing scores of innocent civilians.

However, the strategy of role-taking, if meaningfully appropriated, could help enable negotiators to transcend their own favored ways of thinking about and interpreting the world. If successfully embraced and utilized, this technique could enable decision brokers to perceive the actions of militants and other combatants from their own unique vantage points. This strategy could be particularly worthwhile as peace negotiators endeavored to build improved working relationships among the conflicting groups and their respective members.

Of equal importance in responding to terrorism through law and public policy is the need to focus on its root causes. Hajjar[36] argued that "the conditions that give rise to acts of terrorism must be dealt with as urgently as combating those responsible for such acts if the war on terrorism is to be won." Confronting the institutions that teach the martial aspects of roles, especially those that feed the terrorist identity, is just as important as pursuing those collectives responsible for engaging in militant extremism.

Along these lines, the proposed model could further those existing efforts that endeavor to develop initiatives targeting community responses.[37] For example, as we have described, some militant extremist groups provide much needed social services (e.g., education). However, these school or institutional settings may also double as forums for inculcating hatred and violence.[38] Investing in (or supporting governments that promote) only those educational programs that encourage the expression of nonmartial aspects of roles could be an effective antiterrorism tool over the long term. Thus, art, literature, or dance could be used to verify aspects of these nonmartial role identities.

More generally at the community level, the proposed explanatory model could also help in the implementation of policy reform based on the philosophy of restorative justice. Specifically, the social psychological prism could aid in the strengthening of reconciliation programs focused on rectifying wrongdoing and healing the wounds of victims, offenders, and the international community to which both belong.[39] Here, the framework could function as a serviceable template that enables those groups harmed and those collectives responsible for such harm to understand each other's felt experiences of injustice, thereby promoting the identification of common ground. Admittedly, such an undertaking would entail a willingness on the part of combating participants to seek out workable solutions to violence. In some instances, this willingness might not exist or might only materialize with the passage of some considerable time. However, from our perspective, it is reasonable to suggest that such a strategy, built on the restorative justice insights of forgiveness, compassion, trust, mercy, story-telling, and redemption, could be effectively employed when global acts of hate and international terrorism are addressed.

Advancing Identity Theory and Symbolic Interactionism Relative to Criminal Behavior

From a more macrosocietal perspective, the conceptual framework is suggestive in its account of other forms of criminal behavior or deviant conduct. For example, the study of gang affiliation often relies upon a psychological perspective when researchers account for why some youths gravitate toward such groups. A need for belonging, familial-type bonds, and identity are common themes in such assessments.[40] However, the structural symbolic interactionist model developed in this book also warrants consideration. Indeed, a juvenile's felt sense of victimization, real or imagined, stemming from poverty, racial or ethnic oppression, government-perpetrated injustice, or the threat posed by rival gangs also contributes to one's role-identity as a gang member, or as a recruit or supporter of this collective. Clearly, symbols, the meaning of situations, roles, socialization, and the self-concept figure prominently into this analysis.

Indeed, the interpretation of such symbols and their corresponding link to the definition of the situation probably contributes to the activation of ancient roles embodied in such notions as defending a community or way of life through expressions of courage and heroism. Thus, similar to the way in which racist Skinheads regard themselves as personifying the Nordic racial warrior, images of Aztec and Zulu combatants are, respectively, found in Hispanic American and African American street gang artwork.[41] Consequently, by identifying with certain aspects of these roles, gang collectives arguably develop their own codes of conduct that are faithfully adhered to by group affiliates. Younger generations then learn these subcultural values and norms and verify their role identities through collectivist gang violence.

Finally, the proposed integrated model also works at the level of theory development. In short, it offers a cogent and practical illustration of the way two aspects of Identity Theory can be interwoven to create a more balanced representation of Symbolic Interactionism, especially in terms of society's influence on the self and the social person's impact on the lifeworld. More exactingly, as demonstrated throughout this text, a focus on identity enables one to comprehend how society constitutes the organization of the self through identity salience and commitment and how the social person molds society through the self-verification process. In this respect, the powerful ways in which culture, self, and society interactively function in the construction and maintenance of identity are made manifest through the conceptual framework.

What these observations suggest, then, is the need for continued and more systematic inquiry into the model itself and its many unique features. Indeed, in the final analysis, if terrorism and its threat are to be accounted for, then the integrative and interdisciplinary contributions of psychology, sociology, political science, and international relations must be brought to bear on this complex problem. This is the challenge that awaits researchers, policy analysts, and administrators genuinely invested in abating or forestalling expressions of such global violence. Regrettably, without such sustained attention regarding these very weighty matters, the way identity is formed, nurtured, and sustained such that it gives rise to militant extremism might remain a pivotal, though mostly underexamined, dimension to this deeply devastating human social issue.

Notes

NOTES TO CHAPTER 1

1. Hudson, 1999.
2. Horgan, 2003.
3. See, e.g., Miller, 2005; M. Taylor, 1988, 1991.
4. Böllinger, 1981; Knutson, 1981; Post, 1984; Shaw, 1986.
5. See, e.g., Post, 1986, 1998; Miller, 2005.
6. Taylor and Quayle, 1994.
7. M. Taylor, 1988, 1991.
8. Horgan, 2003.
9. See, Böllinger, 1981; Knutson, 1981; Post, 1984; Shaw, 1986.
10. Fiske and Taylor, 1984; Ross and Fletcher, 1985.
11. Atran, 2003; Silke, 1998.
12. Horgan, 2003.
13. For example, the explanatory power of Böllinger's (1981) examination of West German terrorists was limited because subjects were unwilling to meet with researchers, cooperation from local officials was lacking, and interviewees were only *suspected* terrorists.
14. Mead, 1934/1967.
15. Stryker, 1980.
16. Stryker, 1968; Stryker and Burke, 2000.
17. See Deflem, 2004.
18. Alexander, 2004.
19. Goffman, 1959.
20. Kappeler and Kappeler, 2004.
21. Oberschall, 2004.
22. Silverman, 2002.
23. Brents and Mshigeni (2004: 65) described these as being "descendants of 'indigenous' tribes who are said to come from the intermarriage of mainland Africans and 7th century Arab traders."
24. Brents and Mshigeni, 2004.
25. Akers and Silverman, 2004.

26. Aho, 1990.
27. Aho, 1990.
28. Aho, 1990: 138.
29. Mead, 1934/1967.
30. Dillon, 1998.
31. Dillon, 1998: 21.
32. Dillon, 1998.
33. Juergensmeyer's (2000) "cultures of violence" argument shares some affinities with the work of Taylor and Quayle (1994) and their appropriation of Karl Manneheim's insights.
34. Juergensmeyer, 2000: 185.
35. Berbrier, 1999.
36. Goffman, 1959, 1963.
37. Berbrier, 1999.
38. Arena and Arrigo, 2000.
39. Blee, 2003.
40. Stryker and Burke, 2000: 284.
41. Weigert, Teitge, and Teitge, 1986.
42. Berger and Luckmann, 1966.
43. Gergen, 1999.
44. Best, 1989.
45. Schutz, 1967.
46. See also Arrigo, 1998; Freeman, 1980.
47. Johnson, 1995: 203.
48. Freeman, 1980.
49. See, e.g., Garfinkel, 1967; Hilbert, 1990; Livingston, 1987.
50. Emphasis in the original, Johnson, 1995: 101.
51. Garfinkel, 1967: 11.
52. Gouldner, 1978.
53. Goode, 1996; Lemert, 1994.
54. Fanon, 1965, 1967; Said, 1978.
55. Arrigo, Milovanovic, & Schehr, 2005.
56. Milovanovic, 2003.
57. See, e.g., Chesney-Lind and Sheldon, 1997; Naffine, 1995; Smart, 1995.
58. A distinction exists between psycho-

logical social psychology (PSP) and sociological social psychology (SSP) (Boutilier, Roed, and Svendsen, 1980). The PSP perspective can be defined as an "attempt to understand and explain how the thought, feeling, and behavior of individuals are influenced by the actual, imagined or implied presence of others" (Allport, 1985: 3). A pivotal concept within PSP is Tajfel's conception of the social identity, which he defined as "that part of the individual's self-concept which derives from [one's] knowledge of [one's] membership in a social group (or groups) together with the value and emotional significance attached to that membership" (Tajfel, 1981: 225). *Social Psychology Quarterly* (Scope and Mission, 2000), a journal largely recognized as embracing SSP, defines the field "as the study of the primary relations of individuals to one another, to groups, collectivities, and institutions. It also includes the study of intra-individual processes insofar as they substantially influence, or are influenced by, social structure and process" (3). While the number of studies applying PSP and Social Identity to terrorism is limited (e.g., Brannan, Esler, and Strindberg, 2001; Stevens, 2002), the SSP perspective has all but been ignored in the relevant research.

NOTES TO CHAPTER 2

1. Weigert et al., 1986.
2. Jenkins, 1996: 4.
3. Even when the use of the term "identity" is restricted to psychology and sociology, there is still considerable variability. As Stryker and Burke (2000) pointed out, within these two disciplines there are primarily three usages. The first employs "identity" in a cultural context and draws no distinction between identity and ethnicity (see Calhoun, 1994). According to Stryker and Burke (2000), this usage obscures the theoretical purpose of introducing it in the first place. The second treatment of the term uses "identity" to refer to one's identification with a collectivity or social category as articulated, for example, within Social Identity Theory (Tajfel and Turner, 1986). The third usage, specifically appropriated by Identity Theory, understands the concept as those "parts of the self composed of meanings that persons attach to the multiple roles they typically play in highly differentiated

contemporary society" (Stryker and Burke, 2000: 284).
4. Erikson, 1950, 1959, 1968.
5. Erikson, 1968.
6. Erikson, 1968: 19.
7. Erikson, 1968.
8. Cited in Erikson, 1968: 21–22.
9. Erikson, 1968.
10. Erikson, 1968: 21–22.
11. Jenkins, 1996.
12. Jenkins, 1996.
13. Erikson, 1959: 23.
14. Rice, 2001.
15. Erikson, 1968.
16. Erikson, 1968: 174.
17. Maslow, 1970.
18. Crenshaw, 1986.
19. Crenshaw, 1986.
20. Bollinger, 1981.
21. Post, 1998.
22. Crenshaw, 1986.
23. Crenshaw, 1986: 392.
24. Crenshaw, 1986: 392.
25. Knutson, 1981.
26. Busic, whose cause was the freedom of Croatia in Serbian-controlled Yugoslavia, was arrested and incarcerated for the 1979 hijacking of a Chicago-bound TWA airliner in New York and the placement of a bomb in Grand Central Station. Although the passengers of the plane were released unharmed, the bomb killed a police officer and seriously wounded three others (Knutson, 1981).
27. Erikson, 1968.
28. Knutson, 1981: 136.
29. Knutson, 1981.
30. Knutson, 1981: 113, emphasis in the original.
31. Knutson, 1981: 113.
32. Knutson, 1981.
33. Erikson, 1968.
34. Crenshaw, 1986.
35. Erikson, 1968: 81.
36. Crenshaw, 1986: 391–92.
37. Crenshaw, 1986: 395.
38. Post, 1984.
39. Post, 1984: 247–48, emphasis in the original.
40. Post, 1984: 248.
41. Post, 1984, 1986.
42. Post, 1984, 1986.
43. Post, 1998: 26.
44. Post, 1998: 30–31.
45. Post, 1984.
46. Shaw, 1986.

47. Shaw, 1986: 365–66.
48. Böllinger, 1981.
49. Knutson, 1981.
50. Post, 1984, 1986, 1998.
51. Shaw, 1986.
52. It should be noted that this "conventional" understanding of the terrorist identity appears to be inconsistent with what is known about the September 11, 2001, hijackers and other terrorists who have emerged since the attack on the World Trade Center and Pentagon. For example, Mohamed Atta was born to a middle-class family in Egypt and was a dedicated student who earned a degree from the University of Hamburg (National Commission on Terrorist Attacks upon the United States, 2004). Mohammad Sidique Khan, one of the suspects in the July 7, 2005, bombings of the London transit system, is believed to have been married with a young daughter. He was also a respected teaching assistant at a local primary school (BBC News, 2005, July 18). Neither of the two seems to fit the profile of one who lacked a strong sense of identity, was unable to cope with life's everyday frustrations, or espoused a negative self-image.
53. See, e.g., Böllinger, 1981; Knutson, 1981; Post, 1984, 1986, 1998; Shaw, 1986.
54. In the realm of crime, the positivist school is based on the work of Cesare Lombroso. Lombroso argued that the "antisocial tendencies of criminals [were] the result of their physical and psychic organization, which differs essentially from that of normal individuals" (Lombroso-Ferrero, 1994: 116).
55. Horgan, 2003.
56. Fiske and Taylor, 1984; Ross and Fletcher, 1985.
57. Silke, 1998.
58. Horgan, 2003.
59. Silke, 1998: 53.
60. Shaw, 1986: 361.
61. Horgan, 2003.
62. Horgan, 2003.
63. As cited in Crenshaw, 1986: 382.
64. Horgan, 2003 citing, e.g., Post 1986, 1987a, 1987b; and Pearlstein 1991.
65. Horgan, 2003: 9.
66. Horgan, 2003: 16.
67. Horgan, 2003.
68. Horgan, 2003: 16.
69. Brannan, Esler, and Strindberg, 2001.
70. Brannan et al., 2001: 5.
71. Brannan et al., 2001: 5.

72. Brannan et al., 2001: 5.
73. Tajfel, 1978a, 1978b, 1982a, 1982b; Tajfel and Turner, 1979; Turner, 1975, 1982.
74. The term "social identity theory" was first used by Turner and Brown (1978) in an effort to simplify the various descriptions and ideas used by Tajfel (Turner, 1999).
75. Taylor and Moghaddam, 1994.
76. Taylor and Moghaddam, 1994: 65.
77. Hogg, 1996.
78. Tajfel, 1981.
79. Tajfel, 1981: 225.
80. Deschamps and Devos, 1998.
81. Pelham and Hetts, 1999.
82. Tajfel and Turner, 1986.
83. Tajfel and Turner, 1986: 16.
84. Tajfel and Turner, 1986: 16.
85. Hogg, 1996.
86. Worchel, Marales, Paez, and Deschamps, 1998.
87. Pelham and Hetts, 1999.
88. Tajfel and Turner, 1986.
89. Tajfel and Turner, 1979, 1986.
90. Cairns, 1982.
91. Tajfel, 1978a.
92. Cairns, 1982.
93. Cairns, 1982.
94. See, e.g., Burton, 1978; McCann, 1974; O'Donnell, 1977.
95. Cairns, 1982: 289.
96. Darby, 1973.
97. Darby, 1973.
98. Cairns, 1982.
99. Tajfel, 1978b.
100. Cairns, 1982; Birrell, 1972.
101. Cairns, 1982.
102. Cairns, 1982: 291.
103. Cairns, 1982.
104. Cairns and Mercer, 1984.
105. Cairns and Mercer, 1984: 1101.
106. Seul, 1999.
107. Seul, 1999: 558.
108. Little, 1996.
109. As cited in Seul, 1999: 560.
110. Worchel, 1999.
111. Maslow, 1970.
112. Cooley, 1902.
113. Festinger, 1954.
114. Tajfel and Turner, 1986.
115. Worchel, 1999.
116. Worchel, 1999: 121.
117. Worchel, 1999.
118. Taylor and Fiske, 1975.
119. Ross, 1995.
120. Worchel, 1999.

121. For more on this theory see, Greenberg et al., 1990.
122. Worchel, 1999.
123. Worchel, 1999.
124. Deaux, Dane, and Wrightsman, 1993: 16.
125. Gellner, 1983.
126. Worchel, 1999.
127. Worchel, 1999.
128. Worchel, 1999.
129. Worchel, 1999: 131.
130. Worchel, 1999.
131. Worchel, 1999.
132. Stevens, 2002.
133. Stevens, 2002: 46.
134. Stevens, 2002: 46.
135. Taylor and Louis, 2004.
136. Taylor and Louis, 2004: 171.
137. Taylor and Louis, 2004.
138. Taylor and Louis, 2004.
139. Taylor and Louis, 2004: 172.
140. Taylor and Louis, 2004: 174.
141. Seul, 1999.
142. Taylor and Louis, 2004: 174.
143. Taylor and Louis, 2004: 175.
144. Taylor and Louis, 2004.
145. Taylor and Louis, 2004: 176.
146. Taylor and Louis, 2004.
147. Taylor and Louis, 2004: 179.
148. Taylor and Louis, 2004: 181.
149. Moghaddam, 2004.
150. Moghaddam, 2004: 117.
151. Moghaddam, 2004.
152. Moghaddam, 2004.
153. Moghaddam, 2004.
154. Moghaddam, 2004.
155. 2005.
156. Moghaddam, 2005: 165.
157. Stets and Burke, 2000.
158. Stryker, 2000.
159. Deaux, 1996.
160. Stets and Burke, 2000.

NOTES TO CHAPTER 3

1. Erikson, 1968.
2. Weigert et al., 1986: 1.
3. Blumer, 1937, 1969.
4. Meltzer, Petras, and Reynolds, 1975; Stryker, 1980, 1981.
5. Stryker, 1981.
6. Stryker, 1981.
7. Abercrombie et al., 1994.
8. Stryker, 1981.
9. Stryker, 1980.
10. Farberman, 1985.
11. Longmore, 1998.
12. Farberman, 1985; Stryker, 1981.
13. Cooley, 1996.
14. Cooley, 1996: 63.
15. Weigert et al., 1986: 50.
16. Cooley, 1996.
17. Thomas, 1931.
18. Stryker, 1980.
19. Cooley, 1996.
20. Thomas, 1931: 41.
21. Thomas, 1931.
22. Lauer and Handel, 1983.
23. Stryker, 1980.
24. Mead, 1967.
25. Morris, C. W., 1967; Stryker, 1980.
26. Hewitt, 1976.
27. Weigert et al., 1986: 31.
28. Hoffman, 1998.
29. Mead, 1967: 71.
30. Hewitt, 1976: 49.
31. Mead, 1967.
32. Baldwin, 1986.
33. Hewitt, 1976: 47.
34. Hewitt, 1976: 47.
35. Mead, 1967.
36. As cited in Hewitt, 1976: 48.
37. Mead, 1967.
38. See, Lauer and Boardman, 1971.
39. Jenkins, 1996: 21.
40. Lauer and Boardman, 1971: 139.
41. Hewitt, 1976: 112.
42. Mead, 1967: 73.
43. Mead, 1967.
44. Schaefer, 2000.
45. Mead, 1967.
46. Stryker, 1980: 38.
47. Hewitt, 1976: 55–56.
48. Mead, 1967; see also, Meltzer, 1978.
49. Lauer and Boardman, 1971.
50. Lauer and Boardman, 1971: 140.
51. Mead, 1967: 156.
52. Mead, 1967: 152.
53. Buban, 1986; Couch, Saxton, and Katovich, 1986.
54. Longmore, 1998: 46.
55. Couch et al., 1986: xxi.
56. Longmore, 1998.
57. Mead, 1967.
58. Denzin, 1992; Weigert et al., 1986.
59. Stryker, 1980: 53–55.
60. Stryker, 1980.
61. McCall and Simmons, 1978.
62. The phrase "tools of analysis" was adopted from Lauer and Handel's (1983) work, which identified key concepts in a general Symbolic Interactionism.

63. Mead, 1967.
64. Stryker, 1980: 56–57.
65. Thomas and Thomas, 1928: 567.
66. Lauer and Handel, 1983: 129.
67. Waller, 1970.
68. Waller, 1970: 162.
69. Stryker, 1980.
70. Waller, 1970.
71. Stephan and Stephan, 1985.
72. Parsons, 1951.
73. Merton, 1957.
74. Gross, Mason, and McEachern, 1958.
75. McCall and Simmons, 1978.
76. Johnson, 1995: 237.
77. McCall and Simmons, 1978.
78. Weigert et al., 1986.
79. Lauer and Handel, 1983.
80. Stryker, 1980.
81. Lauer and Handel, 1983.
82. R. Turner, 1962.
83. McCall and Simmons, 1978.
84. Stryker, 1980.
85. Stryker, 1980.
86. Johnson, 1995: 267.
87. Lauer and Handel, 1983.
88. Stryker, 1980: 62.
89. Lauer and Handel, 1983; McCall and Simmons, 1978.
90. McCall and Simmons, 1978.
91. Stryker, 1980.
92. Stryker, 1980.
93. McCall and Simmons, 1978.
94. Stryker and Burke, 2000: 284.
95. Stryker, 1980: 60.
96. Stryker and Serpe, 1994.
97. Markus, 1977: 64.
98. Stryker, 2000: 33.
99. Stryker and Serpe, 1982: 206.
100. Stryker and Burke, 2000.
101. Stryker, 1968.
102. Alexander and Wiley, 1981.
103. McCall and Simmons, 1978.
104. Stryker, 2000.
105. Mead, 1967.
106. Stryker and Burke, 2000.
107. Stryker and Burke, 2000: 285.
108. Mead, 1967.
109. Stryker and Burke, 2000: 285.
110. Burke and Cast, 1997.
111. Stryker, 2000.
112. Stryker, 2000.
113. Stryker and Burke, 2000: 285.
114. Stryker, 2000.
115. Stryker, 1980, 1987.
116. Stryker and Burke, 2000: 286.
117. Stryker, 1968, 1980.
118. Stryker, 1987: 89.
119. Stryker, 1980.
120. Stryker, 1980, 1987.
121. Stryker and Serpe, 1982, 1994.
122. Neufeldt, 1991: 1184.
123. Stryker, 1980.
124. Stryker, 1980.
125. Stryker, 2000: 28.
126. Stryker and Serpe, 1982: 207.
127. Stryker, 2000: 28.
128. Stryker, 1980.
129. Stryker and Serpe, 1982: 207.
130. Stryker, 1980.
131. Serpe, 1987.
132. McCall and Simmons, 1978.
133. McCall and Simmons, 1978.
134. McCall and Simmons, 1978: 72.
135. McCall and Simmons, 1978.
136. Stryker, 1980.
137. McCall and Simmons, 1978.
138. Stryker and Serpe, 1982.
139. Stryker, 2000.
140. Stryker, 2000: 33.
141. Stryker, 2000.
142. Stryker, 2000.
143. Stryker, 2000: 35.
144. Pinel and Swann, 2000.
145. Burke, 1980.
146. Burke and Reitzes, 1991.
147. Stryker and Burke, 2000: 285.
148. Burke and Reitzes, 1991: 239.
149. Burke, 1980.
150. McCall and Simmons, 1978.
151. Goffman, 1959.
152. McCall and Simmons, 1978: 67.
153. McCall and Simmons, 1978.
154. Burke and Stets, 1999: 349.
155. Burke and Reitzes, 1981.
156. Goffman, 1959.
157. McCall and Simmons, 1978: 136.
158. Stryker, 1968.
159. Burke and Tully, 1977.
160. Burke and Reitzes, 1981: 84.
161. Mead, 1967.
162. Burke, 1980.
163. Burke and Reitzes, 1981.
164. Powers, 1973.
165. Burke and Reitzes, 1991.
166. Stryker and Burke, 2000: 287.
167. Burke and Reitzes, 1991.
168. Stryker and Burke, 2000.
169. Burke and Stets, 1999.
170. Swann, 1987.
171. See also, Burke and Stets, 1999.
172. Burke and Stets, 1999.

173. See also McCall and Simmons, 1978.

174. McCall and Simmons, 1978.

175. McCall and Simmons, 1978.

176. McCall and Simmons, 1978.

177. Burke and Reitzes, 1991: 288.

178. Burke and Stets, 1999.

179. Burke and Stets, 1999.

180. Burke and Stets, 1999.

181. Burke and Stets, 1999: 351.

182. Tajfel and Turner, 1986.

183. Stryker, 2000.

184. Deaux, 1996.

185. Stryker, 2000: 30.

186. Social psychologists are beginning to realize the value of both approaches and laying the necessary groundwork for a synthesis of SIT and IT in an effort to advance a more comprehensive and exacting assessment of the identity construct (Deaux, 1996; Stets and Burke, 2000). See Cassidy and Trew (1998) and Stryker, Owens, and White (2000) for applications indirectly related terrorism.

NOTES TO CHAPTER 4

1. See, e.g., Hoffman, 1998; Kushner, 1998a, 1998b; J. R. White, 1998.

2. United Nations on Drugs and Crime, n.d.

3. Schmid and Johgman, 1988: 28.

4. United States Department of State, 2004.

5. As Wooden and Blazak (2001) explained, not all skinheads are racists. Skinheads can be categorized into three groups: nonracist, separatist, and political. In this book, we use the term "racist Skinheads" to refer to those who promote a political agenda based on antigovernment and White-supremacist beliefs through fear, violence, and intimidation.

6. Sheldon, Tracy, and Brown, 2001.

7. Anti-Defamation League, 2002a.

8. Quarles, 1999.

9. Hamm, 1993.

10. Coogan, 1994.

11. J. R. White, 1998.

12. Tonge, 2002.

13. Bell, 1997.

14. Costigan, 1980.

15. Bell, 1997.

16. Hopkinson, 2002.

17. Staunton, 2001.

18. Geraghty, 1998.

19. Anderson, 2002; Coogan, 1994; Tonge, 2002.

20. Bell, 1997; P. Taylor, 1997; R. W. White, 1993.

21. M. Smith, 1995: 91.

22. M. Smith, 1995: 93.

23. As cited in Dillon, 1999: 448.

24. M. Smith, 1995.

25. Toolis, 1995.

26. Horgan and Taylor, 1997; P. Taylor, 1997; R. W. White, 1993.

27. Alonso, 2001.

28. U.S. Department of State, 2004.

29. Horgan and Taylor, 1997.

30. Horgan and Taylor, 1997.

31. Horgan and Taylor, 1997: 2.

32. Patterson, 1997.

33. Alonso, 2001.

34. Knox, 2000.

35. J. R. White, 1998.

36. Vital, 1975.

37. Morris, 1987, 1999.

38. Hourani, 1991.

39. Cohn-Sherbok and El-Alami, 2001; Morris, 1999.

40. Bickerton and Klausner, 1998; Khalidi, 1997.

41. Abu-Amr, 1993; Mitchell, 1993.

42. Barghouti, 1996; Hroub, 2000.

43. Jensen, 1998; Mishal and Sela, 2000.

44. Morris, 1999.

45. Bickerton and Klausner, 1998.

46. Cohn-Sherbok and El-Alami, 2001.

47. Hourani, 1991.

48. Abu-Amr, 1994.

49. Mishal and Sela, 2000.

50. Bickerton and Klausner, 1998.

51. Hourani, 1991.

52. Bickerton and Klausner, 1998.

53. Oren, 2002.

54. Becker, 1984.

55. Abu-Amr, 1993; Hroub, 2000; Mishal and Sela, 2000.

56. Abu-Amr, 1993.

57. Sheikh Yassin continued to act as Hamas's spiritual advisor until his death on March 22, 2004 (Katzman, 2002).

58. Hroub, 2000.

59. As cited in Hroub, 2000: 265.

60. As cited in Hroub, 2000: 265.

61. Mishal and Sela, 2000.

62. Alexander, 2002.

63. Abu-Amr, 1994; Alexander, 2002.

64. As cited in Hroub, 2000: 270.

65. As cited in Hroub, 2000: 273.

66. Nüsse, 1998; O'Ballance, 1997.

67. Alexander, 2002; U.S. Department of State, 2004.

68. Alexander, 2002.

69. Abu-Amr, 1993.

70. Abu-Amr, 1993; Mishal and Sela, 2000.

71. Alexander, 2002.

72. Human Rights Watch, 2002; O'Ballance, 1997.

73. Alexander, 2002; Emerson, 1998.

74. MidEast Web, n.d.

75. CNN.com, 2005.

76. Anderson, 2003; Khalidi, 2003.

77. McCormick, 1988.

78. Degregori, 1990/1991.

79. Fitz-Simons, 1993; "Shining Again," 1997.

80. McCormick, 1988.

81. Strong, 1992.

82. McCormick, 1988; Strong, 1992.

83. Dietz, 1990.

84. McCormick, 1988.

85. Bennett, 1985.

86. Strong, 1992.

87. Strong, 1992.

88. "Shining Bloodstained," 2000.

89. McCormick, 1988; Strong, 1992.

90. As the editor of *El Diario,* the organization's semi-official mouthpiece, explained in an interview, Sendero Luminoso is a pejorative term used by the foreign and bourgeois press (Fokkema, 1990/1991).

91. Dietz, 1990.

92. Wheat, 1990.

93. McCormick, 1990.

94. McCormick, 1988.

95. Berg, 1986; Fitz-Simons, 1993.

96. Amnesty International, 1991; McCormick, 1990; Reid, 1985; Rosenau and Flanagan, 1992.

97. McCormick, 1990.

98. Tarazona-Sevillano, 1990.

99. While researching the daily lives and social relations of those living in three Shining Path bases, del Pino (1998) discovered that many Indian children had been forced against their will into the organization's ranks. This brings up the important point that the motivations of the participants differ at varying levels of the pyramid.

100. Kent, 1993.

101. Palmer, 1992.

102. Burt and Ricci, 1994; Fitz-Simons, 1993.

103. Palmer, 1992.

104. Izaguirre, 1996.

105. U.S. Department of State, 2004.

106. Forero, 2003; Vincent, 2003.

107. U.S. Department of State, 2004.

108. Clutterbuck, 1995; Kay, 1999; Niksch and Sullivan, 1993; Palmer, 1992; Rosenau and Flanagan, 1992.

109. Wilson, 2000.

110. N. Perera, 1998.

111. Pfaffenberger, 1994a: 4.

112. Pfaffenberger, 1994a.

113. O'Ballance, 1989.

114. Manogaran, 1987; Ponnambalam, 1983.

115. The establishment of this centralized government and the amalgamation of two separate nations are cited by Tamil militants as a root cause of the existing conflict (Palacinkam, 1983).

116. A. Wilson, 2000.

117. M. Joshi, 1996.

118. Pfaffenberger, 1994a.

119. Spencer, 1990; A. Wilson, 2000.

120. Pfaffenberger, 1994a; Wilson, 1994.

121. Hellman-Rajanayagam, 1994b, 1994c.

122. O'Ballance, 1989.

123. Pfaffenberger, 1994a: 10.

124. The group was originally called the Tamil New Tigers but was renamed the LTTE in May 1976 (O'Ballance, 1989; Schalk, 1997a).

125. Wilson, 2000.

126. The Liberation Tigers of Tamil Eelam, 1997.

127. Bose, 1994; Joshi, M., 1996; Schalk, 1997a; Wilson, 2000.

128. Senaratne, 1997.

129. M. Joshi, 1996.

130. M. Joshi, 1996.

131. De Silva, 1997; Hoole, Somasundaram, Sritharan, and Thiranagama, 1990; Swamy, 1994.

132. O'Ballance, 1989.

133. U.S. Department of State, 2004.

134. Chalk, 2000.

135. Byman, Chalk, Hoffman, Rosenau, and Brannan, 2001; Fuglerud, 1999; Gunaratna, 1998, 2000a; M. Joshi, 1996.

136. Chalk, 2000; Mazumdar, 1986; U.S. Department of State, 2004.

137. De Silva, 1997; International Policy Institute for Counter-Terrorism, n.d.

138. Gunaratna, 2002.

139. Chalk, 2000; Chandran, 2001; Gunaratna, 2000b.

140. Francis, 2000; Gunaratna, 2000b; C. L. Joshi, 2000.

141. Hoole et al., 1990; C. L. Joshi, 2000; McDonald, 1991; Rogers, Spencer, and Uyangoda, 1998; Somasundaram, 1998.

142. CNN.com, 2003; Tamil Information Centre, 2001.

143. CNN.com, 2003; Naji, 2003.

144. Peace Secretariate of Liberation Tigers of Tamil Eelam, 2004.

145. BBC.com, 2005, August 13.

146. It should be noted that the historical overview of racist Skinheads provided in this subsection is largely based on that provided by Hamm (1993) and Moore (1993).

147. Moore, 1993: 20.

148. Moore, 1993: 20.

149. Etter, 1999; Shelden et al., 2001.

150. Wooden and Blazak, 2001.

151. Moore, 1993.

152. Kaplan, 2000.

153. Moore, 1993.

154. Wooden and Blazak, 2001.

155. Moore, 1993; Shelden et al., 2001; Wooden and Blazak, 2001.

156. Anti-Defamation League, 1995; Etter, 1999; Hamm, 1993.

157. Wooden and Blazak, 2001.

158. "Oi" is a Cockney phrase that means "hey" and is frequently used as a greeting and expression of unity among Skinheads (Christensen, 1994).

159. The racist Skinhead subculture is not limited to Great Britain and North America; indeed, it has become a worldwide phenomenon with striking similarities across cultures and continents (see Anti-Defamation League, 1995; Björgo, 1997; Kaplan and Björgo, 1998).

160. Hamm, 1993; Moore, 1993.

161. Wood, 1999.

162. The National Alliance is one of the largest neo-Nazi organizations in the United States (Burris, Smith, and Strahm, 2000).

163. Hamm, 1993.

164. Dobratz and Shanks-Meile, 1997.

165. Benedict, 1942: 97–98.

166. Dobratz and Shanks-Meile, 1997.

167. Wooden and Blazak, 2001.

168. See Kaplan (1997) and Barkun (1997) for a more detailed description of the various forms of radical religion and the role they play in White supremacist ideology.

169. Barkun, 1997.

170. Barkun, 1997; Ridgeway, 1995.

171. Kaplan, 1997.

172. Dobratz and Shanks-Meile, 1997: 142.

173. Wooden and Blazak, 2001.

174. See Goodrick-Clarke, 1992; Jung, 1936/1947.

175. Kaplan, 1997: 85.

176. Klassen, 1973.

177. Klassen, 1992.

178. Anti-Defamation League, 1996.

179. Anti-Defamation League, 2002a; Dobratz and Shanks-Meile, 1997.

180. Glock and Stark, 1966: 109.

182. Dobratz and Shanks-Meile, 1997; Ridgeway, 1995.

182. Etter, 1999.

183. Anti-Defamation League, 1995; Potok, 2004.

184. Reynolds, 1999.

185. Anti-Defamation League, 2002a.

186. Reynolds, 1999.

187. Anti-Defamation League, 2002a.

188. Moore, 1993: 5.

189. B. L. Smith, 1994.

NOTES TO CHAPTER 5

1. Provisional Irish Republican Army, 1974.

2. Wars and Conflict: The Troubles, n.d.

3. J. R. White, 1998: 169.

4. Moloney, 2002; J. R. White, 1998.

5. English, 2003.

6. P. Taylor, 2001.

7. P. Taylor, 1997.

8. Anderson, B., 2002; English, 2003; Provisional Irish Republican Army, 1974.

9. Provisional Irish Republican Army, 1974.

10. P. Taylor, 1997.

11. Derry was the name of the city prior to the arrival of British inhabitants, who subsequently renamed the city Londonderry.

12. P. Taylor, 2001.

13. P. Taylor, 1997: 137.

14. P. Taylor, 2001.

15. Coogan, 1994.

16. Coogan, 1994; P. Taylor, 1997.

17. Coogan, 1994.

18. P. Taylor, 1997: 137.

19. P. Taylor, 2001.

20. It should be noted that Irish Rebel music has in itself become a powerful symbol within the Republican movement. Sev-

eral ballads contain themes that glorify the IRA, its volunteers, and the battles they have fought while denigrating the British and Loyalists.

21. Katz, 2000; McKittrick and McVea, 2000.

22. McKittrick and McVea, 2000.

23. Coogan, 1994; English, 2003.

24. McKittrick and McVea, 2000.

25. English, 2003; Moloney, 2002.

26. P. Taylor, 1997.

27. Collins, 1986; Wars and Conflict: The Troubles, n.d.

28. Collins, 1986; Moloney, 2002.

29. Collins, 1986; English, 2003; McKittrick and McVea, 2000.

30. Katz, 2000; Sluka, 1997.

31. English, 2003; McKittrick and McVea, 2000.

32. McKittrick and McVea, 2000.

33. Provisional Irish Republican Army, 1974.

34. Provisional Irish Republican Army, 1974: 17.

35. As cited in R. W. White, 1993: 66.

36. Cairns and Darby, 1998.

37. Sinn Féin, n.d.

38. Provisional Irish Republican Army, 1974: 89.

39. Provisional Irish Republican Army, 1974: 20.

40. Provisional Irish Republican Army, 1974.

41. McLaughlin, 1998: 82.

42. P. Taylor, 1997: 327.

43. As cited in Dillon, 1999: 448.

44. O'Brien, 1999: 23.

45. McGarry and O'Leary, 1995.

46. Toolis, 1995.

47. Bell, 2000: 28.

48. R. W. White, 1993.

49. Toolis, 1995.

50. Bell, 2000.

51. Juergensmyer, 2000: 37.

52. Sluka, 1997.

53. Bell, 2000.

54. Dillon, 1998: 86–87.

55. Dillon, 1998.

56. There is a difference between Nationalists and Republicans that needs to be noted. An Irish Nationalist is someone who is in favor of a united Ireland, and a Republican is someone who seeks to separate Ireland from England through armed struggle (Cronin, 1980). Consequently, it is militancy that specifically distinguishes Republicans from Nationalists.

57. Mansergh, 1998.

58. Plato, 1964.

59. As cited in Mansergh, 1998: 41.

60. Bergerot, 1988.

61. As cited in Mansergh, 1998: 46.

62. Mansergh, 1998.

63. Horgan and Taylor, 1997.

64. Toolis, 1995: 24.

65. Toolis, 1995.

66. Horgan and Taylor, 1997.

67. As cited in Dillon, 1999: 459.

68. Coogan, 1994; Tonge, 2002.

69. Irish Republican Army RA, General Headquarters, 1985.

70. Irish Republican Army RA, General Headquarters, 1985: 7.

71. Irish Republican Army RA, General Headquarters, 1985: 8.

72. Irish Republican Army RA, General Headquarters, 1985: 14.

73. Bell, 2000.

74. Sluka, 1997.

75. White and Fraser, 2000.

76. White and Fraser, 2000: 331.

77. As cited in White and Fraser, 2000: 332.

78. Dillon, 1998: 205–6.

79. Dillon, 1998: 206.

80. R. W. White 1993.

81. Bell, 2000: 27.

82. Mead, 1967.

83. Toolis, 1995: 109.

84. Hopkinson, 2002.

85. English, 1998.

86. English, 2003; Hopkinson, 2002.

87. English, 1998: 1.

88. McGuire, 1973.

89. McGuire, 1973: 119.

90. Mish, 1997: 588.

91. Taithe and Thornton, 1999.

92. Wright, 1991.

93. Wright, 1991.

94. White and Fraser, 2000.

95. As cited in White and Fraser, 2000: 328.

96. R. W. White, 1993: 106.

97. R. W. White, 1993: 107.

98. R. W. White, 1993: 127.

99. McKittrick and McVea, 2000; Moloney, 2002; Sluka, 1997; P. Taylor, 1997.

100. P. Taylor, 1997: 291.

101. Bell, 2000.

102. Dillon, 1998.

NOTES TO CHAPTER 6

1. Hroub, 2000; Mishal and Sela, 2000.
2. 1998.
3. Khalidi, 1997: 101.
4. Farsoun and Zacharia, 1997.
5. Bickerton and Klausner, 1998.
6. 1997: 98.
7. Khalidi, 1997.
8. Hroub, 2000.
9. Bickerton and Klausner, 1998.
10. Farsoun and Zacharia, 1997; Khalidi, 1997.
11. Bickerton and Klausner, 1998; Farsoun and Zacharia, 1997.
12. 1990.
13. McDowell, 1995.
14. Bickerton and Klausner, 1998.
15. Hroub, 2000; Palestine-info, 2001.
16. Barghouti, 1996.
17. Hroub, 2000.
18. Cited in Hroub, 2000: 26.
19. 1994.
20. Cited in Hroub, 2000: 28.
21. Hroub, 2000: 28.
22. Jensen, 1998; Litvak, 1998.
23. Hroub, 2000: 30.
24. Abu-Amr, 1994.
25. Reuveny, 2000.
26. Kepel, 2002.
27. Abu-Amr, 1994: 15.
28. Abu-Amr, 1994; Hroub, 2000; Nüsse, 1998.
29. Kepel, 2002.
30. Abu-Amr, 1994: 40.
31. Hroub, 2000.
32. Shlaim, 1994.
33. Reuveny, 2000.
34. Al Jarbawi, 1994; Palestine-info, 2001.
35. Nüsse, 1998.
36. 2000: 232.
37. Nüsse, 1998.
38. Nüsse, 1998: 147.
39. Mishal and Sela, 2000.
40. Kristianasen, 1999.
41. Human Rights Watch, 2002.
42. Nüsse, 1998.
43. Nüsse, 1998: 29.
44. Hamas does not see a significant difference between "Zionist" and "Jew" and uses the words interchangeably; however, it avoids employing the term "Israel" or "Israeli" as a way of resisting the state's recognition (Hroub, 2000; Litvak, 1998).

45. Hroub, 2000; Ismail, 1998; Shaykh, 1997.
46. 1998.
47. Nüsse, 1998.
48. Mishal and Sela, 2000. Nazi Germany's influence on al-Hajj Amin al-Husayni, one of the founders of Palestinian Arab Nationalism, was another notable force in the demonization of Jews/Zionists. Al-Husayni was a Palestinian Arab born in Jerusalem who was appointed the mufti of Jerusalem during British rule over Palestine (Mattar, 1988). After being exiled from Palestine he fled to Germany, where he became a confidant of Hitler and his inner circle and helped form the Muslim Waffen SS.
49. Hroub, 2000: 281.
50. Nüsse, 1998.
51. Hroub, 2000: 273.
52. Litvak, 1998.
53. Palestine-info, 2001.
54. Shaykh, 1998: 151.
55. Taylor and Horgan, 2001.
56. Hroub, 2000.
57. Nüsse, 1998.
58. Litvak, 2003.
59. Litvak, 1998.
60. Mishal and Sela, 2000.
61. 1998: 51–52.
62. Abu-Amr, 1994.
63. Moaddel and Talattof, 2000.
64. Qutb, 2000.
65. Nüsse, 1998.
66. Hroub, 2000: 274.
67. Hroub, 2000.
68. Nüsse, 1998.
69. Mishal and Sela, 2000: 60.
70. Hroub, 2000.
71. Hroub, 2000.
72. Nüsse, 1998.
73. Mishal and Sela, 2000.
74. Palestine-info, 2001.
75. 1997.
76. 1997: 194.
77. Khalidi, 1997.
78. Nüsse, 1998.
79. Hroub, 2000: 11.
80. 1997: 149.
81. Litvak, 1998, 2003.
82. Moussalli, 1998.
83. 2001.
84. Davidson, 1998.
85. Moussalli, 1998, 1999; Tibi, 1998.
86. 1998.
87. Davidson, 1998: 13.

88. Nüsse, 1998; Taylor and Horgan, 2001.
89. Taylor and Horgan, 2001.
90. Davidson, 1998.
91. Kushner, 1996.
92. Juergensmeyer, 2000.
93. 1998b: 24.
94. Bartholet, 1995; Contenta, 2002; Kushner, 1996.
95. Hassan, 2001.
96. Hammer, 2001; Contenta, 2002; Kushner, 1996; Lelyveld, 2001.
97. Bartholet, 1995.
98. 2002.
99. Contenta, 2002: B01.
100. Hroub, 2000: 277.
101. Jensen, 1998.
102. Jensen, 1998.
103. 2003.
104. Ismail, 1998.
105. 2003.
106. P. A17.
107. Hammer, 2001; Stahl, 2003; Zoroya, 2002.
108. Jensen, 1998.
109. Bartholet, 1995.
110. Bartholet, 1995; Hammer, 2001; Kushner, 1998b.
111. 1998b: 33.
112. Anti-Defamation League, 2002b.
113. 2002.
114. 2002.
115. 2004.
116. Nüsse, 1998.
117. Derfner and Toameh, 2000.
118. 1998.
119. Nüsse, 1998: 166.
120. Mishal and Sela, 2000: 6.
121. According to Shikaki (2002), Palestinian support for the Oslo Agreement never dropped below 60 percent between 1993 and 2001, with the exception of 1994.
122. Hroub, 2000: 63.
123. Nüsse, 1998.
124. Nüsse, 1998.
125. Mishal and Sela, 2000: 7.
126. O'Ballance, 1997; Reuveny, 2000.
127. 1997: 1.
128. 2002.
129. Lelyveld, 2001: 50.
130. Lelyveld, 2001: 48.
131. The Middle East Media Research Institute, 2002.
132. The Middle East Media Research Institute, 2002.

133. Guerin, 2002; "Pushed to the Grave," 2002.
134. Guerin, 2002.
135. "Pushed to the Grave," 2002.
136. "Baby Bomber Photo Shocks Israel," 2002; "Pushed to the Grave," 2002.
137. Bartholet, 1995; Levitt, 2004.
138. Jensen, 1998: 207.
139. Jensen, 1998: 208.
140. Jensen, 1998.
141. 1998.
142. The club members interviewed by Jensen (1998) did not openly admit to being members of Hamas, although they identified themselves as supporters. Interestingly, six members of a football team in Hebron became suicide bombers over a span of several months (Simon Wiesenthal Center, 2003).
143. 1991.
144. Chartrand, 1991: A4.
145. 2000: 66.
146. 2000: 77.
147. Barzak, 2002; Juergensmeyer, 2000; Zarembo, 2001.
148. Barzak, 2002.
149. Moghadam, 2003.

NOTES TO CHAPTER 7

1. Communist Party of Peru, 1982.
2. Comrade Gonzalo is Guzmán's *nom de guerre*.
3. Gorriti, 1990/1999.
4. Communist Party of Peru, 1982.
5. Communist Party of Peru, 1982.
6. Strong, 1992.
7. Reid, 1985.
8. Klarén, 2000.
9. Reid, 1985.
10. Vasquez, 1993.
11. Berg, 1986.
12. Fitz-Simons, 1993; McCormick, 1990; Niksch and Sullivan, 1993.
13. 1971.
14. Mariátegui (1971: 30) went on to explain that *gamonalismo* was more than just a social and economic category: that of the *latifundistas* or large landowners. It signifies a whole phenomenon. *Gamonalismo* is represented not only by the *gamonales* but by a long hierarchy of officials, intermediaries, agents, parasites, et cetera. The literate Indian who enters the service of *gamonalismo* turns into an exploiter of his own race. The central factor of the phenomenon is the

hegemony of the semi-feudal landed estate in the policy and mechanism of the government.

15. Mariategui, 1971: 22.

16. Communist Party of Peru, 1982.

17. The "Gang of Four" is a term used to identify four radicals who rose to power during communist China's Cultural Revolution (1966–1976). They dominated political, economic, and cultural life until their arrest and imprisonment in October 1976, only a month after Mao's death. Their overthrow marked the end of radicalism in communist China.

18. McCormick, 1988.

19. Wheat, 1990.

20. McCormick, 1988.

21. Daly, 1997: 41.

22. Niksch and Sullivan, 1993: 8.

23. Palmer, 1992.

24. There is some speculation about whether the lengthy account was really a first-hand interview with Guzmán; nevertheless, it does not diminish "its value as a prolonged sounding board of Sendero thoughts, viewpoints, and ideological opinions" (Dietz, 1990: 133).

25. "Interview with Chairman Gonzalo," 1988.

26. Degregori, 1990/1991; McCormick, 1990.

27. Communist Party of Peru, 1982.

28. Communist Party of Peru, 1982.

29. Niksch and Sullivan, 1993.

30. Dietz, 1990; Fitz-Simmons, 1993.

31. Burt, 1990/1991: 30.

32. Communist Party of Peru, 1982.

33. Communist Party of Peru, 1982.

34. "Interview with Chairman Gonzalo," 1988.

35. Gorriti, 1990/1999.

36. Communist Party of Peru, 1982.

37. Communist Party of Peru, 1982.

38. "Interview with Chairman Gonzalo," 1988.

39. Cited in Degregori, 1990/1991: 12.

40. Niksch and Sullivan, 1993.

41. McCormick, 1990.

42. McCormick, 1988.

43. Tse-Tung, 1975. The term "new democracy" was used to distinguish it from the "old democracy" of the West. The latter was viewed as nothing more than a farce.

44. 1990.

45. McCormick, 1990.

46. Reid, 1985.

47. Tarazona-Sevillano, 1990.

48. McCormick, 1990.

49. Community Party of Peru, 1982.

50. McCormick, 1988; Tarazona-Sevillano, 1990.

51. Tarazona-Sevillano, 1990.

52. McCormick, 1988.

53. Clutterbuck, 1995; Niksch and Sullivan, 1993.

54. Niksch and Sullivan, 1993.

55. McCormick, 1990: 15.

56. McCormick, 1990.

57. Fitz-Simons, 1993.

58. Tarazona-Sevillano, 1990.

59. McCormick, 1988.

60. Fitz-Simons, 1993.

61. Niksch and Sullivan, 1993.

62. McCormick, 1992; Tarazona-Sevillano, 1990.

63. Manrique, 1990/1991.

64. Creoles are those of Spanish descent who were born in the Americas.

65. *Mestizo* is someone of both Spanish and Indian heritage.

66. de Wit and Gianotten, 1994.

67. Niksch and Sullivan, 1993; Vasquez, 1993.

68. de Wit and Gianotten, 1994: 71.

69. Degregori, 1990/1991; Strong, 1992.

70. Degregori, 1994; Fitz-Simons, 1993.

71. Cadena, 1998; Stern, S., 1998.

72. Degregori, 1994: 56.

73. Stern, P. A., 1995.

74. Berg, 1988: 5.

75. Degregori, 1994.

76. 1998.

77. Degregori, 1994: 58.

78. Cited in Degregori, 1994: 58.

79. Fitz-Simons, 1993.

80. Manrique, 1990/1991: 35.

81. 1994: 38.

82. Vasquez, 1993: 212.

83. 1998.

84. del Pino, 1998.

85. Reid, 1985.

86. 1986.

87. Berg, 1986: 187.

88. Isbell, 1994.

89. Berg, 1986: 187.

90. Davis, 1990.

91. Degregori, 1994: 62.

92. Davis, 1990.

93. Daly, 1997; Davis, 1990; Fitz-Simons, 1993; Strong, 1992; Vasquez, 1993.

94. Brennan, 1989.
95. 1990: 75.
96. Strong, 1992.
97. Gorriti, 1990/1999; McCormick, 1990.
98. "Interview with Chairman Gonzalo," 1988.
99. "Interview with Chairman Gonzalo," 1988.
100. Gorriti, 1990/1999; McCormick, 1990.
101. Communist Party of Peru, 1982.
102. Gorriti, 1990/1999: 237.
103. Gorriti, 1990/1999.
104. Manrique, 1990/1991.
105. Degregori, 1990/1991; Fitz-Simons, 1993; Gonzalez, 1989; Kent, 1993. It is important to note that gender roles have also played an important part in the Shining Path movement. Specifically, the involvement of women as leaders and cadres, and the way these positions have influenced the beliefs, values, and behavioral expectations of women in the Peruvian countryside, have all contributed to the group's identity (Andreas, 1990/1991; Tarazona-Sevillano, 1994).
106. Shining Path cadres were made to follow the "three rules." These rules were (a) obey orders during actions, (b) take not a single needle or length of thread from the masses, and (c) turn over everything captured (Gorriti, 1990/1999).
107. Gorriti, 1990/1999. Del Pino (1998) found that while the Indian cadres were expected to abide by these warnings, the Shining Path leaders frequently violated them, especially in the form of taking liberties with indigenous women.
108. McCormick, 1988.
109. Kay, 1999; Kent, 1993; Niksch and Sullivan, 1993.
110. The pro-Cuban Tupac Amaru Revolutionary Movement is a rival counterinsurgency group.
111. Gorriti, 1990/1999; "Interview with Chairman Gonzalo," 1988.
112. McClintock, 1984; Strong, 1992; Tarazona-Sevillano, 1994.
113. Many of the university's students were the Quechua-speaking sons and daughters of the wealthier *campesinos* and small traders from the surrounding regions (Reid, 1985).
114. Kent, 1993; Palmer, 1992; Strong, 1992.

115. McCormick, 1990: 13.
116. McCormick, 1990.
117. McCormick, 1988.
118. Niksch and Sullivan, 1993.
119. Tarazona-Sevillano, 1994.
120. Tarazona-Sevillano, 1994: 197.
121. Daly, 1997; Strong, 1992.
122. McCormick, 1990.
123. Andreas, 1990/1991; Tarazona-Sevillano, 1994.
124. Strong, 1992.
125. 1990/1991.
126. Renique, 1990/1991: 18.
127. Renique, 1990/1991: 18.
128. 1990/1999.
129. P. 245.
130. Gorriti, 1990/1999: 248.
131. Whyte, 1974.
132. Gorriti, 1990/1999.
133. 1990/1999: 180.
134. McCormick, 1988.
135. 1990/1999.
136. McCormick, 1990.
137. Berg, 1986; Fitz-Simons, 1993.
138. McCormick, 1988.
139. "Nicario," 1995.
140. 1994.
141. E.g., 1987.
142. 1992: 95.
143. P. 95.
144. 1990/1991.
145. 1990/1999.
146. Renique, 1990/1991: 18.
147. Kent, 1993.
148. 1993: 452.
149. 1998.
150. Interestingly, however, del Pino (1998) did note that while these social relationship rules were forced upon the Indian masses living at Shining Path bases, they did not necessarily accept all of them.
151. 1990.
152. Strong, 1992.
153. McCormick, 1990: 13.
154. 1990/1999: 30–31.
155. 1990/1999.
156. 1990/1991.
157. Renique, 1990/1991: 18.
158. Communist Party of Peru, 1982.
159. Communist Party of Peru, 1982.
160. "Interview with Chairman Gonzalo," 1988.
161. "Interview with Chairman Gonzalo," 1988.

NOTES TO CHAPTER 8

1. Tamil Information Centre, 2001.
2. Swamy, 1994.
3. Pfaffenberger, 1994a.
4. 1994.
5. Swamy, 1994.
6. O'Ballance, 1989; Wilson, A., 2000.
7. Swamy, 1994.
8. Wilson, A., 2000.
9. Pfaffenberger, 1994a.
10. Swamy, 1994: 20.
11. Ponnambalam, 1983.
12. Wilson, A., 2000.
13. Swamy, 1994.
14. 1984.
15. Senaratne, 1997.
16. Senaratne, 1997.
17. Swamy, 1994.
18. O'Ballance, 1989.
19. Hoole et al., 1990; Senaratne, 1997.
20. Wilson, 2000.
21. Senaratne, 1997; Swamy, 1994.
22. 1997.
23. Piyadasa, 1984; Swamy, 1994.
24. 1994.
25. Swamy, 1994: 104.
26. Hoole et al., 1990; Joshi, M., 1996.
27. Thirunavukkarasu, 1995.
28. Hellmann-Rajanayagam, 1994b; Hoole et al., 1990; Singh, 1986.
29. Ponnambalam, 1983; Wilson, A., 2000.
30. A. Wilson, 2000. On September 25, 1959, a Buddhist monk assassinated Prime Minister Bandaranaike (Swamy, 1994). In July 1960, his widow, Sirimaro Bandaranaike, was elected prime minister. She implemented the Sinhala-Only Act without a Tamil language provision on January 1, 1961.
31. Prime Minister Gandhi would pay the price for his involvement in the events surrounding the Indo–Sri Lanka Peace Accord when a LTTE suicide bomber took his life and those of several others in May of 1991 (Bullion, 1995; Joshi, M., 1996).
32. Bullion, 1995.
33. Bullion, 1995; Hellmann-Rajanayagam, 1994b.
34. Hoole et al., 1990.
35. Balasingham, 2001; Bullion, 1995.
36. Palacinkam, 1983.
37. Liberation Tigers of Tamil Eelam, 1997.
38. 1995.
39. Palacinkam, 1983: 31.

40. Liberation Tigers of Tamil Eelam, 1997; Palacinkam, 1983; Piyadasa, 1984.
41. Liberation Tigers of Tamil Eelam, 1997.
42. Palacinkam, 1983: 8.
43. Manogaran, 1994.
44. Liberation Tigers of Tamil Eelam, 1997.
45. Liberation Tigers of Tamil Eelam, 1997.
46. Chalk, 2000.
47. Prabhakaran delivers the Heroes Day speech every November 27 to honor those who have given their lives in the struggle.
48. Tamil Canadian, n.d.
49. LTTE, 1997.
50. Hopman, 1990.
51. Mazumdar, 1986.
52. EelamWeb, n.d.
53. Singh, 1986. Interestingly, the LTTE's leadership has traditionally been dominated by members of the Karaiyar caste, a fishing caste that is positioned lower on the caste hierarchy (Fuglerud, 1999; McDonald, 1991).
54. 2000.
55. 1994a: 173.
56. Hellmann-Rajanayagam, 1994b.
57. Liberation Tigers of Tamil Eelam, 1997; Thirunavukkarasu, 1995.
58. Liberation Tigers of Tamil Eelam, 1997.
59. Thirunavukkarasu, 1995.
60. International Federation of Tamils, 1992.
61. Australian Tamil Association, 2000.
62. Liberation Tigers of Tamil Eelam, 1997.
63. 1985.
64. It is important to note that the Sri Lankan Tamil role is still being constructed (Wilson, A., 2000). Consistent with this perspective, Fuglerud (1999) suggested that Eelam Tamils may be a more accurate label for those involved in the Tamil struggle. This is the case because the movement also enlists Indian Tamils whose ancestors were brought to the island as plantation laborers while Ceylon was under British control.
65. Schalk, 1997a.
66. Arasaratnam, 1994; Wilson, A., 1994, 2000.
67. Arasaratnam, 1994; Pfaffenberger, 1982, 1994b; Wilson, A., 1994.
68. Wilson, A., 2000.
69. The social mobility provided by the

English instruction served as a foundation for an intense value to be placed on educational pursuits among the Tamil community (Balasingham, 2001; Fuglerud, 1999).

70. Fuglerud, 1999.
71. Daniel, 1997.
72. Fuglerud, 1999.
73. Bose, 1994.
74. Pfaffenberger, 1982, 1994b.
75. Pfaffenberger, 1994a; Shanmugathasan, 1997.
76. Hellmann-Rajanayagam, 1994b; Pfaffenberger, 1994a.
77. Hellmann-Rajanayagam, 1990: 108.
78. Bose, 1994; Wilson, A., 1994.
79. 1983: 4.
80. As cited in Bose, 1994: 104–5. On the battlefield, cadres can be found dining on the same food, fighting together, utilizing the same amenities (or lack thereof), and sacrificing their lives for Tamil Eelam, regardless of social origin, caste, class, religion, gender, rank, or seniority (Bose, 1994). Hence, it appears that the LTTE sincerely espouses the egalitarian philosophy found within its rhetoric.
81. In contrast to other organizations of this kind, the freedom fighter role is not the exclusive domain of men within the LTTE. Consequently, women who have adopted the freedom fighter role have radically transformed the traditional female status in Tamil society (Balasingham, 2001; Schalk, 1994, 1997a).
82. Roberts, 1996.
83. For example, it is customary for LTTE cadres to carry pocket-sized pictures of Prabhakaran (Roberts, 1996). He is a folk hero to many within the Tamil community, the subject of legends, and considered a warrior-lover of the Purananuru age resurrected (Hellmann-Rajanayagam, 1994a).
84. O'Ballance, 1989.
85. Tamil Canadian, n.d.b.
86. November 27 was designated as Great Heroes' Day in 1989 to honor the death of the LTTE's first martyr. Although the date commemorates mourning, it also celebrates edification, rising, and victory in memory of those who sacrificed their lives for the LTTE's objectives (Schalk, 1997b).
87. Tamil Canadian, n.d.b.
88. Tamil Canadian, n.d.b.
89. Cited in Joshi, C. L., 2000: 66.
90. Hellmann-Rajanayagam, 1994b;

Joshi, C. L., 2000; O'Ballance, 1989; Perera, K., 2000; Somasundaram, 1998. This expectation is also conveyed to the cadres through poetry, song, posters, calendars, and other forms of LTTE discourse. In these instances, the popular slogan, "The task (or thirst) of the Tigers (is to achieve) Motherland Tamileelam," frequently appears (Schalk, 1997a: 64).

91. Roberts, 1996; Swamy, 1994.
92. Francis, 2000.
93. Hellmann-Rajanayagam, 1994a; Mazumdar, 1986.
94. Swamy, 1994.
95. Balasingham, 2001; Bose, 1994; West, 1991.
96. Tamil Canadian, n.d.b.
97. McDonald, 1991; Schalk, 1997a.
98. Roberts (1996) traced the LTTE's use of the cyanide vial and subsequent concept of martyrdom back to the suicide death of a seventeen-year-old Tamil student by the name of Ponnadurai Sivakumaran. He ingested the vial he carried after being cornered by authorities in a foiled bank robbery attempt in Jaffna. Sivakumaran's inaugural act sparked what eventually became the LTTE's obsession with devotional sacrifice, martyrdom, and the cyanide vial.
99. 1996: 254–55.
100. Chandran, 2001.
101. 1997a: 68.
102. Schalk, 1997b.
103. Schalk, 1997b.
104. 1997a.
105. Schalk, 1997b.
106. Francis, 2000; Schalk, 1997b.
107. Schalk, 1997b.
108. Schalk, 1997a, 1997b.
109. Roberts (1996) indicated that the devotional themes of the *bhakti* religious tradition could be traced back even further to Tamil literature and poetry of the Cankam period (250 B.C. to 100 A.D.).
110. 1999.
111. 1997a: 66.
112. Schalk, 1997a.
113. Hellmann-Rajanayagam, 1994b.
114. Swamy, 1994.
115. Swamy, 1994.
116. Liberation Tigers of Tamil Eelam, 1984: 79–80.
117. Prabhakaran, 1994.
118. 1994.
119. 1994.
120. Subhash Chandra Bose led the

Indian National Army against British forces in the fight for India's independence.

121. Prabhakaran, 1994.

122. 1994.

123. The film chronicled the exploits of Veerapandia Kattabomman, a Tamil chieftain who led a resistance movement against British imperialists after they began to levy taxes on the native Indian population.

124. Swamy, 1994.

125. Swamy, 1994: 52.

126. 1994.

127. O'Ballance, 1989.

128. 1994.

129. Swamy, 1994: 26.

130. 1994.

131. 1997.

132. University Teachers for Human Rights, 1997: 45.

133. University Teachers for Human Rights, 1997: 47.

134. Chandran, 2002.

135. Roberts, 1996; University Teachers for Human Rights, 1997.

136. 2001.

137. Cited in Joshi, C. L., 2001: 66.

138. University Teachers for Human Rights, 1997.

139. McDonald, 1991: 26.

140. University Teachers for Human Rights, 1997: 46.

141. Bose, 1994; Jansz, 1998.

142. 2001.

143. Hoole et al., 1990.

144. 2001. Although she was technically not an LTTE cadre, the fact that Adele Balasingham lived in flight with her husband and several other cadre members during the occupation of Jaffna sheds light on how an underground life can influence a proscribed identity.

145. Balasingham, 2001: 156.

146. Gunaratna, 2000b.

147. Jansz, 1998.

148. Schalk, 1997a.

149. Gunaratna, 2000b, 2002.

150. Francis, 2000; Gunaratna, 2000b; Joshi, M., 1996.

151. Gunaratna, 2000a.

152. Jansz, 1998.

153. The LTTE was specifically proscribed in the 1989 Emergency Regulations No. 1.

154. 1983.

155. Ponnambalam, 1983.

156. Liberation Tigers of Tamil Eelam, 1997.

157. Gunaratna, 2000b.

158. Tamil Canadian, n.d.a.

159. Tamil Canadian, n.d.a.

160. Tamil Information Centre, 2001.

161. Liberation Tigers of Tamil Eelam, 1997.

162. 1992.

163. Chalk, 2000.

164. Singh, 1986.

165. Mazumdar, 1986.

NOTES TO CHAPTER 9

1. Quarles, 1999.

2. 1997.

3. Dobratz and Shanks-Meile, 1997.

4. Emphasis in the original, Daniels, 1997: 34.

5. 2001.

6. 2001.

7. Anti-Defamation League, 1996; Flynn and Gerhardt, 1989.

8. 1994.

9. P. 105.

10. Dobratz and Shanks-Meile, 1997; Ridgeway, 1995.

11. 1926.

12. Flynn and Gerhardt, 1989.

13. MacDonald, 1978.

14. Flynn and Gerhardt, 1989. *The Turner Diaries* (MacDonald, 1978) was also the blueprint for Timothy McVeigh's bombing of the Federal Building in Oklahoma City (Hamm, 1998).

15. Hamm, 1998.

16. Christensen, 1994.

17. Kaplan, 2000.

18. Christensen, 1994: 46.

19. Anti-Defamation League, 2002a; Christensen, 1994; Wood, 1999.

20. Anti-Defamation League, 2002a.

21. Anti-Defamation League, 2002a.

22. 1994.

23. 2001.

24. Daniels, 1997; Dobratz and Shanks-Meile, 1997.

25. Barkun, 1997; Christensen, 1994.

26. 2000.

27. NAAWP stands for the National Association for the Advancement of White People, an obvious take-off on the NAACP, the National Association for the Advancement of Colored People.

28. Wilson, T., 1982.

29. Dees and Corcoran, 1994.
30. Wooden and Blazak, 2001: 15.
31. Blazak, 2001: 986.
32. Dobratz and Shanks-Meile, 1997: 106.
33. Boots, n.d.
34. 1997.
35. Dobratz and Shanks-Meile, 1997; Hamm, 1993.
36. Dobratz and Shanks-Meile, 1997.
37. Lane, n.d.: 1; as cited in Dobratz and Shanks-Meile, 1997: 109.
38. Flynn and Gerhardt, 1989.
39. Cited in Dobratz and Shanks-Meile, 1997: 109.
40. MacDonald, 1978.
41. Anti-Defamation League, 2002a.
42. Metareligion, n.d.
43. 1994: 17.
44. Moore, 1993: 5.
45. Berbrier, 2000.
46. Daniels, 1997.
47. Berbrier, 2000: 182.
48. 1904/1958.
49. Daniels, 1997.
50. Christensen, 1994: 52.
51. 1993.
52. Daniels, 1997.
53. Brannon, 1976; Doyle, 1995.
54. Christensen, 1994; Daniels, 1997.
55. Anti-Defamation League, 1995; Dobratz and Shanks-Meile, 1997.
56. Anti-Defamation League, 1995; Christensen, 1994.
57. Arena and Arrigo, 2000.
58. 1993: 156.
59. Arena and Arrigo, 2000; Blee, 2003.
60. 1993.
61. Blee, 2003.
62. Christensen, 1994.
63. Daniels, 1997: 39.
64. Christensen, 1994; Daniels, 1997.
65. Christensen, 1994: 52.
66. 2001.
67. Dobratz and Shanks-Meile, 1997; Wooden and Blazak, 2001.
68. Wooden and Blazak, 2001: 150.
69. 1999.
70. 1958.
71. 1999.
72. Kaplan, 2000: 280.
73. Dobratz and Shanks-Meile, 1997.
74. Ezekiel, 1995.
75. Barkun, 1997.
76. 1998: 209.
77. Although Fangan's (1998) comments are in reference to Norwegian racist Skinheads, it is believed that her observations hold true among racist Skinheads in the United States. See Kaplan and Bjorgo (1998) for a more detailed description of the similarities among groups in Europe and the United States.
78. Reynolds, 1999.
79. Christensen, 1994; Etter, 1999; Wooden and Blazak, 2001.
80. 2000.
81. For example, Hamm (1993) determined that most racist Skinheads did not report any physical abuse in their childhood histories. Conversely, Baron (1997) found that most of the Canadian skinheads he interviewed did report such abuse. The contrasting findings might be related to some key differences in the profiles of American versus Canadian Skinheads. Given these discrepancies, more comprehensive research addressing this aspect of the Skinhead profile is warranted.
82. Wooden and Blazak, 2001.
83. Wooden and Blazak, 2000.
84. 1999.
85. 1994.
86. 1994: 11–12.
87. Etter, 1999.
88. Silver and Lester, 1985.
89. Globus, Golan, and Zito, 1985.
90. Feitshans and Cosmatos, 1985.
91. Colonel James "Bo" Gritz claims to be "the living role model for the Rambo films" (Colonel Bo Gritz, n.d.). Gritz was a highly decorated Special Forces officer who served in Vietnam and claims to have led several unsuccessful commando-style operations in Southeast Asia intended to locate and rescue American prisoners of war. He became a prominent figure within the right-wing movement during the late 1980s and early 1990s as a conspiratorial theorist and by providing paramilitary training that he dubbed SPIKE (Specially Prepared Individuals for Key Events) (Southern Poverty Law Center, n.d.). The Anti-Defamation League (n.d.a) purports that Gritz is an adherent of Christian Identity and maintains extensive connections to both White supremacists and antigovernment groups.
92. Dobratz and Shanks-Meile, 1997; Gibson, 1994.
93. 2000.
94. Wiltenburg, 2003.
95. Wiltenburg, 2003.

96. Anti-Defamation League, n.d.b.

97. Wiltenburg, 2003.

98. Christensen, 1994; Etter, 1999; Hamm, 1993; Ridgeway, 1995; Shelden et al., 2001.

99. Whillock, 1995; Young and Craig, 1997.

100. Wooden and Blazak, 2001.

101. Christensen, 1994; Young and Craig, 1997.

102. 1997: 193.

103. 2000.

104. Christensen, 1994.

105. Baron, 1997; Hamm, 1993.

106. Anti-Defamation League, 1995; Etter, 1999.

107. Christensen, 1994; Etter, 1999; Hamm, 1993; Moore, 1993; Ridgeway, 1995.

108. Christensen, 1994: 23.

109. 1997: 193.

110. P. 193.

111. Young and Craig, 1997: 193.

112. 1993.

113. Hamm, 1993: 3–4.

114. Hamm, 1993: 4.

115. Blazak, 2001: 991.

116. Blazak, 2001: 98.

NOTES TO CHAPTER 10

1. E.g., Böllinger, 1981; Knutson, 1981.

2. Crenshaw, 1986; Post, 1984; Shaw, 1986.

3. 2003.

4. Silke, 1998: 53.

5. Clearly, there are exceptions to this rule. Ted Kaczynski, or the Unabomber, is certainly a good example of someone who committed acts of terrorism and was deemed to be mentally ill (Mello, 1999).

6. Stets and Burke, 2000.

7. Thomas and Thomas, 1928: 567.

8. Berbrier, 2000; Holstein and Miller, 1990.

9. Individuals who adopt the martial aspects of the terrorist identity may not be victims themselves but do identify with the victim. For example, animal and environmental extremists who perpetuate violence may not be victims but see themselves as liberators fighting for victims.

10. Schalk, 1997b.

11. While several of the socialization examples emphasized the experiences of young children, this does not mean that only individuals with such a history are inclined to join a militant organization. Indeed, socialization is a lifelong process. Moreover, terrorist groups are known to attract adults. Consistent with our proposed conceptual framework, participants need to be socialized into the group, including being exposed to the core components of the pertinent roles. This process may take place in child or adulthood.

12. Stryker, 1980, 2000.

13. McCall and Simmons, 1978.

14. McCall and Simmons, 1978.

15. In certain circumstances, the martial aspects of the terrorist identity are not unlike those of the soldier. For example, the United States used the 9/11 attacks as a justification for going to war in Iraq. During this conflict, the taking of innocent life was deemed by many as a regrettable, but necessary, evil in order to defend freedom and protect Americans. Clearly, terrorism is a more extreme form of combat as it purposefully targets noncombatants; however, the motivation for terrorism and conventional warfare can stem from the same wellspring.

16. Burke and Reitzes, 1991; Burke and Stets, 1999; Swann, 1987.

17. McCall and Simmons, 1978.

18. To be sure, one must die before fully realizing this identity. Therefore, being a martyr is a postmortem identity (PMI). This is "a technical term for describing the social essence of the self after death" (Weigert et al., 1986: 110). In sum, the PMI of a martyr signifies the self situated in death. According to Lifton (1976, 1979), this symbolic immortality is a way in which individuals shape their remembered identities so that they have a lasting influence on their lineage, their history, the immediate past, the present, and the future.

19. Cited in White, J. R., 1998.

20. Aho, 1990; Juergensmeyer, 2000; Oberschall, 2004; Shaw, 1986.

21. 2000.

22. 2002: 119.

23. Olweean, 2002: 120.

24. 1998.

25. 2003.

26. 1998.

27. 1998: 249.

28. Crenshaw, 1998: 249.

29. 2000.

30. Champion, 2000: 310.

31. 1986: 382.

32. Turvey, 2002.

33. McAndrew, 2000; Scott, 2000. See Sageman (2004) for a comprehensive exploration of the application of social network analysis to terrorist collectives.

34. McAndrew, 2000.

35. This statement is not to be read as endorsing or opposing the use of military force. However, it is a candid expression of the possible repercussions of such activity.

As described throughout this text, interpretations of persecution and victimization have served to swell the ranks of militant extremist groups.

36. 2002: 2.

37. Stout, 2002.

38. Atran, 2004.

39. E.g., Strang and Braithwaite, 2002.

40. Vargas and DiPilato, 1999.

41. Valdez, 1997.

References

Abercrombie, N., Hill, S., & Turner, B. S. (1994). *The Penguin dictionary of sociology* (3rd ed.). New York: Penguin.

Abu-Amr, Z. (1993). Hamas: A historical and political background. *Journal of Palestine Studies, 22*(4), 5–19.

Abu-Amr, Z. (1994). *Islamic fundamentalism in the West Bank and Gaza: Muslim brotherhood and Islamic Jihad.* Bloomington: Indiana University Press.

Aho, J. A. (1990). *The politics of righteousness: Idaho Christian patriotism.* Seattle: University of Washington Press.

Akers, R. L. & Silverman, A. L. (2004). Toward a social learning model of violence and terrorism. In M. Zahn, H. Brownstein, & S. Jackson (Eds.), *Violence: From theory to research* (pp. 19–35). Cincinnati, OH: Lexis-Nexis–Anderson Publishing.

Alexander, C. N., Jr., & Wiley, M. G. (1981). Situated activity and identity formation. In M. Rosenberg & R. Turner (Eds.), *Social psychology: Sociological perspectives* (pp. 269–289). New York: Basic Books.

Alexander, J. C. (2004). From the depths of despair: Performance, counterperformance, and "September 11." *Sociological Theory, 22*(1), 88–105.

Alexander, Y. (2002). *Palestinian religious terrorism: Hamas and Islamic Jihad.* Ardsley, NY: Transitional Publishers.

Alexander, Y. & Martin, K. (2003, July 10). Expanding culture of suicide terrorism. *Washington Times,* A17.

Al Jarbawi, A. (1994). The position of Palestinian Islamists on the Palestine-Israel Accord. *The Muslim World, 84*(1–2), 127–154.

Allport, G. W. (1985). The historical background of social psychology. In G. Lindzey & E. Aronson (Eds.), *Handbook of social psychology* (3rd ed., vol. 1, pp. 1–46). New York: Random House.

Alonso, R. (2001). The modernization in Irish Republican thinking toward the utility of violence. *Studies in Conflict and Terrorism, 24,* 131–144.

Amnesty International. (1991). *Peru: Human rights in a climate of terror.* New York: Amnesty International Publications.

Anderson, B. (2002). *Joe Cahill: A life in the IRA.* Dublin: O'Brien Press.

Anderson, J. W. (2003, June 28). Hamas at historic crossroads; pressure rises to back truce, end bombings. *Washington Post,* A16.

Andreas, C. (1990/1991). Women at war. *NACLA Report on the Americas, 24*(4), 20–27.

Anti-Defamation League. (1995). *The Skinhead international: A worldwide survey of neo-Nazi Skinheads.* New York: Author.

Anti-Defamation League. (1996). *Danger: Extremism; the major vehicles and voices on America's far-right fringe.* New York: Author.

Anti-Defamation League. (2002a). *Extremism in America: A guide.* New York: Anti-Defamation League of B'nai B'rith.

Anti-Defamation League. (2002b). Palestinian kindergartens being schooled in hate. Retrieved August 26, 2002, from http://www.adl.org/Terror/kindergartners.asp.

Anti-Defamation League (n.d.a). *James "Bo" Gritz.* Retrieved September 18, 2005, from http://www.adl.org/learn/ext_us/gritz.asp?LEARN_Cat=Extremism&LEARN_SubCat=Extremism_in_America&xpicked=2&item=5.

Anti-Defamation League. (n.d.b). Racist

groups using computer gaming to promote violence against Blacks, Latinos, and Jews. Retrieved February 4, 2004, from http://www.adl.org/videogames/default.asp.

Arasaratnam, S. (1994). Sri Lanka's Tamils: Under colonial rule. In C. Manogaran & B. Pfaffenberger (Eds.), *The Sri Lankan Tamils: Ethnicity and identity* (pp. 28–53). Boulder, CO: Westview.

Arena, M. P., & Arrigo, B. A. (2000). White supremacist behavior: Toward an integrated social psychological model. *Deviant Behavior, 21,* 213–244.

Arrigo, B. A. (1998). Shattered lives and shelter lies? Anatomy of research deviance in homeless programming and policy. In J. Ferrell & M. Hamm (Eds.), *Ethnography at the edge: Crime, deviance, and field research* (pp. 65–85). Boston: Northeastern University Press.

Arrigo, B. A., Milovanovic, D., & Schehr, R. C. (2005). *The French connection in criminology: Rediscovering crime, law, and social change.* New York: State University of New York Press.

Assadi, M. (2004, March 12). Toys help Palestinian kids prepare for life of war. *Reuters.* Retrieved March 31, 2004, from http://reuters.co.uk/printerFriendlyPopup.jhtml?type=feturesNews&storyID=4556006.

Atran, S. (2003). Genesis of suicide terrorism. *Science, 299*(5612), 1534–1539.

Atran, S. (2004). Mishandling suicide terrorism. *Washington Quarterly, 27*(3), 67–90.

Australian Tamil Association. (2000, July 12). Voice of Tamil Tigers: It is loud and clear about lopsided devoluton proposal. *Tamil Canadian News Room.* Retrieved May 7, 2002, from http://www.news.tamilcanadian.com/news/2000/07/20000712.

"Baby bomber photo" shocks Israel. (2002, June 28). Retrieved October 20, 2004, from http://news.bbc.co.uk/1/hi/world/middle_east/2071561.htm.

Balasingham, A. (2001). *The will to freedom: An inside view of Tamil resistance.* Mitcham, UK: Fairfax.

Baldwin, J. D. (1986). *George Herbert Mead: A unifying theory for sociology.* Beverly Hills, CA: Sage.

Barghouti, I. (1996). Islamist movements in historical Palestine. In A. S. Sidahmed & A. Ehteshami (Eds.), *Islamic fundamentalism* (pp. 163–177). Boulder, CO: Westview.

Barkun, M. (1997). *Religion and the racist right: The origin of the Christian identity movement.* Chapel Hill: University of North Carolina Press.

Baron, S. W. (1997). Canadian male street skinheads: Street gang or street terrorists? *Canadian Review of Sociology and Anthropology, 43,* 125–154.

Bartholet, J. (1995, April 24). A guaranteed trip to heaven. *Newsweek,* 42.

Barzak, I. (2002, December 13). Hamas threatens new attacks at rally. Associated Press. Retrieved December 17, 2002, from http://news.findlaw.com/ap_stories/i/1107/12-13-2002/20021213074501_37.html.

BBC News.com (2005, July 18). Suicide bombers' "ordinary" lives. Retrieved September 18, 2005, from http://news.bbc.co.uk/1/hi/uk/4678837.stm.

BBC News.com (2005, August 13). Timeline: Sri Lanka. Retrieved September 18, 2005, from http://news.bbc.co.uk/1/hi/world/south_asia/1166237.stm.

Becker, J. (1984). *The PLO: The rise and fall of the Palestine Liberation Organization.* New York: St. Martin's Press.

Bell, J. B. (1997). *The secret army: The IRA* (rev. 3rd ed.). New Brunswick, NJ: Transaction Publishers.

Bell, J. B. (2000). *The IRA, 1968–2000: Analysis of a secret army.* Portland, OR: Frank Cass.

Benedict, R. (1942). *Race and racism.* London: Routledge.

Bennett, P. (1985). Pol Pot in Peru: "Shining Path" to a dark future. *New Republic, 3*(654), 16–18.

Berbrier, M. (1999). Impression management for the thinking racist: A case study of intellectualization as stigma transformation in contemporary White supremacist discourse. *Sociological Quarterly, 40,* 411–433.

Berbrier, M. (2000). The victim ideology of White supremacists and White separatists in the United States. *Sociological Focus, 33,* 176–191.

Berg, R. H. (1986). Sendero Luminoso and the peasantry of Andahuaylas. *Journal of Interamerican Studies and World Affairs, 28,* 165–196.

Berg, R. H. (1988). Explaining Sendero

Luminoso. *Program in Latin American Studies Occasional Papers Series, 22,* 1–14.

Berger, P. L., & Luckmann, T. (1966). *The social construction of reality: A treatise in the sociology of knowledge.* Garden City, NY: Doubleday.

Bergerot, B. (1988). *Lazare Hoche.* Paris: Tallandier.

Best, J. (Ed.). (1989). *Images of issues: Typifying contemporary social problems.* New York: De Gruyter.

Bickerton, I. J., & Klausner, C. L. (1998). *A concise history of the Arab-Israeli conflict* (3rd ed.). Upper Saddle River, NJ: Prentice Hall.

Birrell, D. (1972). Relative deprivation as a factor in the conflict in Northern Ireland. *Sociological Review, 20,* 321–343.

Björgo, T. (1997). *Racist and right-wing violence in Scandinavia: Patterns, perpetrators and responses.* Oslo: Tano Aschehougs Foneneserie.

Blazak, R. (2001). White boys to terrorist men: Target recruitment of Nazi skinheads. *American Behavioral Scientist, 44,* 982–1000.

Blee, K. (2003). *Inside organized racism: Women in the hate movement.* Berkeley: University of California Press.

Blumer, H. (1937). Social psychology. In E. Schmidt (Ed.), *Man and society* (pp. 144–198). Englewood Cliffs, NJ: Prentice-Hall.

Blumer, H. (1969). *Symbolic interactionism: Perspective and method.* Los Angeles: University of California Press.

Böllinger, L. (1981). Die Entwicklung zu terroristischen Handeln als psychosozialer Prozess: Begegnungen mit Beteiligten [The development of terrorist actions as a psychosocial process: Encounters with participants]. In H. Jagär, G. Schmidtchen, & L. Süllwold, *Analysen zum terrorismus* [Analysis of terrorism] (Vol. 2: Lebenslauf-Analysen [Biographical analysis], pp. 175–231). Opladen: Westdeutscher Verlag.

Boots, P. (n.d.). Interview with a Hammerskin. Retrieved June 1, 2002, from http://www.88music.net/hammerskins.html.

Bose, S. (1994). *States, nations, sovereignty: Sri Lanka, India and the Tamil Eelam movement.* Thousand Oaks, CA: Sage.

Boutilier, R. G., Roed, J. C., & Svendsen, A. C. (1980). Crisis in the two social psychologies: A critical comparison. *Social Psychology Quarterly, 43,* 5–17.

Brannan, D. W., Esler, P. F., & Strindberg, N. T. A. (2001). Talking to "terrorists": Towards an independent analytical framework for the study of violent substate activism. *Studies in Conflict and Terrorism, 24*(3), 3–24.

Brannon, R. (1976). Ideology, myth, and reality: Sex equality in Israel. *Sex Roles, 6,* 403–419.

Brennan, S. A. (1989). *Ethnicity as a motivating factor of the Sendero Luminoso movement in Peru.* Unpublished master's thesis, University of Texas at Austin.

Brents, B. G. & Mshigeni, D. S. (2004). Terrorism in context: Race, religion, party, and violent conflict in Zanzibar. *American Sociologist, 35*(2), 60–74.

Buban, S. L. (1986). Studying social process: The Chicago and Iowa schools revisited. In C. Couch, S. Saxton, & M. Katovich (Eds.), *Studies in symbolic interaction: Suppl. 2, Part A, The Iowa school* (pp. 25–38). Greenwich, CT: Jai Press.

Bullion, A. J. (1995). *India, Sri Lanka, and the Tamil crisis, 1976–1994: An international perspective.* New York: Pinter.

Burke, P. J. (1980). The self-measurement requirements from an interactionist perspective. *Social Psychology Quarterly, 43*(1), 18–29.

Burke, P. J., & Cast, A. D. (1997). Stability and change in the gender identities of newly married couples. *Social Psychology Quarterly, 60,* 277–290.

Burke, P. J., & Reitzes, D. C. (1981). The link between identity and role performance. *Social Psychology Quarterly, 44,* 83–92.

Burke, P. J., & Reitzes, D. C. (1991). An identity theory approach to commitment. *Social Psychology Quarterly, 54,* 239–251.

Burke, P. J., & Stets, J. E. (1999). Trust and commitment through self-verification. *Social Psychology Quarterly, 62,* 347–360.

Burke, P. J., & Tully, J. (1977). The measurement of role/identity. *Social Forces, 55,* 881–897.

Burris, V., Smith, E., & Strahm, A. (2000). White supremacist networks on the Internet. *Sociological Focus, 33,* 215–235.

Burt, J.-M. (1990/1991). Counterinsurgency equals impunity. *NACLA Report on the Americas, 24*(4), 30–31.

Burt, J.-M., & Ricci, J. L. (1994). Shining Path after Guzmán. *NACLA Report on the Americas, 28*(3), 6–9.

Burton, F. (1978). *The politics of legitimacy.* London: Routledge & Kegan Paul.

Byman, D., Chalk, P., Hoffman, B., Rosenau, W., & Brannan, D. (2001). *Trends in outside support for insurgent movements.* Santa Monica, CA: RAND.

Cadena, M. (1998). From race to class: Insurgent intellectuals *de provincia* in Peru, 1910–1970. In S. Stern (Ed.), *Shining and other paths: War and society in Peru, 1980–1995* (pp. 22–59). Durham, NC: Duke University Press.

Cairns, E. (1982). Intergroup conflict in Northern Ireland. In H. Tajfel (Ed.), *Social identity and intergroup relations* (pp. 227–297). Cambridge, UK: Cambridge University Press.

Cairns, E., & Darby, J. (1998). The conflict in Northern Ireland: Causes, consequences, and controls. *American Psychologist, 53,* 754–760.

Cairns, E., & Mercer, G. W. (1984). Social identity in Northern Ireland. *Human Relations, 37,* 1095–1102.

Calhoun, C. (1994). *Social theory and the politics of identity.* Cambridge, MA: Blackwell.

Cassidy, C., & Trew, K. (1998). Identities in Northern Ireland: A multidimensional approach. *Journal of Social Issues, 54,* 725–740.

Central Intelligence Agency. (2001). *The world factbook 2001.* Retrieved March 13, 2002, from http://cia.gov/cia/publications/factbook/geos/ce.html.

Chalk, P. (2000, March 17). Liberation Tigers of Tamil Eelam's (LTTE) international organization and operations: A preliminary analysis. A publication of the Canadian Security Intelligence Service, Commentary No. 77. Retrieved November 26, 2001, from http://www.fas.org/irp/world/para/docs/com77e.htm.

Champion, D. J. (2000). *Research methods for criminal justice and criminology* (2nd ed.). Upper Saddle River, NJ: Prentice-Hall.

Chandran, S. (2001, October 7). Born to die: The Black Tigers of the LTTE. Retrieved April 8, 2002, from the Institute of Peace and Conflict Studies, Article No. 559, Web site: http://www.ipcs.org/issues/articles/599-s1-suba.html.

Chandran, S. (2002, February 28). An inquiry into suicide terrorism—I: Sociological perspectives. Retrieved May 20, 2002, from the Institute of Peace and Conflict Studies, Article No. 711, Web site: http://www.ipcs.org/issues/700/711-ter-suba.html.

Chartrand, S. (1991, August 22). The veiled look: It's enforced with a vengeance. *New York Times,* A4.

Chesney-Lind, M., and Shelden, R. (1997). *Girls, delinquency and juvenile justice.* Belmont, CA: Wadsworth.

Christensen, L. (1994). *Skinhead street gangs.* Boulder, CO: Paladin Press.

Clutterbuck, R. (1995). Peru: Cocaine, terrorism and corruption. *International Relations, 12*(5), 77–92.

CNN.com (2003, November 11). Timeline: A nation divided. Retrieved December 31, 2003, from http://www.cnn.com/2003/WORLD/asiapcf/south/06/08/srilanka.timeline/index.html.

CNN.com (2005, August 20). Palestinian leader confirms January 25 elections. Retrieved September 18, 2005, from http://www.cnn.com/2005/WORLD/meast/08/20/palestinian.elections/index.html.

Cohn-Sherbok, D., & El-Alami, D. (2001). *The Palestine-Israeli conflict: A beginner's guide.* Oxford, UK: Oneworld.

Collins, T. (1986). *The Irish hunger strike.* Belfast: White Island Book.

Colonel Bo Gritz (n.d.). *Center for Action, Colonel Bo Gritz.* Retrieved September 18, 2005, from http://www.bogritz.com/cfa.htm.

Communist Party of Peru. (1982). *Let us develop the guerrilla war!* (Peru People's Movement, Trans.). Retrieved December 18, 2002, from http://www.redsun.org/pop_doc/pcp_9382.htm.

Contenta, S. (2002, May 26). Why do they detonate. *Toronto Star,* B01.

Coogan, T. P. (1994). *The IRA: A history.* Niwot, CO: Roberts Rinehart.

Cooley, C. H. (1902). *Human order and social order.* New York: Scribner.

Cooley, C. H. (1902, 1996). The social self. In H. N. Pontell (Ed.), *Social deviance: Readings in theory and research* (2nd ed.; pp. 62–63). Upper Saddle River, NJ: Prentice-Hall.

Costigan, G. (1980). *A history of modern Ireland.* Indianapolis, IN: Bobbs-Merrill.

Couch, C. J., Saxton, S. L., & Katovich, M. A. (Eds.). (1986). Introduction. *Studies in symbolic interaction: Suppl. 2, Part A. The Iowa school* (pp. xvii–xxv). Greenwich, CT: Jai Press.

Crenshaw, M. (1986). The psychology of political terrorism. In M. Hermann (Ed.), *Political psychology* (pp. 379–413). San Francisco: Jossey-Bass.

Crenshaw, M. (1998). Questions to be answered, research to be done, knowledge to be applied. In W. Reich (Ed.), *Origins of terrorism: Psychologies, ideologies, theologies, states of mind* (pp. 247–260). Washington, DC: Woodrow Wilson Center Press.

Cronin, S. (1980). *Irish nationalism: A history of its roots and ideology.* Dublin: Academy Press.

Daly, J. C. K. (1997). The USSR and Sendero Luminoso: Marxist rhetoric versus Maoist reality. *Low Intensity Conflict and Law Enforcement, 6*(1), 27–52.

Daniel, E. V. (1997). *Chapters in an anthropography of violence: Sri Lankans, Sinhalas and Tamils.* Delhi: Oxford University Press.

Daniels, J. (1997). *White lies: Race, class, gender, and sexuality in White supremacist discourse.* New York: Routledge.

Darby, J. (1973, Winter). Diversiveness in education. *Northern Teacher, 3*–12.

Davidson, L. (1998). *Islamic fundamentalism.* Westport, CT: Greenwood Press.

Davis, R. B. (1990). Sendero Luminoso and Peru's struggle for survival. *Military Review, 70*(1), 79–88.

Deaux, K. (1996). Social identification. In E. Higgins and A. Kruglanski, *Social psychology: Handbook of basic principles* (pp. 778–798). New York: Guilford.

Deaux, K., Dane, F. C., & Wrightsman, L. S. (1993). *Social psychology in the '90s* (6th ed.). Pacific Grove, CA: Brooks/Cole.

Dees, M., & Corcoran, J. (1994). *Gathering storm: America's militia threat.* New York: HarperCollins.

Deflem, M. (2004). Introduction: Towards a criminological sociology of terrorism and counter-terrorism. In M. Deflem, *Terrorism and Counter-Terrorism: Criminological perspectives, sociology of crime, law, and deviance* (Vol. 5, pp. 1–6). Oxford, UK: Elsevier Science.

Degregori, C. I. (1990/1991). A dwarf star. *NACLA Report on the Americas, 24*(4), 10–16.

Degregori, C. I. (1994). Return to the past. In D. S. Palmer (Ed.), *The shining path of Peru* (2nd ed.; pp. 52–62). New York: St. Martin's Press.

del Pino, P. (1998). Family, culture, and "revolution": Everyday life with Sendero Luminoso. In S. J. Stern (Ed.), *Shining and other paths: War and society in Peru, 1980–1995* (pp. 159–192). Durham, NC: Duke University Press.

Denzin, N. K. (1992). *Symbolic interactionism and cultural studies: The politics of interpretation.* Oxford, UK: Blackwell.

Derfner, L., & Toameh, K. A. (2000, September 18). Just saying "no" to terror. *U.S. News and World Report, 50*–51.

Deschamps, J.-C., & Devos, T. (1998). Regarding the relationship between social identity and personal identity. In S. Worchel, J. Morales., D. Páez, & J. Deschamps (Eds.), *Social identity: International perspectives* (pp. 1–12). Thousand Oaks, CA: Sage.

De Silva, P. L. (1997). Hatred and revenge killings: Construction of political violence in Sri Lanka. In J. Uyangoda & J. Biyanwila (Eds.), *Matters of violence: Reflections on social and political violence in Sri Lanka* (pp. 15–32). Colombo, Sri Lanka: Social Scientists' Association.

de Wit, T., & Gianotten, V. (1994). The center's multiple failures. In D. S. Palmer (Ed.), *The Shining Path of Peru* (2nd ed.; pp. 43–57). New York: St. Martin's Press.

Dickey, C. (2002, April 15). Inside suicide, Inc. *Newsweek, 26*–32.

Dietz, H. (1990). Peru's Sandero Luminoso as a revolutionary movement. *Journal of Political and Military Sociology, 18*(1), 123–150.

Dillon, M. (1998). *God and the gun: The church and Irish terrorism.* New York: Routledge.

Dillon, M. (1999). *The dirty war: Covert strategies and tactics used in political conflicts.* New York: Routledge.

Dobratz, B. A., & Shanks-Meile, S. L. (1997). *White power, white pride: The white separatist movement in the United States.* New York: Twayne.

Doyle, J. A. (1995). *The male experience* (3rd ed.). Dubuque, IA: Brown & Benchmark.

EelamWeb (n.d.). Frequently asked questions. Retrieved March 23, 2002, from http://eelamweb.com/faq/.

Emerson, S. (1998). Terrorism in America: The threat of militant Islamic fundamentalism. In H. Kushner (Ed.), *The future of terrorism: Violence in the new millennium* (pp. 33–54). Thousand Oaks, CA: Sage.

English, R. (1998). *Ernie O'Malley: IRA intellectual.* Oxford: Clarendon Press.

English, R. (2003). *Armed struggle: The history of the IRA.* London: Macmillan.

Erikson, E. (1950). *Childhood and society.* New York: Norton.

Erikson, E. (1959). *Identity and the life cycle: Selected papers by Erik H. Erikson.* New York: International Universities Press.

Erikson, E. (1968). *Identity: Youth and crisis.* New York: Norton.

Etter, G. (1999). Skinheads: Manifestations of the warrior culture of the new urban tribes. *Journal of Gang Research, 6*(3), 9–21.

Ezekiel, R. S. (1995). *The racist mind: The portraits of American neo-Nazis and Klansmen.* New York: Penguin.

Fangan, K. (1998). Living out our ethnic instincts: Ideological beliefs among right-wing activists in Norway. In J. Kaplan & T. Björgo (Eds.), *Nation and race: The developing Euro-American racist subculture* (pp. 202–230). Boston: Northeastern University Press.

Fanon, F. (1965). *The wretched of the earth* (C. Farrington, Trans.). New York: Grove Press.

Fanon, F. (1967). *Black skin, white masks* (C. Markmann, Trans.). New York: Grove Press.

Farberman, H. A. (1985). The foundations of symbolic interactionism: James, Cooley, and Mead. In H. Farberman & R. Perinbanayagam (Eds.), *Foundations of interpretive sociology: Original essays in symbolic interaction; studies in symbolic interaction* (Supp. 1, pp. 13–27). Greenwich, CT: Jai Press.

Farsoun, S. K., & Zacharia, C. E. (1997). *Palestine and the Palestinians.* Boulder, CO: Westview Press.

Feitshans, B. (Producer) & Cosmatos, G. P. (Director). (1985). Rambo: *First blood, part II* [Motion Picture]. Tri-Star.

Festinger, L. (1954). A theory of social comparison processes. *Human Relations, 7,* 117–140.

Fiske, S. T., & Taylor, S. E. (1984). *Social cognition.* Reading, MA: Addison-Wesley.

Fitz-Simons, D. W. (1993). Sendero Luminoso: Case study in insurgency. *Parameters, 23*(2), 64–73.

Flynn, K., & Gerhardt, G. (1989). *The silent brotherhood: Inside America's racist underground.* New York: Free Press.

Fokkema, A. (1990/1991). "There is no other way": An interview with Luis Arce Borja. *NACLA Report on the Americas, 24*(4), 23–25.

Forero, J. (2003, July 23). Shining Path rebels are spreading terror again in Peru. *New York Times,* A4.

Francis, S. (1999, November 19). LTTE's human waves tactics redefine guerrilla warfare. Retrieved April 8, 2002, from the Institute of Peace and Conflict Studies, Article No. 289, Web site: http://www.ipcs.org/issues/articles/289-sl-sabil.html.

Francis, S. (2000, February 4). The uniqueness of LTTE's suicide bombers. Retrieved April 8, 2002, from the Institute of Peace and Conflict Studies, Article No. 321, Web site: http://www.ipcs.org/issues/articles/321-sl-sabil.html.

Freeman, C. R. (1980). Phenomenological sociology and ethnomethodology. In J. D. Douglas (Ed.), *Introduction to the sociologies of everyday life* (pp. 114–130). Boston: Allyn and Bacon.

Freese, L., & Burke, P. J. (1994). Persons' identities and social interaction. In B. Markovky, K. Heimer, & J. O'Brien (Eds.), *Advances in group processes* (pp. 1–24). Greenwich, CT: JAI.

Fuglerud, Ø. (1999). *Life on the outside: The Tamil diaspora and long distance nationalism.* Sterling, VA: Pluto Press.

Garfinkel, H. (1967). *Studies in ethnomethodology.* Englewood Cliffs, NJ: Prentice-Hall.

Gellner, E. (1983). *Nations and nationalism.* Oxford: Blackwell.

Geraghty, T. (1998). *The Irish war.* London: HarperCollins.

Gergen, K. J. (1999). *An invitation to social construction.* Thousand Oaks, CA: Sage.

Gibson, J. W. (1994). *Warrior dreams: Paramilitary culture in post-Vietnam America.* New York: Hill & Wang.

Globus, Y., Golan, M. (Producers), & Zito,

J. (Director). (1985). *Invasion U.S.A.* [Motion Picture]. United States: Cannon.

Glock, C., & Stark, R. (1966). *Christian beliefs and anti-Semitism.* New York: Harper & Row.

Goffman, E. (1959). *The presentation of self in everyday life.* New York: Doubleday.

Goffman, E. (1963). *Stigma: Notes on the management of spoiled identity.* New York: Simon & Schuster.

Gonzalez, R. (1989). Coca's Shining Path. *NACLA Report on the Americas, 22*(6), 22–24.

Goode, E. (1996). On behalf of labeling theory. In H. N. Pontell (Ed.), *Social deviance: Readings in the theory and research* (2nd ed.). Upper Saddle River, NJ: Prentice-Hall.

Goodrick-Clarke, N. (1992). *The occult roots of Nazism: Secret Aryan cults and their influence on Nazi ideology.* New York: New York University Press.

Gorriti, G. (1999). *The Shining Path: A history of the millenarian war in Peru* (R. Kirk, Trans.). Chapel Hill: University of North Carolina Press. (Original work published 1990.)

Gouldner, A. W. (1978). Ethnomethodology. In J. G. Manis & B. N. Meltzer (Eds.), *Symbolic interactionism: A reader in social psychology* (pp. 423–426). Boston: Allyn & Bacon.

Greenberg, J., Pyzczynski, T., Solomon, S., Rosenblatt, A., Veeder, M., Kirkland, S., & Lyon, D. (1990). Evidence for terror management theory II: The effects of mortality salience reactions to those who threaten or bolster cultural worldviews. *Journal of Personality and Social Psychology, 58,* 308–318.

Gross, N., Mason, W. S., & McEachern, A. (1958). *Explorations in role analysis.* New York: Wiley.

Guerin, Orla (2002, June 18). "Pride" of suicide attacker's mother. Retrieved October 20, 2004, from http://news.bbc.co.uk/1/hi/world/middle_east/2050414.stm.

Gunaratna, R. (1998, December 2). International and regional implications of the Sri Lankan Tamil insurgency. Retrieved November 26, 2001, from http://www.ict.org.il/articles/articlesdet.cfm?articleid=57.

Gunaratna, R. (2000a). The LTTE and suicide terrorism. *Frontline, 17*(3). Retrieved April 4, 2002, from http://www.flonnet.com/fl1703/17031060.htm.

Gunaratna, R. (2000b). Piercing a security blanket. *Frontline, 17*(9). Retrieved April 4, 2002, from http://flonnet.com/fl1709/17090610.htm.

Gunaratna, R. (2002). Suicide terrorism in Sri Lanka and India. In Anti-Defamation League and the International Policy Institute for Counter-Terrorism, *Countering suicide terrorism* (2nd ed.; pp. 101–108). New York: Anti-Defamation League.

Hajjar, S. G. (2002, August). Hizballah: Terrorism, national liberation, or menace? *Strategic Studies Institute Publication.* Retrieved June 27, 2003, from http://www.carlisle.army.mil/ssi/pubs/2002/hizbala/hizbala.htm.

Hamm, M. S. (1993). *American Skinheads: The criminology and control of hate crime.* Westport, CT: Praeger.

Hamm, M. S. (1998). The ethnography of terror: Timothy McVeigh and the blue centerlight of evil. In J. Ferrell & M. S. Hamm (Eds.), *Ethnography at the edge* (pp. 111–130). Boston: Northeastern University Press.

Hammer, J. (2001, September 10). Jenin dispatch: Blighted harvest. *New Republic,* 19.

Hassan, N. (2001, November 19). An arsenal of believers: Talking to the "human bombs." *New Yorker,* 37–41.

Hellmann-Rajanayagam, D. (1990). The politics of the Tamil past. In J. Spencer (Ed.), *Sri Lanka: History and the roots of conflict* (pp. 107–122). New York: Routledge.

Hellmann-Rajanayagam, D. (1994a). The "groups" and the rise of militant secessionism. In C. Manogaran & B. Pfaffenberger (Eds.), *The Sri Lankan Tamils: Ethnicity and identity* (pp. 169–207). Boulder, CO: Westview.

Hellmann-Rajanayagam, D. (1994b). *The Tamil tigers: Armed struggle for identity.* Stuttgart, Germany: Verlag.

Hellmann-Rajanayagam, D. (1994c). Tamils and the meaning of history. In C. Manogaran & B. Pfaffenberger (Eds.), *The Sri Lankan Tamils: Ethnicity and identity* (pp. 54–83). Boulder, CO: Westview.

Hendawi, H. (2002, May 14). Gaza's children worship martyrdom. *Washington Post.* Retrieved February 17, 2004, from http://www.aijac.org.au/updates/May-02/160502.html.

Hewitt, J. P. (1976). *Self and society: A symbolic interactionist social psychology.* Boston: Allyn & Bacon.

Hilbert, R. A. (1990). Ethnomethodology and the micro-macro order. *American Sociological Review, 55,* 794–808.

Hoffman, B. (1998). *Inside terrorism.* New York: Columbia University Press.

Hogg, M. A. (1996). Social identity, self-categorization, and the small group. In E. Witte & J. Davis (Eds.), *Understanding group behavior: Small group processes and interpersonal relations* (Vol. 2, pp. 227–253). Mahwah, NJ: Erlbaum.

Holstein, J. A., & Miller, G. (1990). Rethinking victimization: An international approach to victimology. *Symbolic Interaction, 13,* 103–122.

Hoole, R., Somasundaram, D., Sritharan, K., & Thiranagama, R. (1990). *The broken Palmyra: The Tamil crisis in Sri Lanka—an inside account.* Claremont, CA: Harvey Mudd College Press.

Hopkinson, M. (2002). *The Irish war of independence.* Montreal, Canada: McGill-Queen's University Press.

Hopman, K. (1990, April 8). *Sunday Times.* Retrieved April 23, 2002, from http://eelamweb.com/faq/.

Horgan, J. (2003). The search for the terrorist personality. In A. Silke (Ed.), *Terrorists, victims, and society: Psychological perspectives on terrorism and its consequences* (pp. 3–27). West Sussex, UK: Wiley.

Horgan, J., & Taylor, M. (1997). The provisional Irish Republican army: Command and functional structure. *Terrorism and Political Violence, 9*(3), 1–32.

Hourani, A. H. (1991). *A history of the Arab peoples.* Cambridge, MA: Belknap Press of Harvard University Press.

Hroub, K. (2000). *Hamas: Political thought and practice.* Washington, DC: Institute for Palestine Studies.

Hudson, R. A. (1999). *The sociology and psychology of terrorism: Who becomes a terrorist and why?* Washington, DC: Federal Research Division, Library of Congress.

Human Rights Watch. (2002). *Erased in a moment: Suicide bombing attacks against Israeli civilians.* Retrieved March 17, 2004, from http://www.hrw.org/reports/2002/isrl-pa/index.htm.

International Federation of Tamils. (1992, February 15). *The legitimacy of the armed struggle of the Tamil people.* Paper presented at the seminar "Towards a Just Peace" at the School of Oriental and African Studies, University of London. Retrieved September 26, 2001, from http://www.eelam.com/introduction/legitimacy.html.

International Policy Institute for Counter-Terrorism. (n.d.). Liberation tigers of Tamil Eelam (LTTE). Retrieved July 23, 2002, from http://www.ict.org.il/inter_ter/orgdet.cfm?orgid=22.

Interview with Chairman Gonzalo. (1988, July 31). *El Diario* (Peru People's Movement, Trans.). Retrieved September 10, 2002, from http://www.redsun.org/pcp_doc/pcp_0788.htm.

Irish Republican Army, General Headquarters. (1985). *A handbook for volunteers of the Irish Republican Army* [originally issued in 1956]. Boulder, CO: Paladin Press.

Isbell, B. J. (1994). Shining Path and peasant responses in rural Ayacucho. In D. S. Palmer (Ed.), *The Shining Path of Peru* (2nd ed.; pp. 77–99). New York: St. Martin's Press.

Ismail, A. S. (1998). Interview. *Middle East Policy, 6*(1), 116–120.

Izaguirre, C. R. (1996). Shining Path in the 21st century: Actors in search of a new script. *NACLA Report on the Americas, 30*(1), 37–38.

Jansz, F. (1998, March 15). Why do they blow themselves up? *Sunday Times.* Retrieved April 8, 2002, from http://www.lacnet.org/suntimes/980315/plus4.html.

Jenkins, R. (1996). *Social identity.* New York: Routledge.

Jensen, M. I. (1998). Islamism and civil society in the Gaza strip. In A. S. Moussalli (Ed.), *Islamic fundamentalism: Myths and realities* (pp. 197–220). Reading, UK: Garnet.

Johnson, A. G. (1995). *The Blackwell dictionary of sociology: A user's guide to sociological language.* Great Britain: Blackwell Reference.

Joshi, C. L. (2000). Ultimate sacrifice: Faced with harassment and economic deprivation, young Tamils are ready to give up their lives. *Far Eastern Economic Review, 163*(22), 64–67.

Joshi, M. (1996). On the razor's edge:

The Liberation Tigers of Tamil Eelam. *Studies in Conflict and Terrorism, 19,* 19–42.

Juergensmeyer, M. (2000). *Terror in the mind of God: The global rise of religious violence.* Berkeley: University of California Press.

Jung, C. G. (1947). Wotan. In C. Jung, *Essays on contemporary issues.* London: Kegan Paul. (Original work published 1936.)

Kaplan, J. (1997). *Radical religion in America: Millenarian movements from the far right to the children of Noah.* Syracuse, NY: Syracuse University Press.

Kaplan, J. (2000). *Encyclopedia of white power: A sourcebook on the radical racist right.* New York: Altamira Press.

Kaplan, J., & Björgo, T. (1998). *Nation and race: The developing Euro-American racist subculture.* Boston: Northeastern University Press.

Kappeler, Victor E. & Kappeler, Aaron E. (2004). Speaking of evil and terrorism: the political and ideological construction of a moral panic. In M. Deflem, *Terrorism and Counter-Terrorism: Criminological perspectives, Sociology of Crime, Law, and Deviance* (Vol. 5, pp. 175–197). Oxford, UK: Elsevier Science.

Katz, A. (2000). The 1981 Irish hunger strike: Struggle for legitimacy or pathology of terrorism? Retrieved December 1, 2000, from http:www.ict.org.il/articles/1981_ira_hungerstrike.htm.

Katzman, K. (2002). Terrorism: Near Eastern groups and state sponsors, 2002. *CRS Report for Congress.* Washington, DC: Congressional Research Service, Library of Congress.

Kay, B. H. (1999). Violent opportunities: The rise and fall of "King Coca" and Shining Path. *Journal of Interamerican Studies and World Affairs, 41,* 97–127.

Kent, R. B. (1993). Geographical dimensions of the Shining Path insurgency in Peru. *Geographical Review, 83,* 441–454.

Kepel, G. (2002). *Jihad: The trail of political Islam* (A. Roberts, Trans.). Cambridge, MA: Belknap Press of Harvard University Press.

Khalidi, R. (1997). *Palestinian identity: The construction of modern national consciousness.* New York: Columbia University Press.

Khalidi, R. (2003, June 17). Commentary: Can Hamas cut a deal for peace? *Washington Post,* part 2, 15.

Klarén, P. F. (2000). *Peru: Society and nationhood in the Andes.* New York: Oxford University Press.

Klassen, B. (1973). *Nature's eternal religion.* Lighthouse Point, FL: Church of the Creator.

Klassen, B. (1992). *The white man's bible.* Milwaukee, WI: Milwaukee Church of the Creator.

Knox, C. (2000, November). *"See no evil, hear no evil": Insidious paramilitary violence in Northern Ireland.* Paper presented at the 52nd annual meeting of the American Society of Criminology, San Francisco, CA.

Knutson, J. N. (1981). Social and psychodynamic pressures toward a negative identity: The case of an American revolutionary terrorist. In Y. Alexander & J. M. Gleason (Eds.), *Behavioral and quantitative perspectives on terrorism* (pp. 105–150). Elmsford, NY: Pergamon Press.

Kristianasen, W. (1999). Challenge and counterchallenge: Hamas's responses to Oslo. *Journal of Palestine Studies, 28*(3), 19–36.

Kushner, H. W. (1996). Suicide bombers: Business as usual. *Studies in Conflict and Terrorism, 19,* 329–337.

Kushner, H. W. (Ed.). (1998a). *The future of terrorism: Violence in the new millennium.* Thousand Oaks, CA: Sage.

Kushner, H. W. (1998b). *Terrorism in America: A structured approach to understanding the terrorist threat.* Springfield, IL: Thomas.

Lane, D. (n.d.). Dissension within the resistance. *Focus Fourteen, 506,* 1–2.

Lauer, R. H., & Boardman, L. (1971). Role-taking: Theory, typology, and propositions. *Sociology and Social Research, 55,* 137–148.

Lauer, R. H., & Handel, W. H. (1983). *Social psychology: The theory and application of symbolic interactionism.* Englewood Cliffs, NJ: Prentice-Hall.

Lelyveld, J. (2001, October 28). All suicide bombers are not alike. *New York Times Magazine,* 48–53, 62, 78–79.

Lemert, E. M. (1994). Primary and secondary deviation. In J. E. Jacoby (Ed.), *Classics of criminology* (2nd ed.; pp.

261–263). Prospect Heights, IL: Waveland Press.

Levitt, M. A. (2004). Hamas from cradle to grave. *Middle East Quarterly, 11*(1), 3–15.

Liberation Tigers of Tamil Eelam. (1984). *Towards liberation: Selected political documents of the Liberation Tigers of Tamil Eelam.* Published by International Secretariat, Liberation Tigers of Tamil Eelam, Publication No. 8.

Liberation Tigers of Tamil Eelam, International Secretariat. (1997). *A struggle for justice.* Retrieved March 13, 2002, from http://eelam.com/freedom_struggle/ltte_publ/strug_for_just/introduc.html.

Lifton, R. J. (1976). *The life of the self.* New York: Simon & Schuster.

Lifton, R. J. (1979). *The broken connection.* New York: Simon & Schuster.

Little, D. (1996). Belief, ethnicity, and nationalism. *Nationalism and Ethnic Politics, 1,* 284–301.

Litvak, M. (1998). The Islamization of the Palestinian-Israeli conflict: The case of Hamas. *Middle Eastern Studies, 34,* 148–163.

Litvak, M. (2003). The Islamization of the Palestinian identity. Retrieved October 22, 2003, from http://middleeastinfo.org/article3133.html.

Livingston, E. (1987). *Making sense of ethnomethodology.* London: Routledge & Kegan Paul.

Lombroso-Ferrero, G. (1994). Criminal man. In J. E. Jacoby (Ed.), *Classics of criminology* (2nd ed.; pp. 116–131). Prospect Heights, IL: Waveland Press.

Longmore, M. A. (1998). Symbolic interactionism and the study of sexuality. *Journal of Sex Research, 35*(1), 44–57.

MacDonald, A. [William Pierce]. (1978). *The Turner diaries.* Hillsboro, WV: National Vanguard Books.

Manogaran, C. (1987). *Ethnic conflict and reconciliation in Sri Lanka.* Honolulu: University of Hawaii Press.

Manogaran, C. (1994). Colonization as politics: Political use of space in Sri Lanka's ethnic conflict. In C. Manogaran & B. Pfaffenberger (Eds.), *The Sri Lankan Tamils: Ethnicity and identity* (pp. 84–125). Boulder, CO: Westview.

Manrique, N. (1990/1991). Time of fear. *NACLA Report on the Americas, 24*(4), 28–38.

Mansergh, M. (1998). The Republican ideal regained. In N. Porter (Ed.), *Republican ideal: Current perspectives* (pp. 34–61). Belfast: Blackstaff Press.

Maqadima, I. (1994). *Ma'alim fil-tariq ila tahrir filastin* [Guideposts on the road to liberating Palestine]. Gaza: Aleem Institute.

Mariátegui, J. C. (1971). *Seven interpretive essays on Peruvian reality* (M. Urquidi, Trans.). Austin: University of Texas Press.

Markus, H. (1977). Self-schemata and processing information about the self. *Journal of Personality and Social Psychology, 35,* 63–78.

Maslow, A. H. (1970). *Motivation and personality* (2nd ed.). New York: Harper.

Mattar, Philip (1988). *The Mufti of Jerusalem: Al-Hajj Amin al-Husayni and the Palestinian National Movement.* New York: Columbia University Press.

Mazumdar, S. (1986, August 11). The eye of the tiger. *Newsweek.* Retrieved September 26, 2001, from http://www.eelamweb.com/leader/interview/in_eye_1986/.

McAndrew, D. (2000). The structural analysis of criminal networks. In D. Canter & L. Alison (Eds.), *The social psychology of crime: Groups, teams and networks* (pp. 53–94). Burlington, VT: Ashgate.

McCall, G. J., & Simmons, J. L. (1970). The stolen base as a social object. In G. P. Stone & H. A. Farberman (Eds.), *Social psychology through symbolic interaction* (pp. 93–94). Waltham, MA: Ginn-Blaisdell.

McCall, G. J., & Simmons, J. L. (1978). *Identities and interactions: An examination of human associations in everyday life* (Rev. ed.). New York: Free Press.

McCann, E. (1974). *War in an Irish town.* Harmondsworth, UK: Penguin Books.

McClintock, C. (1984). Why peasants rebel: The case of Peru's Sendero Luminoso. *World Politics, 37*(1), 48–84.

McCormick, G. H. (1988). The Shining Path and Peruvian terrorism. In D. Rapoport (Ed.), *Inside terrorist organizations* (pp. 109–126). New York: Columbia University Press.

McCormick, G. H. (1990). *The Shining Path and the future of Peru.* Santa Monica, CA: RAND.

McCormick, G. H. (1992). *From the Sierra to the cities: The urban campaign of the Shining Path.* Santa Monica, CA: RAND.

McDonald, H. (1991, September 21). Cyanide edge. *Far Eastern Economic Review, 153*(37), 26(2).

McDowell, D. (1995). *The Palestinians: The road to nationhood.* London: Minority Rights Group.

McGarry, J., & O'Leary, B. (1995). *Explaining Northern Ireland: Broken images.* Cambridge, MA: Blackwell.

McGuire, M. (1973). *To take arms: My year with the IRA provisionals.* New York: Viking Press.

McKittrick, D., & McVea, D. (2000). *Making sense of the troubles.* Belfast: Blackstaff Press.

McLaughlin, M. (1998). The Republican ideal. In N. Porter (Ed.), *Republican ideal: Current perspectives* (pp. 62–84). Belfast: Blackstaff Press.

Mead, G. H. (1967). *Mind, self, and society from the standpoint of a social behaviorist.* Chicago: University of Chicago Press. (Original work published 1934.)

Mello, M. (1999). *The United States of America vs. Theodore John Kaczynski: Ethics, power and the invention of the Unabomber.* New York: Context Publications.

Meltzer, B. (1978). Mead's social psychology. In J. G. Manis & B. N. Meltzer (Eds.), *Symbolic interaction: A reader in social psychology* (3rd ed.; pp. 15–27). Boston: Allyn & Bacon.

Meltzer, B. N., Petras, J. W., & Reynolds, L. T. (1975). *Symbolic interactionism: Genesis, varieties and criticism.* Boston: Routledge & Kegan Paul.

Merton, R. K. (1957). *Social theory and social structure* (Rev. ed.). New York: Free Press.

Metareligion. (n.d.). Frequently asked questions about Skinheads. Retrieved May 4, 2004, from http://www.metareligion.com/Extremism/White_extremism/Skinheads/frequently_asked_questions_about.htm.

Middle East Media Research Institute (2002, June 19). An interview with the mother of a suicide bomber. Retrieved October 20, 2004, from http://memri.org/bin/opener.cgi?Page=archives&ID=SP39102.

MidEast Web. (n.d.). Timeline of Palestinian Israeli history and the Israeli-Arab conflict. Retrieved September 18, 2005, from http://www.mideastweb.org/timeline.htm.

Miller, L. (2005). The terrorist mind: A psychological and political analysis. *Behavioral Sciences and the Law.*

Miller, W. (1958). Lower-class culture as a generating milieu of gang delinquency. *Journal of Social Issues, 14,* 5–19.

Milovanovic, D. (2003). *Critical criminology at the edge: Postmodern perspectives, integration, and applications.* Westport, CT: Praeger.

Mish, F. C. (Ed.). (1997). *The Merriam-Webster dictionary.* Springfield, MA: Merriam-Webster.

Mishal, S., & Sela, A. (2000). *The Palestinian Hamas: Vision, violence, and coexistence.* New York: Columbia University Press.

Mitchell, R. (1993). *The society of the Muslim brothers.* New York: Oxford University Press.

Moaddel, M., & Talattof, K. (2000). Contemporary debates in Islam: Modernism versus fundamentalism: An anthology of Islamic thought. In M. Moaddel & K. Talattof (Eds.), *Contemporary debates in Islam: An anthology of modernist and fundamentalist thought* (pp. 1–21). New York: St. Martin's.

Moghadam, A. (2003). Palestinian suicide terrorism in the second Intifada: Motivations and organizational aspects. *Studies in Conflict and Terrorism, 26,* 65–92.

Moghaddam, F. M. (2004). Cultural preconditions for potential terrorist groups: Terrorism and societal change. In F. Moghaddam & A. Marsella (Eds.), *Understanding terrorism: Psychological roots, consequences, and interventions* (pp. 103–117). Washington, DC: American Psychological Association.

Moghaddam, F. M. (2005). The staircase to terrorism: A psychological exploration. *American Psychologist, 60*(2), 161–169.

Moloney, E. (2002). *A secret history of the IRA.* London: Norton.

Moore, J. B. (1993). *Skinheads shaved for battle: A cultural history of American Skinheads.* Bowling Green, OH: Bowling Green State University Popular Press.

Morris, B. (1987). *The birth of the Palestinian refugee problem, 1947–1949.* New York: Cambridge University Press.

Morris, B. (1990). *1948 and after: Israel and the Palestinians.* New York: Oxford University Press.

Morris, B. (1999). *Righteous victims: A history of the Zionist-Arab conflict, 1881–1999*. New York: Knopf.

Morris, C. W. (Ed.). (1967). *Mind, self, and society from the standpoint of a social behaviorist*. Chicago: University of Chicago Press.

Moussalli, A. S. (1998). Introduction to Islamic fundamentalism: Realities, ideologies and international politics. In A. S. Moussalli (Ed.), *Islamic fundamentalism: Myths and realities* (pp. 3–39). Reading, UK: Garnet.

Moussalli, A. S. (1999). *Moderate and radical Islamic fundamentalism: The quest for modernity, legitimacy, and the Islamic state*. Gainesville: University of Florida Press.

Naffine, N. (Ed.) (1995). *Gender, crime, and feminism*. Aldershot, UK: Ashgate/Dartmouth Publishing.

Naji, K. (2003, November 27). Power struggle delays peace: Rebel. *CNN.com*. Retrieved December 1, 2003, from http://edition.cnn.com/2003/WORLD/asiapcf/south/11/17/srilanka.tamil/index.html.

National Commission on Terrorist Attacks upon the United States (2004). The 9/11 Commission report. Retrieved September 18, 2005, from http://www.9-11commission.gov/report/index.htm.

Neufeldt, V. (Ed.). (1991). *Webster's new world dictionary* (3rd college ed. of American English). New York: Simon & Schuster.

"Nicario." (1995). Memories of a cadre. In O. Starn, C. I. Degregori, & R. Kirk (Eds.), *The Peru reader: History, culture, politics* (pp. 328–335). Durham, NC: Duke University Press.

Niksch, L. A., & Sullivan, M. P. (1993). Peru's Shining Path: Background on the movement, counterinsurgency strategy, and U.S. policy. *CRS Report for Congress*. Washington, DC: Congressional Research Service, Library of Congress.

Nüsse, A. (1998). *Muslim Palestine: The ideology of Hamas*. Amsterdam, The Netherlands: Harwood Academic.

Nye, F. I., & Bernardo, F. M. (1966). *Emerging conceptual frameworks in family analysis*. New York: Macmillan.

O'Ballance, E. (1989). *The cyanide war: Tamil insurrection in Sri Lanka, 1973–1988*. London: Brassey's.

O'Ballance, E. (1997). *Islamic fundamentalist terrorism, 1979–95: The Iranian connection*. New York: New York University Press.

Oberschall, Anthony (2004). Explaining terrorism: The contribution of collective action theory. *Sociological Theory, 22*(1), 26–37.

O'Brien, B. (1999). *The long war: The IRA and Sinn Féin* (2nd ed.). Syracuse, NY: Syracuse University Press.

O'Donnell, E. E. (1977). *Northern Irish stereotypes*. Dublin: College of Industrial Relations.

Olweean, S. S. (2002). Psychological concepts of the "Other": Embracing the compass of the self. In C. Stout (Ed.), *The psychology of terrorism: Theoretical understandings and perspectives* (Vol. 3, pp. 113–128). Westport, CT: Praeger.

Oren, M. B. (2002). *Six days of war: June 1967 and the making of the modern Middle East*. New York: Oxford University Press.

Palacinkam, E. [Anton Balasingham]. (1983). *Liberation Tigers and Tamil Eelam freedom struggle*. Madras, India: Political Committee Liberation Tigers of Tamil Eelam.

Palestine-info (2001). *About Hamas: General information*. Retrieved December 12, 2001, from www.palestine-info.com/hamas/index.htm.

Palmer, D. S. (1992). Peru, the drug business and Shining Path: Between Scylla and Charybdis? *Journal of Interamerican Studies and World Affairs, 34*(3), 65–88.

Parsons, T. (1951). *The social system*. New York: Free Press.

Patterson, H. (1997). *The politics of illusion: A political history of the IRA*. London: Serif.

Peace Secretariat of Liberation Tigers of Tamil Eelam. (2004). Tigers steadfast in the observation of ceasefire and looking for a powerful government to assume office for resumption of peace talks. Retrieved January 18, 2004, from http://www.lttepeacesecretariat.com/mainpages/n16014.htm.

Pearlstein, R. M. (1991). *The mind of the political terrorist*. Wilmington, DE: Scholarly Resources.

Pelham, B. W., & Hetts, J. J. (1999). Implicit and explicit personal and social identity: Toward a more complete understanding of the social self. In T. Tyler, R. Kramer, & O. John (Eds.), *The psychology of the social self* (pp. 115–143). Mahwah, NJ: Erlbaum.

Perera, K. (2000, June 25). Human bombs spawned by Prabha's cult. *Sunday Times.* Retrieved April 8, 2002, from http://www .lacnet.org/suntimes/000625/plus6.html.

Perera, N. (1998). *Society and space: Colonialism, nationalism, and postcolonial identity in Sri Lanka.* Boulder, CO: Westview.

Pfaffenberger, B. (1982). *Caste in Tamil culture: The religious foundations of Sudra domination in Tamil Sri Lanka.* Syracuse, NY: Maxwell School of Citizenship and Public Affairs, Syracuse University.

Pfaffenberger, B. (1994a). Introduction: The Sri Lankan Tamils. In C. Manogaran & B. Pfaffenberger (Eds.), *The Sri Lankan Tamils: Ethnicity and identity* (pp. 1–27). Boulder, CO: Westview.

Pfaffenberger, B. (1994b). The political construction of defensive nationalism: The 1968 temple entry crisis in Sri Lanka. In C. Manogaran & B. Pfaffenberger (Eds.), *The Sri Lankan Tamils: Ethnicity and identity* (pp. 143–168). Boulder, CO: Westview.

Pinel, E. C., & Swann, W. B., Jr. (2000). Finding the self through others: Self-verification and social movement participation. In S. Stryker, T. J. Owens, & R. White (Eds.), *Self, identity, and social movements* (pp. 132–152). Minneapolis: University of Minnesota Press.

Piyadasa, L. (1984). *Sri Lanka: The Holocaust and after.* London: Marram Books.

Plato. (1964). *The republic* (A. D. Lindsay, Trans.). New York: Dutton.

Ponnambalam, S. (1983). *Sri Lanka: The national question and the Tamil liberation struggle.* London: Zed Books.

Post, J. M. (1984). Notes on a psychodynamic theory of terrorist behavior. *Terrorism: An International Journal, 7,* 241–256.

Post, J. M. (1986). Hostilité, conformité, fraternité: The group dynamics of terrorist behavior. *International Journal of Group Psychotherapy, 36,* 211–224.

Post, J. M. (1987a). Group and organisational dynamics of political terrorism: Implications for counterterrorist policy. In P. Wilkinson & A. Stewart (Eds.), *Contemporary research on terrorism*

(pp. 307–317). Aberdeen, UK: Aberdeen University Press.

Post, J. M. (1987b). Rewarding fire with fire: Effects of retaliation on terrorist group dynamics. *Terrorism, 10,* 23–36.

Post, J. M. (1998). Terrorist psycho-logic: Terrorist behavior as a product of psychological forces. In W. Reich (Ed.), *Origins of terrorism: Psychologies, ideologies, theologies, states of mind* (pp. 25–40). Washington, DC: Woodrow Wilson Center Press.

Potok, M. (2004). The year in hate. *Intelligence Project, 113,* 29–32.

Powers, W. T. (1973). *Behavior: The control of perception.* Chicago: Aldine.

Prabhakaran, V. (Interviewee). (1985, September 29–October 5). We are prepared to pay for freedom with our lives. *Sunday Times.* Retrieved September 26, 2001, from http://www.eelamweb.com/leader/interview/in_1985/.

Prabhakaran, V. (Interviewee). (1994, April/May). How I became a freedom fighter. *Velicham.* Retrieved September 26, 2001, from http://www.eelamweb.com/leader/interview/ikn_199404/.

Provisional Irish Republican Army. (1974). *Freedom struggle by the Provisional Irish Republican Army.* Jackson Heights, NJ: Irish Northern Aid.

Pushed to the grave. (2002, July 4). *The Statesman,* 1.

Quarles, C. L. (1999). *The Ku Klux Klan and related American racialist and anti-Semitic organizations: A history and analysis.* Jefferson, NC: McFarland.

Qutb, S. (2000). War, peace, and Islamic Jihad. In M. Moaddel & K. Talattof (Eds.), *Contemporary debates in Islam: An anthology of modernist and fundamentalist thought* (pp. 223–245). New York: St. Martin's Press.

Reid, M. (1985). *Peru: Paths to poverty.* London: Latin American Bureau.

Renique, J. L. (1990/1991). The revolution behind bars. *NACLA Report on the Americas, 24(4),* 17–19.

Reuveny, R. (2000). Palestinian Islamism and Israeli-Palestinian peace. *Research in Social Movements, Conflicts and Change, 22,* 219–245.

Reynolds, M. (1999). Hammerskin nation. *Intelligence Report, 96,* 37–39. Retrieved April 19, 2004, from http://www

.splcenter.org/intel/intelreport/article.jsp?
aid+310&printable=1.

Rice, F. P. (2001). *Human development* (4th ed.). Upper Saddle River, NJ: Prentice-Hall.

Ridgeway, J. (1995). *Blood in the face: The Ku Klux Klan, Aryan nations, Nazi Skinheads, and the rise of a new white culture* (2nd ed.). New York: Thunder's Mouth Press.

Roberts, M. (1996). Filial devotion in Tamil culture and the tiger cult of martyrdom. *Contributions to Indian Sociology, 30,* 245–272.

Rogers, J. D., Spencer, J., & Uyangoda, J. (1998). Sri Lanka: Political violence and ethnic conflict. *American Psychologist, 53,* 771–777.

Rosenau, W., & Flanagan, L. H. (1992). Blood of the condor: The genocidal talons of Peru's Shining Path. *Policy Review, 59,* 82–85.

Ross, M. H. (1995). Psychocultural interpretation theory and peacemaking in ethnicity conflicts. *Political Psychology, 16,* 523–544.

Ross, M., & Fletcher, G. J. O. (1985). Attribution and social perception. In G. Lindzey & E. Aronson (Eds.), *Handbook of social psychology* (3rd ed.; Vol. 2, pp. 73–122). New York: Random House.

Rouhana, N. N., & Bar-Tal, D. ((1998). Psychological dynamics of intractable ethnonational conflicts: The Israeli-Palestinian case. *American Psychologist, 53,* 761–770.

Said, Edward W. (1978). *Orientalism.* New York, NY: Pantheon Books.

Sageman, Marc (2004). *Understanding terror networks.* Philadelphia: University of Pennsylvania Press.

Schaefer, R. T. (2000). *Sociology: A brief introduction.* Boston: McGraw-Hill.

Schalk, P. (1994). Women fighters of the Liberation Tigers in Tamililam: The martial feminism of Adele Palacinkam. *South Asia Research, 14,* 163–183.

Schalk, P. (1997a). Resistance and martyrdom in the process of state formation of Tamililam. In J. Pettigrew (Ed.), *Martyrdom and political resistance: Essays from Asia and Europe* (pp. 61–83). Amsterdam: VU University Press.

Schalk, P. (1997b). The revival of martyr cults among Llavar. *Studies in Comparative Religion, 33,* 151–190. Retrieved

May 10, 2002, from http://www.tamil canadian.com/eelam/maaveerar/ps2.html.

Schmid, A. P., & Jongman, A. J. (1988). *Political terrorism: A new guide to actors, authors, concepts, data bases, theories and literature.* New Brunswick, NJ: Transaction Books.

Schutz, A. (1967). *The phenomenology of the social world.* Evanston, IL: Northwestern University Press.

Scope and mission. (2000). *Social Psychology Quarterly, 63*(4), 3.

Scott, J. (2000). *Social network analysis: A handbook* (2nd ed.). Thousand Oaks, CA: Sage.

Senaratne, J. P. (1997). *Political violence in Sri Lanka, 1977–1990: Riots, insurrections, counterinsurgencies, foreign intervention.* Amsterdam: VU University Press.

Serpe, R. T. (1987). Stability and change in self: A structural symbolic interactionist explanation. *Social Psychology Quarterly, 50,* 44–55.

Seul, J. R. (1999). "Ours is the way of God": Religion, identity and intergroup conflict. *Journal of Peace Research, 36,* 553–569.

Shanmugathasan, N. (1997). Case struggles in northern Sri Lanka. In J. Uyangoda & J. Biyanwila (Eds.), *Matters of violence: Reflections on social and political violence in Sri Lanka* (pp. 95–105). Colombo, Sri Lanka: Social Scientists' Association.

Shastri, A. (1994). The material basis for separatism: The Tamil Eelam movement in Sri Lanka. In C. Manogaran & B. Pfaffenberger (Eds.), *The Sri Lankan Tamils: Ethnicity and identity* (pp. 208–235). Boulder, CO: Westview.

Shaw, E. D. (1986). Political terrorists: Dangers of diagnosis and an alternative to the psychopathology model. *International Journal of Law and Psychiatry, 8,* 359–368.

Shaykh, A. Y. (1998). Interviews, Gaza Strip, October 1997 (excerpts). *Journal of Palestine Studies, 27,* 150–154.

Shelden, R. G., Tracy, S. K., & Brown, W. B. (2001). *Youth gangs in American society* (2nd ed.). Belmont, CA: Wadsworth.

Shikaki, Khalil (2002, January/February). Palestinians divided. *Foreign Affairs.* Retrieved from http://www.foreignaffairs .org/20020101faessay6559/khalil-shikaki/ palestinians-divided.html.

Shining again. (1997, October 25). *The Economist, 345*, 34.

Shining bloodstained. (2000). *New Internationalist, 331*, 18–21.

Shlaim, A. (1994). The Oslo Accord. *Journal of Palestine Studies, 23*(3), 24–40.

Silke, A. (1998). Cheshire-cat logic: The recurring theme of terrorist abnormality in psychological research. *Psychology, Crime, and Law, 4*, 51–99.

Silke, A. (2003). Becoming a terrorist. In A. Silke (Ed.), *Terrorists, victims and society: Psychological perspectives on terrorism and its consequences* (pp. 29–53). West Sussex, UK: Wiley.

Silver, J. (Producer), & Lester, M. L. (Director). (1985). *Commando* [Motion Picture]. United States: Twentieth-Century Fox.

Silverman, Adam L. (2002). Just war, jihad, and terrorism: A comparison of Western and Islamic norms for the use of political violence. *Journal of Church and State, 44*(1), 73–92.

Simon Wiesenthal Center. (2003, August). Unmasking Hamas' hydra of terror. *Snider Social Action Institute Report*. Retrieved March 30, 2004, from http://www.wiesenthal.com/social/pdf/index.cfm?ItemID=7993.

Singh, J. (1986, March 3). It is the plight of the Tamil people that compelled me to take up arms. I felt outraged at the inhuman atrocities perpetuated against an innocent people. *The Week*. Retrieved September 26, 2001, from http://www.eelamweb.com/leader/interview/in_1986.

Sinn Féin. (n.d.). *Policies: Building an Ireland of equals*. Retrieved April 18, 2004, from http://sinnfein.ie.

Sluka, J. A. (1997). From graves to nations: Political martyrdom and Irish nationalism. In J. Pettigrew (Ed.), *Martyrdom and political resistance: Essays from Asia and Europe* (pp. 35–60). Amsterdam, The Netherlands: VU University Press.

Smart, C. C. (1995). *Law, crime, and sexuality: Essays in feminism*. Thousand Oaks, CA: Sage.

Smith, B. L. (1994). *Terrorism in America: Pipe bombs and pipe dreams*. Albany, NY: State University of New York Press.

Smith, M. (1994). Taking the high ground: Shining Path and the Andes. In D. S. Palmer (Ed.), *The Shining Path of Peru*

(2nd ed.; pp. 33–50). New York: St. Martin's Press.

Smith, M. L. R. (1995). *Fighting for Ireland? The military strategy of the Irish Republican movement*. New York: Routledge.

Somasundaram, D. (1998). *Scarred minds: The psychological impact of war on Sri Lankan Tamils*. Thousand Oaks, CA: Sage.

Southern Poverty Law Center (n.d.). *False patriots*. Retrieved August 30, 2005, from http://www.splcenter.org/intel/intelreport/article.jsp?pid=361#16.

Spencer, J. (1990). Introduction: The power of the past. In J. Spencer (Ed.), *Sri Lanka: History and the roots of conflict* (pp. 1–16). New York: Routledge.

Sri Kantha, S. (2001, June 12). A Brando in the battlefield. In *The Pirabhakaran phenomenon* (part 6). Retrieved April 8, 2002, from http://www.sangam.org/PIRABAKARAN/Part6.htm.

Stack, M. K. (2003, July 17). At camp Hamas, lessons in Intifada. *Los Angeles Times*. Retrieved July 21, 2003, from www.latimes.com.

Stahl, J. (2003, July 9). Palestinian TV urges young men to become martyrs. *Cybercast News Service*. Retrieved July 7, 2003, from http://www.cnsnews.com/ViewForeignBureaus.asp?Page=%5CForeignBureaus%5Carchive%5C200307%5CFOR20030709d.html.

Staunton, E. (2001). *The Nationalists of Northern Ireland: 1918–1973*. Dublin: Columbia Press.

Stephan, C. W., & Stephan, W. G. (1985). *Two social psychologies: An integrative approach*. Homewood, IL: Dorsey Press.

Stern, P. A. (1995). *Sendero Luminoso: An annotated bibliography of the Shining Path guerrilla movement, 1983–1993*. Albuquerque, NM: SALALM Secretariat, General Library, University of New Mexico.

Stern, S. J. (Ed.). (1998). *Shining and other paths: War and society in Peru, 1980–1995*. Durham, NC: Duke University Press.

Stets, J. E., & Burke, P. J. (2000). Identity theory and social identity theory. *Social Psychology Quarterly, 63*, 224–237.

Stevens, M. J. (2002). The unanticipated consequences of globalization: Contextualizing terrorism. In C. Stout (Ed.), *The psychology of terrorism: Theoretical understandings and perspectives* (Vol. 3, pp. 31–56). Westport, CT: Praeger.

Stout, C. (Ed.) (2002). *The psychology of terrorism.* Westport, CT: Praeger.

Strang, H., and Braithwaite, J. (2002). *Restorative justice: Philosophy to practice.* Aldershot, UK: Dartmouth/Ashgate Publishing.

Strong, S. (1992). *Shining Path: The world's deadliest revolutionary force.* London: HarperCollins.

Stryker, S. (1968). Identity salience and role performance. *Journal of Marriage and the Family, 30,* 558–564.

Stryker, S. (1977). Development in "two social psychologies." *Sociometry, 40,* 145–160.

Stryker, S. (1980). *Symbolic interactionism: A social structural version.* Menlo Park, CA: Cummings.

Stryker, S. (1981). Symbolic interactionism: Themes and variations. In M. Rosenberg & R. H. Turner (Eds.), *Social psychology: Sociological perspectives* (pp. 3–29). New York: Basic Books.

Stryker S. (1987). Identity theory: Developments and extensions. In K. Yardley & T. Honess (Eds.), *Self and identity: Psychosocial perspectives* (pp. 83–101). New York: Wiley.

Stryker, S. (2000). Identity competition: Key to differential social movement participation? In S. Stryker, T. J. Owens, & R. White (Eds.), *Self, identity, and social movements* (pp. 21–40). Minneapolis: University of Minnesota Press.

Stryker, S., & Burke, P. J. (2000). The past, present, and future of an identity theory. *Social Psychology Quarterly, 63,* 284–297.

Stryker, S., & Serpe, R. (1982). Commitment, identity salience and role behavior: Theory and research example. In W. Ickes & E. S. Knowles (Eds.), *Personality, roles and social behavior* (pp. 199–218). New York: Springer Verlag.

Stryker, S., & Serpe, R. (1994). Identity salience and psychological centrality: Equivalent, overlapping or complementary concepts? *Social Psychology Quarterly, 57,* 16–35.

Stryker, S., Owens, T. J., & White, R. W. (Eds.). (2000). *Self, identity, and social movements.* Minneapolis: University of Minnesota Press.

Swamy, M. R. N. (1994). *Tigers of Lanka: From boys to guerrillas.* Delhi, India: Konark.

Swann, W., Jr. (1987). Identity negotiation: Where two roads meet. *Journal of Personality and Social Psychology, 53,* 1038–1051.

Taithe, B., & Thornton, T. (1999). *Propaganda: Political rhetoric and identity, 1300–2000.* Gloucestershire, UK: Sutton.

Tajfel, H. (Ed.). (1978a). *Differentiation between social groups: Studies in the social psychology of intergroup relations.* European Monographs in Social Psychology, No. 14. London: Academic Press.

Tajfel, H. (1978b). *The social psychology of minorities* (Report No. 38). London: Minority Rights Group.

Tajfel, H. (1981). *Human groups and social categories.* London: Academic Press.

Tajfel, H. (1982a). *Social identity and intergroup relations.* Cambridge, UK: Cambridge University Press.

Tajfel, H. (1982b). Social psychology of intergroup relations. *Annual Review of Psychology, 33,* 1–39.

Tajfel, H., & Turner, J. C. (1979). An integrative theory of intergroup conflict. In W. G. Austin & S. Worchel (Eds.), *The social psychology of intergroup relations* (pp. 33–47). Monterey, CA: Brooks Cole.

Tajfel, H., & Turner, J. C. (1986). The social identity theory of intergroup behavior. In S. Worchel & W. G. Austin (Eds.), *Psychology of intergroup relations* (2nd ed.; pp. 7–24). Chicago: Nelson-Hall.

Tamil Canadian. (n.d.a). The armed struggle for Tamil Eelam. Retrieved July 19, 2002, from http://www.tamilcanadian.com/cgi-bin/eelam/view.pl?indexview+125-102-100-101-1.

Tamil Canadian. (n.d.b). Pirabakaran's National Heroes Day Speeches (translated into English). Retrieved May 25, 2002, from http://www.tamilcanadian.com/eelam/nl.

Tamil Information Centre. (2001). *Tamils of Sri Lanka: The quest for human dignity.* London: Author.

Tarazona-Sevillano, G. (1990). *Sendero Luminoso and the threat of narcoterrorism.* New York: Praeger.

Tarazona-Sevillano, G. (1994). The organization of Shining Path. In D. S. Palmer (Ed.), *The Shining Path of Peru* (2nd ed.;

pp. 189–208). New York: St. Martin's Press.

Taylor, D. M., & Louis, W. (2004). Terrorism and the quest for identity. In F. Moghaddam & A. Marsella (Eds.), *Understanding terrorism: Psychological roots, consequences, and interventions* (pp. 167–185). Washington, DC: American Psychological Association.

Taylor, D. M., & Moghaddam, F. M. (1994). *Theories of intergroup relations: International social psychological perspectives* (2nd ed.). Westport, CT: Praeger.

Taylor, M. (1988). *The terrorist*. London: Brassey's. Taylor, M. (1991). *The fanatics: A behavioural approach to political violence*. London: Brassey's.

Taylor, M., & Horgan, J. (2001). The psychological and behavioural bases of Islamic fundamentalism. *Terrorism and Political Violence, 13*(4), 37–71.

Taylor, M., & Quayle, E. (1994). *Terrorist lives*. London: Brassey's.

Taylor, P. (1997). *Behind the mask: The IRA and Sinn Féin*. New York: TV Books.

Taylor, P. (2001). *Brits: The war against the IRA*. London: Bloomsbury.

Taylor, S., & Fiske, S. (1975). Point of view and perception of causality. *Journal of Personality and Social Psychology, 32,* 439–445.

Thirunavukkarasu, M. (1995). *Broken promises*. Retrieved March 13, 2002, from http://eelamweb.com/publication/broken_promises/bpl.shtml.

Thomas, W. I. (1931). *The unadjusted girl*. Boston: Little, Brown.

Thomas, W. I., & Thomas, D. S. (1928). *The child in America*. New York: Knopf.

Tibi, B. (1998). *The challenge of fundamentalism: Political Islam and the new world disorder*. Berkeley: University of California Press.

Tonge, J. (2002). *Northern Ireland: Conflict and change* (2nd ed.). Harlow, UK: Longman.

Toolis, K. (1995). *Rebel hearts: Journeys within the IRA's soul*. New York: St. Martin's Press.

Tse-Tung, M. (1975). *Selected works of Mao Tse-Tung* (2nd ed., Vol. 2). Peking: Foreign Languages Press.

Turner, J. C. (1975). Social comparison and social identity: Some prospects for intergroup behaviour. *European Journal of Social Psychology, 5,* 5–34.

Turner, J. C. (1982). Towards a cognitive redefinition of the social group. In H. Tajfel (Ed.), *Social identity and intergroup relations* (pp. 15–40). Cambridge, UK: Cambridge University Press.

Turner, J. C. (1999). Some current issues in research on social identity and self-categorization theories. In N. Ellemers, R. Spears, & B. Doosje (Eds.), *Social identity: Context, commitment, content* (pp. 6–34). Malden, MA: Blackwell.

Turner, J. C., & Brown, R. (1978). Social status, cognitive alternatives and intergroup relations. In H. Tajfel (Ed.), *Differentiation between social groups: Studies in the social psychology of intergroup relations* (pp. 201–234). London: Academic Press.

Turner, R. (1962). Role-taking: Process versus conformity. In A. Rose (Ed.), *Human behavior and social processes* (pp. 20–40). Boston: Houghton Mifflin.

Turvey, B. E. (2002). *Criminal profiling: An introduction to behavioral evidence analysis* (2nd ed.). San Diego, CA: Academic.

United Nations Office on Drugs and Crime. (n.d.). Definitions of terrorism. Retrieved January 19, 2004, from http://www.unodc.org/unodc/terrorism_definitions.html.

University Teachers for Human Rights (Jaffna). (1997). Children in the northeast war: 1985–1995. In J. Uyangoda & J. Biyanwila (Eds.), *Matters of violence: Reflections on social and political violence in Sri Lanka* (pp. 44–51). Colombo, Sri Lanka: Social Scientists' Association.

U.S. Department of State. (2004). *Patterns of global terrorism 2003*. Retrieved May 4, 2004, from http://www.state.gov/s/ct/rls/pgtrpt/2003/c12153.htm.

Valdez, A. (1997). *Gangs: A guide to understanding street gangs*. San Clemente, CA: Law Tech.

Vargas, A. M., & DiPilato, M. (1999). Culture-focused group therapy: Identity issues in gang-involved youth. In C. Branch (Ed.), *Adolescent gangs: Old issues, new approaches* (pp. 159–173). Philadelphia: Taylor & Francis.

Vasquez, G. L. (1993). Peruvian radicalism and the Sendero Luminoso. *Journal of Political and Military Sociology, 21,* 197–217.

Vincent, I. (2003, August 7). Shining Path

marches again. *National Post*. Retrieved August 19, 2003, from http://www.nationalpost.com/search/site/story.asp?id+F2CEE83B-A2EA-4FF9-B4E1-D852A76A1875.

Vital, D. (1975). *The origins of Zionism*. Great Britain: Oxford University Press.

Waller, W. (1970). The definition of the situation. In G. P. Stone & H. A. Farberman (Eds.), *Social psychology through symbolic interaction* (pp. 162–174). Waltham, MA: Ginn-Blaisdell.

Wars and conflict: The troubles. (n.d.). Retrieved April 13, 2004, from http://www.bbc.co.cu/history/war/troubles.

Weber, M. (1958). *The Protestant ethic and the spirit of capitalism* (T. Parsons, Trans.). New York: Scribner. (Original work published 1904.)

Weigert, A. J., Teitge, J. S., & Teitge, D. W. (1986). *Society and identity: Toward a sociological psychology*. New York: Cambridge University Press.

West, J. (1991, March 8). Passage to Jaffna. *Asiaweek*. In S. Kantha, The Pirabhakaran phenomenon (part 7: Violating the Seventh Commandment). Retrieved May 7, 2002, from http://www.sangam.org/PIRABAKARAN/Part7.htm.

Wheat, A. (1990). Shining Path's "fourth sword" ideology. *Journal of Political and Military Sociology, 18*(1), 41–55.

Whillock, D. (1995). Symbolism and the representation of hate in visual discourse. In R. Whillock & D. Slayden (Eds.), *Hate speech* (pp. 122–141). Thousand Oaks, CA: Sage.

White, J. R. (1998). *Terrorism: An introduction*. Belmont, CA: Wadsworth.

White, R. W. (1993). *Provisional Irish Republicans: An oral and interpretative history*. Westport, CT: Greenwood Press.

White, R. W., & Fraser, M. R. (2000). Personal and collective identities and long-term social movement activism: Republican Sinn Féin. In S. Stryker, T. J. Owens, & R. White (Eds.), *Self, identity, and social movements* (pp. 324–346). Minneapolis: University of Minnesota Press.

Whyte, M. K. (1974). *Small groups and political rituals in China*. Los Angeles: University of California Press.

Wilson, A. J. (1994). The Colombo man, the Jaffna man, and the Batticaloa man: Regional identities and the rise of the Federal Party. In C. Manogaran & B. Pfaffenberger (Eds.), *The Sri Lankan Tamils: Ethnicity and identity* (pp. 126–142). Boulder, CO: Westview.

Wilson, A. J. (2000). *Sri Lankan Tamil nationalism*. Vancouver, BC: UBC Press.

Wilson, T. (1982). Suicide rates differ among ethnic groups. *NAAWP News, 15*, p. 12.

Wiltenburg, M. (2003, April 3). More than playing games. *Christian Science Monitor*. Retrieved April 4, 2003, from http://www.csmonitor.com/2003/0403/p14s01-stct.html.

Wood, R. (1999). The indigenous, nonracist origins of the American Skinhead culture. *Youth and Society, 31*, 131–151.

Wooden, W. S., & Blazak, R. (2001). *Renegade kids, suburban outlaw: From youth culture to delinquency* (2nd ed.). Belmont, CA: Wadsworth.

Worchel, S. (1999). *Written in blood: Ethnic identity and the struggle for human harmony*. New York: Worth.

Worchel, S., Morales, F., Páez, D., & Deschamps, J.-C. (Eds.). (1998). *Social identity: International perspectives*. Thousand Oaks, CA: Sage.

Wright, J. (1991). *Terrorist propaganda: The Red Army faction and the Provisional IRA, 1968–86*. New York: St. Martin's Press.

Young, K., & Craig, L. (1997). Beyond White pride: Identity, meaning and contradiction in the Canadian skinhead subculture. *Canadian Review, 34*, 175–206.

Zarembo, A. (2001, October 15). A merger of mosque and state. *Newsweek, 138*, 16, 28.

Zoroya, G. (2002, August 6). Fear, rage fester inside for West Bank children. *USA Today*. Retrieved February 5, 2003, from http://www.usatoday.com/news/world/2002-08-06-curfew-cover_x.htm.

Index

About the Authors

Michael P. Arena is employed by a large state criminal justice agency as an analyst and trainer. He has published in a variety of behavioral and social science journals, including *Deviant Behavior, Professional Psychology: Research and Practice, International Criminal Justice Review, Journal of Forensic Psychology Practice,* and *Behavioral Sciences and the Law.*

Bruce A. Arrigo is Professor of Crime, Law, and Society within the Department of Criminal Justice at the University of North Carolina–Charlotte. He holds additional faculty appointments in the Psychology Department, the Public Policy Program, and the Center for Professional and Applied Ethics. He is the author or editor of numerous books, most recently, with Dragan Milovanovic and Robert Schehr, *The French Connection in Criminology: Rediscovering Crime, Law, and Social Change* (2005); with Christopher R. Williams, *Philosophy, Crime, and Criminology* (2006); and *Criminal Behavior: A Systems Approach* (2006).